INTEREST
GROUPS
IN AMERICAN
SOCIETY

Harmon Zeigler

Department of Political Science
The University of Georgia

PRENTICE-HALL, INC.
ENGLEWOOD CLIFFS, NEW JERSEY

For Michael

Current printing (last digit):
13 12 11 10 9 8 7 6

PRENTICE-HALL INTERNATIONAL, INC., *London*
PRENTICE-HALL OF AUSTRALIA, PTY., LTD., *Sydney*
PRENTICE-HALL OF CANADA, LTD., *Toronto*
PRENTICE-HALL OF INDIA (PRIVATE) LTD., *New Delhi*
PRENTICE-HALL OF JAPAN, INC., *Tokyo*

JK
1118.
.Z4

© 1964 BY PRENTICE-HALL, INC., ENGLEWOOD CLIFFS, N.J.

Library of Congress Catalog Card Number: 64-10841

Printed in the United States of America
C-46928

Preface

This book is an interpretation of the role of formally organized interest groups in the policy formation process. Accordingly, the empirical sections of the book are guided by what is generally referred to as group theory. This particular theory has served a dual function for political scientists. On the one hand it has encouraged numerous case studies of interest group activity, and on the other it has served as a focal point for vigorously conducted methodological debates. Such disputes are touched upon in the earlier sections of the book. However, it may prove useful by way of introduction to provide the reader with a reasonably explicit statement of the author's purpose.

The intention of group theory has been misinterpreted, on occasion, as the establishment of a broad-gauge theory of the political process in the manner of systems theory or structural-functional analysis of political society. This book is *not* built on such a theory. Much misunderstanding of group theory seems to depend on the degree to which a particular writer attempts to explain all political behavior as stemming from some form of group conflict. For example, it can be argued, with considerable justification, that group theory is unable to come to grips with problems of societal integration because of an excessive concern for conflict. In stressing latent and actual conflict, group theory neglects the values, customs, and agencies of socialization that cement the society into a viable operating unit. Such criticism would seem to be founded upon an

55370

accurate description of group theory. Indeed, an explicit conflict model—that public policy is formed as a result of competing pressures—is the framework of this book.

However, such a conflict model is intended to suggest not a theory of politics but rather a theory of the role of organized groups in politics. Hence it neglects, while conceding their importance, instruments of socialization such as schools, churches, and primary groups; and it concentrates upon the distributive aspects of the political process, and upon the distribution of tangible and intangible rewards among competitive portions of the society.

In the process whereby rewards are distributed, organized groups may, under certain conditions, be major actors; but in other situations they may be no more than peripheral and ineffective participants. Under no circumstances do organized interest groups assume the role of *sole* actor. That is to say, organized groups form a portion of the total matrix of pressures flowing in a given direction. Therefore it is a false realism which describes governmental decision makers as passive pawns being pushed and shoved about according to the whims and fancies of "powerful" pressure groups. A brief visit to Washington would be enough to persuade most students of politics that many lobbyists are not very powerful and menacing at all; that they are in fact more dependent upon the good will of elected politicians than the reverse.

An immediate question is: When are organized groups essential components of the pressures surrounding a decision and when are they insignificant? Another way of asking the same question is to inquire into the circumstances which appear to be conducive to the exercising of "power" by an organized group. Such a question is difficult on two counts. First, power is difficult to define and even more difficult to describe, although it is a standard weapon in the arsenal of polemical writers. Second, even if we arrive at a definition of power that will satisfy everyone—an unlikely occurrence—it is a very tricky matter to be able to attribute a particular outcome in policy formation to the efforts of a particular organization or coalition of organizations. Presumably, no one would argue with a definition of power as the ability to get what one wishes to get out of politics, although such a definition is sufficiently inclusive as to make it practically meaningless as a conceptual tool.

Even using such an inclusive definition, is it really feasible to examine the content of governmental decisions for a specific period of time, to determine which interest groups benefited most from these decisions, and to conclude that these groups are influential determinants of the course of public policy? Does the existence of outcome *A*, combined with the observed activity of organization *B* in support of this outcome, mean that the activity "caused" the outcome? Such a conclusion is easy to reach but, unfortunately for those who find single causation systems pleasing, totally unjustified not only by the canons of logic but also by means of empirical exploration. It is equally possible that the outcome would have been the same even if there had been no group effort.

It would seem to this writer that the problem posed above suggests two solutions, neither of which excludes the other. Careful interviewing of public officials and detailed observation of the flow of communication into areas of formal decision may serve to produce an official definition of influence in a particular situation. The spread of the aspirations of behavioral social science to political science has provided methods whereby this can be accomplished. Indeed, research of this nature is already taking place and is recorded in this book. Less difficult but equally important is a ranking of organizations according to the degree to which their stated goals are reflected in language of official policy without any reference to the probability that group activity will contribute to these results.

This latter possibility seems simple, but this is deceptive. In the first place, where does one locate a "final" decision and hence a yardstick? As will be argued in some detail later, in many cases the distribution of values as expressed in a formal document is a far cry from the actual distribution. The appearance of success is more easily obtained than its substance. In the second place, such a ranking of organizations would be limited both temporally and spacially. In a pluralistic society such as ours it is hard to imagine any single set of organizations being powerful except in limited areas and under specified conditions. However, in spite of such obstacles, certain guideposts may prove useful.

Within this book is a series of tentative conclusions concerning the success of interest groups with reference to their rivals. Stated as concisely as possible, interest groups have a good possibility of success if they:

(1) draw their membership from a high-ranking social strata,

(2) espouse goals not in conflict with societal values, and

(3) are accorded legitimacy by those in a position to make authoritative decisions.

These statements invite two comments. First, the "partial" nature of group theory is acknowledged by the inclusion of essentially "non-group" factors: social stratification and societal values. These two factors limit and control interest group aspirations without revealing anything but the faintest connection with group activity. Second, the coercive or threatening aspects of interest group behavior are de-emphasized and the initiative of public officials in sorting through a series of demands is heightened.

I do not, of course, wish to argue that these comments are original. Indeed, the reader will have little trouble in recognizing the impact of the writings of David Truman and V. O. Key, Jr., upon the book. Less immediately obvious, but equally crucial as a formative agent, are the years I spent under the tutelage of Charles Hagan and Murray Edelman at the University of Illinois. Whatever merit the book is judged to possess may be attributed properly to these scholars. Finally, I want to express my appreciation to two people who were involved in trying to make the language of the book more satisfactory than it would have been if left entirely in its original form: my wife, Pat, who read the original drafts, and John Beasley, of Prentice-Hall, who performed his editorial duties with patience and tact.

H. Z.

Contents

Interest Groups
in the
I
Literature
of Political Science

"Like all literature, writings on politics follow fashion," writes Heinz Eulau.[1] This remark should not be taken to mean that political scientists are frivolous in research design but rather to indicate that the study of politics is a constantly expanding discipline. E. Pendleton Herring has written that "political science as a subject of systematic inquiry started with Aristotle. . . ."[2] There is little reason to dispute this claim. However, the purpose of this book is to explore an aspect of politics that has only recently become the object of professional inquiry. Although there may be some justification for Earl Latham's tracing of group theory to the writings of the English philosophical pluralists (Figgis, Maitland, G. D. H. Cole, and Harold Laski), there is a substantial consensus

---

[1] Heinz Eulau, "Political Science," in Bert F. Hoselitz, ed., *A Reader's Guide to the Social Sciences* (New York: The Free Press of Glencoe, Inc., 1959), p. 89.
[2] E. Pendleton Herring, "On the Study of Government," *American Political Science Review*, XLVII (Dec. 1953), 961.

that the study of interest groups was given its first major emphasis with the appearance of Arthur Bentley's *The Process of Government* in 1908.[3] While this may suggest the relative antiquity of the study of interest groups in America, it should be pointed out that Bentley's book was not accepted as a useful contribution until it was resurrected by Bertram Gross, Charles Hagan, and David Truman in the early 1950's. James W. Garner, a leading political scientist of Bentley's era, dismissed *The Process of Government* in the following manner: "A hasty reading of some of these chapters fails to impress the reviewer with their value as a contribution to the literature of political science, though the work as a whole will doubtless interest students of social institutions." [4]

The Institutional Bias of Nineteenth Century Political Research

Garner's implicit assumption that "political science" and "social institutions" are not related will serve as a good means of beginning the intellectual history of interest groups in the literature of American political science. *The Process of Government,* as the title implies, described politics as a system whereby interest groups achieve a favorable allocation of social resources through the institutions of government. This means that the formal institutions of government, considered apart from the system of social pressures in which they function, are of slight significance. Bentley's book came at a period in the history of American political science in which research was heavily oriented toward the study of legally constituted structures. A relatively new discipline in colleges and

---

[3] Arthur Bentley, *The Process of Government* (San Antonio, Texas: Principia Press of Trinity University, 1949).

[4] James W. Garner, Review of *The Process of Government,* in *American Political Science Review,* II (May 1908), 457. The book was given a more favorable notice by Bertram Gross in 1950. However, other disciplines had recognized the value of Bentley's work before the "rediscovery" by political scientists. A standard text in the history of social thought referred to *The Process of Government* as ". . . probably the most valuable contribution made by an American writer to the deeper processes of government since Calhoun published his *Disquisition on Government." See* Harry Elmer Barnes and Howard Becker, *Social Thought from Lore to Science* (Boston: D. C. Heath and Co., 1938), p. 718.

universities, political science depended heavily on European jurisprudence as its intellectual cornerstone. The fundamental characteristic of political science at this time was its preoccupation with
law. This meant that the legal aspects of political relations, particularly those legal aspects embodied in formal constitutions, served
as an adequate guide to the realities of politics. By concerning
themselves exclusively with governmental institutions—those organizations legally designated to perform specified tasks for the
society—political scientists asked themselves only who has formal
authority. The basic problem of discovering the actual centers of
power was not explored. As David Easton rightly declares: "Most
tended to act as though the study of the distribution of power as
delineated in the constitution constituted the core of political research." [5]

THE STATE AS THE CORE OF POLITICAL SCIENCE

A brief survey of some of the writings of this period will serve to
illustrate their institutional bias. Theodore Woolsey's *Political Science or the State* considered the problem of showing how juristic
concepts of "right" give meaning to institutions as manifested in
formal constitutions. This discussion of philosophical rights is narrowly legalistic in that it shows no concern with underlying patterns of activity which operate through the institutions. Nor is
there any interest in the people who helped to form the institutions. Government is thus portrayed as a purely mechanical device,
almost as though it had a will of its own. Underlying this approach
is the utilitarian concept of law as expressed by Jeremy Bentham.
Woolsey, like Bentham, assumed that people are rational creatures.
Therefore, all that is necessary to achieve political change is to issue
laws formally establishing new relations and men will automatically
adjust.[6] Law presumably exists in a sphere beyond the control of
man.

The utilitarian preoccupation with law, as typified by Woolsey,
was combined with reliance in the writings of German historians
to produce the basic unit of research: the state. It was generally

---

[5] David Easton, *The Political System* (New York: Alfred A. Knopf, 1953),
p. 71.
[6] Theodore Woolsey, *Political Science or The State* (New York: Charles
Scribner's Sons, 1878).

agreed that political science achieved the status of a unique academic discipline by means of its concern with the complex of
institutions placed under the heading of "the phenomena of the
state." At the first public meeting of the American Political Science
Association in 1904, Professor Frank J. Goodnow outlined the nature
of the field as "that science that treats of the organization known
as the state." [7] This indicated that political research had merely
extended its concern for law to a consideration of the source of
law for a particular society. However the same lack of awareness
of patterns of activity underlying law became characteristic of the
study of the state. One may rightly ask: What is this institution
known as the state? There was no ready-made answer to this question. One writer records one hundred and forty-five separate definitions.[8] Woolsey defined the state as "the body or community which
thus by permanent law, through its organs administers justice
within certain limits of territory. . . ." [9] However, there was no
real agreement. Some writers, such as W. W. Willoughby, went so
far as to embody the state with a juristic personality, with a life
independent of the society over which it presumably exercised
authority.[10] Political scientists wrote about the state as though the
activities of people were of no importance. For instance, Goodnow
classifies the legitimate fields of political inquiry into: (1) the expression of state will, (2) the content of state will as expressed,
and (3) the execution of state will.

Hence the state was separated from its social context and studied
in isolation. Political science limited itself to the study of the formal
organization of the organs of state. This institutional approach was
essentially static. The resulting method was almost exclusively descriptive and classificatory. The central problems were formal ones:
bicameral government versus unicameral government, the advantages of the American cabinet system versus the British parliamentary system.

[7] Frank J. Goodnow, "The Work of the American Political Science Association," *Proceedings of the American Political Science Association,* 1 (1904), 37.

[8] C. H. Titus, "A Nomenclature in Political Science," *American Political
Science Review,* XXV (Feb. 1931), 45. Cited in Easton, *op. cit.,* p. 107.

[9] In Raymond G. Gettell, *Readings in Political Science* (Boston: Ginn and
Co., 1911), p. 19.

[10] W. W. Willoughby, *The Nature of the State* (New York: The Macmillan
Co., 1896), p. 3. *See also* John W. Garner, "The Relations of Political Science,"
American Journal of Sociology, XII (Nov. 1906), 341-366.

The limitations of this narrow institutionalism are readily apparent. Consider, for example, a legal approach to democracy. From the purely legal standpoint, once a nation has representative government it has democracy. However, it can be verified empirically that such is not the case. Germany, for example, did not become a democracy after World War I although the accouterments of popular government, such as political parties and elections, were present. In other words, the description of a legal distribution of power cannot inquire into the problem of the degree to which the political behavior of the people in a particular society actually conforms to the legal prescription.[11] A legal description of American government would presumably lead one to the conclusion that the Electoral College is a fundamental decision-making unit, while a study of the social patterns underlying the formal constitution would produce a contrary conclusion. To summarize, we paraphrase George E. G. Catlin, who suggested that the exponents of the legal approach assumed that the state is a clock in which we can take for granted the hand that winds it up and confine ourselves to a study of mechanism.[12]

THE REACTION AGAINST LEGALISM

This type of research was not destined to remain long in the vanguard. Indeed, there was a revulsion from the extremities of the legal approach as early as 1885, when Woodrow Wilson published *Congressional Government*.[13] Other political scientists such as A. Lawrence Lowell and James Bryce exhibited a strong belief that political studies must have a relevance to the actualities of practical politics.[14] Noteworthy as these efforts were, they were still confined to formal institutions. Wilson described the representative branch of government in "realistic" terms while Bryce and Lowell were concerned with the activities of political parties. Bryce re-

---

[11] *See* Seymour Martin Lipset, *Political Man* (Garden City, N.Y.: Doubleday and Co., Inc., 1960) for an analysis of the social requisites of democracy.
[12] George E. G. Catlin, *A Study of the Principles of Politics* (London: George Allen and Unwin, 1930), pp. 66-71.
[13] Woodrow Wilson, *Congressional Government* (Boston: Houghton Mifflin Company, 1885).
[14] For a history of the development of realism in political research *see* Bernard Crick, *The American Science of Politics* (Berkeley: University of California Press, 1959), pp. 95-117.

garded the political party as the "great moving force" of politics, and did much in helping to bring about an empirical revolution in political research. Still, inquiry into the process of government as part of a more general social system was lacking. No one had yet sought to explain the importance of nongovernmental organizations such as organized interest groups; nor had the influence of environmental factors like social class, regional identification, and ethnic group loyalties been taken into account. Finally, although there was a growing interest in empirical research, the dominant trends of political science in the nineteenth century were clearly institutional and legal.

Arthur Bentley and Conflict Theory

Such was the nature of political knowledge when Bentley wrote. It would not be entirely correct to say that *The Process of Government* was a refutation of legalism, for Bentley's intellectual development stems from an entirely different tradition. While political science was concentrating on the legal aspects of politics, sociology (the field in which Bentley took his formal training) was dominated by the implications of Social Darwinism. In its original form, Social Darwinism was a rather rudimentary effort to transfer the findings of Darwin from the biological to the social sphere. In their original formulations, the famous doctrines of "the survival of the fittest" and the "struggle for existence" were incorporated into highly normative laissez-faire social theories by Herbert Spencer and William Graham Sumner. However, more systematic studies of society produced a more refined derivative which has been labeled "conflict theory." Among the more significant conflict theorists were Ludwig Gumplowicz, Gustav Ratzenhofer, Rudolph Von Jhering, and Albion Small, with whom Bentley studied at the University of Chicago. While most of these writers are clearly dated and of little significance considered alone, they are important because of the heavy reliance placed upon them by Bentley. Later in the chapter, when a critical evaluation of Bentley is undertaken, it will add to our comprehension if we understand the academic antecedents of the group theory of politics.

Among the conflict theorists who influenced Bentley's thought, there were two distinct schools. One approach, exemplified by Gumplowicz and Von Jhering, minimized the importance of the autonomous individual. The other approach, of which Ratzenhofer and Small are typical, began with the opposite assumption that the fundamental unit in society is the individual. The core of Gumplowicz's system is the doctrine that social change is wholly the product of social groups, intergroup conflict being the social analogue of the biological struggle for existence. In this conflict, the group is the primary element; the individual is entirely a product of group interaction and not a causal force. He maintains that sociologists can never know the origin of society but must assume the existence of social groups in order to start the process.

What are these groups on which social change depends? The groups which Gumplowicz uses in his interpretation are concrete physical entities consisting of people who can be separated from other groups. Actually the Gumplowicz type of group is little more than a refinement of the Marxian class.[15] They are perhaps most aptly described as tribes, hordes, or racial groups.

While the orientation of Gumplowicz is toward the group as a whole, the concern of Ratzenhofer and Small is the individual, who, as a single rational unit, combines with other persons to form groups. According to Ratzenhofer, every individual is endowed with certain inner forces of a psychic character which he called "interests." The social process is the result of interaction between persons with conflicting interests. Both Ratzenhofer and Small developed a category of innate individual interests. While the two categories of individual interests are not important for our purposes, we should keep in mind that for both men the social process is dependent upon conflicts between each individual's perception of his well-being. The individual is a complex package of instincts, needs, or desires conditioned by racial, economic, or other factors. However, it is only through the participation in groups which represent these interests that satisfaction can be achieved. The social process is thus the interaction between individuals who pool their resources with others of similar attitudes. Building from this founda-

---

[15] Emory S. Bogardus, *The Development of Social Thought* (New York, Longmans, Green and Co., Inc., 1940), pp. 364-366.

tion Ratzenhofer states: "The social process is a continual formation of groups around interests and a continual exertion of reciprocal influences by means of group action." [16]

THE INDIVIDUAL AND GROUP AS ACTIVITY

Bentley's place in the development of conflict theory is that of a
synthesizer or amalgamator of the two variant strains of thought.
In an extensive preparatory statement, Bentley refutes the Ratzen-
hoffer-Small position of interpreting the social process in terms of
the feelings, ideas, or attitudes of participants in political events.
The activities of groups, he argues, must be interpreted as a reaction
to the pressures of other groups rather than as a result of individual
interaction. According to Bentley, the psychological attitudes of the
individual are not an appropriate unit of study because there is no
way of establishing a causal relationship between these attitudes
and the formation of public policy. To Bentley, any satisfactory
explanatory system must identify causes. As we have seen, one of
the most commonly advanced "causes" among the conflict theorists
was the individual attitude. Carried to its most extreme statement,
as for example by Franklin Giddings, the argument stated that
there is a measurable correlation between "cultural advancement"
and inherent psychological attributes, the character of the individual
thus forming the character of the society.[17] Rather than undertaking
the tracing of social movements to individual attitudes, Bentley
urged that the student of politics focus his attention on activity.
The individual person as a bearer of attitudes is not a satisfactory
unit of study; the appropriate unit is the activity of the individual.
As stated by Charles B. Hagan, a leading interpreter of Bentley:
"The individual is his activity." [18]

If the individual is his activity, it follows that the groups which
interact in the political process can also be known only through
activity. This means that Bentley's group is not at all similar to

---

[16] Cited in Barnes and Becker, *op. cit.*, p. 718. *See also* Albion Small, "Rat-
zenhoffer's Sociology," *American Journal of Sociology*, XIII (Jan. 1908), 433-
438.

[17] Franklin Giddings, "The Basis of Social Conflict," *American Journal of
Sociology*, XIII (Mar., 1908), 645.

[18] Charles B. Hagan, "The Group in a Political Science," in Roland Young,
ed., *Approaches to the Study of Politics* (Evanston: Northwestern University
Press, 1958), p. 45.

the Small model. Rather than a social aggregate, the Bentleyan group is in reality no more than a mass of purposive activity. In identifying the "raw material" of government, Bentley succinctly emphasizes his concern for activity: "It is first, last and always activity, action, 'something doing,' the shunting by some men of other men's conduct along changed lines, the gathering of forces to overcome resistance to such alterations, or the dispersal of one grouping of forces by another grouping." [19] This clearly means that the individual, in a science of politics, is a fiction. On the other hand, the physical or reified group which characterized Gumplowicz's writings is equally insignificant. The Bentleyan group is no more than a cross section of activity.

The notion of a scientific study of the process of politics, if it is to be based solely upon the group, is perhaps best stated in Bentley's words:

> If we can get our social life stated in terms of activity and nothing else, we have not succeeded in measuring it, but we have at least reached a foundation upon which a coherent system of measurement can be built up. Our technique may be very poor at the start . . . but we shall cease to be blocked by the intervention of immeasurable elements, which claim to be themselves the real causes of all that is happening, and which by their spook-like arbitrariness make impossible any progress toward dependable knowledge.[20]

This passage suggests one of several possible critical evaluations of Bentley based on the obvious fact that his writings are dated by an uncompromising hostility to introspective psychology, which he regarded as an "immeasurable element."

It may be seen that Bentley, while relying on the theories of the sociological conflict school, abstracted only a negligible portion in its original form. To summarize Bentley's definition of the group, it may be stated that the group is a conceptual device through which to view the flow of political activity. It does designate a certain portion of the individuals of a society—a mass of men not cut off physically from other masses but distinguished by a common activity. This does not preclude the people who participate in one pattern of activity from taking part in many simultaneous

---

[19] Arthur Bentley, *The Process of Government*, p. 176.
[20] *Ibid.*, p. 202.

group activities. Group and activity are equivalent terms. The same
may be said for the concept of interest. Whereas Ratzenhofer had
designated interest as the individual's perception of his environment, Bentley equates interest with group activity: "The group and
the interest are not separate. There exists only the one thing, that
is, so many men bound together in or along the path of a certain
activity." [21]

POLITICS AS GROUP CONFLICT

When compared to the legal approach to the study of government, Bentley's *Process of Government* provides a refreshing note
of candor. In assessing the ultimate significance of the book, David
Easton's comment that "Bentley stands as the watershed between
the simple realism of Wilson and the more complex realism of the
group approach . . ." provides an adequate guide.[22] It would be
a mistake to adopt an uncritical acceptance of Bentley's own peculiar approach. However, it would be equally erroneous to dismiss
it because of some of its obvious ambiguities. Consider, for example,
Bentley's approach to the idea of political reality. He maintained
that political scientists had allowed their discipline to die by con-
fining it to a "formal study of the most external characteristics of
governing institutions" and, at most, a study of the action of men
organized into the structure of government. What is lacking is a
description of a deeper level of activity understood as group behavior. Governmental institutions, rather than possessing an independent existence, are products of "lower-lying political groups."
Therefore, the process of government consists of the conflict among
groups for the control of the activity of governmental institutions.
Whereas the legalistic approach divorced governmental organizations from social interaction, Bentley interpreted such institutions
as the product of social conflict: "We shall have to take all these
political groups, and get them stated with their meaning, with
their value, with their representative quality. We shall have to get
hold of political institutions, legislatures, courts, executive officers,
and get them stated as groups, and in terms of groups." [23]

Bentley thus stated that all aspects of government, including the

---

[21] *Ibid.*, p. 211.
[22] Easton, *op. cit.*, p. 177.
[23] Bentley, *op. cit.*, p. 210.

abstract notion of the state, are phenomena of groups pressing against one another. Pressure seems to be transmitted from one group to another in what Easton has described as a "hydraulic" theory of power. It should be noted that this hydraulic theory can exist only on the assumption of a political system, or series of inter-related units. While Bentley dismissed the existence of a social whole or common interest, he did not exclude the idea of a social system. The political process is equated with the "equilibration of interests, the balancing of groups." The balance of group pressures is the existing state of society. Since he defines society as a system of interacting groups, the tendency toward a "balancing" among competing group interests suggests that there is a natural related-ness among the various parts of the process.

Confusion and Agreement

Bentley's "attempt to fashion a tool," as he called his book, lay dormant for many years; many of its implications, and nearly all of its limitations, were left unanswered. However, inquiry into the nature and activities of political interest groups was proceeding independently of the Bentleyan frame of reference. In 1928, Peter Odegard's *Pressure Politics* appeared.[24] This was an exhaustive examination of the origin and activities of the Anti-Saloon League. The history of this organization is traced from its beginnings as an abstract and unorganized social movement to a highly cohesive national lobby. Full attention is given to its extremely complicated techniques and strategies of pressure, and the countergroups arrayed in opposition to the Anti-Saloon League form part of the descrip-tion. While there should be an adequate recognition of the pioneer-ing significance of Odegard's effort, it was essentially a descriptive study with little or no emphasis on theoretical problems.

In 1929, E. Pendleton Herring exhibited a concern for theorizing about the role of groups in the political process. In *Group Repre-sentation Before Congress*, Herring examined the activities of more than 100 formal pressure groups.[25] His classification of these groups

---

[24] Peter H. Odegard, *Pressure Politics: The Story of the Anti-Saloon League* (New York: Columbia University Press, 1928).

[25] E. Pendleton Herring, *Group Representation Before Congress* (Baltimore: Johns Hopkins University Press, 1929).

and his systematic examination of the reasons for their origin appear to be highly viable, and they clearly influenced the work of later writers such as David Truman. More important, Herring viewed the rising significance of organized groups as an indication of a reconstitution of human relationships. Although apparently unfamiliar with Bentley, Herring offers the following concept of the individual: "[the individual] is a mere cipher in a larger and emergent unit: the organized group." [26] While the reliance on organized activity is too narrow, Herring's dismissal of the individual certainly is within the Bentleyan scheme.

Finally, mention should be made of E. E. Schattschneider's *Politics, Pressures and the Tariff*.[27] In describing the activities of economic-oriented organizations during the tariff revision legislation of 1929-1930, Schattschneider not only affords some penetrating insights into group tactics, but also presents a series of categories through which to organize various types of pressure group activity. As valuable as these contributions are, they did not provide much help toward developing an adequate conceptual framework for the study of interest groups. More explicitly, the role of the individual in relation to the group needed further exploration.

PSYCHOLOGICAL ATTRIBUTES AND GROUP NORMS

As we have seen, Bentley recognized the individual only through his activity, never as an autonomous, introspective unit. The study of politics is the study of activity; "there is nothing of the social that is not activity of men." Accordingly, motives, desires, perceptions, and any other individual mental state must be disregarded. This particular aspect of interest group theory has been severely criticized on many grounds. One of the most common grounds for criticism is that Bentley himself was unclear. He seemed unable to rid his theory of individual mental states irrespective of his passionate insistence on the primacy of group activity. For instance, he states on the one hand that ideas and motives "give us absolutely no help in interpreting the doings of social men" and on the other hand:

---

[26] *Ibid.*, pp. 5-6.
[27] E. E. Schattschneider, *Politics, Pressures and the Tariff* (Englewood Cliffs, N.J.: Prentice-Hall, Inc., 1935).

> The "ideas" and "feelings" as set apart concretely, serve to indicate
> the values of the activities which are our raw materials . . . and
> yet there is not a shred of all the activity which does not present
> itself as an affair of feeling and intelligence. It cannot be stated
> with these phases left out . . . It can only be stated as purposive
> activity . . . as the doings of wanting-knowing men in masses.[28]

Perhaps the best way of understanding the role of the individual is
to state that a person's psychological attributes become matters for
inquiry when they are used as a means of orientation toward the
political world in which he participates. "Ideas" and "feelings" serve
to give the individual man his orientation in the social activity in
which he is involved; they serve to define him as an individual.

Professor Vernon Van Dyke, after a careful evaluation of Bentley's
position with respect to the individual, reaches this conclusion:
". . . he tried to drive them [feelings, faculties, ideas, and ideals]
from the field of inquiry—only to find that he could not get along
without them. It seems much more sensible to grant that feelings,
faculties, ideas, and ideals may help to explain behavior." [29] Group
theorists who followed Bentley have, in fact, taken this "more sensible" approach. This is certainly true of David Truman, whose *The
Governmental Process* is an explicit effort to put the formulations of
Bentley to practical use. Truman defines an interest group as "any
group that, on the basis of one or more shared attitudes, makes
certain claims upon other groups in the society for the establishment,
maintenance, or enhancement of forms of behavior that are implied
by the shared attitudes." The individual, rather than serving primarily as an intersection of activity (as in Bentley), becomes the
bearer of attitudes that serve to define the goals of the group. To
understand the group, we must understand the attitudes, or "common interests," of the individuals whose activity comprises the observable behavior of the group.

DAVID TRUMAN'S APPROACH

Truman repudiates the notion that an emphasis on groups means
the invalidation of the individual. He explains that the study of

---

[28] Bentley, *op. cit.*, p. 177.
[29] Vernon Van Dyke, *Political Science: A Philosophical Analysis* (Stanford,
Cal.: Stanford University Press, 1960), p. 148.

interest groups does not involve mystical entities such as the "group mind," which has a personality or will of its own: "a group is real only in the sense that the interactions that are the group can be observed." [30] This does not substitute the group for the individual but only implies that "when men act in consistent patterns, it is reasonable to study these patterns and designate them in collective terms." [31] Therefore, it is necessary on some occasions to study particular individuals, using the methods of the psychologist. The study of groups and the study of individuals are two approaches to the same thing.

A further clarification of Truman's repudiation of the existence of a conflict between individual and group is afforded by his treatment of the phenomena known as overlapping group affiliations. The individual, according to this notion, is never wholly absorbed in any group to which he belongs. Any person characteristically belongs to many groups, ranging from the primary or face to face groups through religious and economic affiliations and formal associations. Each organization or association may play a part in the policy formation process, and the demands of the various groups may conflict. As a consequence of overlapping affiliations, not all members of any given organization support the stated goals of the organization in equal degrees of intensity. There are many illustrations of overlapping affiliations. Consider, for example, the case of labor unions whose leadership is Communist dominated but whose membership is largely Catholic. On the issue of Soviet-American relations, about which the union members were exposed to conflicting influences, the individuals exhibited a strong tendency to withdraw from the conflict by losing interest in the subject.[32]

Truman's treatment of the individual is clearly more reliable than the rather crude Marxian determinism of, for example, Gumplowicz. By treating groups as fluid patterns of interactions rather than as

---

[30] David Truman, *The Governmental Process* (New York: Alfred A. Knopf, Inc., 1951), p. 29.

[31] *Ibid.*

[32] This example is taken from *ibid,* p. 163. For other examples of overlapping affiliations *see* Paul Lazarsfeld, Bernard Berelson, and Hazel Gaudet, *The People's Choice* (New York: Columbia University Press, 1948) and Robert E. Lane, *Political Life* (New York: The Free Press of Glencoe, Inc., 1959), pp. 197-203.

static objects, individual differences are readily incorporated within group theory. It should be made clear that, while interest groups arise as a result of interaction based on shared attitudes, the attitudes themselves are formed by the group identifications of individuals. As soon as a child is old enough to play with groups of other children, he meets group influences and standards. A boy cannot act too differently from his friends if he is to be accepted. Workers may agree on an acceptable speed of production and exert sufficient pressure on "rate busters" who deviate from the accepted norm that the standards of the group will prevail. Such groups deliberately intend to exert pressure for uniformity of attitudes among their members. This is also true of other more formal groups such as churches and political parties. Informal groups induce conformity without the conscious intention of doing so and without the individual's awareness that it is happening. This is generally the case with patterns of interaction which, even though they have not been institutionalized into a formalized structure, may exert significant influence on each member's attitudes by means of informal standards of behavior.

We should not leave Truman's treatment of the individual without noting that he marshalled strong scientific support for his position. In psychology, reaction against the Freudian assumption that the person can be understood apart from his culture is illustrated by modern psychoanalytic theory as typified by Karen Horney and Harry Stack Sullivan. The essential conclusions of this type of psychoanalytic theory are that the basic forms of knowledge are collectivities, not particulars, and that what Freud regarded as "innate" personality traits are in fact induced as a result of interpersonal influences. In the words of George Herbert Mead:

> The behavior of an individual can be understood only in terms of the behavior of the whole social group of which he is a member, since his individual acts are involved in larger social acts which go beyond himself. . . . We are not . . . building up the behavior in terms of the behavior of the separate individuals comprising it; rather we are starting out with a given social whole of complex group activity, into which we analyze (as elements) the behavior of separate individuals composing it.[33]

---

[33] George Herbert Mead, *Mind, Self and Society* (Chicago: University of Chicago Press, 1934), pp. 6-7.

To conclude this section, we have learned that group theory, in its more refined form, rejects the idea that there is "a politics of in-dividuals that opposes a politics of groups." However, the assumption of a group versus individual scheme is not absent from political theory in opposition to the group theory. One of Bentley's critics, Robert MacIver, for example, asserts that the individual is never fully amalgamated by society and always preserves some measure of autonomy. A more realistic statement would be that a person never gives himself completely to any group with which he identi-fies, whether the group is a formally organized pressure group or a barely discernible category such as region or chronological age. Further, there is no individual attitude which is exclusively de-termined by any single group. Nevertheless, attitudes are products of groups; there is no autonomous man. Alfred de Grazia accurately reflects the methodological bias of the group theorists by offering this analysis of "nongroup" attitudes: "Are they not in the last analysis a personal, private and, in an absolute sense, unique com-bination of his group roles? For instance, may not one man be . . . an 'old-socialist-atheist-majoritarian' and another man a 'young-Christian-socialist-pluralist; whereupon both share roles as socialists but never think and act socialist in the same way?" [34]

Variations on a Theme: Politics and Power

The political scientists discussed so far have, with varying de-grees of clarity, defined politics as a struggle among competing groups. Another group of writers accepts this definition implicitly but approaches the problem from another angle. Rather than con-centrating on the actors in the struggle for power (individuals and groups), they focus attention on the "political act." The political act may be understood as the "act of control, or as the act of human or social control." The leading students of the act of control are George E. G. Catlin, Harold Lasswell, and, to a degree, the con-temporary American political scientist V. O. Key.

What is power? First and foremost, it is a relational complex and

---

[34] Alfred de Grazia, "Interest Group Theory in Political Research," *Annals of the American Academy of Political and Social Science* (Sept., 1958), p. 116.

not a tangible object to be possessed. Power cannot exist in a vacuum, but consists essentially of a relationship of "superordination and subordination, of dominance and submission, of the governors and the governed." The popularly voiced statement that a particular group "has" power does not adequately picture the fundamentally relational basis of power. Hence, to say that "big business" or the "labor bosses" have the power is not correct until we realize that there must be some group in relation to which the "powerful" unit is dominant.

GEORGE E. G. CATLIN'S CONCEPT OF POWER

The relational aspects of political power are succinctly put by the English political scientist, George E. G. Catlin. He, like the group theorists, complained against the institutional bias of traditional political science. All through Catlin's writing we find him searching for a science of politics. That is to say, he was groping for a way to develop highly probable generalizations about political behavior, much the same way in which the physical scientist develops generalizations about the behavior of atoms, molecules, and other units of the physical world. The only conceivable way in which this can be accomplished, argues Catlin, is for political scientists to locate a phenomenon which occurs with a frequency sufficient to warrant observation over an extended period of time. If we study the institution known as the state we will not locate enough of them to develop generalizations. The same holds true for other institutions such as legislatures or even organized groups.

The only phenomena which occurs frequently enough to provide a basis for generalization is the political act, the act of control: "It appears . . . well to define politics . . . as a study of the act of control. . . ." [35] In approaching a more specific definition, Catlin enlarges upon the idea of the political act. He begins with the notion of the individual will, that is, with the desire of every individual to satisfy his wants: "The science of politics has two axioms: first, that each man desires to 'have his own way' in life; secondly that man cannot avoid living together." [36] It appears from this statement that Catlin's political act is actually resting on an individualistic basis, much like the earlier Hobbesian struggle for

[35] Catlin, *Principles of Politics,* p. 69.
[36] *Ibid.,* p. 137.

power. This is not entirely accurate, for there is much in Catlin
that resembles the group theories of Ratzenhofer and Small. The
individual is indeed the political unit, or more correctly, the individual will (as distinct from the physiological individual) is what
political scientists must study. The individual does not live in a
world where the will is automatically transferred into the position
of control. Rather, each individual will, in seeking fulfillment, meets
resistance from opposing desires. The clash of wills necessitates a
system of political activity, or struggle. What is the basic unit in
this struggle? Catlin is very explicit on this point: "The unit in the
construction of the political structure must remain the active individual, assenting or dissenting, supporting or weakening that
structure, centripetal or centrifugal to that system. The individual
is autonomous if not uninfluenced."

What role does the group play in this structure? In criticizing the
idea of the state as a unit of study, Catlin maintains that society is
not a collection of individuals bound into any unique organization
such as the state. Society is "an aggregate of individuals organized
into various groups, sometimes contrary, sometimes mutually inclusive, sometimes overlapping." In other words, the individual is
prior to the group and selects on a rational basis the groups through
which he can most readily realize his will. It is an individualistic
ego satisfaction mechanism which lies at the heart of the group
formation process. Groups exist only to magnify the individual's
ego: "The liberty of man lies in his power of selection of the social
group which he will support as order-keeping authority, or of the
group to which he will go for political goods which he may happen to esteem even higher than peace and order. It lies in his
power to choose his political market." [37]

The assumption of the rational, autonomous individual places
Catlin's theory of power at the fringe of group theory as illustrated
by the Bentley-Truman approach. This approach, as we have
learned, posits a rejection of the idea that individuals exist in some
degree of isolation and then form into groups. For example, Truman
attacks the Italian sociologist Gaetano Mosca's assertion that men
have an "instinct" for banding together in groups, on the ground

---

[37] *Ibid.*, pp. 371-375. Much of Catlin's early writings has been reiterated
in *Systematic Politics* (Toronto: University of Toronto Press, 1962).

that the notion of instinct assumes a temporal priority of the individual over the group. Much the same type of argument is offered
by Bentley in his refutation of the theories of Ratzenhofer and
Small that are also built on the foundation of individual desires.

HAROLD LASSWELL'S EMPHASIS ON SYMBOLS

Much more compatible with the development of the theory of
group conflict are the writings of Harold Lasswell. He agrees with
Catlin's emphasis on power, but does not approach the phenomenon
through the narrow device of the autonomous individual. In one of
his earlier studies, *Psychopathology and Politics,* he exhibited a
tendency to rely strongly on the introspective psychoanalytic techniques of Freud in explaining political behavior. However, in 1955,
at the American Psychological Association meeting in San Fran-
cisco, Lasswell read a paper entitled "Psychopathology and Politics:
Twenty-Five Years After" in which he revised many aspects of his
earlier position. Lasswell drew attention to his earlier work: "It is
not surprising to find that Freud continued to talk about 'man' versus
'society' rather than to recognize that it is always a case of 'man in
society' versus (or with) 'man in society.'" [38]

"Man in society versus (or with) man in society" are the participants in the political process. However, Lasswell's more complete
definition of politics does not take as its first premise the struggle
for power as a result of individual wills (which seems to suggest
that those who pursue power adopt power as an end in itself rather
than as a means to an end). A more explicit statement of his concept of the political process is found in *World Politics and Personal
Insecurity*:

> Political analysis is the study of the changes in the shape and com-
> position of the value patterns of society. Representative values are
> safety, income, and deference. Since a few members of any com-
> munity at any given time have the most of each value, a diagram
> of the pattern of distribution of any value resembled a pyramid.
> The few who get the most of any value are the *elite;* the rest are
> the rank and file. An elite preserves its ascendancy by manipulating

---

[38] The first edition of *Psychopathology and Politics* was published by the University of Chicago Press in 1930. The paper referred to above was printed as
an appendix to Harold Lasswell, *Psychopathology and Politics,* rev. ed. (New
York: The Viking Press, Inc., 1960) pp. 269-319.

symbols, controlling supplies, and applying violence. Less formally expressed, politics is the study of *who gets what, when, and how.*[39]

Since the distribution of values depends on the influence of the members of society, the study of politics is a "study of influence and the influential." In *Power and Society,* written in collaboration with Abraham Kaplan, a more comprehensive description of the relation of power to values is given: "The political act takes its origin in a situation in which the actor strives for the attainment of various values for which power is a necessary (and perhaps also sufficient) condition." [40]

Lasswell's framework is useful in understanding the operations of political pressure groups, for we can certainly substitute "group" for "actor" in the political formula defining the political act. Thus politics is a process through which competing patterns of activity (which may take the form of organized groups) seek to enforce forms of behavior consistent with their values. One should be quick to point out, however, that Lasswell did not use the term group as though it were the exclusive actor in the political act. His definition of a group is simply "an organized aggregate" whereas an interest group is "an interest organized for the satisfaction of the interest." The reliance upon organizations as a requisite for the existence of a group is fundamentally different from the definition of either Bentley or Truman. However, Lasswell correctly noted that the political scientist should interest himself neither in individuals nor in groups as "social atoms" but rather in interaction among competitors for the achievement of goals.

A significant contribution by Lasswell, which has only recently come into extensive use, is his treatment of political symbols. None of the major group theorists deal extensively with problems of perception, but Lasswell has always addressed himself to cognitive processes and particularly to nonrational responses to emotionally powerful symbols. He wrote that "politics is the process by which the irrational bases of society are brought out into the open" and that "widespread and disturbing changes in the life-situation of

[39] Harold Lasswell, *World Politics and Personal Insecurity* (New York: The Free Press of Glencoe, Inc., 1950), p. 3.

[40] Harold Lasswell and Abraham Kaplan, *Power and Society* (New Haven: Yale University Press, 1950), p. 240.

many members of society" produce reactions that are stated largely in symbolic terms bearing only a limited relevance to actual needs: "The political symbol becomes ladened with the residue of successive positive and negative identifications, and with the emotional charge of displaced private motives." [41] Lasswell further argues that political symbols, because of their emotional qualities and ambiguities of reference in relation to individual experience, are ideally suited to the satisfaction of group demands. However, Lasswell was not specific as to the conditions under which political symbols play a major role in the political process.

Murray Edelman, a political scientist whose writings are based upon the concept of politics as a struggle among groups, has built upon Lasswell's treatment of symbols. He argues that, although public policy may be understood as "the resultant of the interplay among groups," there are patterns of group activity whose essential characteristic is interest in symbols. The symbol-oriented activity may be distinguished from what Edelman calls "interest in tangible resources." The two varying types of group activity are summarized by Edelman in this manner:

> (1) Pattern A: a relatively high degree of organization–rational, cognitive procedures–precise information–an effective interest in specifically identified, tangible resources–a favorably perceived strategic position with respect to reference groups–relatively small numbers. (2) Pattern B: shared interest in the improvement of status through protest activity–an unfavorably perceived strategic position with respect to reference groups–distorted, stereotyped, inexact information and perception–response to symbols connoting suppression of threats–relative ineffectiveness in securing tangible resources through political activity–little organization for purposeful action–quiescence–relatively large numbers.[42]

---

[41] Lasswell, *Psychopathology and Politics* (New York: The Viking Press, Inc., 1960), pp. 188-193.

[42] Murray Edelman, "Symbols and Political Quiescence," *American Political Science Review*, LIV (Sept. 1960), 701. The patterns of activity described by Edelman offer the possibility of comparison with the theory of William Kornhauser. In his *The Politics of Mass Society* (New York: The Free Press of Glencoe, Inc., 1959) Kornhauser distinguishes between mass or pluralistic movements and elites and suggests that the social strata with the fewest social ties are more responsive to mass movements. Some examples which Kornhauser gives of mass versus elites are: new business versus old business, small business versus big business, unskilled workers versus skilled workers, and poorer farmers and farm laborers versus wealthier farmers. *See* p. 223.

Edelman's contribution to the theory of groups in politics, which consists essentially of a synthesis of Lasswell with more traditional interpretations, provides a useful guide to the study of certain types of political movements, especially the "extremist" type activity.

Group Interest and Public Interest

In the popular vernacular, as well as in more academic discussions, the term "public interest" has come in for more than its share of interpretations. During the Eighty-first Congress, the House of Representatives created a Select Committee on Lobbying Activities (popularly referred to as the Buchanan Committee) to investigate the nature and extent of organized group pressures on the representative branch of government. George Galloway, a political scientist who testified before the Buchanan Committee, presented his view of the responsibility of Congress to the public interest: "The primary responsibility of Congress is to promote the general welfare. . . . No public policy could ever be the mere sum of the demands of organized special interests, . . . for there are vital common interests that cannot be organized by pressure groups." [43] The difficulty of assuming the existence of a public interest is very easily recognized. What are these vital common interests? The Buchanan Committee never undertook the task of specifying such overriding goals, nor has there ever been a clear formulation of the components of a hypothetical general interest. Indeed, even when we list values on which everyone would presumably agree, such as the survival of the nation or the education of the young, we find widely ranging conceptions of the true expression of the general will. In time of war there are pacifists, conscientious objectors, and others who apparently do not agree that the interest of the nation is best pursued by the waging of armed conflict. Can we say that proper education of our children is a common interest when the public authorities of Prince Edward County, Virginia, prefer no education to integrated facilities?

---

[43] House Select Committee on Lobbying Activities, *Hearings, The Role of Lobbying in Representative Self Government,* 81st Cong., 2nd sess. (Washington, D.C.: Government Printing Office, 1950), p. 99.

A REALISTIC APPROACH TO THE PUBLIC INTEREST

The subscribers to the group theory of politics do not agree that it is possible to isolate a national interest beyond that of the interests of the many social aggregates encompassed within the boundaries of the nation. There are, says Bentley, "always some parts of the nation to be found arrayed against other parts." Even before the development of an explicit group theory we find evidence of skepticism about the existence of a common interest. Over a century ago John C. Calhoun said that the general will "instead of being the united opinion of the whole community is usually nothing more than the voice of the strongest interest or combination of interests; and not infrequently a small but energetic and active portion of the people." [44] Compare Calhoun's statement with Bentley's claim that ". . . we shall never find a group interest of society as a whole. . . . The society itself is nothing other than the complex of the groups that compose it" and with Truman's synthesis: "In developing a group interpretation of politics . . . we do not need to account for a totally inclusive interest because one does not exist," and the position of the group theorists may be understood. Stated in its briefest version, the group theorists' doctrine maintains that every public policy helps someone and hurts someone; laws operate to the advantage of some groups and to the disadvantage of others.

The criticism of this aspect of group theory falls into two classes: (1) normative objections based on the assumption that the denial of a common interest undermines the foundations of democratic society and (2) methodological objections claiming that the attribution of primary causal force to groups neglects the integrative function of institutions and political culture. The first charge, that group theory is anti-democratic, is well illustrated by Robert MacIver's criticism of Bentley which, as Richard Taylor points out, is based on a misunderstanding of *The Process of Government*.[45] MacIver interprets Bentley as believing that "a legislative act is always the calculable resultant of a struggle between pressure groups, never a decision

---

[44] John C. Calhoun, *A Disquisition on Government*, in Benjamin F. Wright, ed., *Source Book of American Political Theory* (New York: The Macmillan Company, 1929), p. 537.
[45] Richard W. Taylor, "Arthur F. Bentley's Political Science," *Western Political Quarterly*, V (June 1952), 219.

between opposing conceptions of the national welfare." MacIver concludes that "the fact that the interest in the common welfare cannot be organized after the fashion of specific interest should not conceal from us either its existence or the need to sustain it. Democracy itself is the final organization of the common interest." [46]

Postponing for the moment the necessity of dealing with concepts of democracy, we may easily see that MacIver has attributed to group theory a far more deterministic nature than it actually possesses. Surely it would be useless to maintain that all public policy is a result of the conflict of organized "pressure groups." The slightest inquiry into empirical evidence would convince the student that many laws are passed not only without the support of organized groups but frequently in opposition to the demands of such organizations. When a congressman issues a press release announcing his intention to support or oppose a particular bill in "the interest of the public" in spite of the pressure of "minority interests," we cannot assume that this is merely a rationalization. Surely the congressman believes he is acting in the public interest. This is the key to the problem. Each legislator (or administrator) is an actor in the decision-making process. As an individual he is a member of many groups, yet none of these groups commands his total loyalty. His perception of a particular situation will be the result of the complex pressures of this variety of affiliations. For example, a congressman from a rural, Republican district (to list only two of many possible affiliations) might well believe that the continuation of the foreign aid program is not in the "national interest."

Pendleton Herring adequately expresses a group interpretation of the public interest: "Its value is psychological and does not extend beyond the significance that each responsible [public] servant must find in the phrase for himself. . . ." [47] The evaluation that each person in a position of responsibility gives to opposing presentations of the public interest may well be heavily influenced by the activi-

---

[46] Robert MacIver, *The Web of Government* (New York: The Macmillan Company, 1948), p. 220.

[47] Herring, *Public Administration and the Public Interest* (New York and London: McGraw-Hill Book Company, Inc., 1936), p. 24. For a stimulating analysis of perceptions of group interests by legislators *see* John C. Wahlke, William Buchanan, Heinz Eulau, and LeRoy Ferguson, "American State Legislators' Role Orientations Toward Pressure Groups," *Journal of Politics,* XXII (May 1960), 203-227.

ties of organized lobbying associations, but these associations are not the sole determinants of the content of a decision. In short, instead of public policy "never" resulting from opposing conceptions of the national welfare, as MacIver maintained, it is the position of the group theorists that opposing conceptions of the national welfare constitute the very heart of the political process.

THE IMPORTANCE OF INSTITUTIONS

The second criticism of group theory, that it does not provide an accurate account of the role of institutions and environmental conditions, is more valid. Writing at his particular period in the development of political science, Bentley perhaps overstated his case by urging that we "get hold of political institutions, legislatures, courts, executive officers, and get them stated as groups, and in terms of groups." Is it not possible that these institutions not only react to group pressure, but also help to mold the structure of group action? Later writers, particularly Truman, have given more importance to governmental institutions as actors in the political process. It would be a false realism which described the agencies of government as passive pawns rather than active participants. In many cases, government administrators have identified with the interests of unorganized segments of the population in opposition to cohesive and well organized interests as, for example, in the pursuit of anti-trust litigation.

However, when group theorists are criticized for failing to give proper attention to institutions, the word "institution" is usually employed in a more general sense. In this broader use of the word, institution denotes a stable pattern of behavior. Defined in this way, institutions consist of stylized or regularized patterns of behavior. They reflect conformity in behavior. Merle Fainsod diagnosed the failure of Bentley to come to grips with the broader "institutional matrix" within which groups operate. He maintained that there are "conditional factors" which combine to form the institutional framework within which group conflict is waged.[48]

The institutional context may consist partially of broad, inclusive, or widely shared attitudes which may quite logically be called a

---

[48] Merle Fainsod, "Some Reflections on the Nature of the Regulatory Process," in Carl Freidrich and Edward S. Mason, eds., *Public Policy* (Cambridge: Harvard University Press, 1940).

common interest. Various terms have been given to these widely
shared attitudes. Truman refers to them as "rules of the game";
Austin Ranney speaks of "consensus" while Seymour Lipset prefers
"legitimacy." [49] Whatever the term employed, the essential meaning is the same. In any society there is a "way of doing things." The
continued stability of a political system rests on the degree to which
there is a substantial agreement among the members of the community that they should continue to operate as a community. Truman has greatly improved the reliability of group theory by his
recognition of the existence of a broad social system:

> We cannot deny the obvious fact that we are examining a going
> political system that is supported or accepted by a large proportion
> of the society. We cannot account for such a system by adding up
> in some fashion the National Association of Manufacturers, the
> Congress of Industrial Organizations, the American Farm Bureau
> Federation, the American Legion and other groups that come to
> mind when "lobbies" and "pressure groups" are mentioned. . . .
> Were such the exclusive ingredients of the political process in the
> United States, the entire system would have torn itself apart long
> since.[50]

What Truman is implying is that patterns of group organization
and activity may be derived from factors other than an isolated or
totally inclusive struggle among the groups themselves.

To summarize what we have learned about groups and the social
system we must recognize that whether a group is successful in its
quest for the fulfillment of its goals depends upon its role within
the "total way of life of the population." This includes not only
widely shared attitudes but also more readily observable factors
such as "the degree of separation of formal authority, the degree
of legitimacy accorded formal authority, and the lack of representation of interests in the representative structure of government." [51]

---

[49] Truman, *op. cit.*, p. 159. Lipset, *op. cit.*, pp. 77-83. Austin Ranney and
Willmoore Kendall, *Democracy and the American Party System* (New York:
Harcourt, Brace & World, Inc., 1956), p. 54.

[50] Truman, *op. cit.*, p. 51.

[51] De Grazia, *op. cit.*, p. 115. For criticism of group theory for failure to
account for institutional factors *see* Samuel J. Eldersveld, "American Interest
Groups: A Survey of Research and Some Implications for Theory and Method,"
in Henry W. Ehrman, ed., *Interest Groups on Four Continents* (Pittsburgh:
University of Pittsburgh Press, 1958), p. 187, and Roy C. Macridis, "Interest
Groups in Comparative Analysis," *Journal of Politics,* XXIII (Feb. 1961),
34-38.

It has been the purpose of this introductory chapter to provide a brief outline of the nature of group theory. That it has limitations and is often contradictory may be quickly admitted. Indeed, much of the criticism of the group theory of politics is that none of its exponents have been able to agree on the nature of groups. Nevertheless, the activities of groups have a bearing on the shape of public policy. It now becomes our task to inquire into the manner in which interest groups are able to have some effect on the kinds of decisions made by the political mechanisms of a society.

Interest Groups

II and the American

Democratic Environment

Looking back on the writings of the group theorists, one point stands above all others. This aspect of the theory, which is its most misunderstood, will form the guiding framework for the remainder of the book. "Group interest" is not to be confused with organized associations. Certainly some formal organizations are part of particular interests, but no formal organization is an interest in itself. There are interests in minimum wages, higher parity for farm products, or fair trade legislation. Whoever subscribes to the values or goals of an interest or undertakes activity in support of these goals is part of the group activity no matter to which organization he may belong. There is, of course, a relation between organizations and a particular interest. Virtually all members of the AFL-CIO are part of an interest in higher wages just as many members of the National Association of Retail Druggists are participants in an interest in fair trade legislation. However, some members of these organizations are not parts of these particular interests and may well be adherents of goals which are opposed to the stated aims of

their organizations. In addition, many people who do not belong
to the National Association of Retail Druggists, for example, are
part of the interest in fair trade. People in this category would
include the personnel of government agencies, such as the Federal
Trade Commission, who sympathize with the problems of independent druggists and support legislation on their behalf. Also
included in this interest are congressmen who wish to restrain the
mass buying techniques of large chain corporations, newspapers
who support this position, political parties which have drafted platforms supporting fair trade, and any number of different types of
activity.[1]

Interest Groups, Organizations, and Structures of Power

Public policy, then, is formed as a result of the interplay of group
interests. We are concerned with the role that organized "pressure
groups" play in this process. To begin, it is essential that an operating definition of the term be agreed upon. According to the *Encyclopedia of the Social Sciences,* a pressure group is an "aggregate,
organized or unorganized, which applies pressure tactics." [2] This
definition is helpful, but falls short of the mark in that it does not
provide a key to understanding the role of the formal organizations.
For our purposes, a slightly narrower definition will prove more
useful. A pressure group, as the term is used in this book, is an
organized aggregate which seeks to influence the content of governmental decisions without attempting to place its members in formal
governmental capacities. The definition implies a collection of
individuals who consciously band together, amalgamate their
strength, consult on questions of organization strategy, and undertake action in pursuit of their goals. Obviously, not all organizations
are pressure groups. Since the basic characteristic of the pressure
group is its intention to influence governmental decisions, organizations which do not engage in this activity do not qualify. A local

---

[1] This position is developed from Murray Edelman, "Governmental Organization and Public Policy," *Public Administration Review,* XII (Autumn,
1952), 276-283.

[2] Robert M. MacIver, "Social Pressures," *Encyclopedia of the Social Sciences*
(New York: The Macmillan Company, 1942), XII, 347.

music appreciation group normally would not feel the need to undertake lobbying activities. However, all organizations may *become* pressure groups. The same music appreciation group may desire the establishment of a municipal orchestra supported by taxes and may be opposed by a taxpayers' association. Under these circumstances it is quite likely that the music appreciation advocates will place their case before the city council, which may in turn agree to submit the matter to a referendum. Clearly this situation would involve attempts by both groups to implement their values through favorable governmental decisions. The pattern of their activity will be governed to a certain extent by the peculiarities of the explicit situation. Because of the basic hostility to new taxes, it may be more advantageous to the music appreciation group to try to achieve a decision without undergoing the referendum process. Under different circumstances the issue may be fought out by their trying to influence the outcome of an election by supporting candidates who are favorably disposed to their goals.

THE VALUE OF ORGANIZATION

Pressure politics takes many forms, and many varying types of techniques are utilized. Underlying these patterns, however, there is a basic common denominator of organization. The existence of an organization indicates that a collection of individuals have undergone a perceptive process sufficiently intense to stimulate a frequent rate of interaction. A very important distinction must be made between a purposive aggregate and a mere collection of individuals who happen to have, through no conscious act, something "in common." For instance, it may be said that the individuals who happen to be waiting in line to be admitted to a theatre are a group in the physical sense of the word. The same may be said for any number of other types of similarities. Truman refers to this classification of individuals as "categoric groups." By this he means that there are endless varieties of categories to which every person might belong, such as alcoholics, people who make over $10,000 a year, and so on.[3] The purposive group, however, is distinguished from the categoric group on the basis of interaction among its members. It is the interaction process that is vital. The members

---

[3] David Truman, *The Governmental Process* (New York: Alfred A. Knopf, Inc., 1951), p. 23.

of the purposive aggregate may be observed to interact with one another in certain recurring patterns. Organization occurs when these patterns of interaction have become sufficiently formalized to justify the insurance of stability by institutionalization. Organization, then, represents a stage—a rather advanced stage—in the degree of interaction.

In the competition among interests, the existence of highly organized pressure groups is a factor of crucial importance. Organization represents a concentration of resources toward the realization of political influence. Organized structures of power can wield a predominant force when confronted by diffuse, unorganized interests. Therefore, if one could equalize all other factors it could be said that interests which are supported by organizations have a better chance of success than interests which do not enjoy the participation of organizations. As Latham says: "They [organized groups] are structures of power because they concentrate human wit, energy, and muscle for the achievement of a given purpose."[4]

Pressure Groups and Democratic Values

Organization is only one of many factors which enable us to gauge the probable success of a political movement. As we have observed, pressure groups must operate within a given environment. To be successful, they must come to grips with the total structure of the situation which helps to define the society. Latham offered the following category of devices which may be used in the relationship of groups to their environment: (1) the environment may be made safe and predictable by putting restraints on it, (2) potential areas of hostility may be neutralized, and (3) the environment may be made conciliatory or friendly.[5] A good illustration of these methods may be seen in the efforts of the American Council on Race Relations to secure the passage of state fair employment practices legislation (FEPC). In our society it is considered unfortunate to be accused of having "left wing" support. The existence of such support, whether real or imagined, presumably conflicts with the free enterprise system and hence outrages

---

[4] Earl Latham, *The Group Basis of Politics* (Ithaca: Cornell University Press, 1952), p. 12.
[5] *Ibid.*, pp. 29-33.

loyalties to prevailing institutions and sacred values. Organizations which espouse serious proposals for reform may, if identified with the values of the left, provoke a sense of outrage which obscures a rational response to their arguments. The American Council on Race Relations faced this problem in an actively hostile environment. In a manual prepared to guide those who would participate in campaigns for FEPC legislation, the following evaluation of the tactics of the opposition was offered:

> Proponents of FEPC have dealt with the problem of "left wing" support in many ways. Opponents will make use of every opportunity to describe FEPC as "communist-inspired," and the proponents as "communist-tools." Realistically, there is little that can be done about this except to repudiate such support, and this will not in itself assure that the opponents will view the issue differently. . . . In some states, their support has been repudiated, though occasionally far more violently than one would expect from civil rights advocates. A more positive solution, but one more difficult than the above, is so to organize the elements in the community that the "left wing" groups become an unimportant minority.[6]

Other examples of efforts to manipulate the environment come readily to mind. In many southern states certain organizations such as the National Association for the Advancement of Colored People face similar problems of being labeled as subversive. In Florida, an administrator who had run afoul of certain pressure groups over whom he exercised some degree of control was accused of being a member of the NAACP, a charge which he regarded as contributory to his ultimate dismissal.

TRADITIONAL DISTRUST AND ORGANIZED GROUPS

However careful groups must be to avoid the development of programs which conflict with the values of the community in which they function, all organizations within this country operate to some extent in an atmosphere of latent or actual hostility. From the beginnings of the American republic, the assumption has been made that pressure groups, irrespective of their goals, are evil because they conflict with the fundamental attributes of democracy. James Madison's famous tenth essay in *The Federalist*, while acknowl-

---

[6] Ralph H. Turner and Lewis M. Killian, *Collective Behavior* (Englewood Cliffs: Prentice-Hall, Inc., 1957), p. 290.

edging the inevitability of "factions," argued that one of the best features of the proposed constitution was its "tendency to break and control the violence of faction." Madison described the existence of factions as a "dangerous vice" and one of the most serious threats to popular government.[7] Since Madison's day there has been a prolific stream of anti-pressure group writings, in which some social scientists and public officials have stated the basic thesis that "minority interests" and "democracy" cannot coexist. Our literature is full of warnings that the influence of organized groups is becoming dangerous: "Group organization is one of the perils of our times"; the unfortunate fate of American government is that "there is nothing it can do to protect itself from pressures." From social scientists we have the warning that since the goals of pressure groups are at best the desires of a minority, any effort to implement them would tend to be undemocratic. The only logical conclusion from such a premise is that ". . . every pressure groups tends inevitably to embrace the potentiality for evil."[8]

Official sanction was given to the hostility toward pressure groups by the United States Supreme Court when it refused, in the case of *Trist v. Child,* to uphold a claim for payment by a lobbyist against an individual who had hired him.[9] The basis for the decision was that lobbying was a practice "contrary to sound policy and public morals." Hugo Black, now a Supreme Court Justice, while chairing a Senate investigation committee in 1935, voiced the fear of organized groups in a cogent, if extreme fashion:

> Contrary to tradition, against the public morals, and hostile to good government, the lobby has reached such a position of power that it threatens government itself. Its size, its power, its capacity for evil; its greed, trickery, deception and fraud condemn it to the death it deserves.[10]

This type of criticism is not based merely on the disapproval of some of the more harsh tactics sometimes employed by organiza-

---

[7] James Madison, *The Federalist,* No. X.

[8] Edward M. Freeman, "The Pattern of Pressure," *Sociology and Social Research,* XXXVII (Jan. 1953), 187. For an excellent summary of literature on pressure groups and democracy *see* Lewis A. Bayles, "Are Pressure Groups Threatening American Democracy," *The Midwest Quarterly,* 11 (Oct. 1960), 49-66.

[9] Trist v. Child, 21 Wallace 441 (1875).

[10] Cited in Thomas B. Mechling, "Washington Lobbies Threaten Democracy," *Virginia Quarterly Review,* XXII (Summer, 1946), 341.

tions, but specifies a rejection of the legitimacy of the very existence
of such groups in our society. The furor raised in 1956 when Senator Case of South Dakota reported that an oil lobbyist had attempted to contribute $2,500 to his campaign when he was weigh-
ing the merits of a bill to exempt producers of natural gas from
certain types of federal regulation was directed toward an act regarded beyond the "rules of the game." Few critics questioned the
legitimacy of lobbying.

The criticism exemplified in the writings cited above is based
upon a concept of democracy which is both inadequate and naïve.
There are two basic components of this conception. First, it is maintained that democracy depends on the degree to which the institutions of government provide an accurate reflection of the will of
the people. The will of the people is measured by the device of
majority decision. Therefore any decision which does not implement
the wishes of the majority, which is a concession to the demands
of a "special interest," is undemocratic. This assumption about the
nature of democracy bears close resemblance to the idea of the
general will considered in the first chapter. A democracy is a system
of government in which "the people" rule. The public official acts
only in the name of the public, thus providing direct enforcement
of "public opinion."

The equation of democracy with the will of the people is continually appearing in the speeches of public officials who are har-
assed by the demands of organized groups. Senator Styles Bridges,
Republican of New Hampshire, demonstrates this reaction:

> Do you want your government to be run by pressure groups?
> I ask because there is a danger that our democratic processes
> will be thwarted unless something is done—by you, the voter—
> to put the pressure of public opinion on the pressure groups that
> infest the halls of Congress.
> Now, you will agree that lobbying is wicked when it goes be-
> yond the legitimate expression of opinion as to public issues; when
> it seeks to sway members of Congress in the selfish interest of a
> particular faction. . . . You will concede that any Senator or Rep-
> resentative who yields to the urging of "legislative agents" without
> consideration of the interests of the people ought to be drummed
> out of office.[11]

The problem here is: Who is to decide what the people want? How

---

[11] Styles Bridges, "I Don't Like Pressure," *Pageant*, Sept., 1946, p. 17.

does the Senator or Representative locate the true expression of this will?

Attempts to locate a true public opinion may be seen in the myriad of proposals for political reform in the direction of increasing popular participation in government. Such proposals as the initiative and referendum or direct legislation are supported in the hope that these devices will foster a stable democratic regime. Provisions for the recall of public officials and the adoption of the direct primary as a means of designating party nominees also reflect this concern with the vital nature of public opinion. In 1950 the Committee on Political Parties of the American Political Science Association issued a report which fits well into the scheme of reform. Conceding that direct participation by the citizenry in the day-by-day affairs of government is ill advised, the Committee recommended that a strong, or rigidly disciplined, political party system would provide the best method of resisting the onslaught of organized pressure since "by themselves, the interest groups cannot attempt to define public policy democratically." [12]

The second part of the concept of democracy which expresses hostility to interest groups is concerned with the nature of man. If democracy must reflect the will of the majority, it follows that this majority will is composed of the rational choice of individuals who have carefully evaluated their needs and reached a satisfactory decision. In such a system the interest group is an intruder upon the rational cognitive processes of each person's mind. The idea of the autonomous, rational individual stems not only from abstract theory but also from a portion of the American system of values: the assumption of extreme individualism.

Individualism is a vital part of the political system in that it serves as a symbol, or myth, which helps to cement the society through commitment to an ideal. The use of the word "myth" does not connote disapproval but merely suggests that the idea of individual responsibility serves as a guide for some people as they evaluate public policy. Myths are "the value-impregnated beliefs and notions that men hold, that they live by or live for." [13] Being

---

[12] Committee on Political Parties, American Political Science Association, *Toward A More Responsible Two-Party System* (New York: Holt, Rinehart, & Winston, Inc., 1950), p. 19.

[13] Robert M. MacIver, *The Web of Government* (New York: The Macmillan Company, 1947), p. 4.

basically woven into the values of individuals, myths may continue
to survive irrespective of their objectivity in describing "reality."
Thus, in America we place a high premium on the virtues of individual initiative even though the economy of the society is dominated by large-scale collective enterprise.

This faith in individual responsibility, when amalgamated with the
dogmas of traditional democratic theory, serves as another mechanism to prejudice the average citizen against collective action and,
specifically, against the pressures of organized groups. The view
prevails that each person's own effort toward the solution of his
problems is more worthy than group effort through appeal to government agencies. Pressure groups, so the argument goes, are dominated by single "blind" impulses which tend to "undermine the
honest and rational thinking on which democracy depends" and
"sabotage the struggle toward objective reason." [14]

INTEREST GROUPS AS ESSENTIAL COMPONENTS
OF DEMOCRATIC SOCIETY

If democracy depends on this type of reasoning, then there is
indeed no room for pressure groups. However, as was indicated at
the beginning of this section, this particular view of democracy is
inadequate. In the first place, it is practically impossible for all
governmental decisions to be made by means of the rule of a
majority of the people. Not only are many decisions so complex
that they are beyond the comprehension of the layman, but also
many decisions are beyond his interest. What possible concern have
you or I in the fertilizer development program of the Tennessee
Valley Authority? Whether the TVA administrators elect to use
natural legumes or artificial nitrates is none of our affair. However,
if we are engaged in the production of a particular type of fertilizer,
such a decision may be of primary importance and may determine
whether we can continue to operate a business.

Of course all government decisions are not this narrow, and some
may be so broad as to involve the "nation as a whole" as, for example, a decision to declare war. However, all decisions affect some
people more than others. To German or Italian or Japanese Americans, our entry into World War II possibly stirred a series of con-

---

[14] Freeman, *op. cit.*, 185.

flicting emotions which caused a different perception of the conflict than that of other ethnic groups. Whatever the decision, our interest in the affairs of government is likely to be most intense when we have a personal stake in the resolution of the issue. It is highly unlikely that any public policy will help or hinder us purely in our individual capacities. It is much more probable that our reaction to governmental decisions will be in terms of the groups with which we identify. These groups will thus play a crucial role in enabling us to evaluate the "rightness" or "wrongness" of the action our government is undertaking.

We should have little trouble in agreeing that a working democratic system need rely on the judgment of the voters only on general questions of public policy. The institution of regularly scheduled elections gives the American citizens the opportunity to express approval or disapproval of the *general* course of public policy. Even though the issues are systematically simplified by candidates, this does not produce a high voting turnout. The average citizen is only moderately interested in politics. In the United States about 60 per cent of the eligible voters normally go to the polls. This is considerably lower than the proportion of voters in the other major democracies, such as England.

We are faced, then, with a rather large percentage of people who show no inclination to take an active role in public affairs. Perhaps this is dangerous for democracy and perhaps it is not. It is at least a viable argument to maintain that there is no need to launch elaborate "get out the vote" efforts since those who choose to vote are doing so out of sincere concern for the affairs of their country, state, or city. Who are these people who are politically active? There is a clear correlation between political interest and organizational membership. As Robert E. Lane maintains: "Isolation tends to make a person politically apathetic; group memberships in themselves increase his political interests and activity . . . he is more likely to vote if he has more organizational memberships, no matter where he is in the social system." [15]

Instead of hindering democracy (when defined as response to the public interest) the operation of pressure groups actually functions to strengthen citizen participation.

---

[15] Robert E. Lane, *Political Life* (New York: The Free Press of Glencoe, Inc., 1959), p. 187.

Not only are groups the foundation of attitudes, not only do individuals learn what to think about the world of politics from the range of group affiliations, but also in many groups the individual is encouraged to put his ideas into practice. Political activity is closely related to partisanship. Herbert McClosky illustrated the relation of partisanship to political interest by examining the attitudes of party leaders in contrast to the attitudes of those who held no party position. The interaction between leaders was naturally more intense than communication among the unorganized mass of "followers." The leaders had "party spirit" and perceived genuine differences between the major political parties. In a similar manner, a group provides the individual with information concerning his stake in political decisions and tends to stimulate or even demands participation through voting or other means. There are many groups which insist that their members vote in order to enhance the good of the group. The high turnout of voters in European labor districts reflects the cohesive "working class" organizations which operate abroad. On the other hand, the relatively high degree of apathy found among the American workers may illustrate the fact that they have not developed stable political norms and institutions. There is abundant evidence that workers who belong to unions vote more frequently than non-union laborers.[16]

The evidence therefore would lead one to conclude that the existence of an abundance of pressure groups is natural and healthy for a democracy. In terms of elections, pressure groups perform services in addition to the stimulation of participation. By engaging in active and intense expression of their demands, pressure groups can operate toward the clarification of issues. By insisting on "plain talk" by aspirants for public office, organizations reduce the issues to more understandable terms. Gilbert Y. Steiner notes this important function and maintains that ". . . without this kind of insistence from pressure groups, candidates would avoid making their position clear." [17]

---

[16] Herbert McClosky, Paul J. Hoffmann, and Rosemary O'Hara, "Issue Conflict and Consensus Among Party Leaders and Followers," *American Political Science Review,* LIV (June 1960), 406-427. For an analysis of evidence pertaining to labor voting *see* Seymour Martin Lipset, *Political Man* (Garden City, N.Y.: Doubleday and Company, Inc., 1960), p. 201.

[17] Gilbert Y. Steiner, "Pressure Groups and Elections," *Social Education,* XVI (Oct. 1952), 259.

Interest Groups and the

We have been building to the point of discarding public opinion as a necessary factor in a democratic system. After all, any person's attitudes are functions of his group affiliations. It follows that any person's definition of public opinion flows from the same sources. In recognition of this fact, Irish and Prothro define public opinion as "the verbal expression of attitudes on an issue by the members of any social group." [18] In a similar manner, the rational man becomes irrelevant. What is a rational decision? What does one do when he "makes up his mind?" Basically, the decisional process involves nothing more than a selection of values from the many group identifications of the individual, a process which, while it may be noncognitive, is certainly not necessarily irrational.

What, then, is democracy? A satisfactory definition is given by Seymour Martin Lipset: "Democracy . . . may be defined as a political system which supplies regular constitutional opportunities for the changing of governmental officials, and a social mechanism which permits the largest possible part of the population to influence major decisions by choosing among contenders for public office." [19] In such a system the operations of pressure groups serve as important conditioners of activity. Since the only opinion in democracy is the will of special interest, many of the decisions of the government will be designed to "effect adjustments among the various special wills and purposes which at any given time are pressing for realization." [20] Democracy is therefore a system in which, through compromise, the competing demands of interests may be satisfied while the decision-making mechanisms of government continue to operate.

THE PREVALENCE OF ORGANIZED ACTIVITY

Americans, as Alexis de Tocqueville remarked, are joiners.[21] Just how valid this observation is may be understood from a cursory

[18] Marian D. Irish and James W. Prothro, *The Politics of American Democracy* (Englewood Cliffs, N.J.: Prentice-Hall, Inc., 1959), p. 262.

[19] Lipset, *op. cit.*, p. 45. *See also* Lipset, "Some Social Requisites of Democracy: Economic Development and Political Legitimacy," *American Political Science Review*, LII (Mar. 1959), 69-105.

[20] John Dickinson, "Democratic Realities and Democratic Dogma," *American Political Science Review*, XXIV (May 1930), 291.

[21] Alexis de Tocqueville, *Democracy in America*, Vol. 1 (New York: Vintage Books, 1954), 199.

glance at available statistics concerning the membership of Americans in organizations. The Department of Commerce, in a survey published in 1949, estimated that there were 4,000 national trade, professional, civic, and other associations in existence. In addition to these national organizations, if one were to include their local and branch chapters, add labor unions, neighborhood improvement groups, local "good government" associations, and countless others, the number would range in the hundreds of thousands.[22] While these figures testify to the generalization that most Americans belong to some organization, they tell us nothing about the continued distrust of pressure groups. A curious aspect about our society is the fact that many of us use the word "lobbyist" to refer to something evil while engaging in the very tactics which we condemn. This means that we approve action by groups having goals with which we agree, while condemning as "pressure" similar activities by hostile groups. We see nothing ambiguous in demanding more freedom for business organizations while insisting that labor unions should be abolished. In almost all organizations it is good form to bemoan the evil of "pressure groups" while resolving to organize more effectively to combat this evil.

Recently, a state university, under the auspices of the Citizenship Clearing House, invited several people who were registered as lobbyists at the state capital to explain their work. Without exception, each began his remarks by explaining that his organization was not a pressure group since its goals were in the public interest. Who, then, are the "evil" pressure groups? Those groups with whose goals we disagree. This type of thinking is conspicuous at the local level, where many citizens groups have sought to rid the city of the machine. Consider, for example, this report:

> For years a hotbed of torrid politics, Santa Fe has suddenly seen the light. Last year a group of civic minded citizens, including the League of Women Voters and the Junior Chamber of Commerce, organized the Citizens Union of Santa Fe and enrolled some 400 members pledged to fight for good government and to vote only for able candidates regardless of party.[23]

---

[22] U.S. Department of Commerce, *National Associations of the United States* (Washington, D.C.: Government Printing Office, 1949), p. viii.

[23] "Civic Group Scares Parties Into Nominating Good Candidates," *National Municipal Review*, XLI (June 1952), 317.

This type of group would be appalled at the suggestion that it was organized to achieve a special interest. The goals of the group are those of the city. Another example of this peculiarity in our thinking is afforded in a statement of the Citizen's Council of La Grange, Illinois. The Citizen's Council was founded for the purpose of making nominations for local office. All who accepted membership were obligated to support the candidates of the Council. Yet as part of its articles of association the Council stated: "All members of the Council . . . act as representatives of the village as a whole and do not in any narrow sense represent any organization, business, or social group, or special interest. Each member acts solely in his or her individual capacity." [24]

These examples of self-deception illustrate the essential human drive to seek out people with whom a common interest is shared. In a democracy, with its attendant assumption of freedom of association, such groups are given the added impetus of institutional bias. Indeed, it is hard to imagine a stable democracy without the existence of pressure groups.

The Institutions of American Democracy

Democracy, as defined above, is not dependent upon any given set of governmental institutions. Although we are accustomed to equate our particular form of government with the basic necessities of stable democracy, there are many democratic countries with forms of government different from our own. Nevertheless there are formal patterns of authority which coexist with American democracy. Pressure groups not only must cope with the intellectual environment or cultural atmosphere of the nation but must also operate within the framework of governmental institutions. This section will consider the relation of pressure groups to the following American institutions: (1) federalism, (2) separation of powers, (3) the party system, and (4) rural dominance of legislative bodies.

FEDERALISM AND THE SEPARATION OF POWERS

Federalism and the separation of powers are closely related and will be discussed as a single unit. Federalism may be defined legally

---

[24] The Citizen's Council of La Grange, Illinois, Articles of Association and By-Laws, Revised May 15, 1957 (Mimeograph).

as a system of government in which power is divided between a central government and regional governments, each of which is supreme in its own area of jurisdiction. This system is to be contrasted with the unitary system, in which the central government is supreme and all powers held by regional government are delegated. Of course, such delegated powers may be withdrawn. In the American federal system the states are formally recognized as existing independently of the national government.

The Constitution, as every schoolboy knows, does not contain a formal definition of federalism. However, the Constitution does specify the powers held by the national government and provides, in the Tenth Amendment, that "the powers not delegated to the United States by the Constitution, nor prohibited by it to the States, are reserved to the States respectively, or to the people." The Constitution also includes a system of separation of powers or "checks and balances" among the three branches of the national government. The theoretical argument for these provisions is centered upon the assumption that political power is potentially dangerous. Therefore the best way to reduce the danger is to provide for a balancing of authority between the nation and the states and between the legislative, executive, and judicial branches of the national government. Although one should avoid being so presumptuous as to speak with authority about the *motives* of the framers of the Constitution, it is possible to ascertain from their writings that the system of diffusion of power was designed to provide a barrier to the dominance of "factions" (whether interest group or party). Presumably it would be possible for a faction to gain control of one branch of government only to be thwarted by another; or to control a state government but not *all* the states. As Professor Arthur W. Macmahon states: ". . . federalism lessens the risk of a monopoly of political power by providing a number of independent points where the party that is nationally in the minority at the time can maintain itself while it formulates and partly demonstrates its policies and capabilities and develops new leadership." [25]

To what extent has the diffusion of legal authority succeeded in developing a dispersal of actual or social power? We must be

---

[25] Arthur W. Macmahon, "Problems of Federalism: A Survey," in Arthur W. Macmahon, ed., *Federalism Mature and Emergent* (Garden City, N.Y.: Doubleday and Company, Inc., 1955), p. 11.

cautious in answering this question in order to avoid becoming overly legalistic. First, there is little doubt that actual power is diversified in American society. Still, there is no way in which we can assert that federalism and the separation of powers cause this diversification.[26] The best that can be done is to provide illustrations of the problems encountered by pressure groups in a system of legal dispersion of authority.

In our system of government we observe groups which, although unsuccessful in achieving their goals on a national level, have established positions of power among state governments. One reason for this occurrence is the variation between the responsibilities of state legislatures as opposed to the national Congress. The state legislature has a narrower set of interests within its area of jurisdiction, whereas the national legislature is responsible to the vast array of interests spread among the entire United States.

One of the best examples of an interest group operating from a position of strength at the state level is the perennial conflict between chain stores and independent retailers.[27] In the years following World War I, chain stores had increased their activities to such a point that the economic lives of thousands of independent merchants were threatened. The coming of the depression of the 1930's added to the menace of the chains and increased the fear on the part of the independent businessman that he would be driven from business. The problem was most intense among grocers because chain operations had been most successful in this field. However, other types of retailers and some wholesalers were also affected. Whatever the type of the business, the mass buying techniques of the chains and the subsequent lower prices charged to consumers were techniques against which there was no economic defense.

To meet this threat the retail and wholesale merchants tried unsuccessfully to prevent chain store growth by boycotting manufacturers who sold directly to chains. Next, independent merchants tried to "educate" the public via mass media to the "evils" of chain stores. However, chain sales continued to rise. Finally the problem

---

[26] *See* Franz Neuman, *The Democratic and the Authoritarian State* (New York: The Free Press of Glencoe, Inc., 1957), pp. 216-232 for a discussion of the limitations of the concept of federalism as an independent causal factor.

[27] This description is drawn from Joseph C. Palamountain, *The Politics of Distribution* (Cambridge: Harvard University Press, 1955), pp. 155-187.

was attacked by seeking governmental aid. However, in spite of the fact that chain operations directly injured millions of retailers, no national organization arose to ward off the "chain store menace." Instead, the problem was approached on a state-by-state basis with no connection between the activities of retailers from one state to the next. In most of the states the legislature was urged to enact tax legislation sharply restrictive on the activities of chains. As early as 1927 four states had adopted special taxes on chain stores and thirteen other bills had been introduced but failed to pass. In 1931 the Supreme Court upheld the constitutionality of the chain store tax, and the floodgate was opened. By 1935, two hundred and twenty-five chain tax bills had been introduced and thirteen had passed; by 1939, twenty-seven states had enacted such taxes. One commentator ruefully remarked that "wherever a little band of lawmakers are banded together . . . you may be sure that they are . . . thinking up things they can do to the chain stores." [28]

For our purposes, the significance of this episode is the fact that every success in retaliatory legislation occurred at the state level. Joseph C. Palamountain notes that "taxes vary so extremely from state to state as to show that no national group was able to co-ordinate the activities of its state and local units. . . ." [29] In fact, there is considerable evidence to suggest that, had the proponents of restrictive chain store taxation not worked through the states, the anti-chain campaign would have been much less successful. By the middle 1930's the chains had developed a counterattack program through the use of effective public relations. By skillful propaganda they converted potential supporters to active participants. House-wives, farm organizations, and food processors combined to ebb the tide of tax legislation. In 1936 California voters, in a popular referendum, voted down a chain tax. Thereafter few states con-sidered chain-tax legislation.

The conclusion of the anti-chain drive occurred when an effort was made to have the national Congress adopt a nationwide restric-tive tax in 1938. This would have seriously hampered the operations of chains doing business in several states. However in the arena of

[28] Quoted in Merle Fainsod, Lincoln Gordon, and Joseph C. Palamountain, Jr., *Government and the American Economy* (New York: W. W. Norton and Co., Inc., 1959), p. 545.

[29] Palamountain, *op. cit.*, p. 163.

Congress, the chains were less at a disadvantage than they had been before the state legislatures. At the state level, home town sentiment against "foreign big business" went a long way toward balancing out the lack of money or organization on the part of the independent merchants. Nationally, the independents did not have the resources to compete with the vast potential of the chain stores. Only the National Association of Retail Druggists worked consistently for the legislation, although a few other retailers' groups testified at committee hearings. The chains, however, marshalled a formidable coalition in order to oppose the bill. The chains gained the support of the American Farm Bureau Federation, the National Association of Real Estate Boards, and many large food manufacturers. In addition, the support of labor unions figured prominently in the chain store coalition. Chain stores also had the backing of the Departments of Agriculture and Commerce.

The independent merchants were outmanned once they sought to expand their sphere of influence to the nation as a whole. The chain-tax bill, introduced by Representative Wright Patman of Texas, was lost in a maze of parliamentary delays. No hearings were held until 1940 and the bill never cleared the committee hearing stage. Thus the federal system of government played a part in the solution to a problem of public policy. Although the anti-chain interests were able to secure federal legislation in the form of the Miller-Tydings amendment to the Sherman Act in 1937, the existence of two levels of decision-making bodies enabled one interest to maintain a position of strength that might not have been possible under a unitary system.

The chain store episode is an example of a conflict within the business community in which each had access to a different decision-making area. In this particular case the larger business group, the chain stores, found a more satisfactory environment in the national legislature. Often, however, corporate interests find it more compatible with their goals to advocate the expansion of state jurisdiction at the expense of the national government. Some large corporations have financial resources greater than many state governments. With respect to the regulation of business, many states lack the necessary administrative machinery to provide thorough supervision. Under these circumstances, the cry of "states' rights" has become an important part of the struggle among pressure groups. As Donald C. Blaisdell has noted: "Federalism is particularly pleasing . . . to the managers of industrial enterprise. While their charters to do business are obtained not from the federal but from state government, under federalism they get the benefits of a trade area of continental proportions, at the same time escaping effective federal regulation." [30]

The use of states rights as a symbol or propaganda device is important not only because it serves to clarify the relation of interest groups to the structure of government but also because it plays upon the myths of American society. Indeed the "specter of a centralized federal bureaucracy invading the reserved rights of the states" is invoked on the assumption that our values are biased toward a commitment to "grass roots" democracy.[31]

The use of the states' rights argument by interests seeking to avoid the intervention of the national government into certain economic and social matters began with the surge of industrial expansion after the Civil War, although some businesses still feared the erraticism of the state legislatures and preferred federal regulation. This was the period in which popular reform movements, such as the National Grange, advocated strict regulation of business activity in order to ameliorate the dangers of monopoly. In defense of their status, business interests argued that regulation by the federal government infringed upon the reserved rights of the states while simultaneously maintaining that state regulation was a violation of the right of Congress to regulate under the powers of the commerce clause. A large part of this activity serves to illustrate the use of the doctrine of separation of powers. The normal pattern was for business to challenge regulatory legislation through the courts. Such memorable decisions as *Hammer v. Dagenhart,* in which the Supreme Court invalidated the Child Labor Act as an invasion of the reserved rights of states, reflect this technique.[32] While legislative arenas mirrored the values of those supporting regulation, the courts became the citadel of business.

This technique of "divide and rule," in which federalism was

---

[30] Donald C. Blaisdell, *American Democracy Under Pressure* (New York: The Ronald Press Company, 1957), p. 50.

[31] Robert J. Harris, "States' Rights and Vested Interests," *Journal of Politics,* XV (Nov. 1953), 466.

[32] Hammer v. Dagenhart, 247 U.S. 251 (1918).

used as a vehicle to produce inaction, made it possible for corporations to turn themselves into clusters of private power, sometimes to the extent of dominating the state governments. Many examples from contemporary economic life illustrate this technique. Oil companies interested in controlling the vast reservoirs of tidelands oil have relied extensively on the doctrine of states' rights. Robert J. Harris has written with perception that "the solicitude of the oil companies for states' rights is hardly based on convictions derived from political theory but rather on fears that federal ownership may result in the cancellation or modification of state leases favorable to their interests, their knowledge that they can successfully cope with state oil regulatory agencies, and uncertainty concerning their ability to control a Federal agency." [33]

The position of large dairy chains is comparable to that of the oil companies. Because the marketing of milk is usually perilous due to the highly perishable quality of the product, many states have created agencies to regulate the distribution of milk. These agencies have usually been ineffective in dealing with the huge interstate chains, such as Sealtest, Borden's, and Foremost, which dominate the market. On occasion, overtures have been made to the Federal Trade Commission by states to assist them in the task of regulation, only to face the determined opposition of the dairies.

These examples should serve to illustrate that federalism does not involve a struggle between the nation and the states, but rather a struggle among interests who have favorable access to one of the two levels of government. The recent controversy over integration fits into this assumption. After the Supreme Court had ruled against the continuation of the practice of segregation in public schools, the states' rights argument was well suited for groups of people in the South who sought to defend their regional customs against the dominant attitudes of the rest of the nation. Local and statewide organizations, known variously as White Citizens Councils and States' Rights Councils, demanded, in the name of the right of each sovereign state to exercise the authority of self-determination, that attempts to end segregation cease. Their efforts are given the official sanction of the state governments. State officials regularly attend meetings and pledge the support of the administration. Letters

---

[33] Harris, *op. cit.*, 467.

urging support of these movements are mailed from governors' offices. In Mississippi the state legislature established the State Sovereignty Commission in 1956 to combat integration efforts. The Governor, Ross Barnett, became chairman of this commission and also served as chairman of the Citizens Council, a private organization with the same aims as the official State Sovereignty Commission. The relations between the two bodies became so intimate that the private nature of the Citizens Council was blurred. The legislature actually allocated state funds for the propaganda efforts of the Citizens Council, thus making it a quasi-official body.

In contrast to the warm reception given segregationist groups by the southern state governments, the National Association for the Advancement of Colored People and related organizations have been subjected to constant harassment. Attempts to gain legal access to NAACP records, challenge of tax-exempt status, and other similar tactics continually frustrate the efforts of pro-integration groups. Under these circumstances it is only natural for these organizations to concentrate their efforts at the national government level. The argument between the opposing groups is not, whatever the verbalization, one of the rights of states against an ever-encroaching federal government. Rather the argument concerns more basic values. The states' right argument is an example of the manipulation of symbols for the purpose of creating a satisfactory attitudinal framework for the achievement of political goals. When one realizes that the southern states regularly pay into the federal treasury less than they get back in the form of grants-in-aid, the issue may be seen in a more complete perspective.

Turning to separation of powers, we are confronted with the same patterns of activity expected under any system of divided authority. Access by a particular group to one branch of government does not necessarily mean access to another. Examples of congressional overturning of decisions by the Supreme Court come most readily to mind. The problem of differential access was brought into focus by two recent instances of judicial decisions which damaged the economic security of trade associations that were influential in Congress.

In 1948 the Supreme Court, in the case of *Federal Trade Commission* v. *Cement Institute,* held that the basing-point system of pricing was illegal. Under this system, prices were determined by

formulas which eliminated the right of the consumer to choose between competitive producers. The basing-point system provided
that the price of a commodity delivered anywhere in the United
States included shipping charges estimated from a geographical
basing point, irrespective of the actual point of departure of the
merchandise. The Cement Institute, a trade association organized
in 1929, had administered such a system rigorously. The assumption which guided the tenacity with which the Institute held to its
pricing system was that "ours is an industry above all others that
cannot stand free competition, that must systematically restrain
competition or be ruined." [34]

The reaction to the Court's decision was swift and decisive. The
steel industry, which also used the basing-point system, soon began
to work for legislation that would legalize the system. Representatives from the state of Pennsylvania, national center of steel production, introduced resolutions calling for a moratorium suspending
further action under the decision. United States Steel abandoned
the basing-point system and raised the price of steel seven dollars
per ton, although there is evidence suggesting that the change in
pricing systems actually reduced the cost to the steel companies by
one dollar per ton. The strategy was to raise a demand for legislation among the customers of the steel companies. The clamor finally
resulted in the passage of S.1008. This bill provided that the Federal
Trade Commission Act be amended so as not to regard the absorption of freight charges by sellers as an unfair trade practice. Thus
the Congress had minimized the effects of the Supreme Court's
decision.

However, the political process does not stop with the passage of
a law. There was still another branch of government which had a
role to play. President Truman's sympathies were not usually in
accord with the desires of big business, which had guided the
legislation through Congress. In addition, his political strength was
believed to rest among the lower-income groups. Consequently, the
opponents of the basing-point legislation, unable to bring their
desires into reality in Congress, were in a more favorable position
when they appealed to the President. The congressional delegation
which urged Truman to veto was composed entirely of Democrats

---

[34] Quoted in Latham, *op. cit.*, p. 56.

long conspicuous in their championing of vigorous enforcement of anti-trust legislation such as Senators Kefauver of Tennessee and Douglas of Illinois. In addition, organizations such as the United Automobile Workers of America, the National Association of Retail Druggists, and the United States Wholesale Grocers Association met with the Chairman of the Democratic National Committee. The net result of this activity was a Presidential veto in 1950.

The case of the basing-point legislation gives us a situation in which group interests fought for their goals through the entire national government. Those interests which failed in one area succeeded in another. A similar development can be seen in the Supreme Court decision in *Federal Maritime Board* v. *Isbrandtsen,* handed down in 1958.[35] In this case the Supreme Court struck down the legality of the "dual rate" or "exclusive patronage" contract employed by steamship conferences. Oceangoing carriers have for years been organized into voluntary conferences. These conferences consist only of those vessels furnishing regular service and not the independent lines and "tramps." The principal purpose of these conferences is to establish cargo rates and conditions of carriage. Under normal circumstances such agreements might violate the anti-trust legislation. However, the Shipping Act of 1916 exempted agreements between oceangoing carriers from anti-trust penalties, provided these agreements are approved by the Federal Maritime Board. By 1959 one hundred and ten conferences had negotiated agreements which had subsequently been approved.

One such type of contract was the "dual rate" agreement. This is an agreement binding shippers to transport all cargo loaded or discharged at ports served by the conference in vessels belonging to conference members. The rate charged to shippers who refuse to sign is higher, even for identical items. The "spread" between contract and noncontract rates sometimes was as high as 20 per cent.

However, there was always the question of whether such obviously discriminatory measures did not violate section fourteen of the Shipping Act, which forbids unfair or discriminatory agreements. Although the dual rate agreement had been before the Supreme Court on numerous occasions beginning in 1932, the *Isbrandtsen*

---

[35] Federal Maritime Board v. Isbrandtsen, 356 U.S. 481 (1958). This account is taken from Jerrold L. Walden, "The Dual-Rate Moratorium—End of the Isbrandtsen Odyssey," *Journal of Public Law,* X (Spring, 1961), 78-99.

case was the first time that the Court had faced the question of its legality. This decision literally was felt around the world since over sixty conferences were affected.

Since the decision of the Court threatened serious economic disruption to the shipping industry, an almost frantic appeal was made to Congress through the American Merchant Marine. On the same day that the decision was issued, a bill was introduced in the House legalizing all dual rate agreements. During a hurriedly arranged series of hearings, the only opposition came from a few scattered small traders who were hurt by dual rate agreements. As far as the reaction of congressmen can be ascertained, the shipping industry was believed to present a united front. In approximately one month Congress established a two-year period of immunity for all contracts operative at the date of the *Isbrandtsen* decision. The Shipping Act was amended, with only one opposing vote in either house, to read that "nothing in this section or elsewhere in this Act shall be construed or applied to forbid or make unlawful any dual rate contract arrangement in use by the members of a conference on May 19, 1958. . . ." The stated purpose of the law was to "defer the impact of the Court decision."[36]

These examples of interest groups and separation of powers are not intended to provide an exhaustive account. Indeed, instances such as those cited above could be described almost *ad nauseam.* However, one further point should be made. In the interplay between groups and formal institutions the Executive Office of the President may be checked by strong concentrations of power in the other branches. The famous struggle between President Franklin D. Roosevelt and the Army Corps of Engineers, perhaps the most widely discussed case of successful pressure group opposition to executive goals, will conclude the analysis.[37] The Army Corps of Engineers is legally responsible to the President as Commander in Chief. However, the Corps of Engineers has built a close relationship with Congress primarily through the mechanism of the National Rivers and Harbors Congress, an organization to which many members of Congress belong. The Corps has performed river develop-

---

[36] House Report No. 2055, 85th Cong., 2d sess., 1946, p. 2. Quoted in Walden, *op. cit.,* p. 78.

[37] *See* Robert de Roos and Arthur Maas, "The Lobby that Can't be Licked," *Harper's Magazine,* Aug. 1949, pp. 20-30 for a more complete description of this episode.

ment tasks since the beginning of the nation's history, when it was the only agency with engineers trained for such work. However, since the increasing expansion of government services, the Corps has been almost incessantly involved in struggle with other agencies doing the same thing. The Hoover Commission drew attention to these jurisdictional disputes and concluded that, irrespective of the legal position of the President, the executive branch could not marshal sufficient power to coordinate a water program against the wishes of the influential "rivers and harbors bloc."

The independence of the Corps of Engineers is strikingly borne out in the struggle over the Kings River Project in California. Both the Corps and the Bureau of Reclamation wanted to develop a program to provide more adequate water supply for the arid area surrounding the river. President Roosevelt decided that the project was primarily one of irrigation and consequently should be handled by the Bureau of Reclamation. However, at Congressional hearings on the project the Corps continued to urge that it be given authority. It was supported by its loyal following in Congress, and the final solution had both the Bureau and the Corps authorized to undertake the development of the river. Even though the President's 1945 budget contained an appropriation for the Bureau and none for the Corps, the appropriation acts passed by Congress reversed these positions. President Roosevelt, usually classified as a "strong" President, could not cope with the entrenched strength of the Corps of Engineers built upon Congressional loyalties and close relationships with the National Rivers and Harbors Congress.

THE POLITICAL PARTY SYSTEM

If the formation of pressure groups is the core of the democratic political process, then the existence of political parties is significant. Pressure groups and political parties are both representative of efforts by a substantial number of people to play a role in the formation of public policy. Although the surface similarities between the two types of organization are apparent, there are differences both in technique and in types of goals. The main difference is that political parties seek to have their membership elected to positions within the formal framework of government while pressure groups do not. In addition, the parties' key to success is their ability to convince a majority of the electorate that their particular position is worthy of support. The pressure group takes its demands to legislators, administrators, or judges who are already in office. Admittedly the distinction is frequently blurred. Some pressure groups participate in both types of activity. Some organizations whose interests are far too narrow to attract a majority still persist in running candidates for public office in addition to maintaining the regular type of pressure operation. Also, many influential organizations attempt to have their members appointed to positions on key administrative agencies, usually in advisory capacities.

However, the essential validity of the distinction may be seen in the kinds of programs adopted by political parties. A party which is a serious contender for political influence must present a more general program than the pressure group, and must have a far broader basis of support. Purely on practical grounds, it is impossible for the party to enter into a commitment with the electorate on the thousands of decisions that will be undertaken during its term of office. All the party can do is pledge itself to general approaches to the major issues it expects to face. In this case the voter who supports, for example, a conservative candidate for President can assume that the specific decisions made by the administration will conform to the general precepts represented in the attitudes held by the candidate and his supporters.

In addition to the impracticality of detailed party programs, there are more fundamental reasons. Since the political party is not the sole organizational representative of popular attitudes and goals, but must share its functions with pressure groups, the party must try to direct or control the activities of these groups. Operating in a highly specialized and pluralistic social framework, the party is forced to adopt a program broad enough to satisfy the many narrow demands of diverse and sometimes conflicting interests. For this reason it is very unlikely that a party which is rigidly committed to a set of doctrines or dogmas will succeed. This is true of democratic societies in general, but is particularly true of the United States. Both major parties tend to blur sharply divisive issues and reach a compromise from among the claims of competitive groups. In a society as heterogeneous as ours, the failure of parties to serve as modifiers of group tensions might have serious consequences.

The role of American parties in the segregation struggle serves to illustrate their essentially pragmatic nature.[38] This controversy has been well attended by well-organized interests who have pressed for immediate solutions. On the one hand, there is a group, represented by the NAACP and the more militant Congress on Racial Equality, which regards the ending of all forms of segregation as an immediate necessity. On the other hand, we have a portion of our population, spoken for by the Citizens Councils and allied organizations, which believes that any breach in traditional Negro-white relations will produce utter ruin.

Each set of interests finds allies in both parties. The segregationists have relied upon the Dixiecrat element of the Democratic party for primary support. However, within the Republican party there are certain individuals who, while not favoring segregation, are committed to the preservation of states' rights by means of the reduction of federal intervention and leaving each state free to solve its own problems as it sees fit. They are most reluctant to approve such an invasion of states' rights as is demanded by the integrationists, and have frequently aligned themselves with southern white supremacists on economic issues.

The integrationists likewise have supporters in both parties. Congressional Democrats from the large industrial states of the Northeast usually urge the most rapid enforcement of the Supreme Court's 1954 decision and seek to have the Democratic party adopt an unwavering stand in favor of complete racial equality. Among Republicans, governors, Congressmen, and party leaders from the same area have similar goals. They are less worried about federal intervention than their colleagues from rural areas and are particularly anxious to secure the basic rights of southern Negroes. These Republicans, typified by Chief Justice Earl Warren and former Vice President Richard Nixon, have worked vigorously for the passage of strong civil rights legislation.

Since both parties are divided into factions on the segregation issue, neither party has been able to create the image of being *the* civil rights party. In both parties, moderate elements who seek

---

[38] The best discussion of parties and the Negro question is found in Austin Ranney, "Politics, Parties, and Civil War," in Ivan Hinderaker, ed., *American Government Annual, 1958-1959* (New York: Holt, Rinehart, & Winston, Inc., 1958), pp. 53-73.

a compromise between both extremes have maintained a firm control. While the Democratic party has been plagued with a more spectacular fight between "uncompromising southerners" and the remainder of the party, the southerners have by no means presented a completely united front. Partially as a result of this, Democratic platforms have tended to use language that treads carefully the thin line between extremisms. Since the Democratic party is obviously in no position to become an outspoken champion of civil rights, some Republicans believe that there is a golden opportunity to pick up substantial blocs of support by assuming a more militant posture. However, as is the case with their opponents, the Republican party is dominated by its moderates.

In this case the issue is not one of severe ideological division *between* the parties. The severity of the conflict is more clearly manifested in struggles between social groupings with supporters in both parties. The parties, rather than clarifying the points of difference, have helped repress the severity of group tensions.

The thesis that parties serve as "smoke screens" for potentially explosive issues should not be carried so far as to allow one to conclude that there is no difference between the basic programs of the major parties. In Congress there are certain issues on which there is substantial disagreement between Democrats and Republicans. However, since the firmness of party lines varies from issue to issue, it is impossible to generalize. In determining how he will vote on a certain bill, the congressman's perception of his party affiliation will certainly be one of many pressures operative. Further, despite the notion that parties gravitate toward the blurring of issues, their active party workers appear to be separated by significant differences in their perceptions of programs. These differences agree with the "popular image in which the Democratic party is seen as the more 'progressive' or 'radical,' the Republican as the more 'moderate' or 'conservative' of the two." [39] In a survey of the attitudes of governors, senators, national committeemen, precinct workers, and local officials of both parties, Herbert McClosky and his associates found that these leaders were far apart on many issues. The Republicans strongly opposed government ownership of natural resources while the Democrats were equally vociferous

---

[39] McClosky *et al.*, "Issue Conflict and Consensus among Party Leaders and Followers," *op. cit.*, p. 410.

in favoring it. Republicans favor a reduction of farm price supports; Democrats do not. On the questions of federal aid to education, slum clearance, social security, and minimum wages the
leaders have widely divergent attitudes.[40]

Any simple statement to the effect that the two parties are identical in their principles fails to take into account the attitudes of
party leaders. However, this inquiry into perception of issues should
not be taken to mean that these differences are always translated
into action. Politics, so the saying goes, is the art of the possible. For
example, McClosky's study revealed that the Democratic leaders
expressed more support for ending segregation than did the Republicans. Yet we have seen that neither party has been able to
develop an emphatic program of racial equality.

In addition to contributing to the maintenance of consensus, the
political parties perform the necessary function of supplying leadership. It can be suggested that although the parties are not the sole
or even the best instruments for the development and formulation
of policy, they are ideally suited for the supplying of governmental
majorities. It is generally assumed that the United States has a two-
party system, but this is an oversimplification. It might be more
realistic to say that in any contest for public office there are seldom
more than two serious contenders. In fact, in approximately half
of the congressional districts, the minority party is too insignificant
to finish better than a poor second. In these districts a single party
has a monopoly on election victories and the true opportunity for
choosing among contenders for public office occurs in the party
primary rather than in the general election.

The decentralization of American parties is most apparent in
connection with the nominating function. Although it is obvious
that a federal system of government would tend to buttress the
diffusion of power in the party system, such structural considerations are not in themselves adequate causal factors. A consideration
of the complex array of socio-economic variables which contribute
to the form of party organization might lead one to inquire if the
American party system would have developed its present characteristics even if the framers of the Constitution had adopted a unitary
government. Looking briefly over the sweep of American history,
several possible reasons for decentralization occur. The hetero-

[40] *Ibid.*, pp. 411-413.

geneous qualities of the social structure are to a considerable extent regionalized, and domestic conflicts have maximized these
regional diversities. In the absence of issues of great significance
which may intersect sectional differences, domestic politics takes
full cognizance of attitudes and interests which vary along sectional
lines.[41]

In a very real sense, states and some cities are cultural entities.
North Dakota, economically dominated by wheat farming, is a
strong center of agrarian radicalism. In Utah about 60 per cent of
the people are Mormons and the influence of the Church of Jesus
Christ of Latter-Day Saints is a telling force in the politics of the
state. In Michigan, a highly industrial state, organized labor is
prominent within the Democratic party. In most southern states
urbanization and industrialization have lagged behind and labor is
generally regarded as less important than, for example, the state
Farm Bureau Federations.[42] An element of localism has also been
built into the pattern of American politics by the flow of immigration. With the exception of the Negro question, ethnic issues have
not had much of an impact on national politics. However, the
tendency of ethnic groups to follow similar paths of migration and
concentrate in particular areas has "constituted a means to power
and influence for locally oriented political organizations outside and
inside their own ranks."[43]

Since the electoral system in the United States is designed to
insure the supremacy of local units, it often happens that regional
conflicts are dealt with on a relatively low level. Each party organization will be more responsive to the dominant interests in the
community. For example the Americans for Democratic Action,
an organization dedicated to "liberal" principles, became so aggressive in striving for municipal reform in Philadelphia that it actually
assumed control of the machinery of the Democratic party. The
political activists who operated under the Democratic label in this
election of 1950 were surely not similar in attitude to the Democratic politicians of the South. However, when these differences

---

[41] David Truman, "Federalism and the Party System," in Macmahon, *op. cit.*,
pp. 131-132.
[42] Charles Adrian, *State and Local Governments* (New York: The Macmillan
Company, 1960), p. 4. *See also* John Gunther, *Inside U.S.A.* (New York:
Harper & Row, Publishers, 1947).
[43] Truman, *op. cit.*, p. 132.

reach the national level, they tend to be submerged in the necessity of pooling resources for the election of the President.

Since the Constitution requires that a President receive a majority of the electoral votes, it is necessary for the loose coalition of local and state organizations to forge themselves into a temporary alliance for the purpose of placing their candidate in the White House. This alliance is not based on shared values. Rather, the seeking of office acts as a catalyst. Even in the selection of candidates, localism plays a vital role. The Presidential nominee will be a person who can appeal to the undecided voters while avoiding the alienation of social groupings. Consequently a national platform may be logically inconsistent but satisfying to group demands. Also, those aspiring to Presidential nomination are aware that their best path to success lies in cultivating the support of the state organizations. Once the election is over, the national organizations go into a state of virtual hibernation but the local and state organizations continue to function in preparation for the frequent elections which occur beneath the national level.

One final aspect of the permanence of localized centers of power merits consideration. The isolation of state party organizations makes it possible, and indeed likely, that the interests which coalesce every four years to nominate a president will not continue to function in harmony. This is especially true when the national party organization, personified by the President, attempts coercion of deviant factions within the party. The most remarkable example of the ability of local power structures to resist national pressures toward conformity is the Roosevelt "purge" of 1938.[44] President Roosevelt, in an effort to reduce intraparty opposition to his legislative program, entered selected candidates in state Democratic primaries and lent the full weight of his personal prestige to their campaigns. In addition, he worked "behind the scenes" to develop local organizations in support of these candidates. The purge attempt resulted in a victory for the state organizations, who resented bitterly what they regarded as an intrusion into the right of each state to select its own candidates. In Georgia, where Roosevelt campaigned vigorously against Senator Walter F. George, the President suffered his worst defeat. Senator George, with the full sup-

---

[44] *See* Harmon Zeigler, "Senator Walter George's 1938 Campaign," *Georgia Historical Quarterly*, XLIII (Dec. 1959), 333-352 for a more detailed account.

port of the state party organization and the financial backing of industrial interests such as the influential Georgia Power Company, won over the "New Deal candidate" by a two-to-one margin. The fact that the voters, while soundly trouncing Roosevelt's choice in the senatorial contest, elected a governor running on a New Deal type platform indicates that the resentment of "interference" was a crucial factor.

The essential conclusion of this section is that the political parties, operating on the necessity of a broad base of support, achieve more cohesion in the selection of candidates than in the formulation of public policy. On the other hand, the ideological fuzziness of American parties should not blind us to the fact that each party tends to be more responsive to particular sets of interests within the community. Both in terms of leadership recruitment and "hard core" support the Democratic party has relied upon industrial, urban, low-income groups while the Republicans have traditionally been more representative of financial and manufacturing interests. Translating bases of support into demands for governmental action would lead us to conclude that people of a conservative inclination gravitate toward the Republican party while the "radicals" find a more congenial atmosphere within the Democratic party.

RURAL DOMINANCE OF THE LEGISLATIVE BODIES

The relation between social values and the institutional structure of government is clearly shown in the disproportionate representative strength of rural areas in legislative assemblies. Thomas Jefferson's famous reference to farmers as "the chosen people of God," while using more extreme language than would be acceptable today, expresses quite well the appeal that agrarian ways of life have for many Americans. The presumed virtues associated with the tilling of the soil—honesty, thrift, and individualism—have assumed the role of a myth. In spite of the spectacular surge of migration to the cities and the corresponding decline of rural population, agrarian attitudes are given a high priority in our value system.

As a partial consequence of this attitudinal lag the rural areas, if population is accepted as a basis for representation, are disproportionately influential in legislatures. People living in urban areas —over two-thirds of the American population—have a far weaker voice than their numbers would indicate. The extent of urban under-representation varies from state to state. However, in 1955 only Massachusetts and Wisconsin gave equal representation to their urban areas. At the extreme end of the continuum are Florida, Georgia, California, Delaware, Rhode Island, New Jersey, Maryland, and Connecticut. From this extreme group, Georgia offers the most glaring example of rural dominance. The six largest urban counties, into which 32 per cent of the state's population is concentrated, have 9 per cent of the seats in the lower house and 7 per cent of the Senate seats.[45] In national politics, equal representation of the states in the Senate contributes to the maintenance of rural power. However, it is in the House of Representatives that rural constituencies are given their greatest advantage. The absence of federal regulations enables states to create congressional districts and provide for redistricting in any manner they please. Since the state legislatures themselves are rural dominated, it is not surprising that attempts to achieve a more equitable distribution are usually frustrated.

The relation of pressure groups to this peculiar aspect of our legislative assemblies is that those groups whose goals correspond with agrarian values are at an advantage. Although it is difficult to generalize about the role of pressure groups in state legislatures, some examples of activity surrounding efforts to redistrict may prove useful. Chicago, Illinois, had for many years been underrepresented in the state legislature. Not only was there a problem of rural-urban hostilities involved, but this cleavage was strengthened by the fact that Chicago is predominantly Democratic as contrasted with the Republican loyalties of the remainder of the state. The *status quo* was scrupulously maintained until the movement to the suburbs gave some hope of Republican support within the Chicago area. A constitutional amendment ratified in 1955 authorized the legislature to redistrict, but the final result increased the strength of the suburbs significantly while only slightly improving the status of Chicago. Thus the political climate of intrastate areas appeared to have a crucial role in determining the outcome of the issue. However Gilbert Y. Steiner and Samuel K. Gove, in a case study of the Illinois redistricting controversy, conclude that nonlegislative groups were powerless and did not influence the judgment of legis-

[45] From Gordon E. Baker, *Rural Versus Urban Political Power* (Garden City, N.Y.: Doubleday and Company, Inc., 1955), pp. 16-17.

lators. Legislative leaders regarded this particular matter as an internal affair and did not consult lobbyists as they normally would on substantive matters.[46]

In contrast to the Illinois case, redistricting in California and Georgia has been accompanied by intense activity on the part of nongovernmental associations. In California, an unsuccessful attempt to remedy the disparities in representation by means of a popular referendum was lead by the State Federation of Labor, with the Chamber of Commerce forming the core of the opposition. This struggle, which occurred in 1948, was characterized by pressure groups assuming leading roles in the dissemination of propaganda. The labor groups served as directors for the formation of the Citizens Committee for Equal Representation, while business interests guided the Northern California Committee Against Reapportionment. Thus it appears that urban-rural rivalry was a "smoke screen for another type of cleavage." Business interests found it relatively easy to achieve their legislative goals by influencing representatives from rural areas. "Privately owned utilities, banks, insurance companies and other concerns with crucial legislative programs have discovered some 'cow country' legislators more responsive to their demands and less committed to contrary points of view on key social and economic questions than are urban representatives."[47] Urban representatives were more likely to be influenced by organized labor. Under these circumstances it is hardly surprising that the anti-reapportionment interests relied heavily on propaganda organized around the symbols of "leftist crackpots," "dictatorial labor bosses," and "Commies."

In Georgia, a situation remarkably similar to that of California presents itself. Georgia operated from 1917 until 1962 under the County Unit System. Under this system unit votes were apportioned among the counties according to the following formula. The eight most populous counties each received six unit votes. The thirty next most populous counties received four unit votes and the remaining one hundred and nine counties received two unit votes.

---

[46] Gilbert Y. Steiner and Samuel K. Gove, *Legislative Politics in Illinois* (Urbana: University of Illinois Press, 1960), p. 116.

[47] Dean E. McHenry, "Urban v. Rural in California," *National Municipal Review*, XXXV (July 1946), 353. *See also* Thomas S. Barclay, "The Reapportionment Struggle in California in 1948," *Western Political Quarterly*, IV (June 1951), 313-324.

The candidate receiving a plurality of popular votes within a county was given that county's unit votes. The system applied only to Democratic primaries, but, since the primary is tantamount to election in a one-party state, its effects were far-reaching. For instance, Fulton County with a population of nearly 500,000 is given six votes. These votes could easily be overcome by the combined votes of any three smaller counties which may have as few as three hundred people voting. Thus the key to political success lay in developing strong support in rural areas. The cities could be ignored with reasonable safety.[48]

This institutional bias in favor of rural areas enabled a particular group of candidates and supporting interests to maximize their influence. This coalition, given official leadership by the Talmadge family, is primarily anti-Negro and anti-labor. Valuable support was afforded from various business interests who, while unconcerned with racial questions, were anxious to keep the influence of organized labor at a minimum. In addition, the economic conservatism of the Talmadge faction was well received. This is particularly true of the textile mills and electrical utilities companies, whose economic interests have been well protected. The attitude of business interests toward rural dominance is well stated by Joseph L. Bernd:

> Herman Talmadge won high favor with the industrial leadership because he shifted the burden of new taxes away from corporations and corporation executives and onto the general public with a three per cent sales tax, because he was reasonably amenable to advice from sound business men, because he administered an expanded program of state services with relative efficiency and without major scandal, because he is a defender of states' rights and Southern rights, and because he has developed a habit of success. Interviews with leading members of the industrial hierarchy leave the interviewer with the impression that equal voting rights for Negroes and even token integration are not anathema to the captains of industry. What they seem to want most are stable conditions for business activity and protection against further governmental regulation and taxation.[49]

[48] Lynwood M. Holland, *The Direct Primary in Georgia*, Illinois Studies in the Social Sciences, XXX (Urbana: University of Illinois Press, 1949), 44-46.

[49] Joseph L. Bernd, *Grass Roots Politics in Georgia* (Atlanta: Emory University Research Committee, 1960), p. 35. *Cf.* Baker, *The Politics of Reapportionment in Washington State* (New York: Holt, Rinehart & Winston, Inc., 1960).

Thus the interest group cleavages in Georgia were similar to those of California. In 1950 these cleavages became solidified by an effort on the part of the Talmadge administration to extend the county unit system to the general election. This would require a constitutional amendment ratified by the voters. Opposition quickly developed in urban areas and the backers of the amendment were relatively unorganized. An unexpected defeat stimulated the Talmadge faction to organize for a new and more vigorous campaign. In 1951 the General Assembly passed an amendment providing that all candidates for state office must be nominated by the county unit system, which would have the same effect as the previous amendment. Here again the urban areas formed the core of opposition and were given active support by organized labor. The same arguments and slogans used by business interests in California were heard in Georgia. City voters were described as consisting of "sinister and subversive elements in the form of Negroes, Yankee influences, labor unions, agents of the Soviet Union, etc." [50] However, for once the rural system was unable to dominate since the fate of the amendment was determined by popular vote. Negroes and labor union members were able to cast votes which would be given equal weight with rural votes, thus effectively balancing the influence of the "court house gangs." The defeat of the amendment by 30,000 votes gives telling evidence of the value of the county unit system in protecting rural values.

Urban interests had been seeking judicial relief from the county unit system since 1946, but the Supreme Court held on two occasions that the issue was "political" and hence not subject to judicial intervention. However, following the 1962 *Baker v. Carr* ruling that the Supreme Court possessed jurisdiction on matters of legislative reapportionment, county unit foes in Georgia initiated a new series of lawsuits which resulted in the abolition of the unit system and the reapportionment of the State Senate. These shifts in institutional structure served to awaken urban interests and stimulate them to more sustained activity. The election of a Negro to the Senate seemed to symbolize the fact that Negro organizations were not automatically excluded from legislative representation. For the first time in the recent history of Georgia, the AFL-CIO began to take

---

[50] Bernd, *ibid.*, p. 16.

its lobbying role seriously and pressed for improved unemployment compensation laws, much to the chagrin of the Chamber of Commerce. High on the list of labor's future goals is the abolition of the state's right to work laws.

These examples of rural-urban cleavages are illustrative of one type of interest group alignment whose patterns of activity are influenced by formal government structure. However, as is the case with any group activity, the divisions are not rigid and monolithic. Place of residence is one of a number of influences on behavior and may vary in salience from issue to issue. Businessmen, for example, may divide over the relative merits of backwoods candidates. The Coca Cola Company has usually supported urban-oriented candidates in Georgia, while organized labor is far from unanimous in condemnation of the Talmadge faction. In Alabama it was discovered that a majority of roll-call votes do not result in an urban-rural alignment, but that a considerable number of them do. Among the questions usually decided along rural-urban lines, race relations and reapportionment are conspicuous. In addition, labor-supported legislation was unfavorably received by rural legislators, who also supported prohibitive taxation of trading stamps which small-town merchants regarded as unfair competition. In spite of these issues, rural-urban conflict was not the overbearing theme of the legislative session.[51]

Similar conclusions have been reached about the Illinois and Missouri legislatures. David R. Derge, using 3,662 roll calls and more than 500,000 individual legislator's votes from 1949 through 1957, revealed that conflicts other than those of rural-urban nature are dominant. Derge found that "the city's bitterest opponents in the legislature are political enemies from within its own walls, and those camped in the adjoining suburban areas." Further, when metropolitan legislators can agree among themselves on the solution to a particular problem, nonmetropolitan legislators exhibit a willingness to cooperate. Finally, contrary to the general trend, when urban legislators vote together with high cohesion they are usually on the winning side.[52]

[51] Murray C. Havens, *City Versus Farm?* (University of Alabama: Bureau of Public Administration, 1957).

[52] David R. Derge, "Metropolitan and Outstate Alignments in Illinois and Missouri Legislative Sessions," *American Political Science Review,* LII (Dec. 1958), 1065.

This evidence suggests that both urban and rural societies have important internal differences. These differences may also be seen in national politics. While it is true that the more powerful congressional committees usually contain an exaggerated rural membership, there are conspicuous cleavages among the members of the "farm bloc" which act against full utilization of key positions.[53]

Summary

This chapter has discussed interest groups as they function in the intellectual and institutional environment of American democracy. While it would be erroneous to discuss democracy purely in terms of its institutions, it would be equally erroneous to treat interest groups independent of the social structure in which they must operate and to which they conform in their patterns of activity. Pressure groups help to determine the nature of the institutions but are also channeled by the particular forms of governmental bodies. Democracy itself has become a symbol which makes definition difficult. While some would maintain that interest groups subvert the foundations of democratic government, it has been argued here that the right to form associations for the advancement of special interests is a basic attribute of democracy. Attention has been given to those institutions which, while not essential to democracy, give the American form of government some rather unique characteristics. The decentralization of legal government through the devices of federalism and the separation of powers contributes to a diversification of power among social groups. This tendency is strengthened by the loosely confederated nature of our political parties. The fact that these aspects of American governmental structure work to the advantage of some groups and to the disadvantage of others is illustrated in the legislative process. In the absence of strong party control, a power vacuum exists which is filled by various pressures. In some legislatures the dominance of rural areas contributes to a monopoly of political power, although the chances of monopoly are reduced by the general lack of regional homogeneity.

---

[53] Arthur Capper, *The Agricultural Bloc* (New York: Harcourt, Brace & World, Inc., 1922). *See also* Alvin Boskoff, "The Farm Bloc and Agrarian Ideology," (Master's thesis, Columbia University, 1948), pp. 93-130.

Organized Groups

III   and

Structures of Power

The previous chapter suggested that the institutional structure of American government contributes to a bifurcation of influence. This chapter will inquire into the conditions under which organized groups come into existence and will also offer a comparative description of organizational beginnings, searching for factors conducive to continuity and stability in social movements. Finally, the role of organizations in the power structure of American society will be discussed.

The Creation of Formal Associations

Groups have been described as complexes dependent upon interaction among individuals who possess shared attitudes or a common interest. Yet there is nothing in this definition to explain why some patterns of interaction become formalized while others do not. The best way to approach some understanding of the nature of formal pressure groups is to undertake a comparative description of cultures, both primitive and complex, in order to perceive common occurrences in the formation of political associations.

The most plausible body of theory suggests that increase in task specialization or division of labor provides the most frequent stimulation for the beginning and maintenance of new interaction patterns. The study of primitive societies suggests that, in most cases, associations of a subcommunity type do not exist. Such societies, described by William Graham Sumner as "small groups scattered over a territory," are characterized by a strong feeling of loyalty to the total group.[1] Because of acute physical isolation from other peoples, the primitive community usually develops a strong "we-feeling" directed against all out-groups. "Thus a differentiation arises between ourselves, the we-group or in-group, and everybody else, or the others-groups, out-groups." [2] Despite little communication with outsiders, the primitive community reinforces ethnocentrism by means of intimate internal patterns of communication. The people are very much alike; there is great homogeneity and not much division of labor. "What one man knows and believes is the same as what all men know and believe." [3] This strong feeling of solidarity, minimizing the development to subloyalties, can be seen in Radcliffe-Brown's description of the economics of the Andaman Islanders:

> Within the local group there is no such thing as a division of labor save as between the sexes. Every man is expected to hunt pig, to harpoon turtle, and to catch fish, and also to cut a canal, to make a bow and arrows, and all the other objects that are made by men.[4]

Such a society would afford little opportunity for the development of conflicting interests. In addition to the feeling of total solidarity, social relations within the community are highly ordered by custom

[1] William Graham Sumner, *Folkways* (New York: Mentor Books, 1960), p. 27.

[2] *Ibid.*

[3] Robert Redfield, "The Folk Society," *American Journal of Sociology*, LII (Jan. 1947), 297.

[4] H. R. Radcliffe-Brown, *The Andaman Islanders* (London: Cambridge University Press, 1933), p. 43.

and tradition, which also reduces the chances of conflict. If study-
ing the precedents embodied in tribal lore can solve every new
issue, legislation has no place in the development of social order.
Succession to positions of authority in the social and political
hierarchy is regulated in a similar manner and is subject to only
minimal discussion. The final solution to most social or political
problems that are liable to arouse conflicts of interests is found in
the "cake of custom." [5]

This brief résumé of primitive political organization is an "ideal
type" to which there are exceptions. Some primitive societies have
developed more specialization than others. However, in such societies, associations are usually the product of relations that develop
unintentionally or are the result of complementary usefulness to
members of the group. They are not deliberately entered into in
order to achieve ends implied in shared attitudes. Familial institutions, which are the most durable primitive subgroup, are of this
type. In some cases these institutions, extended beyond the immediate family into clan-like groups, are able to restore equilibrium
in the face of sudden change. Still, these organizations stem from
involuntary characteristics rather than conscious efforts.

Societies which acknowledge subgroup loyalties only in terms of
primary groups generally exhibit a paucity of formal associations.
In some advanced situations, tenacity of primary-group identification reduces the possibility of the development of more broadly
based groups. In Ceylon, for example, although rice and rubber
form the base of the economy, there is sufficient diversity to allow
for the development of conflicting attitudes. Nevertheless, interest
groups on the formal level are almost non-existent and certainly
suffer a high mortality rate. The central government has attempted
to develop trade associations and occupational groups among the
villages, but most of these have become inoperative shortly after
their inception. The growth of special interest groups has been
difficult and tedious because the people are not "easy joiners" and
have little inclination to organize beyond the primary group. Most
interest groups in Ceylonese villages are actually informal leader-

[5] Raymond Firth, "Succession to Chieftanship in Tikopia," *Oceania*, XXX
(Mar. 1960), 161-180. Redfield, *The Folk Culture of Yukatan* (Chicago: University of Chicago Press, 1941).

ship cliques serving the entire village. They function less as special interest groups within the community than as village leadership units directing activity for the entire population.[6]

Other attempts at organization under similar conditions produce comparable results. The transformation of a Navaho society from a pastoral to a wage-earning economy by the construction of a natural gas line over a reservation would seem to create a situation of sufficient challenge to the psychological equilibrium of individuals to require the formation of associations to restore balance. Undergoing their first experience as wage earners, Navaho males were subject to entirely new paths of interaction. However, an attempt to organize them for a strike was a total failure. The Navaho, who had never been accustomed to groups beyond kinship organizations, exhibited no tendency to identify with his fellow workers, felt no solidarity or "class consciousness," and remained unaffected by the appeals of organized labor.[7]

PRIMARY GROUPS AND SECONDARY ASSOCIATIONS

The same conditions proved true for a village in southern Italy and among the small farmers of rural Ireland where the nuclear family dominates.[8] In Ireland, the farm is the center of kinship relations. It is not an economic interest to be exploited, but rather an institution to contribute to the stability of the family system. Small farmers showed no feeling of solidarity with a rural community and felt no desire to interact with members of their occupational group. In spite of economic regressions, the small farmer has clung to traditional patterns of interaction, seeking equilibrium within the kinship system. The family is isolated and fiercely loyal in much the same way as the primitive tribe. "There has never been a vital community larger than the family to act as a focus of cooperation, motivation, or change." [9] On the other hand, larger farm owners, with more contacts outside the family, more specialization in prod-

---

[6] Bruce Ryan, *Sinhalese Village* (Coral Gables: The University of Miami Press, 1958), pp. 148-152.

[7] Gordon F. Streib, "An Attempt to Unionize a Semi-Literate Navaho Group," *Human Organization*, XI (Spring, 1952), 23-31.

[8] Edward C. Banfield, *The Moral Basis of A Backward Society* (New York: The Free Press of Glencoe, Inc., 1958), p. 89.

[9] Ralph Lane, "Change and Organization in *Rural* Ireland," *Human Organization*, XIV (Summer, 1955), 6.

ucts, and a continuous exchange of goods and services with other members of the rural community, are successfully organized into commodity groups and into a general association known as the People of the Soil.

These illustrations suggest that, while associational activity is the result of change in the life-styles of individuals, under some circumstances it is likely that an individual whose life-style has been disturbed will interact with people with whom he has already established tangent relations. "Individuals who need to interact with someone to compensate for the disturbances in the institutions in which they have habitually interacted, do so along channels already in existence." [10] The failure of the individual to interact beyond the traditional primary group in response to chance circumstances seems to depend on the intensity with which perceptions of crisis were geared to the family as an equilibrating mechanism. This intensity of perception may vary from society to society. Generally, however, there is a relation between rapid population shifts and the sufficient differentiation of society to permit the development of formal organizations. While this would lead us to expect that rapid growth of associations is to be expected as a characteristic of urban society, it is incorrect to assume that urbanization *per se* is a fundamental cause of interest groups. Farm organizations are generally conceded to be influential in some aspects of American politics. Nevertheless, the complexities and impersonalization of urban life do lay the groundwork for a rapid growth and greater diversity of organizations. To depart momentarily from primitive culture, the medieval synthesis of church and state made it improbable that the individual could be a member of any other organization. In the late middle ages, guilds developed as a response to the crumbling of traditional loyalties and increasing economic differentiation. Writing on the nature of voluntary organizations, Rose notes that "one of the most characteristic features of the shift from medieval to modern times is the rise of groups with specialized interests *within* the community." [11] One might add that formal interest groups are most likely to develop in the more democratic countries. In modern

---

[10] Eliot D. Chapple and Carleton S. Coon, *Principles of Anthropology* (New York: Holt, Rinehart & Winston, Inc., 1942), p. 418.

[11] Arnold Rose, *Theory and Method in the Social Sciences* (Minneapolis: University of Minnesota Press, 1952), pp. 54-55.

totalitarian societies there are, at least officially, no groups beyond the party or social mechanism that control the apparatus of the state.

Although emotional instability due to rapid urban migration is an incomplete explanation, it is nevertheless worthy of consideration. Studies of political organization in transitional societies are consistent in maintaining that the uprooted and transient feeling of portions of the population reduces the influence of traditional institutions, whether family, tribe, church, or community, and necessitates a substitution of formal associations (secondary groups) to restore stability. In many ways the nineteenth century Industrial Revolution created social and psychological needs that are again evident in the development of new African nations from tribes. Reduced influence of traditional group patterns and rapid growth of special interest groups are characteristic of both periods. Wirth has described the influence of urbanism on organized groups in these words:

> The distinctive features of the urban mode of life have often been described sociologically as consisting of the substitution of secondary for primary contacts, the weakening of the bonds of kinship, and the declining social significance of the family, the disappearance of the neighborhood, and the undermining of the traditional basis of social solidarity. . . . Being reduced to a stage of virtual impotence as an individual, the urbanite is bound to exert himself by joining with others of similar interests into organized groups to obtain his ends.[12]

In West Africa, World War II served as the stimulus toward many different ways of earning a living and many more modes of life than existed in prewar days. As in the era of the Industrial Revolution, much traditional life became disintegrated, and new forms of organization, primarily occupational and professional, arose. Some of the immigrants to the Gold Coast have achieved sufficient solidarity to monopolize certain aspects of economic life. This development can be partially traced to the impersonality of relationships and to the psychological effect of isolation which en-

---

[12] Louis Wirth, "Urbanism as a Way of Life," *American Journal of Sociology,* XLIV (July 1938), 20. *Cf.* S. N. Eisenstadt, "Primitive Political Systems: A Preliminary Comparative Analysis," *American Anthropologist,* LXI (1959), 200-220.

courages the individual to exert himself with others of like interests through the medium of the formal organization.[13]

CHANGES IN THE POLITICAL NATURE
OF ORGANIZATIONS

Perhaps the reason that secondary organizations serve well as reactors to change is that they are initially flexible and easily adjustable to changing circumstances. This explanation is offered by Robert T. Anderson and Gallatin Anderson as a result of their study of the role of voluntary associations in a Danish village facing the problem of relocation of economic enterprise. Technological advances reduced the traditional marine economy of the village to impotence in competition with large commercial fleets. The old form of economic organization, the family-owned fishing boat, could no longer provide a profit. In addition, the village was gradually becoming absorbed as a suburb of Copenhagen. The research indicates that the family unit, losing economic utility, declined in importance, while the special interest organizations assumed the responsibility of adjustment. These organizations met the emergence of changing channels of distribution and marketing by uniting people for concerted action on the basis of shared interests.[14]

The generalization to be abstracted from these examples is that organized groups begin in response to changes in the relationships between individuals when existing institutions are inadequate to provide a means for the re-establishment of stability. Key states, "Most pressure groups . . . originate in an effort to cope with some immediate problem and then persist as an organization to deal with new matters of concern to the membership." [15]

Urbanization is only one example of such change. Social movements occur in rural areas, and there is considerable variation in the participation of urban peoples in voluntary associations. To

[13] Kenneth Little, "The Role of Voluntary Associations in West African Urbanization," *American Anthropologist*, LVII (1957), 579-595.

[14] Robert E. Anderson and Gallatin Anderson, "Voluntary Associations and Urbanization: A Diachronic Analysis," *American Journal of Sociology*, LXV (Nov. 1958), 265-273.

[15] V. O. Key, *Politics, Parties, and Pressure Groups* (New York: Thomas Y. Crowell Company, 1958), p. 49.

suggest other variables, studies of large cities have shown that in all cases primary groups are not replaced by interest groups. Generally, participation in political organizations is more characteristic of higher income groups. In New York 68 per cent of the unskilled workers were without formal affiliation while 98 per cent of the professional people were members of organized groups. Among working-class people, those who did join organizations were most likely to be attracted to a recreational or social club rather than a political organization or occupational group.[16]

It is difficult to generalize about income status as a variable because there are gaps in evidence, and even some contradictory data. For instance, a study of political participation in the 1944 Presidential election in New York City indicated that, although there was no correlation between income status and participation in a political organization, the *direction* of activity was influenced by rank on the social and economic scale. In the Republican organization in support of Dewey, wealthy Protestants were most active, while the lower-income Catholics and Jews were the principal activists in the Roosevelt organization. However, participation in this study was confined to the party organization during an election and does not have immediate bearing on continued participation in nonparty groups.[17]

Another factor which hinders efforts to understand personal motives in participation in political organizations is the fact that these organizations have varying degrees of interest in political issues. Some associations, such as athletic or recreational clubs, function only to satisfy the needs of members in relation to themselves. Others are directed outward and wish to achieve some change or condition in a limited segment of society. Others, usually the "social movement" type, pursue goals which would affect the behavior of all members of society and are not directly related to the immediate satisfaction of their own memberships.[18] The latter kinds of organ-

[16] Mira Komarovsky, "The Voluntary Associations of Urban Dwellers," *American Sociological Review*, II (Dec. 1946), 686-698. This evidence is corroborated in Floyd Dotson, "A Note on Participation in Voluntary Associations in a Mexican City," *ibid.*, XVII (Aug. 1953), 380-386.

[17] Gerhart H. Saenger, "Social Status and Political Behavior," *American Journal of Sociology*, LI (Sep. 1945), 103-113.

[18] For a more precise categorization *see* C. Wayne Gordon and Nicholas Babchuck, "A Typology of Voluntary Organizations," *American Sociological Review*, XXIV (Feb. 1959), 22-29.

ization are of a more political nature but will vary in "politicalness." Even the first type of organization may increase the percentage of its activity devoted to political affairs. Lane places associations into the following categories: (1) political, (2) quasi-political, and (3) others.[19] None of the categories is static or exclusive, and the politicalness of an organization may vary through time. For example, a content analysis of the publications of the Connecticut Manufacturers Association from 1937 to 1946 showed that "there is a general relocation of the focus of attention, an alteration in the attention frame such that government-business relationships occupy a smaller attention area and the problems of production occupy a larger area of business attention."[20] During the same period, labor unions showed an increasing political interest. Thus, the character of the organization may shift after a person has become a member. If the organization satisfies needs of the individual which are not related to politics ("good fellowship," a "feeling of belonging"), then it is possible that the individual will support political objectives in which he initially had little interest.

The Modification of Goals

While formal organizations begin as a reaction to change, and are themselves instruments of change, their goals do not remain constant but rather undergo a series of modifications. Since the goals are directed toward people not formally affiliated with the organization as well as toward the members, interaction between the organization and its environment will introduce some element of outside control. Organizational goal setting is a function of both internal and external forces.[21] Initially, goals may reflect the dominance of a set of stated needs expressed by the group toward whom a political movement is directed. Every group presupposes an ideology which acts as a catalyst for its formation; but the re-

---

[19] Robert E. Lane, *Political Life* (New York: The Free Press of Glencoe, Inc., 1959), 79. The term "politicalness" is borrowed from Lane.

[20] Robert E. Lane, *The Regulation of Businessmen* (New Haven: Yale University Press, 1954), pp. 53-54.

[21] James D. Thompson and William J. McEwen, "Organizational Goals and Environment: Goal-Setting as an Interaction Process," *American Sociological Review*, XXIII (Feb. 1958), 23-31.

sponse of an organization to this ideology need not remain constant. In some cases, particularly those of ethnic-based groups, the intensity of primary-group interaction is extended to the larger group, enabling originally heterogeneous values to become integrated through the mechanism of the formal organization. The Russian Mennonites, for example, were originally recruited from many different strata. Bankers, farmers, merchants, and many other occupational groups formed a subsystem of potentially competing values. However, as the movement progressed and was threatened by the increased hostility of other religious groups and, in some cases, governmental bodies, the internal cross-pressures diminished and were amalgamated in common action against the threat.[22]

EXAMPLES OF IDEOLOGICAL STABILITY

Usually, however, group aims are much less easily developed and maintained. Social movements are presumed to exist "whenever a group of individuals, operating within a community, aim to win the support of that community for the establishment of some innovation in the ways and means of promoting a common interest." [23] A survey of available literature on various social movements leads to the conclusion that these movements have certain common characteristics. They are: (1) the development of an ideology, (2) an organizational framework, and (3) an enduring quality. The last two characteristics frequently operate to produce alterations in the original ideology. Movements may be directed *against* something as well as *toward* a goal. Organizations may seek either to bring about a change in a situation or to prevent a change. Often, the establishment of an organization to institute change will provide the necessary spark to set a *status quo* movement on its feet.

Having distinguished between two types of political movements, it is plausible to suggest that the organization which seeks to prevent a change, to keep things as they are, has a better chance of keeping the original purpose in the forefront. This is due to the essentially *negative* orientation of its operations. It is easier to be in opposition without assuming the responsibility of offering alterna-

---

[22] E. K. Francis, "The Russian Mennonites: From Religious to Ethnic Group," *American Journal of Sociology*, LIV (Sept. 1948), 101-107.

[23] Theodore Abel, "The Pattern of a Successful Political Movement," *American Sociological Review*, II (June 1937), 347.

tive courses of action. Many such organizations concentrate their attention on a perceived threat which may be high in emotional content and unfluctuating even though the conditions which produced the threat have ceased to exist. Negative kinds of groups frequently develop precise symbolization of threats that "resist the discipline of external events." [24] Thus a group may identify "internal Communist subversion" or "Wall Street" as a basic threat, not only to the particular group, but to the total society. The fact that there may be little evidence to substantiate these fears does not alter the continued perception of the danger as immediate.

There appear to be three courses open to a continuing political movement. While the intention to act, whether for or against something, results from some event or series of events impinging upon a value, the direction which an organization takes over time may follow one of these courses: (1) it may decline in activity as the threat becomes less serious and eventually disappear; (2) it may continue to perceive the threat as real, irrespective of its actual seriousness; or (3) it may develop new issues and "causes" to keep alive. A good example of a negative organization which maintains stable goals in the face of changing circumstances is the Ku Klux Klan. The revival of the Klan took place in an atmosphere of steadily rising tension and hostility following the *Brown v. Board of Education* decision of 1954 which declared continued segregation of Negro and white students in public schools to be unconstitutional. In 1956, the crisis temporarily abated and the integration forces instituted a corresponding reduction in their efforts Accordingly, the White Citizens Councils, relatively new organizations, entered a temporary period of relative inactivity. The Ku Klux Klan, on the other hand, continued to operate with its original zeal. While the rapid growth and equally rapid decline of the White Citizens Councils seemed to be hinged to the perception on the part of members of the imminent probability of integration, the Klan apparently functioned independently of the reduction of the external threat. There was no observable correlation between Klan activities and Negro counteractivities.

The explanation of the Klan's deviation from the common-sense assumption that organization breeds counterorganization is to be

---

[24] Harold Lasswell, *Psychopathology and Politics* (New York: The Viking Press, Inc., 1960), p. 314.

found in the social background of Klan members. Klan membership is largely marginal, both socially and economically. Most members are from working class backgrounds, they are usually in the lower brackets of the labor market, and they have been uprooted from traditional life-styles by the rapid industrialization of the South. It was discovered that, while the White Citizens Councils membership is predominately rural, the strength of the Klan is in large cities such as Birmingham, Atlanta, Jacksonville, and Tampa. Klan members are experiencing a transition from one mode of life, that of the rigidly ordered rural community, to another, more ambiguous one, that of the city. Vander Zanden concludes that a lack of the individual to define his role, to "learn his place," causes him to over-conform to what he believes are the values of traditional, middle class America. The ambiguity about one's social role is relieved by the highly tangible group identification provided by the elaborate secret rituals and symbols of the organization. Klan programs are anti-Negro, but they are also much broader in that they represent a conscious effort to convince the membership that they do not occupy an inferior status. The exaggerated emphasis of status symbols (mostly those of "pure" Americanism) in Klan literature helps to placate more extensive anxieties than those produced by the integration question. Hence the Klan goals remain unchanged year after year, since there is no specific action that could be undertaken to satisfy the needs of the members.[25]

SHIFTS IN THE ATTITUDES OF MEMBERS

The essentially irrational nature of the Klan type program, based on status frustrations, is to be contrasted with groups whose *raison d'être* is more directly related to the achievement of a clearly defined, tangible objective. In such groups it is usually true that continued competition and opposition from other groups will produce intense activity, greater membership participation, and more cohesion in goal setting. The lack of these conditions will produce the opposite results. Hence organizations created in response to the more clearly defined type of threat will probably face the problem of continued life once the original goal has either been achieved or has ceased to be salient to those who originally supported it.

---

[25] This analysis is drawn from James W. Vander Zanden, "The Klan Revival," *American Journal of Sociology*, LXV (Mar. 1960), 456-462.

Lipset's study of the Cooperative Commonwealth Federation, which became powerful in rural Saskatchewan in 1944, contains an interesting insight into the change which occurs in people once they have satisfied an immediate need or achieved power in relation to other groups:

> Most of the C.C.F. leaders assume that if farmers are given economic security and increased social services they will continue to support the movement in its efforts to socialize the rest of the economy. Experiences in other countries do not lend weight to this assumption. In fact, the contrary seems to be true—*farmers tend to become conservative when they achieve their economic goals.* The farmer is radical vis-à-vis the larger society when his economic security and land tenure are threatened. He may join other exploited groups, such as the workers, to win his own economic demands. However, *once the farmer achieves these immediate goals and becomes a member of the secure property holders of society, he resents government controls and labor or tax legislation that interfere with the expansion of his business.*[26]

The shift in the attitudes of farmers, which the leaders of the Cooperative Commonwealth Federation faced, was primarily the result of the achievement of a new status. The organization, if it became more conservative, did so in response to demands arising internally. As Turner and Killian suggest, the loss of support by an important "carrier group" may precipitate the demise of the organization if its programs are not re-evaluated.[27] However, goals sometimes are modified when an organization runs into an unexpected amount of external opposition that threatens a disruption of its membership. When the movement toward health insurance began in this country, the American Medical Association denounced both compulsory and voluntary programs as socialistic, Communistic, and inciting to revolution. Opposition grew as voluntary plans increased during the 1930's. It soon became evident that the A.M.A.'s adamant opposition was encouraging the development of new groups which apparently had the ear of the Roosevelt administration: "Liberal physicians and laymen became outspoken in their opposition to what they thought was an untenable stand by the American Medi-

---

[26] Seymour Martin Lipset, *Agrarian Socialism* (Berkeley: University of California Press, 1950), p. 229.

[27] Ralph H. Turner and Lewis M. Killian, *Collective Behavior* (Englewood Cliffs, N.J.: Prentice-Hall, Inc., 1957), 334.

cal Association." [28] Internal squabbles within the medical profession—the American College of Surgeons saw many advantages in the health insurance proposals—coupled with the realization that, in all probability, some action was going to be taken, led the A.M.A. to accept the idea of voluntary private insurance, probably as a hedge against more extreme possibilities.

It seems clear that many organizational goals change, not because they have been achieved, but because of changes in the social environment in which the activities are initiated. On the other hand, Joseph Gusfield's study of the Woman's Christian Temperance Union provides an illuminating example of response to a changing environment which involves not a radical shift in goals but rather a transformation in the audience toward which the organization aimed its appeals. Gusfield notes that changes in American social life manifested in the increasing acceptance of drinking, coupled with a decline in rural population and the vast complex of factors which made possible the repeal of the Eighteenth Amendment, "have presented the W.C.T.U. with an environment more hostile to the doctrine of total abstinence than was true in the years of the organization's formation and development." [29] The political influence of temperance movements, which was once considerable, has diminished almost to the point of non-existence. In the light of this development, Gusfield sought to determine if the change in environment had lead to a change in goals. The conclusion is that the W.C.T.U. has not abandoned its temperance aims. There was no evidence in the literature of the organization to suggest any degree of accommodation. Instead, attention has been shifted to a new audience. While membership has remained numerically constant, the socio-economic status of members has declined. Originally the organization was composed mostly of middle class women who sought to dissuade the working classes from drinking. Now the membership is more lower-middle and lower class and its target has shifted to the drinking habits of the middle class. Rather than experiencing a change of goals, the W.C.T.U. has altered the composition of its membership. Also the techniques of the organization

[28] Joseph Hirsh, "The Compulsory Health Insurance Movement in the United States," *Social Forces*, XVIII (Oct. 1939), 111.

[29] Joseph Gusfield, "Social Structure and Moral Reform: A Study of the Woman's Christian Temperance Union," *American Journal of Sociology*, LXI (Nov. 1955), 221.

have shifted from militant campaigning to "moral indignation." Gusfield concludes:

> Today the W.C.T.U. is an organization in retreat. Contrary to the expectations of theories of institutionalization, the movement has not acted to preserve organizational values at the expense of past doctrine.[30]

ORGANIZATIONS AS RESISTORS OF CHANGE

So far, we have indicated changes in organizational goals resulting from environmental changes and alteration of the ideology of membership upon the achieving of an original goal. A final way in which goals come to be changed, which Gusfield mentioned in the above quotation, might be understood as inherent in the formative process of groups. In the course of their growth, movements generally develop an organizational apparatus consisting of a permanent staff or "bureaucracy." The usual pattern of development is from an informal, amorphous structure to a formal and regimented one. This latter, formal stage is characterized by prescribed patterns of procedure, complexity in structure, standardization of relationships, and a gradual decline in the active participation of the rank and file. These developments are known as the institutionalization or bureaucratization of the movement. Continued apathy may require that the stimulation of participation become the primary object of staff activities, even to the extent of losing sight of the original goals of the organization.[31] Phillip Selznick's theory of bureaucracy states that the running of an organization creates problems not related to original goals. These goals of internal relevance assume an increasing proportion of time and may gradually be substituted for externally directed goals. The day-to-day behavior of the permanent staff and active participants (a minority of the membership) becomes centered around proximate goals of primarily internal importance, modifying or "displacing" the stated goals of the organization.[32]

---

[30] *Ibid.*, 232.

[31] F. Stuart Chapin and John E. Tsouderos, "Formalization Observed in Ten Voluntary Organizations: Concepts, Morphology, Process," *Social Forces*, XXXIII (May 1955), 306-309.

[32] Phillip Selznick, "An Approach to the Theory of Bureaucracy," *American Sociological Review*, VIII (Feb. 1943), 47-54. *See also* David Sills, "Voluntary Associations: Instruments and Objects of Change," *Human Organization*, XVIII (Spring, 1959), 17-21.

The idea of the institutionalization of social movements is related to the concept of goal setting as a function of interaction with environment. Yet bureaucratic inertia seems to exist to some extent in all organizations. Since group norms establish patterns of behavior and tend to preserve them, social or political movements that seek to change the continuing relationships must overcome the resistance of traditional values embedded in the on-going practices of group life. In some cases the conscious planning of the staff may preserve the continuity of the organization by planning for a future after the original purpose has been achieved. For example, The National Foundation for Infantile Paralysis was aware of the probability that a postpolio future would require some adaptation. The structure of the Foundation was so designed that if "National headquarters . . . should decide to embark on a new program, there is no organizational machinery to stand in the way." The local chapters did not need to ratify such a decision and "there are no effective subgroups within the organization which could offer effective resistance to it." Further, members did not view their participation only in terms of a "limited, pragmatic goal," but rather perceived their involvement as a way of life.[33] In short, the membership regarded the organization as a broad reform movement not restricted to a single goal.

In other cases an organization may lose its impetus through a shift in social forces over which it has no control, and, while unable to develop new goals of equal salience, makes continued survival the ultimate goal. The Townsend Organization has nearly vanished because its goal, the alleviation of economic dislocation, has been achieved to some extent, although not as a result of the efforts of the organization.

The Townsend movement achieved its greatest prominence during the depression of the 1930's. The offering of a quick and simple plan to end poverty has enormous appeal to people in the lower income brackets, irrespective of age. Writing in 1941, Cantril observed that "the plan has clearly become a remedy to relieve general economic insecurity." [34] However, passage of the Social Security Act and other forms of social legislation reduced this appeal con-

---

[33] Sills, "The Succession of Goals," in Amitai Etzioni, ed., *Complex Organizations* (New York: Holt, Rinehart & Winston, Inc., 1961), 156-159.

[34] Hadley Cantril, *The Psychology of Social Movements* (New York: John Wiley & Sons, Inc., 1941), p. 192.

siderably. In 1936 the Townsend Organization had over two million members but in 1951 it had only slightly over fifty thousand, a decline of more than 97 per cent. Yet the organization still survives in spite of changes in the relative importance of its original goals. How has this been managed? Sheldon Messinger points out that there has been a tendency to convert membership meetings into social affairs. This development, in addition to other trends, leads Messinger to conclude:

> The organized arms of declining social movements will tend to adapt to these changed conditions in characteristic ways. We can broadly describe this adaptation by asserting that the dominating orientation of leaders and members shifts *from the implementation of the values the organization is taken to represent . . . to maintaining the organizational structure as such,* even at the loss of the organization's central mission.[35]

The Structure of Influence

The change that sets off a political reaction and demands a restoration of equilibrium is thus balanced by the role of organized groups in the maintenance of the status quo and possibly a resistance to further change. Does this mean that political systems reach a position of stability in which the authority of a certain dominant group remains unchallenged and, to paraphrase Key, every group knows its place and keeps it?[36] With respect to the American political process, is there a more or less static ruling class or "power elite" whose decisions are accepted as binding? We have seen that the institutional structure of American government contributes to a diversification of centers of power. However, there is still the possibility that an unusually powerful group can control these institutions.

ECONOMIC CONCENTRATION AND POLITICAL POWER

Such a position is generally maintained by those who tend to equate economic power with political influence. This equation is

[35] Sheldon Messinger, "Organizational Transformation: A Case Study of a Declining Social Movement," *American Sociological Review,* XX (Feb. 1955), 10.

[36] Key, *Politics, Parties, and Pressure Groups,* p. 46.

clearly the articulated major premise of earlier "exposés" of business practices such as the reports of the Temporary National Economic Committee and Robert Brady's *Business as a System of
Power.* Today, the writings of C. Wright Mills and Floyd Hunter
imply the existence of a business "conspiracy" in a more restrained
manner.[37] Basically, the argument states that the concentration of
economic resources enables large corporations to monopolize channels of supply and demand. Politically, these corporations are able
to force the enactment of public policies serving these same ends.
The two types of power are theoretically related since economic
power carries with it the means of influencing government, and,
conversely, political power can be employed to bring the market
under control.

Economists have argued about the degree of concentration in the
American economy. Still, there are some essential aspects of the
economy which are not subject to dispute. More than half of all
industry is concentrated under the control of a few large corporations. In terms of total assets, two hundred corporations own half
of American industry.[38] While other figures might be listed, the
problem is not so much the degree of actual economic concentration but rather the extent to which concentration of economic
power is translated into the achievement of professed political objectives. Can we conclude that wealth is the basic variable in
measuring political power; that "in competition with other groups
the pressure groups of the well-to-do enjoy an immense advantage"? [39]

It is true that in certain selected instances the wealthier pressure
groups have the advantage. In the distribution of defense contracts,
for example, there is a continued tendency to rely on large corporations irrespective of efforts by smaller contractors to receive a more
equitable share. By insisting that small manufacturers should rely
on subcontracts rather than prime contracts, and by allowing large

---

[37] Robert Brady, *Business as a System of Power* (New York: Columbia Uni-
versity Press, 1943). C. Wright Mills, *The Power Elite* (New York: Oxford
University Press, 1956). Floyd Hunter, *Top Leadership, U.S.A.* (Chapel Hill:
University of North Carolina Press, 1959).

[38] M. A. Adelman, "The Measurement of Industrial Concentration," *Review
of Economics and Statistics,* XXXIII (Nov. 1951), 269-296.

[39] Donald C. Blaisdell, *Government Under Pressure* (Public Affairs Pamphlet
No. 67, 1946), p. 24.

contractors to dispense these subcontracts with minimum regulation, the government actually delegates a part of its functions to private concerns and allows the distribution of money by these concerns.

However, this example should not be given more credence than it deserves. While there are certain types of contracts that are suitable for smaller manufacturers, crucial defense needs in the nuclear age necessitate that all considerations other than the building of weapons as quickly and as efficiently as possible be disregarded. In other questions this is not true. In fact, many business organizations believe that policy makers show considerable bias against big business and try to create an image of their particular organization as representative of small or independent enterprises. While available research into public attitudes toward big business reveals that 76 per cent of a sample survey believed the good effects of big business outweighed the bad, observers of regulatory policy making state that the unfavorable image of big business on the part of some office holders is a definite factor in assessing political power.[40] Walter Adams states "let any group become large and economically powerful and its political influence drops." [41] A more specific development of this hypothesis is given by Claire Wilcox:

> When big business restricts output and boosts prices to increase its income, it is said to be engaging in a "conspiracy in restraint of trade" and is subject to punishment by fine and imprisonment. When little business does the same thing, it is said to be practicing "fair trade" and is given official blessing.[42]

COMMUNITY POWER PATTERNS

This evidence would not allow an equation of economic and political power on the ground that the very possession of economic power contributes to hostile attitudes on the part of governmental decision makers. Further, in a federal system, decisions of importance to economic groups may be made beneath the national level. In some sections of the country, business dominates, usually

---

[40] Burton R. Fisher and Stephen B. Withey, *Big Business as the People See It* (University of Michigan: Institute for Social Research, Survey Research Center, Dec. 1959), p. xii.

[41] Walter Adams, "Competition, Monopoly and Countervailing Power," *Quarterly Journal of Economics*, LXVII (Nov. 1953), 472-474.

[42] Claire Wilcox, "Concentration of Power in the American Economy," *Harvard Business Review*, XXVIII (Nov. 1950), 58.

in small towns and villages. A study of a small town in upper New York state revealed that with few exceptions the elected officials are businessmen. These businessmen own most of the real property in the village. Because of the dominant position of this group, the authors of the study conclude that meetings of the village board are usually conducted along lines satisfactory to the business interest:

> Hardly a meeting of the village board passes without some action being justified on the basis of the low tax principle—services are curtailed to avoid a tax raise, purchases of new equipment are postponed in order to avoid expenditures, the trustees complain to each other if street lights are not turned off at sunrise, payrolls are delayed near the end of the fiscal year when funds are short and new taxes have not been collected in order to save interest on a bank loan, state funds and services are accepted and sought "to save the taxpayer's money." [43]

Other community studies reveal that a few people, usually businessmen, are able to exercise varying degrees of control over all decisions of a public nature. In one of the larger southern cities, researchers found that community projects are doomed unless approved by the executives of absentee-owned corporations. On the other hand, some economically powerful leaders may refuse to become involved in community activities for fear of making enemies and damaging the public relations program of the corporation. Thus persons of great economic power may have no influence on public policy.[44]

The available literature on community power structures indicates that the tight "pyramid" of power, in which the people at the top exercise coherent policy decisions, is characteristic of small cities.[45] In larger areas the pyramid is open; no such unified power group exists. To illustrate, a mid-western city of 50,000 contained a small group of influentials but there was no conscious unified leadership

---

[43] Arthur J. Vidich and Joseph Bensman, *Small Town in Mass Society* (Garden City, N.Y.: Doubleday and Company, Inc., 1960), pp. 119-120.

[44] Roland J. Pellegrin and Charles H. Coates, "Absentee-Owned Corporations and Community Power Structure," *American Journal of Sociology*, LXI (Mar. 1956), 413-419. Robert O. Schulze, "The Role of Economic Dominants in Community Power Structure," *American Sociological Review*, XXIII (Feb. 1958), 3-9.

[45] *See*, for example, R. E. Agger and Vincent Ostrom, "The Political Structure of a Small Community," *Public Opinion Quarterly*, XX (Spring, 1956), 81-89.

on the part of this group. Different interests were influential depending upon the issue in question, suggesting a "pluralism of elites" rather than a single ruling elite.[46] In Chicago, a series of case studies dealing with a broad array of issues could locate no single leadership group. Political influence appeared to be a function of the issue rather than the exclusive property of a general leadership group.

Edward C. Banfield, who performed the research on Chicago, offers some reasons for the lack of a dominant business interest. These reasons are generally enough to suggest implications for the study of leadership in any complex area. He suggests first that "there exist fundamental conflicts of interests and opinion among the business leaders." Even if we consider the few individuals who would be at the top of an hypothetical hierarchy of power, these conflicts are sufficient to make concerted activity impossible. Second, "even if there were no such conflicts, the amount of communication that would be required to concert activity in making and carrying out a comprehensive plan would be so great that no time would be left for anything else." Banfield argues that, if there were only a few such leaders, the communication problem would still be difficult since the problem of communication would exist not only among these few principles but also within the large clientele which each controls. In a huge metropolis, the number of individuals would be so large as to make communication nearly impossible. Finally, there is the problem of the bureaucratization of organizations, which has been discussed in this chapter. Assuming that the first two obstacles had been overcome, that differences had been resolved and communication established, an organization would be necessary to carry out agreed upon programs. We know that organization can become an obstacle to comprehensive action "because the desire to maintain and enhance the organization tends to displace the ends for which it was formed; the organization becomes unwilling to act on these ends for fear that by acting it may weaken or destroy itself." For these and other reasons, Banfield concludes:

---

[46] George Belknap and Ralph Smuckler, "Political Power Relations in a Midwest City," *Public Opinion Quarterly*, XX (Spring, 1956), 73-80. The phrase "pluralism of elites" is borrowed from Morton S. Baratz, "Corporate Giants and the Power Structure," *Western Political Quarterly*, IX (June 1956), 406-415.

The notion that "top leaders" run the city is certainly not supported by the facts of the controversies described in this book. On the contrary, in these cases the richest men of Chicago are conspicuous by their absence. Lesser business figures appear, but they do not act concertedly: some of them are on every side of every issue. . . . Businessmen exercise influence (to the extent that they exercise it at all) not so much because they are rich or in a position to make threats and promises as, . . . "by main force of being right." [47]

The single exception to the rule of diversified power in complex areas is Floyd Hunter's study of Atlanta, in which the existence of "top leadership" is claimed. However, even here the power of the elite was greatest at the local level and diminished at higher levels of government.[48] The generalization to be abstracted from these community studies is: as the complexity of the social structure increases, the chances of any single group having a monopoly of influence declines. At the state and national levels, a power elite probably does not exist. "It is the growing complexity and fluidity of American society, with its consequences for power distribution, which must be recognized first. The great technological changes in the U.S., accompanied by specialization, social pluralism, social mobility, and equalization of status, suggests . . . an amorphous, diffuse, 'open' society." [49]

ELITE THEORY: AN EVALUATION

Although the preponderance of evidence suggests a pluralistic power structure, "equal time" will be given to those who seek to refute this evidence. C. Wright Mills's thesis is that there is a concentration of political power in the hands of a small group of military and business leaders. In contrast to the pluralistic assumptions of group theorists, Mills maintains that this Power Elite is well integrated and cohesive. In support of his argument, he points out that the Power Elite controls "command posts" (institutions

---

[47] Edward C. Banfield, *Political Influence* (New York: The Free Press of Glencoe, Inc., 1961), pp. 288, 294-297.

[48] Hunter, *Community Power Structure* (Chapel Hill: University of North Carolina Press, 1953).

[49] Samuel Eldersveld, "American Interest Groups: A Survey of Research and Some Implications for Theory and Method," in Henry W. Ehrman, ed., *Interest Groups on Four Continents* (Pittsburg: University of Pittsburg Press, 1958), p. 190.

where decisions are made). Thus, control of the institutions of power is equated with ability to exercise political influence. Mills does not claim that *all* decisions are made by this small clique, but only the "big decisions." He excludes the "middle range" of decision-making. However, this distinction between the relative importance of decisions is not elaborated upon. Judging from the types of decisions which Mills does select as important (the decision to drop the atomic bomb, for example), we can conclude that most of the issues that create the greatest conflicts of interest are made at the middle level. Presumably Congress itself is part of this middle level.[50] In addition, we need to understand the perception of the importance of issues by the interests which are engaged in a struggle. Phillip Monypenny offers the hypothesis that "the greater the degree to which a given object of activity is indispensable for the maintenance of an optimum state by a given group, the more intense will be the activity of that group." [51] Thus, when a group is more dependent upon a particular objective than are other groups, its activity will be more intense with a greater probability of success.

Political systems may exist in a stable form for relatively short periods with the holders of power remaining unchallenged. However, this equilibrium is frequently disturbed by changes which generate discontent and increase the intensity with which dissatisfied groups view themselves. The pattern varies over time. In the days of McKinley there may have been a "ruling class" of businessmen who could "decide where their interests lay and what editors, lawyers, and legislators might be paid in order to advance them." [52] Groups relatively inactive then are quite active now. Negroes, for example, have changed their behavior patterns from apathy to intense activity. The perception of status with respect to other groups may be one of secondary economic importance and more concerned with social activity. Hence the decline in the power of one group

---

[50] Mills, *op. cit.*, 244-291. For excellent critiques of *The Power Elite*, see Daniel Bell, "The Power Elite Reconsidered," *American Journal of Sociology*, LXIV (Nov. 1958), 238-250 and Talcott Parsons, "Power in American Society," *World Politics*, X (Oct. 1957), 123-143.

[51] Phillip Monypenny, "Political Science and the Study of Groups: Notes to Guide a Research Project," *Western Political Quarterly*, VII (June 1954), 197.

[52] David Riesman, Nathan Glazer, and Reuel Denney, *The Lonely Crowd* (Garden City, N.Y.: Doubleday and Company, Inc., 1955). pp. 246-247.

is not automatically related to the increasing influence of another.

Another aspect of the elite theory open to criticism is the belief that the ruling group interacts frequently on the basis of common interests. We have seen this idea refuted by Banfield. Mills assumes that top corporations are woven together through the mechanism of the National Association of Manufacturers, but there is ample evidence indicating cleavages within the NAM and the big business community in general. There are conflicts among railroads, truckers, and airlines; between export companies and companies with a domestic market; and so on.

A conclusion similar to that of Mills is given by Floyd Hunter: "While disagreements may exist in relation to specific issues, the basic values of the dominant interests, traceable most often to the larger corporate interests, bring about workable unity within the total power structure." [53] This statement is based upon Hunter's discovery that many of the "top" leaders are acquainted with one another, self-awareness being equated with influence. However, he has trouble putting this hypothesis into action since there is very little evidence of an actual decision made by the top leadership. An example of this difficulty is Hunter's list of the most influential organizations. By asking national organizations to nominate leading associations, Hunter compiled a list of one hundred and six "potentially influential" organizations. The top ten are:[54]

   (1) Chamber of Commerce, U.S.A.
   (2) American Federation of Labor
   (3) American Legion
   (4) American Medical Association
   (5) Congress of Industrial Organizations
   (6) National Association of Manufacturers
   (7) American Farm Bureau Federation
   (8) National Council of Churches of Christ in the U.S.A.
   (9) National Education Association
 (10) National Grange

The list was made up entirely from responses to questionnaires by the associations. One may well ask: Who are they to judge? Perhaps a survey of the impressions of governmental leaders would have produced different results, as would a survey of the opinions

---

[53] Hunter, *Top Leadership, U.S.A.*, p. 8.
[54] *Ibid.*, pp. 13-16.

of the members (and nonmembers) of these organizations. One possible measurement of influence is neglected by not ascertaining the reactions of governmental decision makers. Included in the list of the one hundred and six organizations is the National Small Business Men's Association. However, a study of the personnel of the House and Senate Small Business Committees, the units in which the National Small Business Men's Association would be expected to be influential, suggests that these committees are more likely to listen to the advice of the Smaller Business Association of New England, an organization not listed by Hunter.[55] One might ask: Would the Senate or House Banking and Currency Committee be more impressed by the arguments of The National Education Association or the American Bankers Association?

There is also the very plausible hypothesis that associations may vary in influence in correlation with the degree to which the public (nonmembers) looks to them for leadership. Howard E. Freeman and Morris Showell found that, in Washington state, there was a change in the prestige of an association depending upon whose attitudes were tested. The Chamber of Commerce ranked higher among members than nonmembers, but the reverse was true of the American Federation of Labor. Both of these organizations were below the top three (Veterans of Foreign Wars, American Legion, and Grange), whose influence was ranked identically by both members and nonmembers. The prestigious position of these organizations is explained by the large number of veterans and farmers in the Washington population, but influence is not absolutely dependent upon a large number of members. The labor unions had more members than the business groups but ranked lower. This suggests that the larger the group, the smaller the influence over its members.[56] In short, to determine the political influence of an organization we must consider regional variations, differential access to key areas of decision, the nature of the particular issue in dispute, degree of control over members, and the image of the organization with the public.

---

[55] Harmon Zeigler, *The Politics of Small Business* (Washington, D.C.: Public Affairs Press, 1961).

[56] Howard E. Freeman and Morris Showel, "Differential Political Influence of Voluntary Associations," *Public Opinion Quarterly*, XV (Winter, 1951), 703-714.

This critique of the ruling elite model leaves us with the alternative of a diversified structure of power. Riesman and associates have described the structure of power in terms of "veto groups" that have attained sufficient power to stop policies harmful to their interests. Although in some selected areas business is in a position of greater power than other groups on a more or less permanent basis, nationally the influence of groups shifts according to the issue. While each veto group is sufficiently established to be influential in its own area of concern, none is so powerful as to be classified as an elite. It is possible for an aggressive group, usually inactive, to achieve its objectives when none of the large veto groups is sufficiently aroused to take a position. Political influence, then, is "situational and mercurial" rather than static.[57]

---

[57] Riesman et al., op. cit., pp. 246-257.

Business Associations
in
American Politics

For many centuries, businessmen have welded themselves into organizations when it appeared to them that they had a common interest that could be furthered by collective action. The beginning of the capitalistic system in the late middle ages, attended by the growth of guilds, introduced the idea that the making of a profit is, or should be, the fundamental motive underlying a business venture. Since businessmen went to make money, it is reasonable that the achievement and maintenance of a satisfactory margin of profit is a major purpose behind the formation of associations of businessmen. In the complexities of today's economic world, this is not as simple a problem as it once may have been. In some cases a particular segment of the business community engages in "unfair" competitive practices which may threaten to disrupt the stability of a market, thus harrowing the community into subgroups and creating the necessity for protective organization. In other cases, organizations may arise to resist the encroachments of an "outside" foe, such as a militant labor union or a different type of business which seeks to win away traditional customers. Whatever the nature of the threat, business organizations have come into being to cope with change.

Businessmen are indeed a "heterogeneous lot," as may be ascertained easily by a cursory examination of the unbelievably long list of trade associations currently extant.[1] One discovers trade associations with such diverse names and manufacturing roles as the International Association of Photo Engravers, the National Association of Box Manufacturers, the Institute of Makers of Explosives, and the American Paper and Pulp Association, to name but a few.[2] The impressive range in the diversity of economic interests within the business population might well justify one's throwing up his hands in bewilderment at the task of answering such unavoidable questions as: (1) What organizations speak for business? (2) What are the goals of the representative organizations?

The Trade Association Movement

The complexity of business organizations can be partially traced to the growth and diversity of the economy. Before the vast technological changes in the American economy during and after the Civil War, the available historical evidence indicates that organizations of businessmen were usually occasional and local. The functions of such organizations were social and recreational. Little attention was given to public affairs. The sporadic interest of these organizations in governmental problems is the exception which proves the rule. We read, for example, of the baker guild in New York City which, in 1741, was involved in a dispute over a city ordinance fixing the price of bread. Again, in the early nineteenth century, business groupings engaged in some of the internal conflicts predating the War of 1812: "State bank advocates united to support Jackson against the combined opposition of conservative business interests and adherents of the Second Bank of the United States." [3]

These isolated examples are by no means indicative of a trend.

---

[1] V. O. Key, *Politics, Parties, and Pressure Groups* (New York: Thomas Y. Crowell Company, 1958), p. 82.

[2] C. J. Judkins, *Trade and Professional Associations of the United States* (Washington, D.C.: Government Printing Office, 1952).

[3] Clarence E. Bonnett, "The Evolution of Business Groupings," *Annals of the American Academy of Political and Social Science,* 179 (May 1935), 3.

The disturbances were brief and the organizational response temporary. One of the most conspicuous stimulants of aroused business interests, the aggressive labor union, had not yet undertaken sustained activities. Although there were cleavages between employer and employee, the close physical proximity of the parties to a dispute and the relatively small size of businesses tended to contribute to the worker's identifying himself with the success of the business venture. The country was mainly agricultural, there was no genuine labor market, and such grievances as did develop were usually resolved in an informal manner.

A hint of things to come was given with the advent of the factory system in the 1830's. Labor-management relations became less personal as the size of manufacturing establishments increased, although the old "shop" system was still dominant. Local unions sprang up in several of the larger cities and negotiated with newly formed trade associations on questions of wages. This situation was found only in areas of high population density where a fairly extensive number of workers in the same industry was concentrated and where business matters were conducted on an expanding scale.

Although there are examples of employers associations resisting labor's demands, such as the "open shop" movement of the 1830's, the economic conditions of the next two decades contributed to a general decline in organized activity. There were periods of depression from 1838 to 1842 and from 1855 to 1856. During these periods, the existence of a large number of unemployed workers gave employers a strategic advantage. It was not unusual for workers to underbid their companions in order to get or retain jobs. Under these conditions employers were rarely faced with the necessity of presenting a united front.

The pre-Civil War era, then, was characterized by the following conditions: Business associations were confined to urban areas. There were no national associations comparable to those of today, since industries had not developed the complexity which would require these larger organizations. During the period just prior to the Civil War, some industries began to acquire a national basis of operations. Railroads were becoming national in scope and the iron industry was developing rapidly. Embryonic associations in these businesses sprang up under the stresses of war. It is hardly coincidence that railroads and iron manufacturers were among the first to develop elaborate and formal patterns of cooperation. In the iron industry, for example, even as late as 1863, the most likely avenue of repetitive interaction was at the regional level. Machinists and molders unions initiated strikes which met with the resistance of regional managerial groups, who then tried to make contact with other regional associations. One of these groups, the Iron Founders and Machine Builders Association of the Falls of the Ohio, campaigned extensively toward the goal of cooperating with major producers throughout the country. To cope with union efforts, this ᵣegional group tried to interest iron manufacturers in a national blacklist of known labor agitators. A similar effort was being undertaken in the northeastern states by the American Iron Founders Association. These efforts were continued after the war and finally resulted in a truly national organization at the turn of the century.[4]

THE STIMULUS OF COMPLEXITY

The trends predictable in the increasing complexity of business enterprise, sometimes referred to as the "second industrial revolution," reached a temporary peak in the last decades of the nineteenth century. Between 1850 and 1880 the amount of capital invested in manufacturing increased by more than 400 per cent, and there was a comparable rise in the total value of products. Some selected industries exhibited astounding rates of growth. For instance, production of agricultural implements increased 900 per cent, machinery nearly 700 per cent, and pig iron slightly over 600 per cent.[5] Natural resources were exploited greedily while the entire economy expanded with almost bewildering speed. Accompanying this growth were changes in the structure of the economy. Encouraged by technological advances, enterprises became more corporate in nature. Rather than an economy typified by bankers, merchants, and other types of small units, a shift occurred to a manufacturing economy with mass production as the key. The door was opened to large-scale enterprise.

As the economy shifted to mass production, the informal problem-solving techniques of the past were no longer adequate. No longer

---

[4] Clarence E. Bonnett, *Employers' Associations in the United States* (New York: The Macmillan Company, 1922), p. 146.

[5] Merle Fainsod, Lincoln Gordon, and Joseph C. Palamountain, Jr., *Government and the American Economy* (New York: W. W. Norton and Company, Inc., 1959), pp. 5-6.

were workers skilled artisans who knew their employer personally and strove toward the same goal. No longer was competition largely a matter of tiny competitive units absorbing a small share of the market. The famous trust of this period undertook well planned and sometimes quite ruthless attempts to reduce the number of competitors. Vertical and horizontal integration, pools to regulate pricing and output, and various types of holding company operations contributed to a virtual corporate revolution.

For our purposes, it is sufficient to draw attention to the breakup of a single entrepreneurial function into specialized managerial tasks, and the concurrent differentiation between labor and ownership. Workers, entering into a more formal arrangement with their employers, began to hold out for higher wages and were no longer underbid. The decline in the informality of interpersonal relationships between the worker and his boss enabled them to drift more naturally into rival camps. Each group came to regard the other not as mutual contributors toward the same end but as enemies toward whom nothing would be yielded except under compulsion. Whereas unions had formerly been ephemeral and ineffective, great strides toward cohesion were made in order to provide more reliable instruments of negotiation with respect to large businesses. The year 1886 was notable for the violence of its strikes. In the years following, organized labor showed employers and the remainder of the nation that it was henceforth to be taken seriously. This was the period in which the Knights of Labor realized its largest membership and the American Federation of Labor was founded.

THE "OPEN SHOP" MOVEMENT

The most immediate response to this surge of power was the "open shop" movement which lasted until World War I. To guide this defensive effort, most of the major industries of the country formed associations whose major (or even single) purpose was to develop a counterattack, to counterbalance the new power of labor. Organization was met with organization. The intensity with which employers shared the attitudes of hostility to labor is illustrated by an examination of the goals of the Employers Central Executive Committee, which directed the labor relations activities of the building trades: "It would be well for employers to discourage labor unions by every fair means; by insisting on their right to employ workers independent of restrictions imposed by a combination of men. . . ." [6] Under the persistence of a threat to their security, businessmen found the common interest, so long lacking, which led to the creation of national associations. Typical of the period, many of these associations included the word "defense" in their titles. However, the relative stability of organizations begun in this period may be attributed to the fact that the threat against which a defense was necessary gave every indication of becoming a permanent part of the businessman's environment.

There is no doubt that insecurity and perhaps fear were of primary motivational significance. To select one example from many, consider the National Metal Trades Association. In July 1889, the metal pattern workers struck on a national scale. At informal meetings, employers initially agreed, without exception, that there would be no concessions, irrespective of the ultimate cost of this decision. However, as the strike continued, the employers realized that, if they were to remain committed to their position, a more formal type of arrangement to "police" possible deviants would be necessary. Thus the National Metal Trades Association was born. Several manufacturers, acting on their own initiative, had negotiated agreements with the International Association of Machinists, but at the first organizational meeting of the new association all prior agreements were declared null and void. The methods of defense and attack agreed upon and later carried out indicate that the newly established association did not feel constrained by the rules of "fair play" adopted by some earlier movements. The National Metal Trades Association provided its members with "labor spies" (employees who pretended to be sympathetic to labor but reported all organization attempts to management), strikebreakers, and strikebreaking funds. The association recruited a skilled corps of officers who provided guidance to members threatened with labor troubles. In exchange for these services, members surrendered all authority relating to negotiations to the association. If any member compromised or began individual negotiations he was immediately expelled. The protective aspirations of the National Metal Trades Association are well stated in one of a series of advertisements that were circulated among prospective members:

------

[6] Quoted in Clarence E. Bonnett, *History of Employers' Association in the U.S.* (New York: The Vantage Press, 1956), p. 213.

If unopposed, the unions of metal workers will develop sufficient strength to dominate *your* shop. . . . The National Metal Trades Association . . . is the most powerful defense organization in existence and the one most feared by labor leaders. . . . *It gives its members a feeling of security obtainable in no other way* . . . the mere fact of membership has prevented many strikes.[7]

Here is emphasized the overt appeal to the insecurity of business-men who are forced to adjust to alterations in their patterns of relationship with workers. In fact, the services of the association were used frequently and with such results that the machinists union suffered declining membership and, by the 1920's, was nearly destroyed.

The almost frantic appeals, the violent methods, and the un-compromising attitudes of this organization were typical of a par-ticular era of our economic history. As organized labor became an established part of the economic community, it settled into a more pacific type of struggle with management. The open shop move-ment, at least in its more belligerent aspects, had ground to a halt by the time of World War I. The vast number of associations created in response to a particular type of threat, from which the National Metal Trades Association has been selected as an example, discovered that there was still a need for a more moderate type of body, found other problems unrelated to the labor market that required a coordinated effort, or disbanded.

ASSOCIATIONS AND THE RESTRAINT
OF COMPETITION

Although this initial reaction to organized labor was perhaps the most spectacular of the disturbances in the business community, the problems unique to this reaction were only a portion of the total economic life of a businessman. Equally as crucial and infinitely more complex is the problem of market control. Unrestricted competition, while idealized in the "rags to riches" myth and for-malized in that rather nebulous body of thought referred to as the American business creed, is ill-suited to the economic survival of a great many types of businesses. Operating with only the most informal channels of communication, members of an industry are

---

[7] Senate Committee on Education and Labor, *Violations of Free Speech and Rights of Labor*, Senate Report No. 6, 76th Cong., 1st sess., 1939 (Washington, D.C.: Government Printing Office, 1939), p. 22.

frequently tempted to play one competitor against another. This can be accomplished by selling below cost in order to drive down a business whose volume is not large enough to enable it to absorb losses, granting special concessions (usually in the form of rebates or volume discounts) to favored customers to guarantee the maintenance of a stable clientele, and any number of elaborate devices designed to reduce the rigors of competition. These practices occur both among the members of an industry or distribution operation and between two types of businesses competing for the same market. The frequent "price wars" among gasoline distributors and milk producers illustrate the first type. To use the example of milk distribution, one large dairy within an area may offer an equally large retail customer (usually a chain store) a cash discount. This discount may be met by a second dairy, which will necessitate the improving of the first dairy's original offer. Thus begins a vicious circle of price cutting. Although lower consumer prices are frequently the result of this type of competitive behavior, it can be ruinous to businesses that cannot continue to operate at a profit yet are left with no alternative but to play the deadly game.

Associations with the primary purpose of self-regulation of competitive practices are as characteristic of the period since World War I as were the anti-labor associations of the previous period. While associations of this kind were on the upswing during World War I, there was a sharp decline immediately after the war. The prosperous 1920's saw another surge, which ended in the depression. Then, with the creation of the National Recovery Administration in 1933, the number of associations again increased. Under the direct prodding of the government and with the advantage of quasi-public status, "trade associations became the *sine qua non* for every industry." [8] The movement tapered off again after the United States Supreme Court ruled the National Industrial Recovery Act unconstitutional, but trade associations helped businessmen to meet the demands of World War II. Since the end of the war, the total number of associations has remained fairly constant.

There is a conspicuous aspect of this briefest of histories that merits comment: The increase in the total number of voluntary associations among businessmen seems to correlate roughly with periods of prosperity or war; and a decline in the number of these

[8] Fainsod *et al., op. cit.,* p. 468.

associations corresponds to periods of depression. The relation between war and associations is easily understandable. Here indeed is a situation of changing environments, demanding mechanisms of adjustment. Depression also is productive of flux. Why should we not expect more intense effort at cooperation during these years? Key has called our attention to the measurable relation between farmer agitation and periods of economic disadvantage for agriculture.[9] Yet the opposite conclusion seems to be indicated here. While no explanation should be regarded as absolutely conclusive, periods of economic crisis do not affect all types of businessmen in a similar manner. Indeed, we have seen that changes in the economic structure are accelerated during periods of relative prosperity. While some types of businesses may be victims of change during depressions, it is quite likely that others may enter a period of the *status quo*. Differences between industries in the areas of scales of production, marketing methods, and price complexes are acute. Taking the years 1929 to 1933 as an example, prices of agricultural commodities fell 63 per cent but production fell only 6 per cent. On the other hand, prices of agricultural implements fell 6 per cent and production declined by 80 per cent.

In some cases the depression economy apparently creates the need for organization but also creates attitudes of such hostility that businessmen lose the inclination toward associational activities. Such a situation would hold true when members of an industry compete among themselves for a limited market, rather than when two separate industries compete for the same market. This problem was noted by the Temporary National Economic Committee:

> Industries that faced a depressed market in many cases evidently had a desperate need for cooperation, but it was under such circumstances that association was most difficult; the conflicts between members of an industry are likely to be most pronounced when they are struggling for a limited market, and during such time many of them feel that they can ill afford to share the burden of support of an association.[10]

Another aspect of the development of trade associations which is striking is the active role played by the federal government. The

---

[9] Key, *op. cit.*, p. 30.

[10] U.S. Temporary National Economic Committee, *Trade Association Survey*, Monograph No. 18 (Washington, D.C.: Government Printing Office, 1941), p. 19.

most obvious example of the active role of the government is, of course, the National Recovery Administration of 1933. Congressional declaration of policy stated that the purpose of the National Industrial Recovery Act was ". . . to provide for the general welfare by promoting the organization of industry for the purpose of co-operative action among trade groups, to induce and maintain united action of labor and management under adequate governmental sanctions and supervision, to eliminate unfair competitive practices. . . ." [11] To achieve these goals, NRA encouraged industries to submit "codes of fair competition" which, if approved, would serve as basic law for an industry. If no code was forthcoming, the President could impose one after notice and hearing. However, the law provided for the development of codes through representative associations. This essentially "carrot and stick" approach would naturally encourage those industries which did not have associations to organize as quickly as possible.

The NRA is the most outstanding example of governmental encouragement of trade associations. However, it is far from a single example. Many agencies of the federal government, and some Congressional committees, have sought to establish a working relationship with the particular portion of the population with which they are uniquely concerned, and have instigated organization efforts to facilitate the creation of clear channels of communication and influence. The Department of Commerce, the Federal Trade Commission, and the Department of Defense, to cite several examples, have encouraged the formation of associations. In some cases the active intervention of a federal agency serves as the spark to ignite organizational efforts in industries that had previously been unable to iron out factional squabbles. In other cases, the influence of the government is more indirect. Two examples, each reflecting a different relation between an industry and the government, will serve as illustrations.

The Sugar Institute, which operated from 1928 until 1936, had as its basic purpose the control and stability of prices and the stand-

---

[11] For an assessment of the NRA activities see Committee on Industrial Analysis, *The National Recovery Administration*, House Document No. 158, 75th Cong., 1st sess., 1937 (Washington, D.C.: Government Printing Office, 1937).

ardization of competitive practices in the sugar refining industry.[12] The Sugar Institute, in policing the activities of its members, became a private government of significant influence. An examination of the industry over which it governed will help us to understand why this association functioned as it did. In the earliest days of the sugar refining industry, the years following the Civil War, there were more than twenty companies, each of which accounted for a relatively small percentage of the total market. However, in 1887, seventeen companies merged to form the American Sugar Refining Company, which then continued to buy up the remaining companies. By 1891 only five companies remained outside the combination, and by 1899 this number had been reduced to one. Ninety per cent of the sugar refining business of the country was concentrated in a single firm. It was as a result of this situation that the famous case of *U.S.* v. *E. C. Knight* emerged in 1895. After the ruling that the combination did not violate the Sherman Act, American Sugar undertook sustained efforts to buy up the stock of the remaining independents, but was unable to achieve the desired amount of control. As American continued to buy up stock of existing companies, new and persistent independents arose to thwart its efforts. One effect of the inability of the largest company to control the market was a severe price war which erupted in the early 1900's. When the country entered World War I, an expanded demand enabled these independent companies to keep alive and, with the help of government control of prices and production quotas, to realize a satisfactory profit. However, when control was relaxed in 1920, the industry also faced a reduced demand. The multiplicity of competing units for this lower demand seriously damaged the dominant position of America; and with the reduction of the influence of the "natural" leader, unrestrained competition became the rule. In 1927, the year the idea of a Sugar Institute began to germinate, American had about one-fourth of the market, its nearest competitor 22 per cent, and no other company more than 10 per cent.

It was only natural that members of the industry looked nostalgically upon the war years in comparison with the completely undisciplined market behavior typical of the postwar years. With no

---

[12] A longer account of this episode may be found in U.S. Temporary National Economic Committee, *op. cit.,* pp. 106-143.

single unit in a position to exercise leadership, sugar refiners resorted to a variety of semisecret devices to attract customers. Secret discounts, split brokerage systems, absorption of freight charges, and delayed billing to extend the period of cash discounts were tried first by one refiner and then by his competitors. A minority of "ethical" refiners refused to resort to these hidden types of rebates and met competition by openly announced discounts; but most of the sugar delivered was sold under the stipulations of some form of secret agreement. A final blow to the unstable industry was delivered in 1927 by the "slimness" campaign of a cigarette manufacturer whose slogan "reach for a Lucky instead of a sweet" was reputed to have damaged the sales of several refineries. In an effort to introduce order into the relationships among competitors, the "unethical" refiners, led by the American and the National Sugar Refining Corporation, promoted the establishment of the Sugar Institute. This organization was to set both prices and quotas while outlawing any form of secret agreement.

During its life the Sugar Institute was able to perform its tasks in a reasonably efficient manner, but the industry contained diverse interests whose antagonistic attitudes made quick solutions to emergent problems difficult. With the exception of Louisiana and Florida cane, which accounted for perhaps a fifth of production, domestic refiners used sugar beets. Sugar beets are produced both in the eastern states of Indiana, Ohio, and Michigan, and on irrigated land west of the Mississippi. Cost of production is higher in the eastern states, and there was some fear that the relatively inexpensive production of the western areas might provide an incentive for dispute with respect to price schedules. The refiners who were members of the Sugar Institute were only peripherally affected by these antagonisms, since none of the domestic sugar production was economical in comparison with world standards. Therefore the members of the Institute were largely refiners of imported raw sugar. The Institute was therefore more properly understood as a continental refiners' association with potentially conflicting interests in relation to the total industry. The Sugar Institute was held to be a violation of the Sherman Act in 1936, but many of its members re-aligned themselves into the United States Cane Sugar Refiners Association. This new group, with less rigorous controls over membership than its predecessor, was able to achieve a substantial portion of its goals in the Sugar Acts of 1937 and 1948. In the first Act, the interests of the continental refiners were protected by the placing of tonnage limits on the sugar that could be imported in finished form; in the subsequent Act, although Puerto Rico and Hawaii sought to increase their refining quotas, these efforts were successfully resisted.

Consider now the case of railroads that faced outside competition of a more severe nature than could be expected to develop from within the industry. This competition became most severe during the depression years, when conditions particularly favorable to truckers existed. Shippers who normally used railroads discovered that there were many advantages offered by trucks, which could not be matched by railroads. Lower rates (except for long distance hauling), door to door pick up and delivery, and comparable inducements enabled truckers to make inroads into the freight business of railroads. The railroads, which, unlike the truckers, had exceptionally high overhead costs, could do little to meet this competition. The amount of business lost to truckers continued to soar until by 1938 it was estimated that two billion dollars annually were being lost.[13] However, before the condition of the industry had reached this point, corrective action by collective means was undertaken. In 1932, railroad executives formed statewide organizations to seek legal harassment of trucking firms. In this year the trucking industry had become ready to compete with railroads for the transportation market in terms of technology and business firm organization. A few rudimentary associations among the larger trucking firms had sprung up.

The tactics of the railroads, although restricted to regional efforts, were ingenious and successful. The Iowa railroads, for example, employed Joseph Hays to undertake the task of eliminating competition from trucks. His methods were to seek rigid enforcement of weight and length laws then in existence while encouraging municipalities to enact more rigorous restrictions. Municipalities were supplied with weighing mechanisms by the railroads. In addition, Hays sought anti-trailer laws that would have practically de-

---

[13] Senate Committee on Interstate Commerce, *Investigation of Railroads, Holding Companies, and Affiliated Companies,* Senate Report No. 26, part 2, 77th Cong., 1st sess., 1941 (Washington, D.C.: Government Printing Office, 1941), p. 2.

stroyed the long haul capabilities of trucks. The cities that were selected for this type of pressure were located at strategic points within the state which would "set up a wall of these ordinances at the Mississippi River" and thus impede long hauls.[14] In support of these goals, taxpayers' groups (composed of people not directly connected with railroads) were urged to demand legislation. The railroad employees themselves were organized into an intelligence system to discover and report violations. Courses in the estimation of weights were given to the employees, who then roamed the highways seeking violators.

Unfortunately, from the point of view of the railroads, many of the most obviously discriminatory laws were declared unconstitutional. However, the reaction to the extra-industry competition was beneficial in terms of organized activity. Such organizations as the Western Association of Railway Executives existed primarily to pursue those methods presumed to act as impediments to the continued health of the trucking industry. However, these methods were certainly not productive of long-range solutions to the problems. Railroads began to look with increasing favor at the possibility of seeking a solution through the offices of the Interstate Commerce Commission. Ironically, the truckers were experiencing problems within their industry that made many of them favor regulation by the I.C.C. Unlike railroads, entrance into the trucking market requires little capital. Consequently, businessmen who used trucks for their own purposes found it possible to hire out for extra service, charging whatever rates the market would stand. This competition from intermittent truckers, when combined with the overt hostility of railroads, led the larger trucking firms to establish the American Highway Freight Association in 1932.

The organizational efforts of truckers were given impetus with the establishment of the National Recovery Administration, while at the same time they spurned competition among rival groups for the position of legitimate representative of the industry. The American Highway Freight Association was challenged by the truck division of the National Automobile Chamber of Commerce. NRA arranged for the rival factions to meet, but rigidly adhered to its demand that a single representative association present a code of

---

[14] *Ibid.*, p. 9.

fair competition. Faced with no alternative but to merge into a single unit, the trucking industry submerged its differences and created the American Truckers Association, still a highly influential organization. Here, the role of the government was paramount: ". . . that the NRA brought the industry together into a powerful association cannot be denied." [15]

Meanwhile, compelling forces were moving the railroads toward a comparable organization, or, in the words of Earl Latham, a "more perfect union." [16] In 1933, the post of Federal Coordinator of Transportation was created to cope with, among other things, the problem of the continued loss of business by railroads. Joseph B. Eastman, who served as coordinator, lamented the fact that the railroads ". . . form a single national system, but they are separately owned and the bonds of union between them which enable them to deal with matters of common concern are rather loose and ineffective, and the question is whether they can't form a more perfect union, as the states did through the adoption of the Constitution." [17] Eastman lent further support to the unity movement in his *First Report*. In this document he made mention of the American Railway Association, which was established in 1891, and the Association of Railway Executives, created in 1914. Neither of these organizations, said Eastman, was sufficient to provide coordination on a national basis. In addition to Eastman, the Interstate Commerce Commission and even President Franklin D. Roosevelt had criticized the unnecessary confusion in the railroad industry.

While the sources of government support were clear, Latham has discovered that ". . . the specific movement that led to the formation of the Association of American Railroads was started by a group of security holders." [18] However, the specific recommendations of this group were not well received by the Association of Railway Executives, which, rather than agreeing with the security holders, made a separate set of recommendations leading to the merger of all existing associations. This plan was discussed at a joint meeting of the Association of Railway Executives and the

[15] Meyer H. Fishbein, "The Trucking Industry and the National Recovery Administration," *Social Forces*, XXXIV (Dec. 1955), 178.

[16] Earl Latham, *The Politics of Railroad Coordination: 1933-1936* (Cambridge: Harvard University Press, 1959), p. 164.

[17] *Ibid.*, p. 165.

[18] *Ibid.*, p. 168.

American Railway Association, and these two organizations were subsequently merged into the Association of American Railroads in 1934. A more ambitious plan, to bring all existing regional and national associations under the same roof, was discarded, and most of the offices of the new association were filled by executives who had held positions in the two major associations prior to amalgamation.

These case studies in the formation of trade associations are illustrative of the insecurity, the need for the establishment of stable interaction patterns which underlay the basic theory of the development of organization. While the importance of the federal government in providing the impetus for the unification of a hitherto chaotic industry cannot be denied, the existence of shared attitudes on the part of potential members of the organization should not be overlooked. The existence of such attitudes had to be the foundation or governmental pleas for unity would have been to no avail. For purposes of analysis it is fortunate that the National Recovery Administration, which was directly responsible for the creation of a large number of associations, was declared unconstitutional in 1935. What happened to these organizations? Many are still extant. An impressive minority, however, were dissolved shortly after the demise of NRA. In these cases, the hastily assembled associations, whose major purpose was the short-term job of developing a code or having the NRA do it for them, contained elements of such a divisive nature that continued existence was neither desired nor possible. NRA, in attempting to bring sanctions to bear against portions of an industry, actually produced the unanticipated consequence of raising to the surface underlying conflicts between members of an association, thus jeopardizing any potential stability. In seeking to simplify its administrative tasks, NRA encouraged groupings of related but quite different types of enterprise which lacked the foundations for continued interaction. A similar situation can be pointed to in the Small Business Conference of 1938, which was sponsored by the Department of Commerce. The purpose of this conference was to create some recognizable area of support for President Roosevelt's policies. However, there were so many different attitudes expressed at this conference that the Department of Commerce's attempt to establish a representative organization resulted in numerous and ephemeral groups with sharply divergent goals, each claiming to be the "true" expression of the needs of small business. A conspicuous example of the opposite tendency is the trucking industry, which, after 1935, pooled its resources with the bus companies to support the Motor Carrier Act, which placed trucks under the jurisdiction of the Interstate Commerce Commission.

The Unity of Business

This description of the trade association movement has emphasized the many conflicts of interest within the business community and has, by implication, muted the more pervasive attitudes that may be common to all businessmen. If there is a lesson to be learned here, it is that the easy habit of referring to "businessmen" as though this word described a complex of homogeneous values and behavior patterns is misleading. Nevertheless, there are organizations, such as the National Association of Manufacturers and the Chamber of Commerce, perhaps the most well-known of all business associations, that seek to represent and speak for the interests of every businessman irrespective of occupation. The National Association of Manufacturers and the Chamber of Commerce of the United States are not trade associations; they are not the special advocates of the grievances of any one segment of the business population. The existence of these organizations does imply some goals that are common to all businessmen; some goals that transcend more narrowly perceived occupational interests. Key, while not referring specifically to these two organizations, maintains that ". . . a network of common interests pulls the business community together when its security is threatened . . . within the business community powerful factors operate to bring conformity to dominant views. Unanimity is rare, but a predominant business sentiment usually crystalizes and makes itself heard on major issues." [19]

THE NATIONAL ASSOCIATION OF MANUFACTURERS

If Key is correct, and it is unlikely that he would draw such a conclusion without sufficient evidence, the goals of the Chamber of Commerce and the National Association of Manufacturers should

---

[19] Key, *op. cit.*, p. 83.

provide a microcosmic indicator of the common values of American business. The NAM was formally organized in 1895, although the unsettled condition of the economy during the previous two years was the catalyst for the organization effort. The year 1895, if we can use the Supreme Court's emasculation of the Sherman Act and invalidation of the income tax as a partial indication, was one in which business interests were being treated with deference. Industrial depression had, nevertheless, plagued business during 1893 and 1894. These conditions, according to the official dogma of the NAM, necessitated a national organization to put business on a more equal footing with other economic interests.

During 1894 a southern journalist and businessman, Thomas H. Martin, ". . . wrote and circulated vigorous editorials urging the industrialists of the United States to organize for the purpose of placing their common experience and ability at the service of their fellows and the nation, finding a way out of the existing situation and assuming a permanent leadership in the promotion of the industrial future of the country." [20] This plea fell on the receptive ears of a group of Cincinnati manufacturers who extended an invitation to businessmen in all parts of the country to assemble for the purpose of creating a permanent organization. The response brought three hundred and eighty-three businessmen to Cincinnati on January 22, 23, and 24, 1895.

Accustomed as we are to identify the NAM as a "management" organization, and to imply by this that the major efforts of the organization are in the direction of labor relations, the results of this first meeting are curious. Although the exact disturbances in the economy that led to the meeting are only vaguely defined, there is a conspicuous lack of the fear of organized labor so characteristic of the beginnings of other business organizations. A plausible explanation of this lack of concern might be abstracted from the fact of the depression. As noted previously, depression serves to reduce the bargaining power of organized labor; and these were years of depression. There were no major strikes in iron and steel industries or in the building industries, which previously had been ridden with labor problems. Also, from 1890 to 1895 the member-

---

[20] Senate Committee on Education and Labor, *Hearings, Violations of Free Speech and Rights of Labor*, 76th Cong., 1st sess., 1939 (Washington, D.C.: Government Printing Office, 1939), p. 14025.

ship of the American Federation of Labor had not increased but rather had shown a slight decline. While 1894 was notable for its strikes, irrespective of the depression, the year 1895 was a "calm between the storms." Bonnett's survey of union activity leads him to observe that "most union leaders had . . . learned that there was a depression too deep for major wage advances. . . ." [21]

Perhaps a continuation of strikes would have caused a more belligerent attitude on the part of the founders of the NAM, but, at the time of the Cincinnati meeting, industrial peace was prevalent. The fundamental evil for which this original group sought a solution was the "tariff for revenue only" policy of President Grover Cleveland. The inclusion of William McKinley, an unwavering advocate of high protective tariffs, as the guest of honor was symbolic of this area of concern. The early activities of the NAM, which were certainly inauspicious by comparison with later periods, were almost entirely concerned with the promotion of trade and commerce. The relatively innocuous nature of these activities may be ascertained from the first NAM program. Included in its aims were: the extension of home and foreign markets, establishment of the principle of reciprocity in national legislation, restoration and completion of the merchant marine, construction of a government-owned and -operated canal to connect the Atlantic and Pacific Oceans, and the improvement and extension of natural and artificial waterways.

The NAM did not flourish with these goals. In 1896 its total income was $30,748.34 and its disbursements were $39,429.80, hardly indicative of a dynamic organization. We need make no more mention of the early years of the NAM until 1903, when the goals of the association underwent such a vast change that Truman feels justified in the assertion that "1903 marked the beginning of a new organization." [22] The reorientation of NAM goals can be seen from its statement that "formal cognizance was taken of the increasing activity of organized labor." [23] This increasing activity is well reflected in the astounding increase in the membership of the American Federation of Labor from less than 350,000 in 1895 to

---

[21] Bonnett, *History of Employers' Association in the U.S.* (1956), p. 396.

[22] David Truman, *The Governmental Process* (New York: Alfred A Knopf, Inc., 1951), p. 81.

[23] Senate Committee on Education and Labor, *Hearings* (Washington, D.C.: Government Printing Office, 1939), p. 14025.

nearly 1,750,000 in 1903. Unionism was on the move and, among the specialized trade associations, an open shop movement was gaining momentum. The "new" NAM took the role of coordinating the open shop activities of the previously unconnected associations into a consolidated open shop campaign. Its literature was no longer devoted to questions of merchant marine and artificial waterways but was directed toward a "declaration of labor principles" which bore strong resemblance to the earlier program of the National Metal Trades Association. NAM President David M. Parry's vigorous leadership and prolonged campaign of oratory against unions ("organized labor knows but one law, and that is the law of physical force . . . the law of the savage") encouraged local employer groups to form "citizen's alliances" and finally resulted in the establishment in 1907 of the National Council of Industrial Defense.[24] This organization, whose officers were NAM officials, was composed of national employers groups and such relatively new combinations as the Anti-Boycott Association. The National Council of Industrial Defense (later known as the National Industrial Council) became the lobbying arm of the NAM.

From the rebirth of NAM until the 1920's, practically all of its energy was expended in leading the open shop movement, lobbying against labor-approved legislation, combating strikes, and developing a public relations program to "sell" its labor policy. Compared to its meager beginnings, NAM became an organization of impressive vitality. In 1904 NAM received $153,256.61 and spent $156,138.03, nearly five times as much as it received and spent in its first year; by 1926 these totals were nearly tripled. This period of growth and expansion is described by the Senate Committee on Education and Labor:

> . . . the National Association of Manufacturers has taken the leadership in mobilizing the organization and resources of corporate interests . . . during the two periods prior to 1933 when labor organization acquired strength and momentum under the leadership of the American Federation of Labor.[25]

So greatly were the efforts of the NAM centered around labor problems that a postrebirth statement attributed its beginnings not to

---

[24] Senate Committee on Education and Labor, *Violations of Free Speech and Rights of Labor* (Washington, D.C.: Government Printing Office, 1939), p. 15.
[25] *Ibid.*, p. 42.

the tariff but to labor: "Labor was already united, labor was moving as one man; labor in splendid phalanx-like precision was moving like an army to the accomplishment of its great design. Capital was disorganized, had no coherent force, had no definite, united policy to interpose against the aggressions that might be made upon its interests." [26]

During the 1920's NAM activities became more diversified, more general and, although not relegating labor to a position of unimportance, less overtly belligerent. Accordingly, James W. Prothro's analysis of business ideas in the 1920's is restricted to the NAM and the Chamber of Commerce, on the grounds that "it was the ideas of these two groups, whether an accurate or distorted reflection of actual business opinion, that entered the stream of American political thought during the 1920's as *the* business viewpoint." [27]

THE CHAMBER OF COMMERCE

Before undertaking an investigation of this viewpoint, some attention to the origin and development of the Chamber of Commerce is required. Here the common pattern occurs: "The dominant . . . factor which first appeared in the historical development of . . . the Chamber . . . was a sense of insecurity." In addition to insecurity generated by the standard fear of labor, businessmen thought they saw tangible evidence of a "persecution of business." Instances of such presumably hostile attitudes were the passage of the Sherman and Clayton Acts, the vigorous prosecution of trusts by the Theodore Roosevelt Administration, and the growing demands of disadvantaged groups for increased regulation of business.

Certainly the Chamber was not unique in assuming this defensive posture. In addition to the organizations considered in this chapter, a direct predecessor of the Chamber, the National Board of Trade, exhibited a consciousness of fear. This latter association, begun shortly after the Civil War, did not develop as a sufficiently representative organization for the purpose of reduction of anxieties; otherwise, it is unlikely that the need for a new organization would have been felt. Prior to 1912, when the Chamber of Commerce was

---

[26] Quoted in Bonnett, *Employers' Associations in the United States* (New York: The Macmillan Company, 1922), p. 300.

[27] James W. Prothro, *The Dollar Decade* (Baton Rouge: Louisiana State University Press, 1954), p. viii.

begun, several efforts to make the National Board of Trade representative of a broad base of business opinion were unsuccessful. The National Association of Manufacturers was actually a federation of trade associations with only auxiliary connections with business interests on a localized basis. Consequently, when businessmen expressed their conviction that the government was discriminating against certain economic interests, a common response was that there was no basic agreement among these economic interests and thus no organization that could present a reliable business viewpoint except on the question of labor.

The first overt step toward a remedy was taken by an official of the national government, Secretary of Commerce and Labor, Charles Nagel. He wrote that when he first assumed his duties "there was an organization in existence which I think was called the National Council, or something to that effect. . . . After one or two meetings, I concluded . . . that if commerce and industry . . . were to organize with any hope of exerting an influence, it would have to be done upon a larger basis." [28] Nagel's dissatisfaction with the current situation was shared by a considerable number of local Chambers of Commerce, and, after a series of preliminary negotiations, a meeting at the offices of the Department of Commerce and Labor was arranged for February 12, 1912. The purpose of this meeting, which was attended by representatives of local Chambers and the National Association of Manufacturers, was to devise a plan whereby the Chamber of Commerce could receive its credentials as a legitimate spokesman for the business community. This was achieved partially by means of the establishment of two general types of membership: organization and individual. Each state or local Chamber became an organizational member and the door was open to trade association affiliation. An individual member was designated as any person who is a member of an organization that belongs to the national Chamber. At a more general meeting on April 22 at which President Taft was present, these membership regulations were adopted by delegates of 2,000 local Chambers.

This classification of membership was fortunate in that it provided the opportunity for the new organization to build upon the established prestige of the existing local groups. In addition to this ad-

---

[28] Quoted in Harwood Childs, *Labor and Capital in National Politics* (Columbus: The Ohio State University Press, 1930), p. 10.

vantage, Harwood Childs, whose *Labor and Capital in National Politics* is the authoritative account of the history of the Chamber, calls attention to fortuitous circumstances surrounding its beginnings: "The Chamber idea seems to have taken place at an opportune moment, and the wide publicity given to the undertaking, the quasi-governmental endorsement of the move, the general feeling of insecurity among a large number of business interests during the political upheaval in 1912-1913 . . . served to facilitate somewhat the early problems of recruiting." [29]

BUSINESS GOALS: CONTINUITY AND CHANGE

From its beginning, the Chamber has maintained a stable pattern of goals and, with the exception of the years from 1921 to 1924, has gradually increased its membership. On the other hand, the membership of the National Association of Manufacturers showed an alarming decrease during the 1920's. After increasing from 3,600 in 1913 to 5,700 in 1922, NAM membership declined to a low of 1,469 by 1933. It is instructive that the period in which these organizations assume the role of legitimate spokesman for business can be correlated with a decline in influence as measured by responses of members and potential members. Although the Chamber does not experience membership fluctuations with the decline of a threat, the "normalcy" of the 1920's was nearly disastrous for the NAM. The temporary predominance of business values, typified by the laissez-faire disposition of the Republican administrations of the era, reduced the appeal of a belligerent, ever-vigilant type of association. Having achieved some hindrance of organized labor, and with the prevailing political atmosphere more in harmony with their goals, the frantic effort to impede what had appeared an impending social upheaval became unnecessary, and the NAM seemed to relax their efforts during the years of prosperity.

Both organizations expressed broadly stated and widely shared goals, such as the promulgation of the "survival of the fittest" doctrine and other expressions of "hard-headed" conservatism. Viewing any attack on this premise as a threat to the business system and to the community at large, the spokesmen for business held fast to the ideas in the face of the depression. To relieve un-

---

[29] *Ibid.,* p. 24.

employment, for example, would be to reward sin, since poverty as well as wealth is the result of individual capabilities. The major point which Prothro seeks to make is that these business organizations did revise their goals to accommodate shifting circumstances in the economy. He states that "the very inflexibility with which the old assumptions were applied revealed the extreme degree to which conservative thought in America had degenerated. . . . The dedication of business to the cause of property against persons was no more exclusive or complete in 1930 than it had been in 1920, but the circumstances were such as to reveal this dedication in a more naked and unappealing light." [30] Prothro thus suggests that the position of businessmen as leaders, so clearly established during the preceding decade, was damaged by their refusal to adopt a more flexible and hence useful position. With the coming of the New Deal there was a manifestation of the shift of business goals from a position of dominance to one of a militant opposition. This vigorous opposition is brought home by Cleveland's research which indicates that, of thirty-eight major laws enacted between 1933 and 1941, the NAM opposed thirty-one.[31]

Business had received a jolt from the rise of interests that formerly had been more quiescent. Its reaction, that of holding firm to rigorous dogma, may have reduced its claim to a more general leadership but it most certainly contributed to a revitalization of business organizations. NAM checked its decline in membership quickly and by 1937 had recouped a substantial portion of its losses. Its new role of "whipping boy" was clearly advantageous: ". . . by its uncompromising, bitter-end battle against Franklin D. Roosevelt's New Deal, the NAM rescued itself from the grave, reunited its membership, reinforced its treasury, and established itself as the St. George of certain benighted U.S. businessmen." [32] This long-range correlation between internal strength and external threat can become a matter of a slackening off after a specific legislative victory. Thus, NAM membership again suffered a sharp decline after the passage of the Taft-Hartley Act in 1948.

---

[30] Prothro, "Business Ideas and the American Tradition," *Journal of Politics*, XV (Feb. 1953), 82.

[31] Alfred S. Cleveland, "NAM: Spokesman for Industry?" *Harvard Business Review*, XXVI (May 1948), 357.

[32] "Renovation in NAM?" *Fortune*, XXXVIII (July 19, 1948), 74.

The Response to Regulation

This survey of the goals and attitudes of the two inclusive organizations leads to the conclusion that the business interest they represent is stated in broadly phrased terms and is stable. Most businessmen can presumably agree in opposition to "welfare socialism" and deficit financing. They can support a reduction in the bargaining position of organized labor and a minimization of the tax burden, all of which amounts to a declaration in favor of free enterprise. Yet there is an undercurrent of conflict which quite often makes these goals meaningful only symbolically. This is particularly true with respect to the ever-present problem of government regulation. Thus, irrespective of frequent protests that a continued expansion of regulation will lead to the demise of private enterprise, businessmen frequently support certain types of government supervision. Marver Bernstein refers to the willingness of businessmen to accept regulation as the "basic contradiction." Bernstein explains that, although businessmen deplore interference in their affairs as contributory to an upsetting of the natural order, they welcome aid that will promote the health of business even if it involves regulation: "While the businessman describes the operation of the economy in terms of absolute laissez-faire concepts, he himself does not rely exclusively on these natural forces to preserve his position in society. Instead he seeks to utilize the coercive authority of government to enhance his interests." [33]

FROM HOSTILITY TO COOPERATION

We have seen an illustration of Bernstein's thesis in the development of trade associations, and it is given further validity in the operation of the regulatory agencies of today. Although some types of regulatory policies were instituted to satisfy the demands of dissatisfied interests within an industry, other demands for regulation of business originated with pressure from extraindustry interests that sought a more equitable position in the total economy. In such

---

[33] Marver H. Bernstein, "Political Ideas of Selected American Business Journals," *Public Opinion Quarterly*, XVIII (Summer, 1953), 258-267.

cases, the industry to be regulated vigorously opposes any restriction upon its freedom.

The initial demands for the regulation of rail transportation as voiced by farmers and small merchants illustrates this point. Although the rapid expansion of railroads after the Civil War was initially a blessing, the depressions of following years produced a change in attitude. Farmers and merchants, who relied almost exclusively on railroads for the shipping of goods, complained that rates were too high and that railroads conspired to eliminate competition. This agitation for change was manifested in the Grange, the National Anti-Monopoly League, and numerous other protest groups, and was given legislative sanction by the passage of "Granger legislation" by several midwestern states. Railroads fought against this activity, but were unable to stem a tide that culminated in the passage of the Interstate Commerce Act in 1886. The movement toward regulation was begun and pursued by shippers, while the railroads, the party to be regulated, were hostile: "the burden of sponsoring regulation was . . . shouldered by shippers; the objects of the original act to regulate commerce were shippers objectives." [34]

If the history of regulation were to remain unchanged, there is every reason to expect that a relation of hostility between the agency and the regulated party would typify most aspects of the regulatory problem. However, it frequently happens that, after an initial period of hostility, the regulated businesses adopt a more cooperative attitude. Lane presents the thesis that we can trace the attitude of business toward regulation as hostility that is gradually replaced by acceptance and eventually overt preference.[35] What are the reasons for this modification of attitude? Substantial evidence can be marshalled to indicate that the promises of regulatory statutes to distribute benefits to relatively broad and diverse interests do not materialize. Edelman's survey of the literature on the administration of regulatory statutes indicates that "there is virtually unanimous agreement among students of the anti-trust laws, the Clayton and Federal

---

[34] Fainsod, Gordon, and Palamountain, *op. cit.*, p. 258. *See also* Lee Benson, *Merchants, Farmers, and Railroads* (Cambridge: Harvard University Press, 1955).

[35] Robert E. Lane, "Law and Opinion in the Business Community," *Public Opinion Quarterly*, XVII (Summer, 1953), 239-257.

Trade Commission Acts, the Interstate Commerce Acts, the public utility statutes and the right to work laws, for example, that through much of the history of their administration these statutes have been ineffective in the sense that many of the values they have promised have not in fact been realized." [36] Few policies have been pursued unless they have been approved by the well organized groups who are being regulated.

THE "LIFE CYCLE" OF REGULATORY AGENCIES

Marver Bernstein's "life cycle" theory of regulation is in line with Edelman's conclusion. Bernstein suggests that, at the time of its creation, the intentions of a regulatory agency conflict with the goals of the regulated groups. The agency operates in an environment of organized, hostile interests which, having lost the legislative struggle, try to protect themselves from what they regard as the "onslaught" of administrators. In this atmosphere of animosity, the regulating agency frequently adopts an aggressive or crusading resolve to meet its opposition and not surrender its ambitions.[37] However, although the regulated groups have lost the first round, as borne out by the passage of the enabling legislation, they can be influential both in the operation of the agency and in the securing of "sound" men as appointees. Even at the outset, fear was expressed that the Interstate Commerce Commission, irrespective of the intentions of the legislation, would become dominated by railroad interests. Representative John Reagan of Texas, long a partisan in the movement toward regulation, feared that "the railroad interests will combine their power to control the appointment of commissioners in their own interests." [38]

It is doubtful if so simple an explanation as suggested by Reagan could explain the administrative history of the I.C.C. Bernstein suggests that the momentum of pressure which builds up during the "gestation" period reaches a climax with the passage of the regulatory statute and begins a decline from this point. Support reaches a peak; the combatant interests are tired and have earned a rest. It

[36] Murray Edelman, "Symbols and Political Quiescence," *American Political Science Review,* LIV (Sept. 1960), 696.

[37] Marver Bernstein, *Regulating Business by Independent Commission* (Princeton: Princeton University Press, 1955), pp. 74-102.

[38] As early as 1878 Reagan had introduced legislation prohibiting discriminatory rates, rebates, and pools for the distribution of freight earnings.

is natural that these interests would tend to regard administration as following automatically from legislation. In the case of the Interstate Commerce Commission, the support of shippers simply ceased to exist; the I.C.C. gradually committed itself to the welfare of the railroad industry and became identified as a "railroad agency."[39] In its developing stages the I.C.C. developed policies that were gradually modified as, for example, in the Transportation Act of 1920. The purpose of this act was to strengthen the economic position of railroads through consolidation and merger. The guidance by the I.C.C. of the integration into a smaller number of systems was far removed from its beginning premise of prevention of unfair rates. It was not the shippers, but rather the railroads themselves that were protected.

Under such circumstances it is not surprising that defense of regulation comes from the business community which was initially hostile. Under a system which permits business in its more organized aspects to pursue its interests under protection of legal sanction, it would be economically unsound to do anything but defend a regulatory agency against demands that its functions be abolished or transferred. The writer's study of the Florida Milk Commission shows that the most formidable defenders of regulation were the larger dairies while the demands for "free enterprise" came from loosely organized and ephemeral citizens committees whose members were aggrieved that the retail price of milk in Florida had at times been the highest in the nation.[40]

The Role of the Corporation in Politics

Having surveyed the activities of organizations of businessmen, we turn finally to a consideration of an aspect of contemporary politics that is attracting increasing attention on the part of both social scientists and interested laymen: the role of the giant corporation in the political process. An emerging trend is noticeable in the tendency of these corporations to "strike out on their own" without the use of the good offices of trade or business associations.

[39] Samuel Huntington, "The Marasmus of the ICC?" *Yale Law Journal*, 61 (Apr. 1952), 467-509.
[40] Harmon Zeigler, *The Florida Milk Commission Changes Minimum Prices* (New York: The Inter-University Case Program, 1963).

Although it is possible that this independence indicates a dissatisfaction with the representation of very large businesses in the activities of associations, it is more probable that corporations have limited interests and funds ample enough to make it undesirable for them to be fettered by the necessity of participation in intraorganizational disputes.

We have heard and read much about the "businessmen in politics" programs of large corporations such as General Electric and Gulf Oil.[41] These programs involve a wide range of activities usually focused upon the electoral process. Here we concern ourselves with some theoretical and practical implications of the role of the corporation as an actor in the political process. Hacker has raised an important question for students of democracy: Whom does the corporation represent? In our treatment of trade associations we have seen them as responsive to the needs of identifiable groups of people. Hence they are representative devices. Even if the decision-making in such organizations is delegated to a minority that tends to be self-sustaining, some measure of "legitimacy" is ascribed to them as the "voice of the sentiments of the individual citizens who comprise their memberships." Hacker therefore ascribes legitimacy to the organized pressure group because it can be shown to act on the "behalf of discrete individuals." [42]

RESPONSIBILITY AND RESTRAINT

The corporation—sometimes described as a self-governing, self-perpetuating bureaucracy—can actually substantiate no such claim. While it is true that, as a consequence of its operations, employment for large numbers of individuals is provided, it is equally true that the corporation would "welcome the chance to operate with no employees at all." [43] No argument that the corporation speaks for its employees can be taken seriously. The responsibility of the corporation to its stockholders is of a more debatable nature. Are not stockholders in a similar relation to corporation management

---

[41] See "Business and the Political Process," *The Conference Board Business Record*, XVI (Sept. 1959), 424-431, and "Business Gets Political Urge," *Business Week*, Oct. 11, 1958, pp. 125-129 for comments on this trend.

[42] Andrew Hacker, "The Corporation and Campaign Politics: Power and Legitimacy" (Paper presented to the American Political Science Association Meeting, Sept. 7, 1961), p. 23.

[43] *Ibid.*

as association members are to their officers? A portion of American folklore, and a comparable portion of institutional advertising, suggest that the final arbiters of corporation policy disputes are the millions of individuals who own stock certificates. Accepting this argument at face value leads one to wonder to what extent such widely diversified stock could possibly provide control of corporation management. A large corporation may have a million "owners," a situation that would naturally cause actual power to locate with the company executives. However, Berle points to a new development in stock ownership which reduces the authority of the stockholder even further. Nearly half of all outstanding stock in American industry is held, not by individuals, but by fiduciary organizations, institutions, foundations, pension funds, and mutual trusts.[44] With the individual holder, support of present management becomes a matter of habit or inertia. Berle notes that "not once in a decade is control of a minor giant . . . threatened. Managements of the major giants are, for all practical purposes, impregnable." [45] However, Hacker believes that, in the case of the institutional holdings, support of management is a "considered policy." This means that, even if a "revolt" among individual holders developed, the balance of power would be with management and that "the acquiescence of individual stockholders coupled with the interest of institutional stockholders gives management a free hand." [46]

This rather dramatic picture of corporations as a modern type of feudal monarchy need not be carried to extreme proportions. Certainly corporation management is acutely conscious of "public opinion" as evidenced by the vast amounts of capital invested in institutional advertising to create a favorable climate of opinion. Also, the threat of political intervention through the mechanism of the state should not be discounted, although the crucial position of the giants in the economy may serve to reduce this intervention to mere harassment. Assuming, with Hacker, that the corporation is not legitimate because it does not speak for any identifiable segment of the population, we should not allow ourselves to impute "evil" to its political efforts. Berle, with considerable persuasion,

---

[44] Adolph A. Berle, *Power Without Property* (New York: Harcourt, Brace & World, Inc., 1959), pp. 59-76.

[45] *Ibid.*, p. 63.

[46] Hacker, *op. cit.*, p. 24.

argues that the *function* of the corporation is not merely to make money but to produce and distribute goods and services. The use of political power in the pursuit of this function is therefore justified. So dependent is the nation upon the proper performance by corporations of their function that community reliance attaches a semipublic image to the legally private enterprise: "the corporation having won its place in the economic system must fill it." [47]

THE POLITICS OF NATIONAL DEFENSE

The function of a great many minor and major giants is that of supplying the nation with an adequate defense against external aggression. Since the federal government is responsible for the coordination of the defense effort, the dependence of the nation on the corporations is matched by the dependence of the corporations upon the government. Government contracts make up 70 to 90 per cent of the sales in many corporations whose major products are aircraft. For example, about 85 per cent of Lockheed's sales may be expected to be to the federal government. Even in so diversified a company as General Electric, about 25 per cent of sales are the result of government contracts.

Competition for contracts is keen, and these corporations have gradually shifted from using law firms to represent their interest to the employment of skilled lobbyists. Unlike the usual trade association representative, the activities of these corporation representatives have little to do with legislation. Most of their efforts are instead directed toward locating available contracts and securing these contracts for their companies. While the corporation representative keeps an "ear to the ground" on possible harmful legislation, most actual participation is arranged by the National Association of Manufacturers, the Chamber of Commerce, or a trade association. There are exceptions, of course, and if the corporation chose to concentrate upon legislation it might be considered to have a

---

[47] Berle, *op. cit.*, p. 102. Berle's use of the concept of function seems to be drawn from the function-dysfunction theories of Robert Merton. Any structure is said to have a function if it contributes to the fulfillment of the social needs of a system; a dysfunction if it hinders the fulfillment of these needs. Function is to be distinguished from purpose, which is a conscious formulation, since it is an objective consequence of action. *See* Merton, *Social Theory and Social Structure* (New York: The Free Press of Glencoe, Inc., 1957), pp. 19-84.

high power potential. Some of the representatives express the opinion that, because a particular corporation may contribute substantially to the well-being of a congressional district, the company representative will have ready access to a congressman. Further, because many corporations who hold prime government contracts engage in subcontracting involving many thousands of smaller companies, the economic effects of the corporation can extend to every congressional district in the country. On the debit side, it is likely that the company which is owned and managed locally will command more attention from the congressman of a district.[48] The corporations engage in strenuous competition to sell to the government, leaving legislation for the most part to the associations. This competition is quite restricted. As one representative of a large corporation phrased it: "I think the league is too big for small companies. There is very little place for them except under special situations. . . . It is not going to be a league they can play in." [49] This impression is given validity by a consideration of the extent to which a few companies are given most of the responsibility for providing for the national defense. During World War II, $175 billion in prime contracts was awarded; two thirds of this ($117 billion) went to the one hundred largest corporations. These figures remained substantially unchanged during the Korean War, while today these same select few hold approximately 75 per cent of all contracts.[50] The league is indeed too big for any save the largest and strongest.

The peculiar way in which most contracts are awarded, by negotiation rather than open bidding, further increases the exclu-

---

[48] This is the suggestion of Hacker. On the other hand, when a contract for the construction of a particular weapon or aircraft is cancelled the effect may extend to the economic life of the community in which the corporation is located. The cancellation of Chance-Vaught's Crusader III jet fighter resulted in the layoff of 2,500 workers and the cancellation of North American's Navaho missile cost 5,000 jobs. Also, subcontracts extending into many congressional districts beyond that of the prime contractor are lost. Hence it is not surprising to find congressmen from the affected areas trying to prevent cancellations. The representatives from Los Angeles exerted efforts on behalf of North American, and the Washington state delegation is eager to defend the Boeing B-52 program.

[49] Paul W. Cherington and Ralph L. Gillen, "The Company Representative in Washington," *Harvard Business Review*, 39 (May-June 1961), 113.

[50] Walter Adams and Horace M. Gray, *Monopoly in America* (New York: The Macmillan Company, 1955), p. 102.

siveness of the "league." A high premium is placed upon political sophistication and technical know-how. Only the largest companies can afford to keep a full-time representative on constant alert for new contracts. A new actor in this closed political arena is the former military officer or government official, who, because of expertise and personal contacts, is in an advantageous position in the securing of contracts. A recent check indicated that nearly 1,500 retired officers were on the staffs of companies holding 80 per cent of outstanding contracts.

The increasing activity of these corporations has led to the recognition of an interest which has been designated—with derogatory connotations—as the "munitions lobby." The extreme fringe of the counterinterest accuse this interest of working toward the prevention of disarmament. It is obviously an oversimplification of a complex problem to attribute to large contractors causal force in the deterioration of Russian-American relations. While it is tempting to consider these prime contractors as a cohesive group whose interests will be in opposition to those of, for example, the Committee for a Sane Nuclear Policy, a more realistic appraisal indicates that a great part of the political activity surrounds rivalry between the military branches and their industrial allies. Thus, in its dispute with the Army, the Air Force is supported by the Aircraft Industries Association, the Air Force Association, the Arnold Society, and the Air Division of the American Legion National Security Commission. These associations provide liaison between the industry and the Air Force in a relation of symbiosis. In addition, the various labor unions whose members are employed in defense industries can be relied upon to support the industry-military coalition. The International Association of Machinists, which represents two-thirds of the organized workers in aircraft industries, thus describes itself as "synonomous with the aircraft industry." [51]

Understanding the importance of the function of the corporation, in conjunction with the realization of the degree to which the economic well-being of the corporation is dependent upon the largess of the government, impels us to conclude on the question of accountability and restraint of private units of power. While we have seen that organization breeds counterorganization, we

[51] Quoted in Al Toffler, "Salesmen in Uniform," *The Nation*, Nov. 30, 1957, p. 404.

have also noted that the only balancing of power with respect to contracts is the restricted competition of the few. While labor might well act as a restraint of corporation power in matters of labor relations, the two have an identical interest in defense spending; hence the ranks are closed. There are organizations—the Electronics Small Business Council and the Strategic Industries Association— that seek to wrest contracts from the giants, but their efforts are not likely to be successful. The dilemma then becomes one of determining the degree to which a government should become dependent upon a monopoly and perhaps enable that monopoly to prescribe the terms upon which the job that needs to be done will be done.

Organized Labor:

V Protest

and Defeat

"No political democracy has offered a more hostile environment to unionism than has the United States. And this hostility has imparted to American unionism a character and temper unlike those of any other labor movement." [1] Unlike the organization movement among businessmen, labor activity, as the above quotation indicates, has faced the impediment of transmitting an image which deviates from social norms. Although there is increasing evidence of a growing social acceptance of unions, it is nevertheless true that, even though the New Deal afforded increasing attention to a wide variety of presumably disadvantaged groups, organized labor has had a difficult time developing itself into a unit of power set against the influence of business.

---

[1] Jack Barbash, *Labor Unions in Action* (New York: Harper & Row, Publishers, 1948), p. 1. *See also* Robin Williams, *American Society* (New York: Alfred A. Knopf, Inc., 1960), p. 203.

Labor as a Protest Movement

Industrialism, the root "cause" of labor organizations, provided a made-to-order set of leaders for our society. Businessmen, so demonstrably successful in putting into practice the creed of individualism, afforded models of what could be attained through individual initiative. In short, business, during the formative period of unionism, could represent itself as a defender of the *status quo* of our "business civilization," while labor was of necessity a protest movement. Playing the role of emergent power challenging dominant power institutions has of necessity contributed to the particular form, that of militancy, which labor has assumed through most of its history. Perlman's theory of the labor movement stresses the very high "resistance power" of American capitalism in the face of a threat to the long-held values of the society.[2] The prestige of the resisting group is enhanced because the greater part of the society accepts capitalist ideals such as the principles of private property, private initiative, and the notion that businessmen are equipped with the unique knowledge of how to operate the economy. While it may be argued that the dominant ideology of labor has, with notable exceptions, been one of acceptance of the capitalist system rather than its destruction, there can be no question that the object of union activity is to reduce in some measure the control of the employer over his property. Consequently, it is no less than ironic that a labor movement which has exerted considerable energy in divorcing itself from revolutionary leanings has nevertheless been met with calculated attempts at repression of a rather violent nature.

THE TRADITION OF VIOLENCE

In Europe, where much of labor organization has been of a more radical nature, we find few examples of strikebreakers and labor spies comparable to those employed by American industry. Violent struggles such as the armed battle at Homestead in 1892 be-

---

[2] Selig Perlman, *A Theory of the Labor Movement* (New York: The Macmillan Company, 1928), Chap. 5.

tween the strikers and hundreds of Pinkerton detectives hired by Carnegie Steel, the anthracite strike of 1902, the Ludlow "massacre" of 1913, where the state government of Colorado served entirely as an instrument of Colorado Fuel and Iron Corporation in breaking the strike, and the 1919 steel strike, while startling, are not obscure exceptions to the rule of violence. These examples illustrate that, with respect to violence, the formative years of unionism came only to a partial end with the Roosevelt administration; customary, indeed accepted, techniques in labor-management struggles were intimidation, assault, and murder.

Although the struggles involved high economic stakes, money was hardly the only issue. Laborers were struggling for status against dominant interests. Businessmen were fighting against a subversion of the traditional social system, against "anarchism" and "socialism." These great captains of industry were self-made men of the highest degree of conformity to the American dream. In accord with the reigning values of self interest, they did not hesitate to employ ruthlessly all weapons at their disposal for the challenger's destruction. Since the struggles involved an adjustment of property rights, employees felt themselves entitled to police protection of rights sanctioned by law. Labor therefore had to fight not only property owners but police and government officials. This situation is well illustrated by the famous reply of a coal mine operator to a minister who pleaded for some concession to striking miners during the anthracite strike of 1902: "The rights and interests of the laboring man will be protected and cared for, not by labor agitators, but by the Christian men to whom God in His infinite wisdom has given control of the property interests of the country." [3]

INSTITUTIONALIZATION AND ORDERED CONFLICT

Continued interaction leads to stabilization, and union-management relations have exhibited a more mature attitude on the part, of both participants in recent years. For years the right of workers to bargain collectively was resisted by violence, which, though perpetrated by employers, was perhaps sanctioned by a wider segment of the public. One of the directors of the Colorado Fuel and

[3] Barbash, *op. cit.*, p. 4.

Iron Corporation at the time of the Ludlow strike, stated that the killing of people was preferable to recognizing the right of unions to represent workers for bargaining purposes, and equated his opposition to collective bargaining with the principles of the War of the Revolution. The passage of the National Labor Relations Act of 1935, which gave legal guarantee of employees' right to bargain collectively, although strenuously opposed by employers, eventually served to remove from debate one of the most emotional aspects of the problem.

THE QUESTIONABLE STATUS OF UNION LEADERSHIP

A wider acceptance of unionism has altered labor-management relations from conflict to orderly interaction. Surveying the historical development of unions in the fashion of an overview, stages of management hostility, neutrality, and cooperation may be discerned. A paucity of evidence makes it fruitless to attempt to identify these stages except in broadest terms. However, a public opinion poll in 1957 showed that 76 per cent of the population expressed approval of unions. Lowest approval (60 per cent) came from farmers; highest, from skilled workers (84 per cent); but approval by professional and business occupation groups was 73 per cent. Nevertheless, these statistics hardly indicate that labor or labor leaders are as prestigious as business leaders.[4] Labor began as a protest movement. Of necessity its leaders were predominately deviants—those whose aspirations were regarded with suspicion. America experienced the sudden rise to considerable power of men whose background was foreign to the customary career pattern of success, that of the business and professional people. As a result of their deviance, labor leaders past and present can attain wealth and varying degrees of influence but not necessarily the social acceptance that usually accompanies such attributes: "The labor leader's social status is equivalent to that of a street car conductor."[5] The businessman can work his way up from the bottom and find not only

---

[4] Melvin J. Vincent and Jackson Mayers, *New Foundations for Industrial Sociology* (Princeton: D. Van Nostrand Co., Inc., 1959), p. 272.

[5] A. A. Imberman, "Labor Leaders and Society," *Harvard Business Review,* XXVII (Jan. 1950), 53. *See also* Melvin Nadell, "Labor Leaders and Industrial Values," *Sociology and Social Research,* XXXIII (Nov.-Dec. 1948), 106-112.

financial but social rewards awaiting him. The labor union leader can follow a similar path and find only ostracism. Actually, the Horatio Alger success story is less true for business executives than for labor leaders. Mills believes that only 10 per cent of the business executives rose through the ranks, while 60 per cent of the labor leaders did so.[6] It is therefore the case that the American trade unions, unlike the European labor movement which drew leadership from the middle and even upper strata of society, have been led almost wholly by men with working class backgrounds. The well-born would not be attracted to a movement that offers so little in the way of social advancement.

As organizations go through a maturing process, the type of leadership needs will change. Unions, in their early stages, were attempting to achieve a significant altering in the balance of privilege. They were aggressive and stimulated vigorous external opposition. They were fighting not only for goals considered by substantial portions of the population as radical, but also for their very existence. The type of leadership this situation demanded was the agitator, the man of action. Later, as unions gradually won some degree of acceptance, transformation in goals and leadership occurred. The crusader against the enemy was replaced by the skillful manager. Nevertheless, while the character of union leadership has shifted, the social background of the leaders has remained substantially the same. This has implications for the success of unions in the achieving of their political goals. The essence of what we have learned so far is that union leaders have not gained community status and ordinarily feel unsuccessful in fitting themselves into a middle class milieu. Truman's theory of overlapping group affiliations includes the affiliations of public officials: "Since an elected representative cannot give up his already existing attitudes and relationships, the legislature and various political interest groups inevitably overlap in membership." [7] In support of his thesis, Truman cites the generally accepted conclusion that the organized bar is given an advantage due to the unusually high proportion of lawyers who are legislators.

---

[6] C. Wright Mills, *The New Men of Power* (New York: Harcourt, Brace & World, Inc., 1948), p. 107.

[7] David Truman, *The Governmental Process* (New York: Alfred A. Knopf, Inc., 1961), p. 336.

CONTRASTING SOCIAL BACKGROUNDS
OF LABOR LEADERS AND PUBLIC OFFICIALS

The disadvantage would seem to lie with labor if we consider the occupational origins of, for example, United States Senators. Matthews' study of the backgrounds of senators for the years 1947-1957 shows that the senators were, with very few exceptions, sons of people with middle or upper class occupations: "The children of low-salaried workers, wage earners, servants, and farm laborers . . . contributed only 7 per cent of the postwar senators." [8] Very few senators, whether Republican or Democrat, were born in working-class families. The senators themselves reflect this class origin. Although 6 per cent began their work careers as industrial wage earners, none was engaged in this occupation for a long enough length of time to have it designated as his principal livelihood. By extending his investigation to other branches of government, Matthews draws a similar conclusion: ". . . American political decision-makers . . . are, with very few exceptions, sons of professional men, proprietors and officials, and farmers. A very small minority were the sons of wage earners, low-salaried workers, farm laborers or servants." [9]

These data reflect the less prestigious rank of labor than what are generally understood to be the middle class occupations in our society. Society places different evaluations on occupations, and it is expected that to the more "worthy" individuals who fill these occupational roles will accrue the rewards of public office.

Although on the basis of overlapping group affiliations based upon occupation labor is at a disadvantage, there is another aspect which needs to be explored. There is the possibility of an *intellectual* overlapping which may serve to ameliorate labor's lack of access to key points of decision-making. When we compare Matthews' findings with those of C. Wright Mills, it is hard to understand why labor has been able to achieve any success at all. Mills reveals that 59 per cent of the AFL's leaders and 61 per cent of the CIO's leaders came from families of the wage-earning class: "The big

---

[8] Donald R. Matthews, *United States Senators and Their World* (Chapel Hill: The University of North Carolina Press, 1960), p. 19.

[9] Donald R. Matthews, *The Social Background of Political Decision-Makers* (Garden City, N.Y.: Doubleday and Company, Inc., 1954), pp. 23-24.

fact about the occupational origins of labor leaders is that they are predominantly from labor's own ranks. Six out of ten, in both the AFL and the CIO, derive from fathers who were wage workers, most from the foreman or skilled labor ranks." [10] The leaders reflect their origins as shown by the fact that "the great bulk—seven or eight out of ten—were wage workers before they became union officials." [11] The great disparity between the class affiliations of labor and those of public officials is surely a disadvantage to labor in its political competition with other groups.

The widely stated belief that, on the whole, Democrats are more sensitive to labor interests than Republicans cannot be explained as a consequence of the occupational affiliations of Democratic politicians. It is true that labor generally finds more satisfactory access to the Democratic party, but this is due to the "symbolic and reference-group identification of the two parties, and in their underlying values." [12] McClosky and associates found that, in the 1956 conventions, only 14 per cent of the Democrats belonged to trade unions. Although only 4 per cent of the Republicans were trade unionists, this disparity is hardly sufficient to explain the substantial difference in attitudes toward labor. McClosky notes that many more Democratic than Republican leaders are apt to take advice from trade unions rather than from business associations.[13] The conspicuous example of a Democratic Senator of working-class background who actively championed the cause of labor is Robert Wagner of New York, whose father was a janitor. Wagner is believed to have had a great affect on the shape of the legislation that bore his name, the Wagner Labor Relations Act, and was prominent in the sponsoring of other legislation beneficial to labor. However, this relatively singular exception merely goes to prove the rule.

If the group affiliations of public officials do not automatically dispose them against labor, can we not draw the conclusion that these affiliations do not necessarily work to the advantage of business? The preceding chapter described the many different kinds of businessmen and the conflict of values within the business community.

[10] Mills, *op. cit.*, p. 88.

[11] *Ibid.*, p. 91.

[12] Herbert McClosky *et al.*, "Issue Conflict and Consensus Among Party Leaders and Followers," *American Political Science Review,* LIV (June 1960), 416.

[13] *Ibid.*, p. 417.

Despite the dominance of business and professional occupational origins of legislators, Hacker shows that, in the case of the Senate, the "image of the business world is cast largely in provincial terms."[14] Although most of the legislators are not antagonistic to the business community and are sympathetic to the needs of business, the majority have had little experience in national corporations. They may have had some familiarity with small businesses or branches of corporations within their constituencies, but "have little appreciation of the national outlook of the large firms."[15] Hacker believes that, while the legislators are apparently anxious to oblige the corporations, a break in communication has resulted in the dissatisfaction of the "economic elite" with the performance of senators. Large corporations do not feel that their interests are comprehended by lawmakers. Evidence of this is seen in the repeated assertion that Congress is dominated by labor unions, in spite of the fact that the trend since passage of the Taft-Hartley Act has been to place further restrictions on unions. The "businessmen in politics" movement, referred to in the previous chapter, is a further symptom of this dissatisfaction.

THE IMAGE OF LABOR IN THE MASS MEDIA

A final evaluation of the place of labor within the American environment can be ascertained by surveying the treatment of union activities by mass media. Generally, coverage is unfavorable. The peaceful aspects of unions are de-emphasized while the strikes and violence are reported in great detail. The degree of hostility to labor in newspapers varies considerably from, for example, the extremely antagonistic *Chicago Tribune* to the more moderate *New York Times*. Nevertheless, few newspapers report labor news with as much detail as they do business news. There are no sections devoted exclusively to labor affairs as there are to business news. This increases the chances that only the more spectacular aspects of union activities will be considered newsworthy. The AFL-CIO is, of course, unsatisfied with this treatment. This recent statement is typical of labor's frustration: "Under the . . . labor news story formula, unions are—of course—evil. Either they strike (against

---

[14] Andrew Hacker, "The Elected and the Anointed," *American Political Science Review,* LV (Sept. 1961), 547.
[15] *Ibid.,* 458.

the public interest) or they settle (for exorbitant increases against the public interest). There is no such thing as stubborn management forcing a strike, nor is there, by definition, a contract settlement equitable to all parties including the public." [16]

What is true for newspapers was also true for radio networks, according to a 1944 study. This study reported that the division of opinion about labor and management ran five to one against labor.[17] We should also take notice of the role of mass media as promulgators of popular culture. Reflecting perhaps the dominant values of our society, television soap operas and dramatic shows, comic strips, and movies almost never use labor leaders or unions as material. The heroes of mass culture are usually professional or business people of solid, middle class respectability.

A Short History of the Labor Movement

The unusual amount of violence and less overt hostility accompanying the American labor movement helped shape the history of union organization. In addition, factors emanating from the social value system, the structure of the economy, and the characteristics of the laboring population contributed to the development of distinctive features. Robin Williams notes that the absence of traditional social ties encouraged the commercialization of labor. In an economy of promising resources but relatively meager population, labor became a "market commodity in an individualistic economy." [18] As was the case with business organizations, we can point to scattered local unions before the growth of large-scale economy after the Civil War. However, it was not until American industry developed its mass production techniques that the wage earner, economically and physically separated from his employer, became a "commodity" in the capitalistic market economy. As is the case with any market, the job market fluctuated and workers had to face the insecurity of losing their jobs.

---

[16] "Our Objective Press," *I.U.D. Digest*, VI (Winter, 1961), 20.
[17] Lila W. Sussman, "Labor in the Radio News, an Analysis of Content," *Journalism Quarterly*, XXII (Sept. 1945), 207-214.
[18] Williams, *American Society*, 201.

INDUSTRIALIZATION AND "FIRST GENERATION"
FACTORY WORKERS

Industrialization during and after the Civil War not only contributed to the insecurity of tenure of workers, but also contributed to the development of a large labor force as a permanent part of the economy. This rapid transformation of the economy produced a group of "first generation" factory workers. Most of the new workers did not come from working class families since these were relatively few, but rather were the sons of farmers. Factory discipline was often demanding, and this constituted a severe break with former styles of life. Not only were hours long and wages low, but restraint of personal freedom was severe; working conditions were frequently unsanitary or unsafe, and work rules humiliating.[19] Thus, while economic insecurity contributed to the rise of unionism, the status insecurities associated with a rapid and total break with prior life-style made economic determinism a shallow explanatory system. Although the law assumed equality in bargaining, the lone worker was not able to bargain with his employer on an equal basis. A device which would make it possible for the worker to "fight back" would allow him to improve his feeling of worth, to achieve "the erect posture of something like a human being." [20] Vincent and Mayers believe that "this is the worker's main status-achieving device; without it, he is helpless before automatic machinery and forces he cannot control." [21]

THE NATIONAL LABOR UNION AND THE KNIGHTS
OF LABOR

The drive toward unionism has been hampered since its inception by a heterogeneous labor population. Not only did the workers have no factory experience, but they were recruited from both European and American communities. Hence ethnic cleavages impeded the formation of a group of people with a sufficiency of shared attitudes leading to the creation of a cohesive organization. As Robin Williams says:

---

[19] *See* John R. Commons, *History of Labor in the United States,* 2 Vols. (New York: The Macmillan Company, 1918).

[20] Clyde E. Dankert, *Introduction to Labor* (Englewood Cliffs, N.J.: Prentice-Hall, Inc., 1954), pp. 146-147.

[21] Vincent and Mayers, *op. cit.,* p. 265.

. . . the labor force was constituted mainly of heterogeneous, un-organized, relatively unskilled workers without factory experience, who hoped soon to escape from wage work. They were spread over a vast territory, often disunited in creed and language, subject to incessant shifts in the labor market and rapid technological innovations.[22]

These factors, when combined with the apparent conformity by workers to the ideals of individual responsibility and the departure from the ranks of labor through personal effort, reduced the chances of a "class consciousness."

The social background of the laboring population was reflected in the failures of several serious post-Civil War efforts to form a national labor organization. In 1866, the National Labor Union, a loose confederation of local unions, a few national trade unions, and reform organizations not strictly concerned with labor problems, was organized. The National Labor Union was never able to develop a clear idea of what it sought, and consequently concerned itself with a variety of "causes" such as land reform and cooperatives. Unable to develop a trade union program, it nevertheless undertook direct political action by organizing the National Labor Reform Party and making a nomination for the presidency in 1872. Most of its union members had little interest in the reformist goals of the organization and, after a series of disputes, withdrew.

The same sort of vagueness of purpose characterized the Knights of Labor. Originally a secret organization, the Knights experienced a rapid increase in membership during the decade of the 1880's. Originally made up of local labor organizations, during its period of growth it expanded into the West and diluted its membership with farmers, small businessmen, and others who had little interest in the immediate problems of the wage earner. Under its rallying slogan of "an injury to one is the concern of all," the Knights attracted 700,000 members by 1886—the equivalent of approximately 10 per cent of the labor force.[23] The Knights experienced some success in negotiating agreements with corporations but were generally disinclined to use the strike for the achievement of short-term gains. Rather than concentrating on the immediate welfare of the job-conscious worker, the leaders sought a more general and far-reach-

[22] Williams, *op. cit.*, pp. 201-202.
[23] Lee Wolman, *The Growth of American Trade Unions, 1880-1923* (New York: National Bureau of Economic Research, Inc., 1924), pp. 29-32.

ing goal: the substitution of a cooperative society for the wage system. This goal was, at least formally, based on the assumption that wage earners and other disadvantaged segments of the population could achieve a unity of interest which could be institutionalized in the common brotherhood of one union.

This ideal dictated a pattern of organization which proved to be unworkable. If they were to be one big union they had to admit everyone, but at the same time the natural trend toward occupational particularism could not be neglected. While the ideals of the union required one pattern of organization, its success depended on another. Hence, the structure of the Knights consisted of both "mixed" local assemblies and "trade" locals. The mixed local contained every type of wage earner within a particular area and was found generally in rural or semirural locations, while the trade locals were dominant in the cities. This effort to accommodate occupational groupings contributed to conflict between the skilled workers, who began to leave the mixed locals and to form autonomous trade unions, and those who clung rigorously to the ideal of fundamental unity. The utopian goals of the Knights were not in harmony with the needs of its union membership, and the resultant organizational structure enhanced this ideological cleavage.[24] The quick surge in membership was followed by an equally rapid decline. Terence V. Powderly, the Grand Master, recognized the transient appeal of the organization's stated goals by remarking that, of the 700,000 members "at least 400,000 came in from curiosity and caused more damage than good." [25] By 1893 the membership had declined to 74,635. Although the Knights of Labor continued to exist until 1917 its membership was taken over almost entirely by socialist and other reform groups.

THE AMERICAN FEDERATION OF LABOR
AND BUSINESS UNIONISM

Although the Knights of Labor leadership discouraged trade organizations, several craft unions—the telegraphers, window glass, and shoe workers—obtained national craft autonomy. The con-

---

[24] William C. Birdsall, "The Problem of Structure in the Knights of Labor," *Industrial and Labor Relations Review*, VI (July 1953), 532-546.

[25] Terence V. Powderly, *The Path I Trod* (New York: Columbia University Press, 1940), p. 60.

tinuation of this conflict of interest led to the formation of the
Federation of Organized Trades and Labor Unions, which in 1886
became the American Federation of Labor. This new organization,
with Samuel Gompers as President, was in direct contrast to the
Knights both in goals and organization. While the Knights generally
deplored strikes, preferred evolution to revolution, and assumed no
irreconcilable conflict between employee and employer, its expansive goals contributed to its identification with more extreme manifestations of discontent. For example, the Haymarket Riot in
Chicago in 1886 produced renewed opposition on the part of
corporations, churches, and courts, and generated a defensive attitude in the ranks of labor. Although there is no evidence that the
Knights were associated with the riot, they were bitterly criticized
in the period of general condemnation which followed. The American Federation of Labor made explicit its more conservative aims.
Rather than urging an ambitious program of social reform, the AFL
kept within the framework of day-by-day objectives. In a statement
before a Senate Committee in 1883, Adolph Strasser, president of
the Cigar Makers Union, said: "We have no ultimate ends. . . . We
are fighting only for immediate objects—objects that can be realized
in a few years." [26]

The AFL believed in the capitalistic system and worked to improve the lot of the worker within that system. While seeking the
avoidance of more radical doctrines of class warfare or the abolition
of capitalism, the AFL sought to utilize to their fullest advantage
such short-term tactics as the strike and picketing. Further, an implicit premise on the part of the leadership was that the occupation of laborer was one of relative permanence. Accepting the
status, the objectives were the improvement of that status rather
than departure from it. This "business unionism," as it has come
to be called, was more in harmony with the needs of the labor
force. In terms of organizational response to insecurity, it offered
a more tangible set of benefits than the promise of a new society.
AFL goals developed not only as a response to the demands of a
clientele, but also as a result of the restrictions placed upon the
labor movement by the environment. These goals developed in a
period characterized by hostile public sentiment and antagonistic

---

[26] Quoted in Harold U. Faulkner and Mark Starr, *Labor in America* (New
York: Harper & Row, Publishers, 1949), p. 115.

employer attitudes. The President of the United States, as well as the governors of some states, used troops against strikers. Laws limiting the effect of boycotts and strikes were passed. The Sherman Act, passed presumably to prevent illegal combinations by corporations, was applied by the courts against combinations of workers, hence against the idea of the legality of the union.

Under such circumstances it is understandable that Gompers and the other leaders tended to adopt a laissez-faire approach to the use of the government for the furtherance of the position of organized labor. While the AFL did seek to prevent the use of government agencies by corporations to the disadvantage of labor, it rarely sought governmental institutions as a positive ally. Blocked on the political front, Gompers led the AFL into a strategy aimed at building union strength to the point at which a successful direct relation with the employers could be achieved. This involved building strong, financially sound unions which could bargain from a position of strength. The tactics were thus to increase the scope of unionization while at the same time disassociating labor from extremist elements; to build public support and tolerance for the time when labor would find itself engaged in a struggle with management.

"REALISM" AS A MEANS OF SURVIVAL

In contrast to the Knights of Labor, the AFL was organized along craft lines. Each participating union had its own constitution and rules for internal government. In no case were people who were not working at the trade but sympathetic with the aims of the union permitted to join. The restricted aims and restricted membership of the AFL proved to be a durable basis for survival. In contrast to previous depression periods, the unions affiliated with the AFL held their own during the severe depression of the 1890's. These early years were not favorable to the continued existence of union organization. Unsuccessful strikes such as the Pullman, the extension of the use of the injunction by the courts, rivalry from socialists and those interested in forming a labor party, and depressed economic conditions contributing to intense employer hostility operated to keep AFL membership stationary from 1892 to 1898. However, the fact that membership was stable rather than declining shows the success of AFL as contrasted with earlier experiences of unions during depressions. The return of prosperity at the beginning of the twentieth century saw AFL membership increase at a rapid rate from less than 300,000 in 1898 to more than 1,675,000 in 1904. That the AFL's particular brand of unionism appealed to the rank and file workers can be seen not only from its membership increase of approximately 360 per cent but also from the fact that the total membership in unions in 1904 was 2,022,300. Thus AFL member- ship included all but a fraction of the unionized workers in the country.[27]

SHIFTING GOALS IN RESPONSE
TO INTERNAL DEMANDS AND EXTERNAL HOSTILITY

This growth in AFL membership was accompanied by a change in policy with respect to political activity. We have described the response of management to the growth of unionism and discussed the role of the National Association of Manufacturers as a deterrent. In spite of its increasing membership, organized labor was not realizing benefits commensurate with its power potential. In addi- tion to opposition from without, the AFL was experiencing internal pressures to assume a more aggressive approach. An important split occurred in 1897 when the Western Federation of Miners withdrew and formed the American Labor Union three years later. Organized on an industrial basis and living in a region more identi- fied with the lawlessness of the frontier, the miners were more in- clined to direct action than to the conservative traditions of eastern craft unionism. In 1905, the American Labor Party and the Socialist Labor Party, together with other dissatisfied unions, created the In- dustrial Workers of the World. While its membership never ad- vanced beyond 50,000 the "wobblies," with their inclination toward direct and extreme action, indicated that AFL leadership needed to reconsider its assumptions.[28]

In addition to the internal pressures, AFL goals were subject to another influence. Before undertaking a more positive political program, Gompers believed that a labor union, as a group working against the *status quo*, could not hope for success unless it arranged

---

[27] Harwood Childs, *Labor and Capital in National Politics* (Columbus: The Ohio State University Press, 1930), p. 23.

[28] Philip Taft, "The I.W.W. in the Grain Belt," *Labor History*, I (Winter, 1960), 53-67.

alliances with groups more representative of middle class sentiment. The business unionism ideal was attractive not only to a large
portion of the working class but also to the less recalcitrant employees. Consequently, an expression of support from labor came
from such essentially middle class organizations as the National
Consumers League, the National Civic Federation (with Marcus A.
Hanna as president), the National Child Labor Committee, and the
American Association for Labor Legislation. Labor was thus improving the possibility of achieving access to governmental institutions by identifying itself with social groups traditionally favored.

These factors, plus the growing aggressiveness of the employers
associations supporting the National Association of Manufacturers,
led to a change in policy with respect to legislative and general
political activity. Beginning in 1906, the AFL pursued the tactics
of rewarding the friends and defeating the political enemies of
labor. No immediate results of this more aggressive policy are discernible. The growing and well organized opposition to labor responded to the new policy with a determined effort; some of the
public support acquired in past years seemed to be dissipated, and
AFL membership declined. However, the AFL had formulated some
basic objectives to which it had given high priority and the pursuit
of these objectives continued. It supported a wide variety of
measures ranging from the direct election of senators to the initiative and referendum and other devices designed to increase popular
participation in governmental affairs. However, one of the most
compelling reasons for the new policy was the use of injunctions in
labor disputes. In 1908, AFL urged both major parties to introduce
an anti-injunction plank in their platforms but were successful in
persuading only the Democrats. Thereafter, Gompers and other
leaders supported Bryan in 1908 and Wilson in 1912.

By 1911, AFL membership was again on the increase and the
government appeared to show concern for labor-management relations. The Department of Labor was created in 1913 with Cabinet
rank for its secretary. Although important as a symbol of the recognition of labor as a legitimate component of the social system,
thus enhancing the prestige of a hitherto neglected group, the
establishment of the Department of Labor did no more than suggest a more equalitarian relationship. Not until the 1930's did the
Department shift from an agency dominated by the Immigration

and Naturalization Service and, "touching lightly or not at all the lives of America's labor force," to an agency exercising influence in developing programs for the protection for workers.[29] More suggestive of tangible reward, at least in intention, was the Clayton Act of 1914, which exempted unions from prosecution as conspiracies in restraint of trade and which attempted to limit the use of injunctions by federal courts. Although referred to by Gompers as labor's "Magna Charta," hostile treatment by the courts soon made it evident that the Clayton Act promised more than it was able to deliver.

AFL GAINS DURING WORLD WAR I

During World War I, the position of the AFL was enhanced by its prompt assurance of cooperation with the government in the mobilization effort. In exchange for the removal of restrictions and suspensions that might hamper the war effort, the principle of labor representation on government agencies was accepted. Gompers became a member of the advisory commission to the Council of National Defense, and other labor leaders were appointed to most of the emergency war boards created by the government. In addition, in those industries which the government operated for the duration of the war, sanction was given to the right of workers to undertake collective bargaining. Under such favorable auspices AFL membership surged from 2,100,000 in 1915 to a peak of 4,000,-000 in 1920. Also to the advantage of the AFL was the virtual disappearance of the troublesome Industrial Workers of the World during the war years. As a consequence of its anti-war position, the members of the I.W.W. were suspected and accused of subversion. Previously Gompers had led the executive committee of the AFL in opposing its radical rival while the I.W.W. had tried to bore into AFL membership at the local level. Since the departure of the Western Federation of Miners in 1907 the I.W.W. had become largely an agitating organization more given to spectacular strikes and colorful propaganda than organizing on a stable basis. The hostility toward socialism or any form of radicalism which was typical of the war years brought action against the I.W.W. on the

---

[29] Murray Edelman, "New Deal Sensitivity to Labor Interests," in Milton Derber and Edwin Young, eds., *Labor and the New Deal* (Madison: The University of Wisconsin Press, 1957), p. 161.

part of the Department of Justice and local governments. Many of its leaders were imprisoned and its headquarters closed under authority of the criminal syndicalist laws. After the war, harassment by legal authorities and tacitly sanctioned vigilante action succeeded in destroying the organization. Thus ended a serious threat to the AFL.

POSTWAR REACTION

Although labor, and the AFL in particular, emerged from the war in a strengthened position, these advantages were short in duration. Several major trends during the "roaring twenties" present us with the paradox of decline in membership during a period of prosperity. After the enforced truce between labor and management, active government participation in labor relations ended, thus releasing the unions from wartime restraints. With the continued expansion in business following the Armistice, workers continued to join unions in increasing numbers until the peak year of 1920. This expansion brought renewed efforts to extend collective bargaining, which in turn produced many bitter disputes. In 1919, over four million workers were involved in strikes, many of which were to obtain or strengthen collective bargaining arrangements. Particularly significant was the union organizing campaign in the steel industry. While unionization had been successful in most of the industries connected with the war effort, industrial relations in the steel industry had not altered. At the 1918 convention of the AFL, those unions having membership in the steel industry appointed a special committee for the purpose of organizing in iron and steel factories. This campaign met with widespread success and the employers responded with the discharge of the new union members. Led by U.S. Steel, the industry remained firm in its open shop position and a strike involving over 350,000 workers was called. For reasons to be discussed later, the strike failed and the workers gradually returned to their jobs.

It was clear that the battle lines were being drawn over the issue of the open shop. President Wilson sought to reduce the animosity by calling a labor-management conference in October 1919 but this conference immediately split over the issue of collective bargaining and broke up with nothing achieved. However, the success of U.S. Steel encouraged an open shop movement similar to the one at the beginning of the century. Manufacturers' associations, chambers of commerce, bankers' and front-type citizens' groups, and even the National Grange united in supporting the "American plan" to prevent union organization. Open shop organizations thrived in every major industrial center in the country conducting "patronize the open shop" campaigns, supplying employers with blacklists of union members, and furnishing money and strikebreakers to employers involved in strikes.

Unions began to lose their war and their immediate postwar gains under the onslaught of anti-union drives and wage cuts which were introduced during the brief recession of 1921 and 1922. The larger packing companies declared themselves no longer bound by the union agreement accepted during the war, they established company unions to subvert the Amalgamated Meat Cutter and Butcher Workmen, and they restored the packing industry to the open shop. The seamen's union lost a two-month strike and was reduced to one-fifth its former size. In Chicago, the Illinois Manufacturers Association and the Chicago Chamber of Commerce were successful in maintaining open shop conditions, and even the organized building trades could not escape the anti-union drives.

The question which comes most readily to mind when we view this anti-union activity is: What was the response of the unions? As the AFL saw its once secure position under constant and successful attack, what were the countermeasures undertaken to reduce the severity of the threat? The AFL was poorly equipped to serve as an adequate organization in this hostile environment. Following its earlier period of aggressiveness, the AFL chose now to revert to its traditional attitude. With respect to AFL doctrine, Key has noted that "dogmas, philosophies, and ideas have a strength of their own," [30] indicating that the idea of business unionism, while not expedient under the circumstances, was rigidly adhered to beyond its period of usefulness. On the other hand, there seemed to be some logic behind the inertia of the AFL. We have seen that, while labor is described as a protest movement, it has had to resist the infiltration of those with truly revolutionary schemes. During the "normalcy" of the 1920's the AFL was in no position to risk identification with the goals of the socialists and communists, but rather saw a

---

[30] V. O. Key, *Politics, Parties, and Pressure Groups* (New York: Thomas Y. Crowell Company, 1958), p. 67.

distinct advantage in conforming to what seemed to be the dominant pattern of beliefs. While other unions were reaching toward the government as a means of achieving economic security, the AFL persisted in its laissez-faire dogma. Thus the Railroad Brotherhoods, which were independent, vigorously supported the candidacy of the LaFollette Progressives in 1924, while the AFL did so in a half-hearted manner.

OCCUPATIONAL SHIFTS AND AFL INERTIA

Although the reluctance to go against the grain certainly contributed to the AFL's doctrine, there is a relation between structure and ideology which cannot be overlooked. That the AFL tended to grow "old and comfortable" during the prosperous decade of the 1920's may be attributed partially to its strength among skilled craftsmen.[31] Although it included some industrial unions such as coal mining and women's garment industries, the core of its strength lay with the skilled craftsmen such as those in the building trades, certain branches of the metal industries, and the printing trades. The members of these craft unions were usually concentrated in smaller enterprises and hence did not face the problem of bargaining with giant corporations. The craft form of organization, on the other hand, could not take into account the burgeoning of semiskilled workers in the new industrial giants. In the automobile, steel, rubber, and electrical industries, for example, new machines and processes were substituting semiskilled machine tenders for skilled craftsmen working with tools. Machinery and a rigid division of labor had largely broken down craft skills. In any mass production industry a minority of skilled workers remained, often submerged in a mass of unskilled and semiskilled workers. However, this minority of skilled craftsmen included men trained in many different skills, who, under AFL organizing rules, were divided into national unions built around the particular crafts. Without legal recognition of the right to organize, and in the face of determined corporation opposition, successful organization of the mass production industries required the ability to win bitter strikes. The diffusion of power demanded by the craft system proved incapable of resisting the concentrated attack of the company.

---

[31] Joel Seidman, "Efforts Toward Merger," *Industrial and Labor Relations Review*, IX (Apr. 1956), 353.

The steel strike of 1919 is a notable example of the inability of the craft-oriented AFL to cope with the stubborn resistance of a giant corporation. Further, it is clear that the AFL failed to throw its full power behind the strike. This suggests that the AFL was less than eager to organize the mass production industries. While each union would gain if more members were added, there was the possibility that a torrent of semiskilled workers flowing into the AFL would strengthen the position of semiskilled workers already in the federation, such as the miners and garment workers, against the dominant craft union leadership. There seemed little to be gained by challenging industrial giants.

Although AFL membership was declining, most of the craft unions, subsequent to reversals in the early postwar years, were able to maintain and in some cases increase their membership. The printing and building trades, for example, had higher memberships in 1929 than at any time in the past. These unions had always formed the dominant wing in AFL power structure. On the other hand, the industrial unions within the AFL suffered serious losses in membership. Membership in coal mining was reduced by half; John L. Lewis of the coal miners made the only serious challenge to the re-election of Gompers in 1921. Thus, although AFL membership fell under the impact of employers' offensives and dipped below three million for most of the decade of the prosperous twenties, this occurrence served to strengthen the position of craft unions within the AFL. Thus whole industries, such as automobiles and rubber, remained untouched. It was in these industries that employers took the extra precaution of adopting programs which they hoped would make unions unnecessary. The twenties marked the peak of "company unions" whereby the need to organize was recognized but control was retained by management. Withdrawing into the industries of entrenched strength, the AFL failed to grow, proved incapable of organizing the giants of American industry, and seemed perfectly satisfied.

However, the severe depression of the early 1930's found even the craft unions losing membership, the building trades being particularly affected. Faced with this situation, encouraged by the upturn of business in mid-1933, and having apparent access to the new Democratic administration, AFL leaders took an active part in drafting the National Industrial Recovery Act. Section 7a gave governmental approval to the right of workers to organize and bargain collectively. As a result, the AFL made an effort to organize the mass production industries, but the effort was no more strenuous than its previous forays into industrial unionism had been. In the mass production industries, unions appeared spontaneously and applied for AFL charters. This was indeed the opportunity for the AFL to prove adjustable to new demands, and, had it done so, some observers believe the forthcoming establishment of the Congress of Industrial Organizations would not have occurred. However, the strength of custom is strong, and the AFL was not willing to join the locals, organized on an industrial basis, into national industrial unions. Instead it looked upon these local industrial unions as temporary forms of organization, to be tolerated only until the skilled workers could be segregated and transferred to their appropriate craft unions.

This form of organization was as unsuited to the realities of the situation as the old "mixed local" structure of the Knights of Labor. The initial enthusiasm of the months following the passage of the National Industrial Recovery Act was replaced with apathy; the surge of local industrial unions declined and company unions usually sprang up in their place. The reluctance of the AFL to change its ways of organizing is well illustrated by its efforts toward auto workers. From 1933 until 1936 the AFL tried to organize the automobile industry but met opposition from both workers and management. Moving cautiously into the industry, the AFL did not encourage strikes and actively opposed the creation of an international union. The situation settled into a stalemate between the local union and the AFL with the former pressing for a general strike and the latter applying the "red" label to such tactics.[32]

THE RISE OF THE CONGRESS
OF INDUSTRIAL ORGANIZATIONS

Since the AFL remained rigid in spite of the shifting needs of its clientele, it was only a matter of time until a rival organization more in harmony with the interests of the workers in mass production industries would arise. At the October 1934 AFL convention a group of unions led by John L. Lewis of the United Mine Workers

[32] Jack Skeels, "The Background of U. A. W. Factionalism," *Labor History,* II (Spring, 1961), 158-181.

urged the organization of the mass production industries on an industrial basis. However, a compromise plan was adopted which called for the protection of craft union jurisdictional rights where craft lines could be discerned but for the issuance of charters on an industrial basis where appropriate. This resolution, initially presumed to be a victory for the forces of industrial unionism, seemed hollow when months passed without implementation of the resolution and bountiful organizing opportunities disappeared. Nearly a year elapsed before charters were issued to automobile and rubber workers, and these charters did not permit complete industrial organization. At the 1935 convention, the industrial unionists demanded unrestricted industrial union charters for the mass production industries. However, the craft union majority insisted that craftsmen in such industries be enrolled in the appropriate craft union. Following this defeat, the presidents of eight unions created the Committee for Industrial Organization with the intention of organizing industrial unions within the AFL structure. Although President William Green of the AFL demanded its immediate dissolution, the Committee began energetic organizing drives which culminated in the formation of the separate Congress of Industrial Organizations in 1938.

The result of these organizing drives was startling in contrast to the sputtering efforts of the AFL. In the automobile industry, where the AFL had condemned strikes as a tactical device, a series of strikes culminated in 1937 in recognition of the CIO by General Motors; Chrysler followed shortly after. These successes, coupled with the Supreme Court's ruling in favor of the constitutionality of the National Labor Relations Act, made it evident that the CIO was not merely a dissident faction but a permanent break with the past. Although Ford remained non-union and labor suffered a major setback in the failure of the "little steel" strike in 1937, CIO membership rose to nearly four million while the AFL found itself beneath the three million mark. Under such a formidable assault why did the AFL not wither away, as had the Knights of Labor? Its structure was still geared to the needs of the skilled workmen, and it built from this nucleus by launching a vigorous organizing effort which included a modified form of industrial unionism. Rather than declining, the AFL's response to the challenge was sufficiently flexible and imaginative to allow the federation to increase steadily until, at the time of the merger in 1955, it was more than twice the size of the CIO.

This breach in the labor movement continued its formal phase until the 1955 merger, but, due to the fact that far more than the obvious difference in structure was involved, legal merging did not reduce the severity of conflict to any appreciable degree. From the outset, the CIO and AFL attracted different clientele, developed different types of leaders, and espoused different goals. Made up primarily of lesser skilled workmen who lacked the more stable economic position of craftsmen, the CIO unions were more dependent upon government legislation to supplement the achievements of collective bargaining. These unions showed interest in the level of minimum wages, public housing for low income groups, social security, and other similar measures necessitating considerable attention to political developments at the national level. The AFL, by contrast, seemed far less concerned with broad gauge goals and more occupied with government at the local level where authority over building codes, for example, lay. Until 1932 it opposed unemployment insurance and supported the 1938 Wage and Hour Act with greatest misgiving.

An examination of representative publications of the two organizations supports the assumption that the AFL has regarded the social structure as basically sound and requiring little improvement while the CIO sought more fundamental alterations in the structure of society. Hence AFL publications emphasized individualism and the rewards of individual ability while the CIO was more inclined to emphasize the value of collective or cooperative endeavor. By classifying "progressive values" in union publications, Rosenberg and Bellin were able to conclude that, with a mean of 73.9, the CIO had a progressive index of 86.6, while the AFL ranked much lower with 52.5.[33] A final note on the differences between the unions is provided by Mills's study of the backgrounds of their leaders. He writes: "The AFL is a gerontocracy: at its top are older men who are relatively poorly educated and who have authority over much younger men who are relatively better educated. . . . The CIO is a professional bureaucracy: at its top are slightly older men who

---

[33] Morris Rosenberg and Seymour Bellin, "Value Patterns in the Trade Union Press," *International Journal of Opinion and Attitude Research,* III (Winter, 1949-1950), 555-586.

are quite well educated, and those better-educated leaders exercise authority over slightly younger and less well-educated men." [34] The younger "intellectuals" found more of a home in the CIO.

THE ADVERSE CONSEQUENCES OF DIVIDED LABOR

While the history of the labor movement is certainly a "perpetual struggle to keep the organization from going to pieces for want of inner cohesion," this is certainly not a unique problem.[35] Truman's remark that "complete stability within any interest group is a fiction" is intended to suggest that a basic component of any organization is internal conflict.[36] We shall describe the efforts of interest groups to overcome or neutralize this centrifugal tendency in a later chapter. On the other hand, it would be a mistake to overlook the very likely possibility that the inability of unions to achieve unity has consequences as they challenge groups whose goals are more in line with established ideologies. If we compare labor's activities during the two world wars, some evidence of the adverse consequences of the formal split appear. While the pattern in both cases was for a moratorium on industrial disputes, the cooperative effort of labor was damaged by several severe disputes which in turn contributed to a more hostile congressional attitude than had been evidenced in the earlier New Deal period. Appointment of CIO and AFL representatives to the National Defense Mediation Board provided institutional implementation of labor's internal frictions. Shortly after it was established, the Board became the center of a dispute between the CIO—which, led by John L. Lewis of the United Mine Workers, demanded the implementation of the union shop as official policy—and management representatives, who were unwilling to accept such a proposal. A management victory precipitated a coal strike, but even more significant was the vote of the AFL representatives against the union shop and the resignation of the CIO members as a result of this action. This dispute effectively wrecked the Mediation Board which was replaced by the National War Labor Board.[37] The War Labor Board, originally

[34] Mills, *The New Men of Power*, p. 73.

[35] Perlman, *A Theory of the Labor Movement*, p. 154.

[36] Truman, *The Governmental Process*, p. 156.

[37] James Burns, "Maintenance of Membership: A Study in Administrative Statesmanship," *Journal of Politics*, X (Feb. 1948), 101-116.

established by executive order, was established by law, over the President's veto, in 1943. The War Labor Disputes Act aimed at the prevention of interruption of production by authorizing governmental seizure of industry and forbidding strikes in such industry after the government assumed the responsibility for its operation. Although this legislation had little immediate effect, it provided evidence of growing strength of anti-union sentiment. The act also prohibited contributions by labor organizations in national elections, showing that the reaction extended beyond the immediate issue. While this act provided a hint of even more restrictive legislation which was to come, it did not serve to bring the warring factions closer together. A dispute erupted over the policies of the National Labor Relations Board, with the AFL charging the board with a bias toward industrial unionism. Further, while both unions were in support of New Deal candidates, the AFL objected to the vigorous tactics of the CIO Political Action Committee, which was established in 1944 to mobilize support for Roosevelt. There was also disagreement with regard to fair employment practice legislation, which the CIO supported and the AFL opposed.

LABOR'S POSTWAR DECLINE

Thus, although the leaders of the unions found themselves cooperating on many of the issues that arose during the war, the position of labor seemed weaker after the war. On the other hand, business interests which, as we have seen, lost substantial prestige during the depression enjoyed a revival of prestige partially as a result of their successful contribution to the war effort. There emerged a pattern of attacks on unions akin to those following World War I, and labor found itself unable to muster an effective counterattack. The obvious manifestation of the shift in the power structure was the mounting success of management in passing restrictive legislation. Even with a Democratic Congress, the tide of such legislation was rising and the Republican victory in the congressional elections of Fall, 1946 indicated growing hostility. This activity came to a climax with the passage of the Taft-Hartley Act in 1947. The inability of the AFL and CIO to prevent passage is instructive in the damaging effects of lack of cohesion. The National Association of Manufacturers engaged in a strenuous effort to secure the passage of the act, which, among other things, prohibited interfering with a person's right not to join a union and forbade discrimination against non-union labor. There was a struggle in the NAM between the larger and smaller manufacturers which resulted in a victory for the latter. The NAM advised Congress to keep a substantial portion of the Wagner Act in the writing of new legislation.[38] However, the NAM was able to settle its differences before it became necessary to present a program and consequently was united in the legislative struggle.

In sharp contrast to management, labor's differences were carried over into the legislative debate. While both the AFL and CIO viewed the Taft-Hartley Act as a threat to their existence and committed themselves vigorously against the proposed revision, the open, sharp disagreement over what course of action should be taken reflected well their past differences. The AFL felt that the National Labor Relations Board, established under the auspices of the Wagner Act, was biased in favor of the CIO. Consequently, the AFL opposed the CIO's idea of keeping the Wagner Act intact and favored merely an adherence to the "spirit" of the earlier act. The Taft-Hartley Act, while more restrictive than its predecessor, facilitated the separation of craft unions from industrial unions and thus offered some advantage to the AFL.

The passage of Taft-Hartley over the opposition of President Truman contributed to unity efforts. While the act was still taking shape, the CIO suggested negotiations which ended in failure. The passage of the law frightened both groups and impressed upon them that combined action would be needed if the Act were to be repealed and even more restrictive legislation to be averted. The changing complexion of Congress converted the AFL to the need for more aggression, and it created Labor's League for Political Education, which was similar in objectives and method to the CIO's Political Action Committee. The election of Truman in 1948, with repeal of Taft-Hartley a major issue in his campaign, provided added incentive, for the time seemed right to recoup labor's losses. Immediately after the election, labor sought to utilize the "mandate" of Truman's victory to press for repeal, but again it ran into the snares of dissension. As was expected, the CIO wanted absolute return to the Wagner Act and the AFL did not. Cleavage was not

---

[38] Robert E. Lane, "Law and Opinion in the Business Community," *Public Opinion Quarterly*, XVII (Summer, 1953), 239-257.

limited to the dispute at the highest level. The CIO, in favoring a simple repeal, was reflecting its growing inability to control deviant interests within its structure. Its member unions, particularly the more left-wing groups, had clearly formulated ideas about labor legislation. Some wanted abolition of injunctions in national emergency strikes; others sought legalization of the closed shop; still others insisted that the requirement that union officers take a noncommunist oath be abolished. With this array of competing interests, the CIO preferred not to become involved with complex revision, since this would necessitate the consideration of competing demands, with the assignment of priorities to some and the disregarding of others. The difficulty of remaining united while approving some demands and rejecting others was therefore a primary consideration.[39]

The problem was intensified because of the basic organizational principle of union autonomy of which more will be said later. The CIO had followed the AFL principle of leaving each national union relatively free to manage its own affairs and subject to no central agency. With each union able to determine its own policy, the CIO found some of its more aggressive unions taking positions opposed to what it believed to be the most tenable position, and consequently laid down detailed regulations for the conduct of all lobbyists. The AFL, by contrast, seemed more suited to the formulation of feasible objectives.

PRESSURES TOWARD MERGER

Although these examples of labor's failure to agree certainly contributed to its loss of ground, the realization of failure which accompanied these legislative defeats stimulated the leadership of both unions to seek reconciliation. In addition to the Taft-Hartley Act, the passage of state "right to work" laws suggested a widespread hostility to the continued health of organized labor. The passage of these laws galvanized the AFL toward vigorous political action and, in the ensuing political experience, many of its leaders saw the possible benefits of cooperation. These laws brought home in a vivid manner the realization that labor was a deviant type movement and could ill afford to expend its energy fighting internally.

---

[39] Gerald Pomper, "Labor and Congress: The Repeal of Taft-Hartley," *Labor History*, II (Fall, 1961), 323-343

Finally, the election of 1952 brought into office an administration considered unfriendly by most labor unions. If the labor movement had been declining under the friendly auspices of the New and Fair Deals, no improvement could be expected from the Republicans. The fear that it would be difficult to do business with the new administration was borne out by the Eisenhower appointments to the National Labor Relations Board, although Republican leadership was far from unanimous in its opinions of the proper line to take.[40]

In addition to these external pressures toward unification, factors within the labor movement were working toward the same end. Unity negotiations had been conducted periodically since the split, and, despite frequent failures, the two unions were drawing closer together. Successfully negotiated no-raiding pacts and improved cooperation during the Korean War played a large role. Industrial unionism was also reduced as a divisive issue when the AFL chartered industrial unions or authorized craft unions to operate on that basis. Within the CIO, a major step was taken by the expulsion of some communist-dominated unions in 1950. These unions opposed the Marshall Plan and supported Henry Wallace for President in 1948 contrary to specific CIO policy. In addition to incurring the wrath of the more conservative AFL leadership, these communist-dominated unions had the most to fear from a merger. Their expulsion, therefore, removed a source of pressure and gave CIO leaders a measure of independence. However, the CIO continued to be plagued by cleavages which threatened disintegration and made it a distinct possibility that a continued separate existence would diminish its strength. Leadership changes also had an effect. In the Fall of 1952, William Green, AFL president since 1924, and Philip Murray, who had headed the CIO since 1940, both died and were succeeded by George Meany of the Plumbers and Walter Reuther of the United Automobile Workers. Both of the former presidents were deeply imbued with the spirit of the split and, as the separate organizations continued, each seemed to be developing institutional patterns and group norms which contributed to the maintenance of the *status quo*. The old symbols and shibboleths

---

[40] Seymour Scher, "Regulatory Agency Control Through Appointment: The Case of the Eisenhower Administration and the NLRB," *Journal of Politics*, XXIII (Nov. 1961), 667-688.

continued to be utilized on frequent occasions. The appeals from the AFL to the CIO, for example, were phrased as though they were directed to truant school children. The new AFL leadership dropped this tone of moral superiority and Meany's more equalitarian approach made the older union easier to deal with.

The change of leadership in the CIO, while improving the chances of unity, did so on a different basis. Murray had been, as Max Weber would say, a charismatic leader able to hold the warring factions together.[41] With his death there occurred a power struggle between the heads of two powerful CIO unions, Reuther and David McDonald, who succeeded Murray as president of the steel workers. The steel workers and a number of smaller unions opposed Reuther, who nevertheless won by a narrow vote. Thereafter, McDonald made it clear that he was unsatisfied with CIO leadership and, unless a merger was achieved quickly, would consider taking his union out of the CIO. Further, Reuther had received support in his election from some of the other unions only on condition that he would move quickly for merger. The pressures from within were, if anything, more intense than the external factors.

Assessing Labor's Power

The merger of December 5, 1955 brought more than fifteen million workers together under a single banner. Did the merger enhance labor's political power? Did the cleavages of more than twenty years suddenly dissipate or become negligible? A simple answer is impossible since labor's strength varies through time and from place to place. Yet one can certainly say that its aims remain divided and its goals generally unrealized.

FORMAL UNITY WITH CONTINUED STRESS

Why is this the case? First, the formal union of the AFL and CIO did not erase past grievances and the unity of the AFL-CIO is easily strained. Since the AFL was the stronger of the two at the time of merger, it was given a proportionate share of the offices: the

---

[41] Charisma is, of course, an ideal type of leadership. Murray was both legal and charismatic. *See* Hans Gerth and C. Wright Mills, *From Max Weber* (New York: Oxford University Press, Inc., 1958), pp. 51-55.

president and secretary-treasurer were to come from the AFL but the Industrial Union Department, with Reuther as president, was to serve the interests of the old CIO unions. This provided an organizational basis for continuing the old craft-industrial conflict which has, in fact, grown severe. Prior to the 1961 AFL-CIO convention in Miami, the conflict was brought into the open by Reuther, who lamented that the "high hopes born at the time of the merger have failed to materialize." [42] While the fight does not seem to be drawn purely on the basis of a division between former CIO and AFL unions, the building trades which were an important segment of the old AFL are the source of greatest conflict with the Industrial Union Department. Unions affiliated with the Building and Construction Trades Department have joined employers in promoting "project maintenance" agreements which provide for the contracting-out of work by industrial concerns that have traditionally used their own employees for maintenance work. This induces industrial employees to disregard collective bargaining agreements with industrial unions. The IUD regards this as collusion and asserts that such agreements "have been used . . . as a union-busting and strike-breaking instrument of the employers." [43] Further examples of discord are the boycotting by craft unions of products of industrial unions and even the "raiding of industrial unions by craft unions in defiance of the orders of the AFL-CIO Executive Council." For example, the Sheet Metal Workers sought to displace the Steelworkers during a strike by the latter—the certified bargaining representative—at the Carrier Corporation. Although twice defeated in elections by Carrier employees, the Sheet Metal Workers refused to withdraw in spite of an Executive Council order, and, with the Steelworkers still picketing, finally won an NLRB election at the Carrier plant. These and other examples suggest that union strength is dissipated in what AFL-CIO president Meany calls "useless internal bickering." [44]

THE RISE OF THE WHITE COLLAR WORKER

Consider now the changes that are taking place in the occupational structure of the United States. In treating the labor move-

---

[42] "Reuther Calls for End of Strife," *I.U.D. Bulletin*, VI (Dec. 1961), 3.
[43] "Action on Internal Disputes," *ibid.*, 7.
[44] "Meany Asks End of Fights So Labor Can Go Forward," *ibid.*, 11.

ment, we have called attention to the fact that the emergence of a new occupational group, the industrial group, the industrial worker, produced needs and demands which were met by the emergence of formal organizations: labor unions. Notice has been given to the increase in the number of employees in mass production industries which made the traditional organizations inadequate and created the need for new institutional arrangements: the CIO. There is a further trend in occupational mobility that may have consequences for the political effectiveness of organized labor: the growth of professional and other white collar occupations and the levelling off of factory workers in proportion to the total labor force. Taking 1880 as a starting point, the number of white collar workers has increased in each decade at a degree in excess of the increase among manual workers. Further, the degree of increase seems to be continually rising. In the years from 1940 to 1950, for example, white collar workers increased by 34.3 per cent while manual workers increased by 17.8 per cent.

The question then becomes: has labor penetrated the readily organizable segments of the labor force or can it move from the "blue collar" workers in large corporations in urban centers to small firms, service industries, retail trades, and the white collar workers? Since World War II, union membership has increased from thirteen to eighteen million, or 39 per cent. However the "real" membership (membership as a percentage of the civilian labor force) increased only from 24.8 to 26.2. Eliminating agricultural employment would still show an increase of 33.4 to 35.0. This slow rate of increase, in the face of the rise of the white collar worker, suggests that perhaps labor organizations will have to modify their goals or face shrinking membership. In fact, twenty-eight unions lost members between 1956 and 1958. Even in the manufacturing segments of the working population, union membership is only 54 per cent and the rate of growth is slowing down.[45]

In addition to the problem of the white collar worker, unions will have to consider the trend of women in the labor force. By 1965 about one-third of the labor force is expected to be female.

---

[45] Irving Bernstein, "The Growth of American Unions, 1945-1960," *Labor History,* II (Spring, 1961), 155. *See also* Donald J. Bogue, *The Population of the United States* (New York: The Free Press of Glencoe, Inc., 1959), p. 478.

Will women prove more difficult to organize than men? Also, today two-thirds of all union membership is concentrated in ten
states. Even if total mobilization were somehow achieved, this
geographical concentration presents an obstacle. Can labor extend
for example, into the rapidly industrializing South? While unions
have been unable to organize the older southern factories, the newer
ones have been more accessible.[46] Here we might encounter the
same problem which faced the earliest unions. Just as the first workers drawn from the rural areas were not used to factory industrial
discipline, the modern southern worker has not had a working
class background. Friction over racial equality in unions is only one
obvious possibility existing from the overlapping affiliation of the
southern worker. Is he a southerner or a union member? Under-
standably, the AFL-CIO has had to tread lightly in this problem
area. While new industries pour into the South, the bulk of its
workers remain largely unorganized and in those industries which
are organized, local-national friction is an acute problem.

A fundamental theory of sociologists is that, as needs change, institutions to implement these needs make corresponding adjustments.[47] If the needs of a southern clientele differ from needs expressed in the North, what can we say of the needs of the relatively
unorganized white collar workers? This is not the place to discuss
the labor vote in detail, but it should be noted that white collar
workers favor the Republican party while union leadership substantially supports Democratic candidates.[48] The inference would be
that if union organization is to expand it will have to adjust to the
needs of those who exhibit attitudes different from those which
leaders have assumed to be the foundation of union membership.
Although it is not necessary to regard the lack of union penetration
into white collar strata as permanent—airline pilots and musicians
have strong unions—there is every reason to expect that the
emotional release of the strike, symbolizing solidarity against
"them," will not be as satisfactory a catalyst as it has been in the

---

[46] Industrial Union Department, AFL-CIO, *The Southern Labor Story.*

[47] Norman F. Washburne, *Interpreting Social Change in America* (New York:
Random House, 1954), pp. 9-11.

[48] Max M. Kampelman, "Labor in Politics," in Industrial Relations Research
Association, *Interpreting the Labor Movement* (Madison: Industrial Relations
Research Association, 1952).

past. As one observer states: "they have not hated the boss enough." [49]

If this is the occupational trend, what of those who remain in the manual labor strata? It is possible, of course, that continued separation from the mainstream of occupational development will serve to intensify their identification with a more narrowly conceived labor interest.[50] If the white collar workers are drifting toward a business point of view, will the manual laborers, as they become a smaller proportion of the total labor force, achieve more cohesion than has heretofore been possible? The evidence now available seems to suggest that workers, with the exception of those at the bottom of the ladder, do not regard themselves as primarily union members but rather as one of a variety of potentially conflicting identifications. It is significant that, again excluding those at the bottom of the occupational structure, most workers regard self-employment in a small business as a highly desirable goal.[51] If labor leaders must proselytize potential followers to their goals, it would appear that the conformity to middle class ideology would be a good selling point.

THE PROBLEM OF APATHY

Given the general identification of labor with middle class values —and hence the absorption by the society of a potentially disruptive force—there still remains the problem of apathy. As a general rule, political participation increases as one travels up the income or occupational ladder. Thus, those at lowest levels of the occupational structure, those more clearly resigned to a stable, underprivileged status, are also those least likely to be roused from apathy. Of course, if a worker's plant has a union shop contract, he has to join the union whether he wants to or not. Even in open shop plants there is considerable evidence that the joining of a union is not based on logical reasoning in which economic self-interest plays a considerable part, but upon expediency; a reaction to immediate pressures such as informal group pressure. Seidman, London, and

---

[49] F. C. Smith, "Why White Collar Workers Don't Join Unions," *Personnel Journal,* XXVIII (Oct. 1949), 171.

[50] This suggestion is made in Key, *op. cit.,* p. 58.

[51] Eli Chinoy, "The Tradition of Opportunity and the Aspiration of Automobile Workers," *American Journal of Sociology,* LVII (Mar. 1952), 453-459. *See also* Chinoy, *Automobile Workers and the American Dream* (Garden City, N.Y.: Doubleday and Company, 1958).

Karsh estimate that, in the local union—which is synonymous with the labor movement for most of the members—nearly 40 per cent of the rank and file members joined with neither conviction nor sympathy. Surely this core of apathetic workers cannot be counted upon as a reliable basis of political support. The political activity of the union left 95 per cent of these members unmoved and untouched. They looked to competing groups—ethnic, religious, familial—for orientation and guidance. A humorous illustration of the separation of the member from the political aspirations of union leadership is afforded by the recorded response of "who's he?" to a query about the P.A.C. (Political Action Committee). In the eyes of the members, union political activities are peripheral rather than a core function.[52] Collective bargaining is far more crucial and is supported by most of the members who are indifferent about more broadly gauged political activity. As Hudson and Rosen say: "present political strength of the union seems limited more by the members' lack of positive enthusiasm or by their uncertainty than by a strong disapproval of political activity."[53] There would seem to be a considerable failure by the leadership to impress upon the rank and file the utility of purposive political action. Bruner, a former union staff man, ruefully describes a typical political meeting in these words: "the conference breaks up and the delegates adjourn to the bar, grumbling about the length of the sessions and the monotony of the speeches. After that nothing much happens."[54]

Thus labor has never exercised the political power which many of its more persistent enemies attribute to it. Senator Goldwater's fear that "the President of the United States will be picked by labor leaders" is not justified.[55] In discussing the role of interest groups in elections we will see, for the reasons cited above, labor cannot exercise the electoral strength which its numbers would seem to confer upon it.

---

[52] Joel Seidman, Jack London, and Bernard Karsh, "Why Workers Join Unions," *Annals of the American Academy of Political and Social Science* (Mar. 1951), 75-84. *See also* Seidman, London, and Karsh, "Political Consciousness in a Local Union," *Public Opinion Quarterly*, XV (Winter, 1951-1952), 692-702.

[53] Ruth Alice Hudson and Hjalmar Rosen, "Union Political Action: The Member Speaks," *Industrial and Labor Relations Review*, VII (Apr. 1954), 418.

[54] Dick Bruner, "Labor Should Get Out of Politics," *Harpers Magazine*, Aug. 1958, p. 24.

[55] *Ibid.*, p. 21.

Agrarian Politics:

VI

The Triumph
of Formal Organization

We have learned in the theoretical sections of this book that the development of specialization—or division of labor—in society is a prerequisite for the development of groups whose goals can be distinguished from more general social needs. The development of agricultural organizations is well suited to illustrate this premise. From the Revolution to the Civil War, agriculture was primarily a self-sufficient enterprise built around the family. Economic independence meant that the income of the family farm was not dependent upon price supports or any similar government aid program; there was no surplus of products and the market generally favored the producer in a situation of scarcity. It was not even necessary to venture into cooperative arrangements with neighboring farmers or small-town businessmen, for what was needed was produced on the farm. Such a system was well suited to the ideals of individualism so eloquently spoken of by Jefferson and other apologists for the agrarian way of life. The farmer, described as ". . . the most noble and independent man in society," could hardly have been anything but independent since physical isolation required that farm production be directed principally to the supply of home consumption needs.[1]

The Agrarian Century

Coupled with this individualism, we note that the period prior to the Civil War has been labeled the "agrarian century." By this is meant that the dominant themes in our developing culture were rurally oriented. The major share of the national income was derived from farming or related enterprises, and most of the population of the country was employed in primary occupations. Farm organizations as we know them today did not come into being until this self-sufficient pattern was impaired by the commercialization of farming and the attendant specialization in the tasks of agriculture: "the most thrifty and efficient farmer might fail through no fault of his own. Forces were set in motion over which the farmer individually had no control." [2] The farming population was becoming economically integrated with the complexities of industrial society at the same time that the labor force began to be transferred from agriculture to the manufacturing industries.

EMERGING ATTITUDES

The notion of physical isolation as a barrier to collective action should not be overdrawn. There is evidence to indicate that during the "agrarian century" much of the eulogistic praise of rural life was defensive against perceived attacks. The farm journals of these days seemed overly concerned with refuting aspersions cast upon farm people and agrarian customs. Farmers were urged to be proud of their occupations but at the same time were exhorted to acquire the education and social graces that would make such criticism meaningless. Scorn was heaped upon a "certain class of individuals

---

[1] Paul H. Johnstone, "Old Ideals Versus New Ideas in Farm Life," in *Farmers in a Changing World,* 1940 Yearbook of Agriculture (Washington, D.C.: Government Printing Office, 1940), p. 117.

[2] Everett M. Rogers, *Social Change in Rural Society* (New York: Appleton-Century-Crofts, Inc., 1960), p. 253.

. . . who treat the cultivators of the soil as an inferior caste." [3] This certain class was urban dwellers toward whom particularly vociferous attacks were directed. Urban areas were described by reference to such emotive symbols of "royalty" and "aristocracy" as contrasted with the "real, unsophisticated American; a virtuous, intelligent, brave, hardy and generous yeoman." [4] Such hypersensitivity to supposed hostility also took the form of distrust of the institutions of urban life, particularly banks. Fear was expressed that the "loan sharks" could, by taking unscrupulous advantage of the farmer's poor grasp of financial affairs, immerse the unsuspecting victim in a morass of debt from which he could never emerge: "A farmer should shun the doors of a bank as he would the approach of the plague or cholera." [5]

Thus, while the agrarian century was characterized by a strong faith in the advancement and future of agriculture, there seemed to be a feeling that the cities of the eastern seaboard represented an adversary. [6] Since agricultural values were more dominant in the West and South, these sections, through institutions of formal government, cooperated to prevent control of the economy by the eastern portions of the country. We recall, for example, the denunciations of the Hamiltonian policies of encouraging industrial expansion by portions of the agricultural community. The dissolving of the second U.S. bank under Jackson and the strenuous opposition of southern planters to protective tariffs gives evidence of a "powerful attack upon one symbol of putative Eastern oppression." [7] In addition to this hostility, the westward expansion of agriculture brought demands that public lands be disposed of on favorable terms, while pressure was brought to bear on both state and national governments to improve transportation routes from farm to market.

Although isolation and "individualism" of farmers were obstacles to long term stable organizations during the agrarian century, there were manifestations of the farmers' willingness to act in coordination for brief periods. Lacking institutionalized mechanisms for the ex-

---

[3] Johnstone, *op. cit.*, p. 118.
[4] *Ibid.*
[5] *Ibid.*
[6] See Alvin Boskoff, "The Farm Bloc and Agrarian Ideology" (Master's thesis, Columbia University, 1948), pp. 9-23 for a more complete discussion of early rural-urban hostility.
[7] Boskoff, *op. cit.*, p. 20.

pression of grievances, early farmers' movements took the form of armed conflict. Shay's Rebellion and the Whiskey Rebellion are the most widely cited examples of the reaction against conditions harmful to agriculture. These sporadic outbursts, plus the agrarian support given to the Jacksonian Democrats by the smaller farmers and to the Whigs by wealthier planters, suggest that farmers were groping for some viable device to direct shared attitudes into purposive forms.

THE DECLINE OF ECONOMIC ISOLATION

The breaking of the self-sufficient pattern occurred during the emergence of industrialism as the dominant social pattern of American life. The shift from "peasant farming" to commercial farming, or the shift from farming as a means of providing basic needs to farming as a business enterprise, carried with it the increased reliance upon agricultural machinery.[8] Mechanized farming, in turn, increased the dependent position of the farmer. In the agrarian century, land was easy to obtain and the market still expanding. However, land became scarce while land values were jumping to almost prohibitive levels. This served to increase competition and required the use of more efficient instruments. In addition, the pressures of competition led many farmers to turn toward specialization in crops, rendering the rural population dependent upon urban areas for many if not most of their supplies. Not only was there a growth in dependency with regard to farm implements, but there was also a lack of ready capital which could be supplied only by the banks. Technology required the purchase of expensive equipment and large quantities of capital, thus plunging many farmers into long periods of indebtedness to the "loan sharks."

The first consequence of the industrialization of the society and the growing subordination of agriculture is found in the shifting relations between farmers and railroads. Mention has been made of the pleasure with which farmers welcomed the expansion of railroads into the hinterlands and how this pleasure soon turned to dismay with the discovery of discriminatory freight rates and other unfair practices. During the Civil War period, farmers, pros-

---

[8] Carl C. Taylor, "Significant Trends and Direction of Change," in Carl C. Taylor *et al.*, eds., *Rural Life in the United States* (New York: Alfred A. Knopf, Inc., 1949), p. 523.

pering with the increased demands of the war economy, invested heavily in railroad companies. However with the tumbling of farm prices which followed the reduced demand after the cessation of hostilities, the farmer found that the dividends expected from his investments did not materialize. Thus, while suspicious railroad activities were only a portion of the farmers' woes, the railroads became a symbol providing a scapegoat to simplify a complexity of causes of economic insecurity. The goal of economic success, which had been previously described as a function of individual initiative, was now dependent upon the utilization of means beyond the grasp of the farmer. All the thrift and initiative a reasonable man could expect a farmer to muster were to no avail without credit and transportation at a reasonable cost.

First Moves Toward Organization: The Grange

The conditions were ideal for the emergence of a formal organization with the goals of obtaining some measure of control over these new forces, and one was soon forthcoming. Since it was no longer adequate for the farmer to think solely in terms of his own success, some method of obtaining an estimate of his condition in relation to other economic groups was required. This was achieved to some degree by the utilization of the Patrons of Husbandry (the Grange) and the reformulation of its goals. The Grange was organized in 1867 on an educational and fraternal basis. With objectives similar to many of the local farm organizations, the early years revealed the Grange as an organization dedicated to improving and exhibiting farm crops, increasing production, and making farm life a little less dull by providing recreation and cultural diversions. Perhaps the farmer's sense of his decline in relative importance was psychologically compensated for by the elaborate and secret ritual. Although the founders of the Grange had visions of a huge membership extending to all regions of the country, the organization found little acceptance in rural America. Distressed farmers whose crops were their only source of income were not attracted. At the end of its first year the Grange could point to few members and subordinate units in only three states. However, the leaders of the Grange had sufficient vision—and employed sufficiently adept pro-

moters—to seize upon the growing unrest and turn the organization into a satisfactory instrument to express agrarian dissatisfaction by collective means. Why should the farmer study methods of
scientific production when corn was practically worthless because
of "middle men's profits and exorbitant prices of transportation?" [9]
One of the founders of the Grange, Oliver H. Kelley, caught the
temper of the times and gave his recognition to the necessity for
developing more meaningful goals when he described the reaction
to Grange membership drives: "The idea of discussions upon how
to raise crops is stale. They all want some plan of work to oppose
the *infernal monopolies.*" [10]

FROM QUIESCENCE TO ACTIVISM

The recognition that the promise of financial advantage was a
greater incentive to support the movement than intellectual better-
ment led the Grange to leap into the growing tide of pressure for
the regulation of railroad freight rates by states. This movement has
been labeled as the "Granger Movement," but this perhaps assigns
to the Grange more influence than it was actually able to exert.
Recent research has suggested that farmers were only one of several
participating groups and that the Grange played at most a "supporting role." Although the Grange did supply a portion of mass
support—usually by supporting the campaigns of sympathetic aspirants for public office—mercantile interest, particularly small
shippers, "set the movements rolling and generally directed their
course." [11] In Illinois, where the Constitution of 1870 provided for
railroad regulation as authorized by the General Assembly, Chicago merchants represented by the Chicago Board of Trade worked
carefully to persuade farmers of the necessity for regulation and
had achieved at least part of their objectives before the Grange had
created a formal organization.

Nevertheless, the Grange continued to thrive and reached an
estimated membership of 858,050 in 1875. With units in every state
except Rhode Island, the rejuvenated organization began programs

---

[9] DeWitt C. Wing, "Trends in National Farm Organizations," in *Farmers in
a Changing World,* 1940 Yearbook of Agriculture (Washington, D.C.: Government Printing Office, 1940), p. 946.

[10] *Ibid.*

[11] Lee Benson, *Merchants, Farmers, and Railroads* (Cambridge: Harvard
University Press, 1955), p. 25.

of economic cooperation to eliminate middle-man costs; Grange cooperative stores, shipping associations, and even insurance companies sprang up in quick succession. It was but a short step to more advanced schemes, such as the cooperative manufacturing of heavy equipment. But these more complicated schemes were doomed to failure and contributed to scepticism and disillusion among the members.

DISSIPATION AND DECLINE

Such schemes were typical of the groping, unsure methods of the Grange. With the exception of its foray into the struggle for regulation of railroads, most of its political activities were oriented toward the formation of various third parties along the general lines of protest against monopolies. Known variously as Farmers' parties, Anti-Monopoly parties, Independent or Reform parties, these movements hoped to attract a broad base of support from all disadvantaged segments of the population. These schemes eventually dissolved under the persistent pressure of the major parties and, coupled with the unsatisfactory results of many of the Grange's economic ventures, contributed to a decline in membership as spectacular as the flurry of support which it attracted during the high point of the railroad rate regulation effort. At its peak, the Grange probably had the sympathy, if not the active participation, of a large portion of the agricultural population, but by 1889 only about a hundred thousand had not deserted. It is hard to locate a "cause" for this sudden loss of favor among the segments of the population which had originally endorsed the Grange so enthusiastically. The dissipation of energy on projects which were unworkable certainly contributed to disillusionment. The economic advantages of the organization had been quite obviously overestimated. Further, when membership in a local Grange chapter meant that the farmer had invested in a cooperative enterprise, the failure of such an enterprise meant more than the mere sacrifice of membership dues. When the Grange stores began to fail, the personal possessions of the farmers were lost.

However, taking the Grange in the general context of the ebb and flow of agrarian movements of the time, this organization suffered a fate quite similar to that of comparable movements. Key calls our attention to the instability and high mortality rate in farm organizations until the twentieth century.[12] These movements achieved their greatest numerical strength during periods of economic distress and declined as soon as the effects of the immediate threat were alleviated. Farmers' organizations, much as the earlier labor unions, could only identify with a vaguely felt sense of deprivation and seek the fruitless avenues of third-party alliances to pursue their goals. When the Grange was at the height of flourishing expansion, it did in fact seek out labor leaders for the purpose of forming a society to protect the interests of the have-nots. While it would be belaboring the point to attempt to show direct connections between the Grange and the Knights of Labor, the formal declarations of the two organizations exhibit a substantial degree of similarity.

SHIFTS IN GEOGRAPHICAL NUCLEI

For a short span of time the Grange did locate and attack a specific "evil" and, with the guidance of mercantile groups, achieve some degree of success. However, after about 1880 the demands for business regulation became diffused and the specific identification of these demands with the Grange declined. The Grange was able to check its decline and begin an arduous rebuilding process so that today its membership is probably about the same as it was at its peak in 1875. However, these figures do not account for a shift in the geographical location of its clientele, which began simultaneously with the decline in total membership. The Grange had prospered vigorously in the Midwest, where crop specialization had progressed to the point at which most farmers were dependent upon meat or grain for their incomes. This dependence upon commodities tended to produce a consistent reaction to economic stress. Temporarily, this resulted in more unity than was possible as the Grange migrated toward the Atlantic coast where diversification was more pronounced. Not only did diversification ameliorate financial hazards, but it also reduced the possibility of a cohesive farmers' movement. Using New York as a test case, Benson points to other reasons why the Grange could not extend its influence. He notes that, in spite of rural isolation, "the impress of urban thought patterns, urban interests, and urban influences was much more per-

---

[12] V. O. Key, *Politics, Parties, and Pressure Groups* (New York: Thomas Y. Crowell Company, 1958), p. 35.

vasive in New York agrarian areas than in other regions." [13] Agriculture was clearly subordinate to other groups in its ability to influence the content of community decisions and was less receptive to the new militant posture of the Grange than were farmers in the West.

As farming continued on its path of commercialization and specialization, the Grange rose to a position of greater influence in New England, and gradually increased its power in New York, Ohio, Pennsylvania, and the Pacific West, while its prestige declined sharply in the areas of its greatest initial strength, the Midwest and South. The shifting of membership of the Grange (two-thirds of its members are now located in New England) was accompanied by a toning down of its early radical indignation. Reflecting the restrained conservatism of farmers more favorably situated to markets than their prairie counterparts, the Grange gradually came to adopt a position in favor of keeping the government as far from the agricultural segment of the economy as possible.

Frustration and Defeat

Following the decline of the Grange, there occurred a wave of organizations, each enjoying a brief surge of support and then fading away as others arose to take their place. Most spectacular of these movements was the Farmers' Alliance, which enjoyed the position of filling the vacuum created by the departure of the Grange. It absorbed several of its floundering competitors, spread from the South into the West, and became the largest organization of farmers ever to exist in this country, with nearly two million members. With a similar organization in the Northwest, the National Alliance, the farmers' movement began to repeat the history of agrarian discontent. During the upheavals of the 1880's and 1890's, the Farmers' Alliance devoted a great portion of its efforts to the creation of the Populist Party and to its electoral success. While this "Populist revolt" is indicative of unrest and of the need for organization to contribute to a more equitable distribution of economic rewards, it is also suggestive of the continuing frustration of organizations

---

[13] Benson, *op. cit.*, p. 87.

unable to operate within a framework of clearly articulated needs. Following its commitment to rely upon the electoral process, the Populist Party, and with it the Farmers' Alliance, gradually lost its identity in the stubborn stream of the two-party pattern.

THE FARMERS UNION AND THE PERPETUATION
OF POPULISM

While the Grange was declining and the Alliance was turning to the idea of a farmer-labor coalition, another organization arose which was able to achieve permanence in an area of rapid change. At the turn of the century, organizational activity had approached quiescence, even though the prosperity of the Spanish-American War was followed by depression. The first sign of renewed activity was the appearance of the Farmers Union, which began in Texas in 1902, spread to the cotton farmers in the South, and by 1915 had shifted to the wheat regions of the Midwest. In terms of clientele, the Farmers Union filled the vacuum left by the demise of the Alliance and the migration of the Grange eastward. Many of the leadership positions in the Farmers Union were filled by former Alliance leaders, who exhibited much of the exuberant radicalism of the earlier organization. This exuberance manifested itself in such union policies as a campaign to have its members destroy portions of their crops while holding the remainder for higher prices. The Farmers Union thus showed itself to be typical of the pattern in rural organizations. Like its predecessors, it took a flyer in party politics by supporting the Non-Partisan League, a movement in the Great Lakes and Plains regions undertaken in 1915. The goals of the Non-Partisan League were reminiscent of "grass roots" movements following the Civil War. It was a sectional protest against the impositions of middle men and the railroads, and exhibited particular frustrations with the supposed acquiescence of the party system. For a brief period, it was able to gain some control of the primary elections of both parties, but the combined hostility of the major parties forced the League into the posture of a third party, and by 1920 had eliminated it as a threat.

During this period of development, the Farmers Union underwent the expected pattern of growth and decline. After the initial enthusiasm had subsided, membership declined considerably, leaving the Farmers Union with a small nucleus in the Dakotas, Montana, and Oklahoma. However, there had been a continual controversy within the Farmers Union as to the techniques which would be most suitable for maximization of the organization's potential. Against the dominant belief in the old way of doing things, a faction arose which urged less emphasis on direct economic schemes and fewer flirtations with the established party system and more concern with utilization of the existing system to improve the power position of the agricultural segment.

Although this faction rose to power following World War I, its development must be considered in relation to dramatic changes in the economy which set the mold for the patterns of agrarian politics which exist today. As the nation solved some of the more pressing problems of postwar adjustment, it began to enjoy a period of remarkable prosperity. However, after a short boom in farm commodity and land prices had passed its peak in 1920, the prices of farm products began to drop downward at a rate even sharper than the rate of increase during the war. By 1921 agriculture found itself in a more unfavorable position than it had been at any prior time. The prices that farmers were required to pay for implements and other necessities reflected the prosperous years, but the purchasing power of farm products in terms of nonagricultural products was down to 63 per cent as compared to the prewar base.[14] Inflated farm incomes in the war years contributed to free spending in the rural areas, a tendency which continued through the first postwar years. Increased buying power was applied not only to automobiles and tractors, which were then coming into general use, but also to land and livestock. When the purchasing power of farm products began its decline, farmers were dismayed that the price of farm land could also go down. Consequently, many farms were carrying large debts contracted during the speculative boom of the preceding years. Further, costs of operation were increasing at a time when farmers were overextended and unable to borrow even the capital required for day-to-day farm management.

---

[14] Murray R. Benedict, *Farm Policies of the United States, 1790-1950* (New York: The Twentieth Century Fund, 1953), p. 174.

The American Farm Bureau Federation:
Pioneer and Innovator

Out of this morass of debt emerged a new farm organization, the American Farm Bureau Federation, whose membership reflected the increasing mechanization and specialization of farming. The Farmers Union and the Grange were clearly representative of particular regions and particular types of farming, and the new organization filled a regional gap by achieving its greatest strength in the cotton South and the corn-hog Midwest. Although the appearance of the Federation as a vigorous attempt to galvanize farmers into political action coincides with a low ebb in the economic fortunes of farmers, the origins of the organization are rooted in the period of relative prosperity immediately prior to the outbreak of war. The American Farm Bureau Federation was formally constituted in November, 1919, by a union of state farm bureaus. These farm bureaus had developed parallel to the educational extension movement in agriculture. In 1862, the Morrill Act ceded public lands to the states for the purpose of establishing colleges for the teaching of courses "related to agriculture and the mechanic arts." These "land grant" colleges, under authority of the Hatch Act of 1887, established experiment stations in order to further agricultural research, and, by the beginning of the twentieth century, were conducting off-campus educational programs. This idea of extension was carried on in various forms but generally involved "corn seed gospel trains" distributing demonstration materials and bringing college professors into the farm areas. However, there was usually a firm suspicion on the part of the colleges that such materials were soon discarded as the farmers reverted to the standard farming methods. The suggestion that a permanent extension worker—a county agent—who would operate as a permanent part of the community was therefore broached.

THE USES OF AGRICULTURAL EXTENSION

This suggestion came to fruition with the passage of the Smith-Lever Act in 1914. As administered, the Act offered federal grants to states which were willing to organize county farm bureaus for the purpose of cooperation with extension agents of the U.S. Department of Agriculture. The states were permitted to match federal grants with state, local, or private funds, and, as the states began to comply, the pattern developed of granting funds only to counties which had organized a specified number of farmers. Under these circumstances, the extension workers became diligent supporters of farm bureaus.[15] There is little doubt that the farm bureaus, as originally constituted, were to do no more than concern themselves with improving the educational and demonstration programs. However, the bureaus tended to attract the more prosperous farmers in an area—those able and willing to defray some of the expenses. As the number of bureaus increased, interaction on a statewide basis between local bureaus became widespread, and, as the economic position of agriculture began its decline, the farm bureau leaders explored ways and means of achieving effective expression of the agricultural point of view. The county agents, although pressured by state administrators to confine their activities to authorized programs, sympathized with the aspirations of their clients. At a meeting of the National Association of County Agricultural Agents in 1919, resolutions were adopted urging the formation of state and national farm bureau federations which would not only advise farmers on production operations but would also aid them in economic conflicts with other interests.

The movement toward a national organization was given further impetus by the increasing tendency toward the formation of state farm bureaus. One of the strongest of these was the New York Bureau which, with the cooperation of midwestern state bureaus, began a drive to form every county organization into a state bureau and eventually into a national federation. Finally, in 1919 a national convention was held in Chicago.[16] At this convention, there was a struggle for supremacy between two factions as to the type of program that a federation should undertake. The eastern and southern representatives proposed that the organization remain purely educational, but the midwestern group, made up of more prosperous farmers, wanted a policy oriented more toward the achieving of

---

[15] William J. Block, *The Separation of the Farm Bureau and the Extension Service*, Illinois Studies in the Social Sciences, Vol. 47 (Urbana: University of Illinois Press, 1960), 10.

[16] *Ibid.*

political success. This divergence of opinion paralleled a similar division in both the Grange and the Farmers Union, and, as was the case with these organizations, the more aggressive attitude won out.

The new organization, with the purpose of furthering the farmer's economic objectives through the influencing of public policy, was not "spontaneous" but rather had an evolutionary growth from well-financed, governmentally supported local units. The catastrophic decline in farm prices, which helped to make farmers aware of the need for union, combined with a firm groundwork of organizational structure laid by the agricultural extension program, enabled the American Farm Bureau Federation to become a more influential agricultural organization than its competitors and to revolutionize the scope of farm lobbying. The Farmers Union and the Grange were alarmed at the emergence of the Federation, especially since the privileged relationship between farm bureaus and extension agents had contributed to the strong position of the Federation at a time when the older organizations were not expanding.

THE FARM BLOC

The rise of the American Farm Bureau Federation seemed to galvanize the Farmers Union and the Grange into action. During hearings before the House Committee on Agriculture, held in 1920, other farm organizations used the "privileged relationship of county farm bureaus as the focal point of their attack." [17] State Grange and Farmers Union units charged that the Farm Bureau Federation was trying to "capture" portions of their membership, and material inserted into the record brought out the preference of extension workers to operate through the farm bureaus rather than attempting to use other organizations. At the same time, members of state Farmers Unions sought to have their state legislatures refuse to appropriate money for extension services.

The stimulus of a new and powerful rival, combined with the serious economic plight of the farmer, encouraged the Grange and Farmers Union to follow the example of the American Farm Bureau

---

[17] *Ibid.*, 11. This conflict resulted in the True-Howard Agreement of 1921 which provided that county agents should not be partial to any particular organization, but it allowed the Farm Bureau to continue to contribute funds. It proved to be virtually unenforceable.

Federation and establish Washington offices for the purpose of influencing legislation by whatever techniques seemed appropriate. The farm organizations had made a genuine break with the past. There was to be no effort to build a new party. Instead, efforts would be concentrated toward contributing to the election of sympathetic congressmen of both parties and the molding of these congressmen into a reliable bloc. The "Farm Bloc" was officially constituted on May 9, 1921, at the Washington office of the American Farm Bureau Federation. Representatives of the Farm Bureau Federation, the National Grange, the Farmers Union, and some lesser organizations had been meeting since April 11 with a group of government officials to discuss a possible legislative program to alleviate agrarian economic distress. The high priority of this meeting can be ascertained from the prominence of the officials in attendance: Henry Wallace (Secretary of Agriculture), Herbert Hoover (Secretary of Commerce), among others. The May 9 meeting was formally requested by Senator Kenyon of Iowa, but the idea for the meeting was obviously not inspired by him but by the farm organizations. Prior to the Washington meetings, Farm Bureau leaders in Iowa had held a caucus with the Iowa delegation and, with the help of Henry Wallace, secured a bipartisan pledge to support the needs of agriculture. It was natural, therefore, for Kenyon to call the final meeting. The purpose of the May 9 meeting was to establish ways of initiating and passing a legislative program desired by the agricultural organization. The group was composed of senators from the dominantly agricultural states from both parties. The Washington representative of the American Farm Bureau Federation, Gray Silver, assumed the responsibility of outlining to the meeting the things the farmers felt they needed, and Senator Kenyon was designated chairman of the continuing organization.[18]

Almost immediately following its formation, the farm bloc showed itself able to achieve a high degree of coordination. Its geographical support was wide, its leadership (spearheaded by the Farm Bureau) was aggressive, and its techniques a far cry from the

---

[18] For descriptions of these events in more detail *see* Arthur Capper, *The Agricultural Bloc* (New York: Harcourt, Brace & World, Inc., 1922) and Wesley McCune, *The Farm Bloc* (Garden City, N.Y.: Doubleday & Company, Inc., 1943).

fumbling efforts which prevailed at the turn of the century. McCune notes that the farm bloc "functioned through committee meetings, cloakroom intrigue, telephones in each congressman's office, button-holing in the stone cold lobbies of the Capitol, logrolling in the House of Representatives and Senate, and—occasionally—an old fashioned oration before the microphone of either house." [19] One great strength of the group was its ability to maintain an organizational structure which cut across party lines. It set up a committee system for evaluation of legislation simultaneously before the official committees of Congress and, in the Senate Committee on Agriculture, a majority of committee members were affiliated with the farm bloc. Thus it was quite possible that, in the event the program of the bloc conflicted with the program of the majority party in the Agriculture Committee, the former would prevail.

The influence of the farm bloc was apparent as the Senate sought to adjourn in the summer of 1921. Early adjournment was desired by the leaders of the majority party as a means of concentrating on tariff legislation, but such adjournment would have meant sacrificing legislation desired by the farm bloc. However, by agreement with leaders of both houses and the support of the President, five of the measures considered crucial by the farm bloc were passed and signed prior to adjournment. These laws dealt with the most immediate problem of the farm bloc: improving the balance between agriculture and the industrial segments of the economy. The Emergency Agricultural Credits Act and the Intermediate Credits Act (1923) reflected the firm opinion of the farm bloc that contraction of credit had been the major factor in the price decline of 1920 and 1921. After these initial successes, Congress was presented with a flood of bloc-sponsored legislation from 1921 until 1925, out of which emerged a dozen or so acts on cooperative marketing, agricultural tariffs, supervision of the packing industry, and grain futures regulation. However, after 1926 the influence of the bloc slumped badly. The next few years were characterized by internal squabbles, clumsy attempts at lobbying, and legislative defeats. Senator Kenyon, who built the bipartisan alliance, was appointed to a federal judgeship in February 1922, and was replaced by Arthur Capper of Kansas. Capper worked more closely with the

---

[19] McCune, *op. cit.*, p. 1.

established party leadership but the Republican administration continued to oppose the farm bloc as a threat to party discipline. Also, during its rapid mobilization period, the farm bloc had accomplished many of its original goals. It is difficult enough to maintain stability in formal organizations once initial objectives have been achieved. With such a hastily assembled marriage of convenience among diverse elements, the problem was even more severe. No formal effort to organize the bloc was made after 1923, and, although there continued to be a bipartisan group in both the House and Senate which supported agricultural legislation, the farm organizations gradually went their separate ways.

CHALLENGES TO THE DOMINANT PATTERN

Even while the farm bloc was functioning with maximum effect there was evidence of divisive influences within the agrarian community. The Nonpartisan League, although past its peak by 1922, institutionalized demands for a different direction of activity. During the war a loosely organized federation known as the Farmers' National War Council had begun operations. Made up of "Progressive State Granges," state Farmers Unions, and other groups dissatisfied with the believed complacency of the major organizations, the Farmers' National Council (as it was later called) advocated government ownership of natural resources and railroads. This program represented the Council's efforts to establish cooperation with labor organizations and to maintain a separate existence from the growing orthodoxy of the mainstream of the agrarian movement. Also active during the period of the farm bloc was the National Board of Farm Organizations, which took form under the leadership of the Farmers Union. The legislative program of this group was, however, not very different from that of the Grange and American Farm Bureau Federation. In spite of persistent bickering, the tendency of the National Board of Farm Organizations was to cooperate with the farm bloc. Finally, a rival bloc under the leadership of Senator La Follette's "Progressive Bloc" symbolized the anxiety of the more extreme farm groups to unite with labor to force the national government to consider more comprehensive relief measures. In December 1922, the Progressive Bloc launched an organization comparable to that of the farm bloc but with support coming more from the direction of the western farm states. Attempting to accumulate a broader base of political support, the Progressive Bloc "intended to supersede the Farm Bloc with an organized congressional force based more broadly upon the general welfare." [20] Regardless of these ambitions, the Progressive Bloc, not unlike the other potential challengers to dominant farm leadership, found it expedient to cooperate with the Farm Bloc. Unfortunately for the life of the Progressive Bloc, it drifted into a third party movement under the urging of the Conference for Progressive Political Action. This organization, an amalgam of various dissident elements with a farmer-labor leaning, had been active in establishing the congressional organization of the Progressive Bloc and was able to guide most of the components of the bloc into supporting La Follette for the Presidency in 1924.

Agrarian Organization at Low Ebb

Although the members of the Farm Bloc had resisted any move away from soliciting support from both major parties, its declining influence necessitated the exploration of other possible channels of influence. Even though the Farm Bloc was no longer more than an informal clique, the American Farm Bureau Federation continued to base its legislative techniques upon the hopes of a fusion of the agricultural sections. The efforts of the Farm Bureau Federation, and the frustrations it suffered as the Farm Bloc disintegrated, are best illustrated by the conflicts surrounding the McNary-Haugen bills—conflicts which typified the activity surrounding farm legislation during the second half of the decade. Five McNary-Haugen bills came under consideration from the years 1924 through 1928, but all were basically the same. The proposal was that a government export corporation be established with the authority to buy up specified agricultural commodities at a rate sufficient to bring the domestic price up to the "ratio-price" (that price which would bear the same relation to the general price level as the price of the commodity had borne to the general price level in the period prior to the war).

---

[20] James H. Shideler, *Farm Crisis, 1919-1923* (Berkeley: University of California Press, 1957), p. 238.

THE MC NARY-HAUGEN EPISODE

The main support for the plan developed in the wheat states but not in the corn belt where the American Farm Bureau Federation was strongest. Although the idea underlying the McNary-Haugen bills was presented to the Federation for its support as early as 1921, it was not until 1924 that it began active support. The reluctance of the Federation was partially because of internal cleavages which had been present in the organization from its inception. Prior to the formation of the Farm Bloc, the American Farm Bureau Federation had begun a vigorous program of encouraging cooperative marketing, based upon its preference for self-help over long-term government financing. Support for this idea was particularly strong in the South where the Federation was less effectively organized and desirous of expanding its control. Moreover, it appeared that those sections most clearly committed to cooperative marketing were also firmly opposed to McNary-Haugenism. A strong center of opposition was built around the nucleus of the Illinois Farm Bureau, which, while not particularly enthusiastic about plans involving government managed export of farm surpluses, was extremely hostile to a cooperative emphasis, perhaps recalling the debacle of the early Granger schemes.[21] The Farm Bureau was ripped asunder during this controversy and was required to devote most of its energies toward the solution of the internal conflict.

The Farm Bureau continued to support cooperative marketing for a brief period. Its membership was in a period of decline and its legislative successes had not materially improved the economic position of the farmer. While the paying membership of the Farm Bureau declined from 967,279 in November 1921 to 363,481 in December 1922, the National Council of Farmer Cooperative Marketing Associations had suddenly ridden the waves of discontent to become, in 1922, the largest of the farm organizations. The Farm Bureau was drifting while its members feuded. In 1923, however, the strength of the anti-cooperative faction appeared on the upswing. At the convention of that year the opposing views erupted into open conflict from which the opponents of cooperatives

---

[21] Grant McConnell, *The Decline of Agrarian Democracy* (Berkeley: University of California Press, 1959), pp. 59-61.

emerged as the stronger. It was clear that cooperative marketing would assume a subordinate place in the Federation scheme of things which would treat such ventures as "fads." Edward A. O'Neal of Alabama, who survived these struggles as a leader of the anti-cooperative faction, gained in personal influence and later became president of the organization.

At the time the Federation was beating down its cooperative faction, the movement for the McNary-Haugen bill was reaching a peak. The Farm Bureau was still losing membership and had explicit plans for farm relief. It was in this situation that the decision in favor of concentrating upon political action was made; the McNary-Haugen bill was the most readily available choice. Not surprisingly, the Federation's support of the first McNary-Haugen bill was less than enthusiastic. The bill was defeated in the House by a southern-eastern coalition, which suggested not only that the Farm Bloc was not functioning but also that the Federation still was unable to satisfy its southern members who were suspicious of the export-dumping features of the plan. However, the election of Sam Thompson of Illinois as president in 1925 signaled the beginning of the active support of the Federation. In the meantime, a second and third set of McNary-Haugen bills failed to pass. Finally, in 1927 a fourth effort was successful but was vetoed by President Coolidge; a fifth met the same fate in 1928.

THE RELUCTANT COMMITMENT TO PARTISANSHIP

Faced with this continuous string of defeats, the forces pressing for the McNary-Haugen idea, including the American Farm Bureau Federation, the Grange, and the Farmers Union, tried a direct approach to the political parties. Unsuccessful with the Republicans, who nominated Herbert Hoover, the McNary-Haugen advocates won a moderately favorable plank in the 1928 Democratic platform. The election of the Republican candidate therefore left the American Farm Bureau Federation in the very position which it had sought to avoid during its management of the Farm Bloc. Grant McConnell calls attention to the unsatisfactory consequences of this course of action: "In supporting a party policy—a policy which was neither its own work nor particularly satisfactory in substance—the Farm Bureau was in effect acknowledging its own weakness as a pressure group. This was a confession that the making of policy yet remained a party matter. It was a position which the leadership of the Farm Bureau did not relish." [22]

The position of the farm organizations during the early years of the depression was unfavorable. The hardships of the depression were perhaps less of a shock since, while the remainder of the nation prospered during the 1920's, the farmers had suffered their own private slump. Still, these organizations were compromised by the necessity of trying to do what they could with the Hoover administration—an administration from which little could be expected. In terms of specific programs, farm leaders continued to stress the need for direct aid to agriculture and were noticeably aloof toward the more general efforts of the administration to restore urban prosperity. Prior to the depression, farm organizations habitually maintained that agriculture was the nation's foremost industry and that the only logical approach to national policy must begin with the assumption that agriculture should be made profitable. Even though urban business had prospered while agriculture was in a depression, the old dogma continued to exact loyalty. During the Hoover administration, the position of farm groups had crystallized into rigid protectionism. Most of the farm organizations gave increasing support to protective tariffs, as illustrated in their demands that the Philippine Islands become independent so that domestic agriculture might be protected against products coming from that area.

It is not surprising, given these attitudes, that the Hoover administration's farm program was not well received. The Agricultural Marketing Act of 1929 suggested no concession to the demands for direct relief as incorporated in the McNary-Haugen bills. The Act created the Federal Farm Board whose primary function was to make loans to cooperatives. Since the American Farm Bureau Federation had recently resolved its internal dispute in favor of deemphasizing cooperative marketing, it naturally regarded the Federal Farm Board as impotent. In the Farmers Union, a similar conflict between legislative emphasis and cooperative marketing had been resolved in favor of the former in 1929. This organization, like the Farm Bureau, could only regard the Federal Farm Board as an unsatisfactory substitute. Moreover, during the early 1930's the survival of both organizations was threatened. Persistent declines

---

[22] *Ibid.*, p. 64.

in membership reflected the failure of the organizations to accomplish their aims through legislation.

This drift toward apathy was arrested to some extent by the new leadership of the Farm Bureau. The organization had, with considerable reluctance, supported the Federal Farm Board. In 1931 President Hoover requested that Farm Bureau President Sam Thompson join the Board—a request which could hardly be ignored since it meant recognition of the Farm Bureau as a legitimate spokesman for agriculture, and, it was hoped that such recognition would provide a crutch for the sagging prestige of the organization. This appointment cleared the way for Edward O'Neal to become president. With O'Neal of Alabama as president and Charles Hearst of Iowa elected vice president, the Farm Bureau hoped to forge a lasting alliance between the southern and midwestern segments of the organization.

The Farm Bureau and the New Deal

However, O'Neal's first step was to thrust the Farm Bureau into leading a unity drive among the major farm organizations. The outgrowth of these efforts was a series of meetings held in 1931 and, finally, a legislative program agreed to by the Farm Bureau, Grange, and Farmers Union. These legislative recommendations were hardly comprehensive. If anything, their vagueness reflected the glaring cleavages which would militate against the existence of a pervasive organization within the agricultural community. The Agricultural Marketing Act was to be continued, but amended to include some plan that "will make it effective in controlling surpluses. . . ."[23] Thus the program was noncommittal on the essential question of raising farm prices.

The Farm Bureau and the Farmers Union were, at best, uneasy partners in the alliance. However, the Farm Bureau was able to place itself at the head of what appeared to be a resurgent movement and to profit by this leverage. The National Agricultural Conference, as the union was called, appeared at the critical time of the 1932 elections. The Farm Bureau was anxious to identify itself in such a way that its voice would be heard when the new ad-

---

[23] Benedict, *op. cit.*, p. 271.

ministration began, and, although it did not openly endorse Roosevelt, there was little doubt about its sympathies. O'Neal apparently
did not regard the events of 1928 as a deterrent to open cooperation
with a major party. After the election of Roosevelt, the Farm
Bureau could look with pride upon the success of its venture for the
new administration appeared ready to award the organization a
place of leadership. McConnell tells us that "Roosevelt sent Mor-
ganthau, Tugwell, and W. I. Myers as his representatives to the
conference of the Farm Bureau in December 1932. Here was assurance that the 'voice of agriculture' would have some kind of a
say in measures to come." [24] Apparently, Roosevelt's choice of
Henry Wallace as Secretary of Agriculture was approved by the
Farm Bureau and cooperation between the Department of Agriculture and the Farm Bureau leadership was close until the early
1940's. Significantly, the "united front" had ceased to exist by 1934
but the Farm Bureau was again on the upswing with membership
rising and the treasury growing.

THE STRATIFICATION OF AGRICULTURE

Students of agrarian politics, including, but not limited to, its
official historian O. M. Kile, have maintained that the Farm Bureau
is the most powerful of the three major farm organizations.[25] If this
is true—and the author can find little evidence to dispute the claim
—then it is apparent that the Farm Bureau attained its influential
position during the New Deal. As the leader of the agricultural
lobby, the Farm Bureau institutionalizes important shifts in the
structure of the farm population and mirrors a change in the direction of group goals. For the first time since the inception of agricultural organizations, farm groups were working in opposition to
each other. The agricultural movement began with specialization
and commercialization but nevertheless exhibited consistency in
attitude arising from a socially homogeneous agricultural community. Farm tenancy was moderate in the greater part of the
period from the Civil War to World War I. Also, the crystallization
of agriculture into distinct crop areas and agricultural belts was not

[24] McConnell, *op. cit.*, p. 70.
[25] O. M. Kile, *The Farm Bureau Movement* (New York: The Macmillan
Company, 1921). *See also* Kile, *The Farm Bureau Through Three Decades*
(Baltimore: The Waverly Press, 1948).

completed until after the turn of the century. More significant is the absence of differentiation in agriculture with respect to income and the production of farm products. As late as 1899, agricultural income was relatively evenly distributed. Eighty per cent of the farmers earned $1,000 or less and this 80 per cent produced nearly one-half of the commercial value of farm products. Large farms (2.7 per cent with incomes over $2,500) produced only 19.9 per cent of the total value of farm products.[26] The populistic spirit which pervaded the farmer agitation then was that of the "underdog." The wrath of the farmer was directed toward bankers, big business, and "Wall Street." Conversely, the farmers' movements of the time extended a sympathetic hand to labor movements, since both expressed hostility toward the same adversary.

During the Farm Bureau's period of ascendancy, stratification of agriculture had become advanced. In place of a homogeneity of poverty, farmers could be differentiated into low, medium, and high income groups. In 1929, almost 18 per cent earned $2,000 or more while 54 per cent earned $1,000 or less. Between these two extremes a "middle income" group of 28 per cent earned between $1,000 and $2,000. Stratification was even more obvious in the production of commercial farm products. Farms reporting incomes of $1,000 or less (about half) produced only one-tenth of the value of commercial farm products. The large farms, those with incomes of $2,500 or more (one-fifth), produced more than three-fifths of the value of commercial farm products.[27] Later census reports reveal the continuation of this trend toward stratification.

ORGANIZATIONAL MEMBERSHIP

The membership and policies of the Farm Bureau indicate quite clearly that it is primarily the representative of the upper strata of the farm population. In contrast to the sympathy of the earlier movements toward labor, the Farm Bureau's more prosperous

---

[26] U.S. Bureau of the Census, *Sixteenth Census of the United States,* 1940 (Washington, D.C.: Government Printing Office, 1943). *Agriculture,* III, 874.

[27] *Ibid.,* 912; *Ibid., Analysis of Specified Farm Characteristics for Farms Classified by Total Value of Products,* p. 30. *See also* Evan Z. Vogt, Jr., "Social Stratification in the Rural Midwest: A Structural Analysis," *Rural Sociology,* XII (Dec. 1947), 364-375. Arthur J. Vidich and Joseph Bensman show the effects of rural stratification on local and national politics in *Small Town in Mass Society* (Garden City, N.Y.: Doubleday & Company, 1960).

membership identified with the values of business and the urban and small-town middle class. This orientation was immediately evident in the boasts of the Farm Bureau that it helped to keep down "unrest" among the farmers in the 1920's and that it avoided any policy which would "align organized farmers with the radicals of other organizations." One of the early struggles in the Farm Bureau involved a decision on whether the organization should hold to the original purposes of the county farm bureaus—education for the average farmer—or whether the organization should operate as a business and legislative agency for larger farmers. The latter view won out and overt support from business groups signaled a major alteration in the course of farm politics. In the mid-1930's O'Neal's solicitation of the South paid off in a rapid increase of Farm Bureau membership among large southern planters which, combined with the nucleus of the Midwest, assured the Farm Bureau that the "farmer in a business suit" would serve as the object of its representative efforts.[28]

While the image of the Farm Bureau is one of prosperity, it would be a mistake to assume that its membership does not include some low and medium income farmers. Some tenants and share-croppers are members through the auspices of landlords or employers, especially in the South. This membership would not materially affect the structure of power. One good way to ascertain levels of membership is to compare the income of farmers in strong Farm Bureau states with that of farmers in strong Farmers Union states since it is commonly assumed that the latter organization represents the more impoverished classes. To begin, we must recall the fact that organizational membership is lower in rural than in urban areas, and also that organizational membership is more pronounced in the higher economic strata of the rural areas. Therefore, organized farmers, irrespective of the particular association to which they belong, will have a higher social and economic status than unorganized farmers. Hence both the Farm Bureau and Farmers Union membership have greater gross farm income, greater family income, more formal education, and operate larger farms than the

---

[28] John Davis and Kenneth Hinshaw, *Farmer in a Business Suit* (New York: Simon and Schuster, Inc., 1957). *See also* Wayne C. Rohrer, "Conservatism-Liberalism and the Farm Organizations," *Rural Sociology,* XXVII (June 1957), 163-166.

unorganized portions of the farm populations. Indeed, a study of organized farmers in Oklahoma revealed that, although Farm Bureau members had a somewhat higher socio-economic status than Farmers Union members, the differences were not statistically significant and that the "hypothesis that Farm Bureau members represent a considerably more privileged position within agriculture than Farmers Union members is not substantiated by the data." [29]

Yet this evidence was gathered in a single state which is usually considered a stronghold of the Farmers Union. To get a more accurate picture, let us take a group of "typical" Farm Bureau states —Indiana, Illinois, Iowa, and Minnesota—and compare income patterns with "typical" Farmers Union states—North and South Dakota, Nebraska, and Kansas. The Farmers Union group of states contains a larger proportion of low-income farmers and a much smaller proportion of well-to-do farmers than does the Farm Bureau group. Under these circumstances it is not altogether surprising that we find an informal alliance between the Farm Bureau and major business groups. While the alliance is no more than an informal agreement and fluctuates considerably in its intensity, there is a substantial meeting of the minds between Farm Bureau leadership and that of the National Association of Manufacturers and the Chamber of Commerce. Although the Farm Bureau-business accord declined to some extent during the 1930's, it became quite distinct in the 1940's and has continued to operate since then. Particularly evident is the cooperation between the Farm Bureau, the National Association of Manufacturers, the Chamber of Commerce, and occasionally the Grange on matters of the tariff, wage control, and price control. It is frequently reported that the legislative director of the Farm Bureau spends as much time in the offices of the Chamber of Commerce as he does in his own. More useful as an index of the attitudes reflected by the Farm Bureau is that the American Federation of Labor, which had enjoyed moderately sympathetic understanding from agriculture, broke off friendly relations with the Grange and Farm Bureau in 1951. We might also mention that state right to work laws have usually been passed in legislatures more conspicuously dominated by rural areas and that

---

[29] Robert A. Rohwer, "Organized Farmers in Oklahoma," *Rural Sociology,* XVII (Mar. 1952), 46.

the American Farm Bureau Federation filed a brief with the United
States Supreme Court in 1956 supporting these laws.[30]

THE FARM BUREAU AS LEADER
OF THE AGRICULTURAL LOBBY

During the New Deal, the influence of the Farm Bureau increased considerably due to its ability to establish and maintain
close relationships in the administration of the Agricultural Adjustment Administration. It was also establishing itself as leader of a re-
aligned agricultural bloc that strongly mirrored the stratification
of farmers by income, in addition to commodity. Particularly significant was an informal partnership with the Grange, whose greatest membership was among dairy, truck, and fruit farmers of New
England and the Pacific West Coast. The Grange, with a reputation
for longevity, was a logical partner for the more politically oriented
Farm Bureau. While emphasizing the ritualistic and fraternal aspects
of organization as a technique for survival, the Grange was nevertheless possessed of a sizable membership, which, by means of
agreements between association leaders, added influence to the
activities of the Farm Bureau. In addition, the National Council of
Farmer Cooperatives and the National Cooperative Milk Producers
Federation found frequent ideological identification with the Farm
Bureau.

The "big four," as this bloc was called, operated through the
Farm Bureau as coordinator of legislative activities while the Farmers Union was unable to function in alliance with other agricultural
organizations. During the 1930's, the position of the Farmers Union
as "wallflower" was unmistakable.

THE AGRICULTURAL ADJUSTMENT ADMINISTRATION

The weighting of influence in the farm lobby is well illustrated by
the operation of the Agricultural Adjustment Administration. A bill
containing the essentials of the Agricultural Adjustment Act was considered by Congress in 1932 but failed to pass. At this point, the
agricultural unity movement had not disintegrated and the Farm
Bureau's O'Neal testified as a representative of the Grange and

---

[30] Lowry Nelson, "Rural Life in a Mass-Industrial Society," *Rural Sociology*,
XXII (Mar. 1957), 20-30.

Farmers Union in addition to his own organization. However, by the time of the passage of the Act in May 1933, the Farmers Union had swung into a position of opposition. The basic idea of the Act was production control. Production was to be restricted on the basis of a quota system drawn from previous uses of acreage. Reduction of acreage was to be accomplished by voluntary agreements with farmers, and a subsidy program financed by a processing tax was to provide sufficient inducement to encourage farmers to enter agreements. It will be recalled that production control was one of the earlier schemes of the Farmers Union but was too expansive an effort to be successfully performed by a private organization. The Grange and Farm Bureau had never been unusually concerned with reduction of acreage but did come to accept the idea. The Farmers Union, on the other hand, had lost its faith in production control and was anxious that any relief program include the idea of "cost of production." Cost of production would be figured on the basis of the current crop year (which would work to the advantage of the smaller farmer) and prices would include operation costs, interest on loans, medical and school expenses, plus a surplus payment sufficient to establish living conditions equal to the "American standard of living."

The Farmers Union tried vainly to get cost of production written into the Agricultural Adjustment Act but was opposed by the Farm Bureau. The Farm Bureau recognized that such a plan would benefit high cost producers whereas the larger farms concentrated on low production costs. The argument, so typical of the ideals of the Farm Bureau, was that cost of production would "penalize efficiency." The Farm Bureau position was accepted in the drafting of the legislation and the Farmers Union was eventually forced to abandon cost of production as a major portion of its program. When the first Agricultural Adjustment Act was invalidated by the Supreme Court on the basis of its processing tax, the Farmers Union again sought cost of production. However, the Agricultural Adjustment Act of 1938 went even further away from an emphasis on production. Although price maintenance was stressed more than in the first act, this maintenance was to be achieved by controlling surpluses rather than production. Accepting defeat with respect to the guiding principles of the Agricultural Adjustment Administration, the Farmers Union then tried to have limits set on the size of large payments while an increase was sought in the amount of minimum payments for acreage reduction to buttress the position of the small farmer. Once again, the influence of the Farm Bureau proved insurmountable.

In addition to the advantages which accrued to the Farm Bureau by reason of the policy of the Agricultural Adjustment Administration, a tightly drawn web between the administrative structure of the government agency and that of the private association produced a coalition of monopolistic proportions. The source of the Farm Bureau foothold in administering the Agricultural Adjustment Act lay in its long standing affiliation with the Extension Service. The county farmers association, having the responsibility of assigning quotas and insuring compliance was a basic part of the AAA program. Since the Extension Service was already operating in the field, it was the logical agency to administer the program. While the AAA machinery was being established, the Farm Bureau, working through the Extension Service, actually supervised the establishment of local units. Farm Bureau representatives performed the task of delivering benefit checks to farmers, which symbolized the organization as a dispenser of the public largess and, on occasion, deducted organizational dues before final transmittal. After the initial organizational phase of the AAA, the Farm Bureau-Extension administration continued to be the center of reliance for the farmer. The parent organization confined its operation to central review in Washington.[31]

THE FARMERS UNION AS "POOR RELATION"

The Farm Bureau had made the AAA "its own in administration as well as in policy," an achievement which paid ample dividends in steadily rising membership during the New Deal.[32] During this period the Grange was not as enthusiastic in support of the AAA but was content to endorse it as "sound." The Farmers Union, on the other hand, suffered considerably and was weakened by internal cleavages at the very time that the Farm Bureau was cementing its regional variations into a cohesive body. As carrier of the old Populist traditions, the Farmers Union was clearly a poor relation of the dominant farm groups. Its radical fringe, formed into the

[31] McCune, *op. cit.*, p. 166.
[32] McConnell, *op. cit.*, p. 75.

Farm Holiday Association, advocated violent and revolutionary solutions to farm problems and, in 1933, organized a campaign to cut
off public support for the Extension agents and to persuade Farm
Bureau members to resign. While the Farm Holiday Association
lasted only a few years, its supporting clientele continued to reduce
the potential influence of the Farmers Union. Indeed, the leadership of the Farmers Union seemed unwilling to solve the conflict,
perhaps reflecting the prevalent image of the organization. However, the election of James Patton as president in 1940 signaled the
end of the influence of the Farm Holiday element much as O'Neal's
election as president of the Farm Bureau had indicated the new
direction of that organization. During Roosevelt's third term, relations between the Farmers Union and the White House became
cordial, although access to the Department of Agriculture was not
improved. The position of the Farmers Union within the Department of Agriculture improved substantially, primarily because it
was found that larger farmers were producing at near capacity rates
and, with the increased market during war, other sources of production were needed. Accordingly, the AAA began to regard the Farmers Union as a possible agent to enlist broader support for the war
production program since the Union had a monopoly in the organization of small farmers.

Emerging Patterns

During the war the economic interests of the divergent segments
of the farm population tended to coalesce, but there were schisms
beneath the surface of policy which were only temporarily ob-
scured. The Farmers Union, for example, had condemned the 52
to 75 per cent of parity loan provision of the Agricultural Adjustment Act of 1938 and maintained that payments should equal the
difference between market price and parity whatever the percentage. The Farm Bureau, while preferring commodity support loans
to direct subsidy, indirectly contributed to the enhancement of
Farmers Union objectives. Thus, when the Emergency Price Control Bill was being considered in 1942, farm pressures were able to
secure an amendment forbidding the imposition of ceilings on
specified farm commodities below 110 per cent of parity. In addi-

tion, the Farm Bureau supported the Bankhead Commodity Loan Act of 1941 which required loans for basic commodities at 85 per cent of parity and the Steagall Amendment to the Stabilization Act of 1942 requiring loans at 90 per cent of parity for two years after the war had ended.

ALTERATIONS IN OFFICIAL SUPPORT

While the policy successes of the Farm Bureau during the war were reminiscent of the old farm bloc of the 1920's in that the major farm organizations agreed on basic objectives, the Farm Bureau itself was drifting into a hostile position in its relations with the Department of Agriculture. There had already been one clash between the Farm Bureau and President Roosevelt over the Emergency Price Control Bill of 1942. Roosevelt and the Department of Agriculture wanted 100 per cent of parity but the Farm Bureau's demands for 110 per cent prevailed. Even more indicative of an alteration in the pattern of official support for the Farm Bureau was the growing independence of the Agricultural Adjustment Administration. A gradual separation of the AAA from the Farm Bureau-dominated Extension Service had occurred. The AAA was developing its own regional offices and AAA employees with Extension Service backgrounds were being replaced. Partially as a consequence of its release from Farm Bureau control, the AAA fell more in line with the New Deal idea of helping smaller farmers, a policy which had never been implemented to any considerable degree. Specifically, the AAA sought to cooperate with farmers organized through Farm Security Administration committees, soil conservation district committees, and other mechanisms constituting a clear threat to the Farm Bureau's heretofore near-perfect monopoly of information and benefit dissemination. In 1943 and 1944 the AAA-Farm Bureau conflict erupted into open warfare with the result that AAA appropriations were severely cut in 1944 and it was forbidden to provide technical information to farmers.

While the goal of the Farm Bureau in its struggle with the AAA was clearly the reduction of the influence of any rival with the Extension Service, it did have the support of the Grange and Farmers Union against efforts by the Secretary of Agriculture to reduce the independence of the AAA by means of departmental reorganization. On the other hand, the Farmers Union again left the union over the question of the Farm Security Administration. Shortly after the passage of the Bankhead-Jones Farm Tenant Act of 1937 the Secretary of Agriculture created the Farm Security Administration to administer a program of helping underprivileged farmers—those who were left at the bottom of the economic scale when agriculture became commercialized. Since AAA loans were distributed in proportion to output, only a small portion of these benefits reached the marginal or family farms, while fully half of the total payments were extended to the commercial farmers least in need of assistance. Due to the commitment to support of the poorer farmers, the bulk of FSA clients were tenants and sharecroppers of the South. However, the program was within the psychological orbit of the Farmers Union which quickly became an FSA ally, in truth the lone supporter. Actually the FSA came to be regarded as the marginal farmer's own Department of Agriculture. Most of the work of the FSA involved camps for migrants, rehabilitation loans, tenant purchase loans, educational programs to improve housing, and the development of medical care.

This type of program coincided with the Farmers Union idea of "social parity," a label loosely applied to any scheme to secure for the rural population the same opportunities assured the urban populations. On the other hand, the FSA was viewed as a threat by the Farm Bureau and, to a lesser extent, by the Grange. The FSA cooperative programs, for example, were entirely consumer cooperatives or joint purchasing associations. The Farm Bureau, even during its period of support for cooperatives, had always envisoned producer associations. Consequently, the Farm Bureau denounced the FSA cooperatives as collectivist schemes not unlike the Soviet system, especially when merchants began to lose business. Commercial farmers and southern landlords naturally denounced measures designed to increase the independence of tenants, which, in the case of the South, could be viewed as a challenge to the sharecropping system and hence white supremacy.

This was indeed a radical departure from the main trends in agrarian politics and suggested a decline in the influence of the Farm Bureau in the operations of the Department of Agriculture. The threat to its position was made more meaningful by the fact that FSA personnel were recruited from beyond the Extension-land grant college orbit and were usually more infused with "New Deal-

ism" than the traditional Department of Agriculture employee. Just
as the Farm Bureau prospered through its connection with the Extension Service, the Farmers Union gave evidence of developing a
similar relationship with the FSA. The Farm Bureau, as spearhead
for commercial farmers, began an intense campaign first to transfer
most FSA functions to the Extension Service and eventually to destroy the FSA. The issue of large versus small farms, reflecting the
social and economic stratification of the agricultural community in
a graphic manner, was brought to a head and the Farm Bureau
again proved to be the most powerful voice. It turned to a traditional source of support, the Congressmen from the farm bloc areas
who were still in control of the agricultural committees. As a result,
the FSA suffered such harassment that it was finally liquidated.[33]

The FSA incident showed that there was no effective counter-
pressure to the commercial farmers. It meant that the Farm Bureau
could well defend its boast that any plan "opposed by the AFBF
is not likely to get far." [34] More immediately, the Farm Bureau was
finding it difficult if not impossible to cooperate with Democratic
administrations and more valuable to seek friends in the ranks of
the Republicans. The pattern of partisanship which was set during
this struggle remains intact. This pattern became cemented during
the postwar years when it became necessary to develop a long-
range agricultural policy. Now the battleground shifted to the
problem of flexible versus rigid price supports but the social bases
of support and opposition remained the same. The short-lived postwar price rise divided the agricultural community into two groups:
one favoring rigid supports at the cost of other controls (cotton and
tobacco farmers in the South and western wheat farmers); the
other, a coalition of midwestern corn and hog farmers and farmers
of the northeast and west coast, whose production costs would be
raised by high supports, advocating the flexible plan. This division
cut across organizational lines to some extent. While the Farmers
Union entirely embraced the high support farmers and the Grange's
membership was drawn from the flexible support areas, the Farm

---

[33] The Farmers Home Administration Act of 1946 abolished the FSA and
provided for the liquidation of all labor supply centers and resettlement and
rehabilitation projects. Land purchasing and land leasing associations were
also abolished.

[34] Kile, *The Farm Bureau Through Three Decades* (Baltimore: The Waverly
Press, 1948), p. 389.

Bureau with its delicate sectional balance contained adherents of both positions. However, the Farm Bureau split, while serious, was resolved quickly in favor of the midwestern farmers, whose comfortable income persuaded them that there was much to be gained from unrestricted production.

THE BRANNAN PLAN

Once the Farm Bureau had settled its squabble, the division was clear: the Farm Bureau, Grange, and most Republican congressmen would back flexible supports while the Farmers Union and the congressional Democrats would press for rigid supports. In 1948, the Republican-controlled Eightieth Congress passed the Hope-Aiken Act which allowed price supports to drop as low as 60 per cent of parity, and the Farm Bureau leadership played a major role in securing passage. However, the Democratic Secretary of Agriculture, Charles F. Brannan, developed his "Brannan Plan" as an alternative to the Farm Bureau position. It is significant, not only that the Brannan Plan was highly pleasing to the Farmers Union, but also that the plan was formulated without consultation with the Farm Bureau, a practice that had become almost unwritten law. Without a technical examination of the plan, one can still ascertain that it contemplated extremely high levels of payment. Further, payments were to be made directly to farmers rather than by maintenance of prices at the market. Finally, there was to be a limit on the size of farm that would be eligible to receive support for total output. The Brannan Plan was, because of its egalitarian aspects, the antithesis of Farm Bureau goals and stimulated the most sustained attack on the Department of Agriculture in the history of the organization. With the support of the Grange, the National Council of Farmer Cooperatives, and the remainder of the commodity groups, the Farm Bureau had no trouble in turning back the Department of Agriculture-Farmers Union assault. The balance of power could not be altered.

FROM UTOPIA TO IDEOLOGY

The pattern of agrarian politics has remained basically the same since the Farm Bureau became identified as a large-farmer spokesman. When the Republicans won the 1952 Presidential election, the Farm Bureau resumed cordial relations. Eisenhower's Secretary of

Agriculture, Ezra Taft Benson, ably represented the Farm Bureau position that regulation should be kept to a minimum. Cooperation was improved by the recruiting of Farm Bureau officers into the Department of Agriculture as, for example, vice president Romeo Short who served for a time as Assistant Secretary of Agriculture. The Grange also benefited from the Republican administration by way of appointments, while the Farmers Union, intimately connected with the Department of Agriculture under Brannan, was left in the role of outsider. Whereas the Brannan Department had been friendly toward labor—indeed the Brannan plan was certainly designed to unite farmers and labor by supporting farm prices while allowing food prices to find their natural level—the Benson Department was decidedly hostile to labor and oriented toward the business point of view. In exchange, the Farm Bureau and the Grange defended Benson when his policies were challenged by Democratic Congresses.[35] The situation reverted to the pre-Benson era with the election of John Kennedy and the appointment of Orville Freeman, with Farmers Union endorsement, as Secretary of Agriculture. Freeman's plan for marketing quotas and farmer committees appointed by the Secretary seemed suggestive of the philosophy behind the Brannan plan and was quickly condemned by the Farm Bureau and Grange with the Farmers Union again playing the dissenting role.

With the major cleavages in agriculture now channeled in partisan directions, the position of the Farm Bureau as the source of policy has been challenged but not overcome. The dominant farm spokesmen have veered toward the ideological perspectives of the industrialism they originally sought to combat and the utopian values of dissident elements are overshadowed.[36] If there is to be a change, it will have to come from those who control the expression of agrarian beliefs. The Farm Bureau, with 1.6 million members, and the Grange, with 789,000 members, perform this func-

---

[35] Charles M. Hardin, "The Republican Department of Agriculture—a Political Interpretation," *Journal of Farm Economics*, XXXVI (May 1954), 210-227.

[36] Karl Mannheim defines an ideological perspective as one which is concerned with the maintenance of the *status quo* because it has become interest bound to that situation. A utopian perspective describes the attitudes of a group whose interest is with the breaking of the prevailing order. *See* Mannheim, *Ideology and Utopia* (New York: Harcourt, Brace & World, Inc., 1936), pp. 36, 51.

tion. Although the dominant organizations have had to cope with internal dissension, the conservatism of the leaders has remained intact. Most recently, the midwestern sections of the Farm Bureau have expressed dissatisfaction with official policy. The National Farm Organization was created in 1955, with most of its strength in Missouri and Iowa (a traditional Farm Bureau state) as an open challenge to prevailing ideology; and the Illinois Agricultural Association, the largest Farm Bureau affiliate, passed a resolution in favor of compulsory acreage retirement although the parent organization was able to keep the resolution from being adopted at the annual convention.[37] There have been rumblings of discontent before and there will be more in the future, but the way in which these tensions are resolved will surely provide the key to understanding the vagaries of agrarian politics.

[37] Lauren K. Soth, "Farm Policy, Foreign Policy, and Farm Opinion," *Annals of the American Academy of Political and Social Science* (Sept. 1960), pp. 103-109.

VII

Group Politics

in a

Mass Society

America has been called a "mass society," a term generally used to describe an erosion of primary identifications. Daniel Bell's summary of the concept of mass society illustrates why this is so. He writes:

> The revolutions in transport and communications have brought men into closer contact with each other and bound them in new ways; the division of labor has made them more interdependent; tremors in one part of society affect all others. Despite this interdependence, however, individuals have grown more estranged from one another. The old primary group ties of family and local community have been shattered; ancient parochial faiths are questioned; few unifying values have taken their place.[1]

If this is the case, it follows that the people of a mass society will be differentiated on the basis of a great many characteristics. In addition to occupation, which has been discussed in the preceding

---

[1] Daniel Bell, *The End of Ideology* (New York: The Crowell-Collier Publishing Co., 1961), p. 21.

chapters, we would expect a mass society to include subgroups based on social class, political affiliation, race, nationality, religion, and ideological preference. Further, since the mass society is typified by the reduction of personal relationships it is inevitable that these subgroups be institutionalized by formal organizations. In this chapter we shall consider some of the more prominent organizations produced by our heterogeneous society, and basic patterns which appear to persist in the structure of these organizations. In addition, the techniques employed by interest groups to control their membership (persuasive efforts to keep the official ideology intact) and to influence the opinions of a broader public will be examined.

Professional Associations

Of the many professional associations currently operative, the American Bar Association and the American Medical Association provide the most fruitful data for political analysis. Both have had long careers in pressure politics and the developmental pattern of both is similar. David Truman notes that medical associations appeared in the last years of the eighteenth century although the American Medical Association did not develop as a national, representative organization until 1901.[2] In the same way, state associations formed the nucleus of the American Bar Association which was formally constituted in 1878 but did not achieve any appreciable degree of national coordination until it was reconstituted in 1936.[3]

MEMBERSHIP RECRUITMENT AND PRESTIGE

The professional association, typified by those selected for inclusion here, is unique in that its membership consists of persons who have been specially trained by formal education for entry into the profession. While it is true of other organizations that their membership is composed of those of similar environmental and educa-

---

[2] David Truman, *The Governmental Process* (New York: Alfred A. Knopf, Inc., 1951), p. 94.
[3] *Ibid.*, p. 95.

tional background, this is more an accident of circumstance than a deliberate choice. Hence it is a major task of the professional association to maintain as much influence as is possible over standards of admission to the profession, and the relation between the association and the professional school is close. Drawing upon a preconstituted reservoir of membership gives the professional association the opportunity to extend its sphere of influence. Both the ABA and the AMA are the dominant organizations among their potential clientele; the National Association of Manufacturers is only one of many business groups, although its influence is not reduced substantially by its competition.

Similarities between the two organizations also extend to the realm of status. The membership of both is drawn from the middle and upper-middle classes, and the associations, taking the content of their official publications as a measuring device, reflect the ascribed values of their class: both are described as "conservative," meaning that they tend to respect the *status quo* and view proposals for serious change with jaundiced eye. However, there is a very substantial difference between doctors and lawyers with respect to occupational prestige. Truman calls our attention to the importance of the status of a group in the structure of the society as a factor affecting access to key governmental decision makers.[4] While the status of doctors has always been high, the lawyers have had their ups and downs. Shortly after the American Revolution, the loss of trade and resulting financial instability suffered by the new nation served to put the legal profession in the unfortunate position of functioning primarily in the collection of debts. The resulting ill feeling, the tendency to blame the lawyers for misfortunes, was cogently stated by John Quincy Adams: "The mere title of lawyer is sufficient to deprive a man of public confidence."[5] However, the legal profession recovered as the country prospered and lawyers began to assume the role in public life for which their training prepared them. By the time de Tocqueville wrote his famous essay on the nature of American social and political life, lawyers were believed to be possessed of "special information" (knowledge of the

---

[4] *Ibid.*, p. 265.
[5] Quoted in John T. Doby, "The Lawyer as a Political Leader" (Master's thesis, University of Wisconsin, 1948), p. 90.

intricacies of government) which made them the highest political class.[6] Since the possession of unique technical skills tends to raise occupational prestige, the recognition that lawyers, like doctors, had a body of specialized learning at their command worked to the advantage of the legal profession. One cannot practice law as a personal right; one must undergo explicit training. Further, the notion of "a government of laws, not of men" placed the expertise of the lawyer in an especially favorable position.

On the other hand, it is easier to become a lawyer than a doctor. Night school "diploma mills" have increased access to the profession considerably, and perhaps this less exclusive nature serves to reduce the profession's status. Recently the American Bar Association lamented that "despite the indispensable contributions of the legal profession to our American society and economy, lawyers are all too often regarded by laymen as experts in sharp practice and legal legerdemain."[7] The overrepresentation of lawyers in formal governmental positions might also contribute to this "shyster" image since the results of public opinion surveys suggest that the "average man" does not regard politics as a very desirable occupation. Yet this same man "knows what it is to save life and health, and almost worships the medical profession for preserving them for himself and his loved ones."[8] The American Bar Association believes that lawyers "no longer rank in every community as the unchallenged leader of the professional group" and the halcyon days of de Tocqueville have slipped from view.[9] One might be skeptical were it not for the existence of the North-Hatt scale which is designed to measure occupational prestige. According to this scale, physicians rank second only to Justices of the United States Supreme Court while lawyers rank eighteenth. Lawyers fall beneath such categories as college professors, mayors of large cities, scientists, bankers, minis-

---

[6] Alexis de Tocqueville, *Democracy in America,* ed. Phillips Bradley (New York: Vintage Books, 1954), Vol. 1, 283. *See also* Joseph Schlesinger, "Lawyers and American Politics: A Clarified View," *Midwest Journal of Political Science,* 1 (May 1957), 26-39.

[7] American Bar Association, Standing Committee on Public Relations, *Public Relations for Bar Associations* (1953), p. 1.

[8] *Ibid.*

[9] *Ibid.,* p. 2.

ters, architects, and dentists. Yet lawyers still rank in the high status categories. The average score was 69.8 with forty-seven occupations exceeding the average; the lawyers' score was eighty-six and the doctors' ninety-three.[10]

Given the status advantage of doctors, it is ironic in view of evidence indicating that political participation increases with socioeconomic status that they are less disposed to sustained political activities than lawyers. Training for the practice of law is, as we have seen, productive of skills and attitudes which contribute to a compatibility between law and politics; but medical training is of a different type. Studies of the attitudes of medical students indicate that they rank high in theoretical and scientific values and low in political and economic values, while similar studies of law students indicate the reverse cluster of values.[11] Both groups, according to their socio-economic status, are disposed toward participation in political processes and indeed doctors tend to vote in a higher proportion than other high income groups. However, voting is only one measure of participation. It is quite another matter to create sustained interest in the affairs of the American Medical Association, especially when this involves "grass roots" lobbying by doctors. Doctors tend, along with the general population, to see politics as bad and politicians as less than trustworthy. Trained to expect a clear scientific decision to a problem, they develop a patronizing attitude toward the compromise inherent in the solution to political problems. These variations in occupational preparation help explain why lawyers, with less income, are more interested in politics. Thus, one of the early organizational meetings of the American Bar Association declared its function to be "extending the benefit of true reforms and publishing the failure of unsuccessful experiments in legislation." [12]

---

[10] Cecil C. North and Paul K. Hatt, "Jobs and Occupations: A Popular Evaluation," *Opinion News* (Sept. 1947), 3-13. For recent developments of the scale *see* Albert J. Reiss, Otis Duncan, Paul K. Hatt, and Cecil C. North, *Occupations and Social Status* (New York: The Free Press of Glencoe, Inc., 1962).

[11] William A. Glaser, "Doctors and Politics," *American Journal of Sociology,* LXVI (Nov. 1960), 237.

[12] Tappan Gregory, *The American Bar Association* (Chicago: Junior Bar Conference, American Bar Association, 1949), p. 5.

COMPARATIVE POLITICAL INVOLVEMENT

One would expect, from the above data, that the American Bar Association would be continuously involved in the influence process while the American Medical Association would tend to concentrate more on purely professional matters. However, the AMA has surely been far more spectacular in its political activities, as illustrated by its long and intense struggle against compulsory health insurance. The ABA's efforts have generally been less likely to arouse widespread interest. Whereas every citizen may be expected to be affected by any arrangement involving expenditures for medical services, few have knowledge or interest in such ABA supported legislation as a uniform simplification of the Fiduciary Security Transfer Act, bills to revise federal legal services, and bills to permit transfer of cases between district courts and the Court of Claims. The ABA's position only occasionally becomes involved with a wider set of values. Its strenuous opposition to Franklin Roosevelt's "court packing" plan of 1938, its support of the Bricker Amendment, and its opposition to the recall of judges would fall into this category.[13] It will be noticed that none of these goals involves the lawyer-client relationship whereas compulsory health insurance clearly has implications for the relation between doctor and patient. Since the physician is presumably intellectually committed to the pursuit of scientific truths, the suggestion that their services be controlled to any extent by unqualified nonprofessionals has proven sufficient to activate them in support of the AMA. The opposition to the King-Anderson Bill, incorporating President Kennedy's wish that medical insurance be financed through social security contributions, may be viewed as another manifestation of the desire of the AMA and of the doctors who support its declarations to keep "politics" out of the practice of medicine.

Paradoxically, this fear of the political requires that doctors participate in the very process of compromise and group conflict which they abhor. This suggests that the group identification of doctors is

[13] Jack W. Peltason, *Federal Courts in the Political Process* (Garden City, N.Y.: Doubleday & Company, Inc., 1955), p. 27. *See also* American Bar Association, Special Committee on the Supreme Court Proposal, *Reorganization of the Federal Judiciary* (Chicago: American Bar Association, 1937).

fairly intense only in this particular instance, but, since there is no competing institutionalization of political activity, the AMA has been able to translate this attitude into effective action. Although doctors have seemed restrained by professional ethics and have had to be goaded into participation by the plea that the special status of the medical profession requires organization to protect the public, resistance to compulsory health insurance has been maintained with only strategic retreats. Lawyers, however, having the greater tendency toward political activity, have divided their energies, thus siphoning off some of the potential strength of the American Bar Association.

Any organization will suffer a reduction of political effectiveness by reason of internal conflict, and the associations being considered here are no exceptions. Within both there is a clear division between teachers and practitioners. Law professors, expressing themselves through the legal periodicals, quite often take positions in opposition to the ABA; teachers of medicine and doctors attached to foundations or universities in research capacities have expressed dissatisfaction with the AMA. During the AMA's opposition to President Truman's medical insurance program, and, in fact, ever since the issue arose and was acted upon by the AMA, an active minority of research physicians has spoken out against the official doctrines.[14] There is an interesting type of conflict among competing values here. While doctors as a class are "predisposed toward conventional conservative values" and have greater Republican leanings than other classes of similar economic standing, the official ideology of the profession emphasizes concern for the poor—Glaser refers to this as a "Robin Hood" attitude.[15] Frequent contact with people of relatively impoverished circumstances—contact not likely to occur in the experience of the AMA professional staff nor of the wealthier specialists who are usually delegates to AMA conventions—would serve to increase the possibility of internal cleavages. The trend toward specialization in private practice—56 per cent of

[14] Milton Mayer, "The Rise and Fall of Dr. Fishbein," *Harpers Magazine,* Nov. 1949, pp. 76-85. *See also* Oliver Garceau, *The Political Life of the American Medical Association* (Cambridge: Harvard University Press, 1941).

[15] Glaser, *op. cit.,* 241. *Cf.* Howard S. Becker and Blance Geer, "The Fate of Idealism in Medical School," *American Sociological Review,* XXIII (Feb. 1958), 50-56.

the medical population is accounted for by specialists as compared to 37 per cent in 1950—contributes to a crystallization of opposition between researchers and practitioners.[16]

Among those doctors in private practice, general support of AMA policies is indicated. Seventy-five per cent agree that hospital care should not be included in social security coverage and 75 per cent do not believe that doctors' services should be financed by social security. In both cases 20 per cent opposed the AMA position. If we look beyond these most public of the AMA's policies, however, we find some examples of rank and file deviation from official policy. The AMA has consistently opposed inclusion of self-employed physicians under social security, but 51 per cent of the sample approved of this plan. On this issue the specialists and rural general practitioners voted in consensus against social security (70 per cent) leaving the urban general practitioners in opposition. Another example of disagreement within the organization which is of interest is the AMA's opposition to medical school teachers also conducting private practice.[17] During the struggles over compulsory medical insurance, the AMA staff has tended to isolate the teacher opposition by referring to the teachers as men in "plaster towers." Truman writes that "the teaching and research men in medicine have been more sensitive to disturbing changes because of differences in their experience as individuals and as a group. Using the low esteem in which teaching is held by men of affairs in the culture, the AMA has attempted to isolate them from the main body of practicing physicians . . . by classifying them as trouble-making, impractical dreamers." [18] Hence the official opposition to teachers engaging in private practice might be interpreted as part of the isolation program. However, 53 per cent of the sample disagreed with this position. The basic support for the AMA's policy declarations came in this instance

---

[16] Pearl Barland, "Now It's Official: Specialists Outnumber G.P.'s," *Medical Economics,* Apr. 24, 1961, p. 72.

[17] Herbert H. Kauffman, "Does the A.M.A. Heed Your Views?", *Medical Economics,* June 5, 1961, pp. 76-84.

[18] Truman, *op. cit.,* pp. 172-173.

from physicians in group practice because, since teachers tend to practice along group lines, the nonschool physicians see them as competitors.[19]

These tensions are illustrative of the impossibility of any organization achieving total mobilization. The glaring frictions within the ranks of organized labor, described previously, are no more than exaggerated examples (perhaps intensified by the mass membership basis of the organizations) of what is to be expected in every instance of formally coordinated political activity. All organizations are characterized by what Truman calls the "active minority"—in the AMA this minority has usually been urban specialists.[20] In comparison, the active minority of the National Association of Manufacturers has been the officers of the larger, financially solvent manufacturing concerns.[21] Although active minorities tend to perpetuate themselves, they are forced to operate within the limitations imposed by the necessity of having to satisfy the aspirations of enough of the membership to avoid open rebellion. Dr. Morris Fishbein, almost legendary editor of the AMA *Journal,* suffered the consequences of threatened revolt by angering the researchers (who opposed his objectives) and a group of more conservative practitioners (who thought Fishbein's flamboyant lobbying tactics to be not in keeping with the ethics of the profession). As a result, Fishbein's powers were substantially reduced.[22] In the NAM, factions opposing the dominant views have not been able to muster enough support to make themselves a serious threat. For example, large and small manufacturer members of the NAM differed over the policy of the organization concerning the National Labor Relations Board after the election of Eisenhower. Smaller manufacturers preferred a complete reorganization of the NLRB while large manufacturers were willing to rely on a Republican President to make "sound" appointments and thus reduce the bias which they believed was operating within the Board

---

[19] Kauffman, *op. cit.,* p. 78.

[20] Kauffman writes of the delegates to the AMA conventions that "they're almost all specialists [and] have served long apprenticeships in county and state society offices before being tapped for the House of Delegates." *See* Kauffman, *op. cit.,* p. 76. *See also* Garceau, *Pol. Life of A.M.A.,* p. 54.

[21] Alfred S. Cleveland, "N.A.M.: Spokesman for Industry?" *Harvard Business Review, XXVI* (May 1948), 353-371.

[22] Mayer, *op. cit.,* pp. 76-85.

under Democratic Presidents. The President ultimately went along with most of what the large manufacturers wanted.[23]

In the case of the research doctors within the AMA, the ability to make alliances with prestigious members of the association undoubtedly helped the cause. Also, doctors affiliated with research institutions command considerable respect among laymen. When such doctors lobby independently of the AMA, they speak for the National Institute of Health, the National Cancer Institute, and similar groups, and they enjoy considerable success.[24] Apparently the least prestigious members of the medical profession are the public health doctors, who might be considered a type of deviant specialist. Medical training develops qualities different from those needed in public health and there is considerable pressure within the profession against public health careers; the evidence indicates that public health doctors are drawn from the least popular students. Accordingly, while public health doctors differed with the AMA on issues such as the Kennedy medicare program, their status did not allow them to contribute to a successful coalition against the hierarchy.[25]

Both the AMA and ABA have similar formal organizations. Formal authority is placed in a House of Delegates. However, within the American Bar Association, there exists a very nebulous relationship between the state associations and the national body. For many years, membership in state bar associations was more impressive than membership in the American Bar Association. This situation is reflected in the ABA's device of allowing the members of the *national* association from each state to elect delegates to the annual convention. These delegates form the nominating committee and, while members of state and local associations are allowed to attend (provided the local association has eight hundred members, 25 per cent of whom are members of the American Bar Association) they cannot participate in the nominating process.[26] The American Medi-

---

[23] Seymour Scher, "Regulatory Agency Control Through Appointment: The Case of the Eisenhower Administration and the NLRB," *Journal of Politics,* XXIII (Nov. 1961), 667-688.

[24] Lois R. Chevalier, "Doctors Are the Greatest Lobbyists!" *Medical Economics,* Sept. 1, 1958, pp. 131-149.

[25] "New Study Finds Public Health Men 'Different,'" *Medical Economics,* Sept. 1, 1958, p. 56.

[26] Gregory, *op. cit.,* p. 10.

cal Association allows each state medical society to send delegates, few of whom are given binding instructions by the sponsoring society.[27] In these associations, as is the general rule, the tendency is for the delegates to be selected from among the political actives. Among doctors only about 50 per cent attend more than half of the local medical society meetings, leaving to the "medical politicians" the responsibility of deciding among alternate courses of action within the national association.[28] The natural tendency toward oligarchy leaves the formal staff of the AMA and the actives at the local level (usually specialists) free to develop informal control mechanisms. For example, Dr. Fishbein was said to have known "ten thousand practitioners by name, and among those ten thousand were . . . 'the men who count,' the local medical politicians who have to be seen and who, having been seen, run the constituent county and state societies of the AMA through a politically innocent general membership."[29]

Although the AMA has, for most of its existence, included a substantial portion of the medical population (AMA membership is now 180,000 out of a possible 254,000), both it and the American Bar Association (with 102,000 members out of 286,000 lawyers) have been engaged in activities to make their respective organizations more inclusive. Compulsory membership in the AMA has been approved by twelve state medical associations. In these states, membership in the state society automatically includes the payment of dues to the AMA and when the twelfth state, New York, recently approved compulsory membership it did so over the objections of two of its largest components, Manhattan and Brooklyn.[30] It can easily be seen that the ABA has a less inclusive membership, perhaps because of the tendency of lawyers to identify with their clients rather than with their profession. This diversification of affiliations has contributed to the existence of the National Lawyers Guild as a minor competitor to the American Bar Association. Thus, the issue of the "integrated bar" (membership in the state bar as a requirement to practice) is not without justification. Yet the smaller ABA has never suffered the loss of cohesion which characterizes the

---

[27] Kauffman, *op. cit.*, p. 76.
[28] *Ibid.*, p. 82.
[29] Mayer, *op. cit.*, p. 77.
[30] *Medical Economics*, June 5, 1961, p. 1.

more inclusive AMA. As long as the medical profession incorporates men of diverse environments, comments such as the following will be expected: "never in the history of the organization [have] so many dedicated conscientious physicians felt that the hierarchy did not speak for them . . . Either the Association will be rebuilt from within or a competing National Academy of Health, which [now] has support from medical leaders all over the country, will appear." [31]

Minority Groups

While members of professional associations are educated toward group affiliation at a rather late stage in their lives, members of minority groups are provided with group identification on the basis of "race, religion, immigrant status, and origins in other than Anglo-Saxon countries" at a much earlier age. [32] Studies of children of nursery school age and very early primary school age indicate that identifications on the basis of racial, religious, and national differences are present. Negro and white children within this age group are aware of racial differences expressed in physical characteristics and many use racial terms which imply the perception of differences in the social roles of Negroes and whites. [33] The same findings apply to Jewish children of the same age group, as illustrated by the remarks of a second grade Jewish girl:

> I'm Jewish. . . . Jews are the best people, mother said. You know I'm a Jew. . . . I'm not allowed to go [to church]. Only synagogue. [Churches] ain't no good. Synagogue is better. Catholics don't like Jews. Make fun of Jews. [34]

Of great significance is the conclusion that the minority group children show earlier and greater identification than majority group children of the same age. Negro children show more concern with

[31] *Ibid.*, Mar. 26, 1962, p. 2.
[32] Robert E. Lane, *Political Life* (New York: The Free Press of Glencoe, Inc., 1959), p. 235.
[33] Mary E. Goodman, *Race Awareness in Young Children* (Reading, Mass.: Addison-Wesley Publishing Co., Inc., 1952).
[34] Marian Radke Yarrow, "Personality Development and Minority Group Membership," in Marshall Sklare, ed., *The Jews* (New York: The Free Press of Glencoe, Inc., 1958), p. 455.

their racial characteristics than white children; Jewish children are more conscious of their own group than Protestant; and Catholics are more group conscious than Protestants but less than Jews.

PRESSURES TOWARD MINORITY GROUP SOLIDARITY

However convincing this evidence may be, it is a mistake to assume that a member of a minority group is automatically desirous of identifying himself with the customs and traditions of his family and immediate associates. There is nothing in the personality structure of a person that makes him inclined to identify, interact, and undertake political activity on behalf of a minority group any more than there is in the personalities of members of any other broadly defined aggregate or "categoric group." Members of minority groups have overlapping affiliations with other groups which may be easily activated while minority group affiliation remains dormant. For example, a Polish druggist could easily be motivated to support fair trade legislation through the auspices of the National Association of Retail Druggists in cooperation with other druggists of varying ethnic or religious backgrounds. There must be some reason for identification and, as is the case with all interest groups, such identification is produced by "pressure from the outside and the consequences of that pressure." [35] Whereas the outside pressure operating upon other types of potential interests might be ideological or economic, the pressures imposed upon a minority group may be categorized by the word "prejudice." While many definitions of prejudice may be found, one of the most useful is Allport's: "an avertive or hostile attitude toward a person who belongs to a group, simply because he belongs to that group, and is therefore presumed to have the objectionable qualities ascribed to the group." [36] While it is fruitless to attempt to argue that there is perfect correlation between degree of prejudice and minority group identification, it is fairly obvious that, in the United States, opposition to majority prejudice is a strong catalyst to minority protest movements.

In some cases, group identification occurs without visible prejudice; in others the minority group is the object of prejudice, yet has

---

[35] Arnold and Caroline Rose, *America Divided* (New York: Alfred A. Knopf, Inc., 1949), p. 178.

[36] Gordon W. Allport, *The Nature of Prejudice* (Garden City, N.Y.: Doubleday & Company, Inc., 1958), p. 8.

ineffective group identification. In the latter case, the desire is usually to escape identity as a member of a minority by means of name changing and the avoidance of contact with other members of the group. No effective organization to protest discrimination will occur, since the only shared characteristic of the members of such a group is being identified by the majority as possessing certain undesirable qualities. The conditions under which minority groups will normally undertake political activity are described by Wirth: "The continued subordination over a long period of time of any special class in the population, when coupled with the concentration of that group in large numbers, with social visibility based on racial traits or cultural characteristics, with intense competition with the dominant group, and with rising levels of education, generally results in the emergence of group-consciousness and eventually the overt struggle for recognition." [37] The reader will have no trouble in applying this description to the status of the American Negro whom Wirth believes to be the "principal shock absorber of the antiminority sentiment of the dominant whites." [38] Hence the persistent struggle of Negro organizations toward the attaining of "first class citizenship" has attracted more attention than the efforts of other minorities, such as Catholics and Jews.

THE COMPONENTS OF MINORITY STATUS

A proper comprehension of the concept of the minority is very crucial to the understanding of the politics of minorities. The word refers not to numerical characteristics but rather to physical or cultural characteristics which cause a "singling out" from others and a consequent unequal treatment. Although the size of the group apparently has a direct relation to the treatment the minority may expect from the majority, it is quite possible that people whom we consider to be a minority are a numerical majority. In the southern black belt, where the population is 50 per cent or more Negro, there is no question that Negroes are placed in the status of a minority in the sense that they are totally subordinate to the white community. Clearly, the density of minority group population in-

---

[37] Louis Wirth, "The Present Position of Minorities in the United States," in Elizabeth Wirth Marvick and Albert J. Reiss, Jr., eds., *Community Life and Social Policy* (Chicago: University of Chicago Press, 1956), p. 228.
[38] Wirth, "The Problem of Minority Groups," *ibid.*, p. 243.

creases prejudice and organizational reactions to prejudice. In the case of both the Jews and Catholics, discrimination did not become a problem until the impetus of increased immigration was provided. If the group is small, the chances of assimilation increase while the probability of prejudice decreases (although this "law of density" cannot stand alone). Examples of this situation would be the Jew in China, the Negro in Brazil, or the Hindu in America. In each of these cases, if the minority population were to increase markedly, there is little doubt that the pattern of assimilation would be reversed.[39]

The United States is liberally sprinkled with minority groups, and, since the distribution of many minority groups is regional, many patterns of discrimination are localized and the protest activity is correspondingly restricted to a particular area. In addition, many of the ethnic minority groups were organized primarily for the purpose of maintaining loyalty to the "old country" and not for the pursuit of goals through participation in the domestic political process.[40] Thomas and Znaniecki describe the Polish community in America as operating through the Polish National Alliance to "turn the Polish immigrants in this country into a strong and coherent part of the Polish Nation." [41] Another instructive example is the Japanese of the West Coast. Here, the Japanese American Citizens' League grew under the guidance of the Nisei who opposed the tendency of the older generation to support the militarist activities of the Japanese government. In this case, events taking place abroad had consequences for the nationality group whose position in the host society was threatened.[42] It is natural that minority groups with foreign identifications take unusual interest in foreign policy, and there is much evidence of gradual shifts in party loyalty among such groups according to the position taken on a particular issue by one of the two major parties. Occasionally, minority activities in foreign policy take the form of direct pressure on office holders as illustrated by President Harry Tru-

---

[39] Allport, *op. cit.*, pp. 220-222.

[40] Lane, *op. cit.*, p. 247.

[41] William I. Thomas and Florian Znaniecki, *The Polish Peasant in Europe and America* (Boston: Richard G. Badger, 1918), Vol. 5, 113. Cited in Lane, *op. cit.*, p. 247.

[42] Rose, *op. cit.*, pp. 201-204. *See also* Morton Grodzins, *The Loyal and Disloyal* (Chicago: University of Chicago Press, 1956).

man's statement that, during the United Nations debate over the partitioning of Palestine, "I do not think I ever had so much pressure and propaganda aimed at the White House as I had in this instance." President Truman continued by saying that "the persistence of a few of the extreme Zionist leaders—actuated by political motives and engaging in political threats—disturbed and annoyed me. . . . The Jewish pressure on the White House did not diminish in the days following the partition vote in the U.N." [43] While other examples of internationalist type pressure may be found, we are more interested at this point in "nationalist" organizations whose attention is largely concentrated domestically, those representing Negroes, Catholics, and Jews.

CATHOLICS: THE POLITICAL SOCIALIZATION OF RELIGION

Catholicism is given political expression primarily through the instrument of the Church, rather than through voluntary secular associations. The reasons for this assumption of the role of political agent by the Church may be found both in the nature of the Catholic faith (and consequent structure of the Church) and in the social composition of the Catholic laity. Many of the immigrant groups are Roman Catholic and there is considerable overlapping between identification as a minority on the basis of nationality and minority religious status. To some extent, national solidarity has been transformed into religious solidarity, especially when assimilation into the larger society is impeded. Certainly there are many examples of hostility between the Catholic groups—Poles and Italians object to the domination of the Irish in the affairs of the Church—but there is still a very basic unifying function performed by the Church as an institution. The initial anti-Catholic movements in this country did not develop until the beginnings of Irish immigration and the later Italian immigration. However, as a nationality group the Irish now encounter so little prejudice that it is doubtful if they can be considered a minority. The Irish are,

---

[43] Harry S Truman, *Years of Trial and Hope* (Garden City, N.Y.: Doubleday & Company, Inc., 1956), Vol. 2, 158, 160. *See also* Louis L. Gerson, "Immigrant Groups and Foreign Policy," in George L. Anderson, ed., *Issues and Conflicts: Studies in Twentieth Century American Diplomacy* (Lawrence: University of Kansas Press, 1959), pp. 171-192.

nevertheless, held together by their loyalty to the Catholic Church, and the extent to which they remain a minority will be on this basis rather than nationality. The Italians, by way of contrast, retain the stereotype of "foreigners" and this, as well as their Catholicism, contributes to their minority status. Yet the probability of assimilation is sufficient to enable one to advance the thesis that the Italians will gradually retain minority status primarily through Catholicism.

The transfer of the tensions of prejudice to the religious area has generated a reaction which might be described as the political socialization of religious biases. Discrimination against people simply because they are Catholics is negligible, but religious conflict between the two major religions has increased. Since the Catholic Church does not acknowledge any separation between church and state, and since the Church is formally organized to promote internal unity, it is ideally suited for political activity: ". . . all acts by human beings have religious significance, and [the Church] realistically recognizes that all acts of the churches have political significance if they affect the relative power of groups." [44] Consequently, it is usually the Catholic clergy which is given the responsibility of speaking to political questions. For example, during the Spanish Civil War the Church strongly supported Franco and condemned the Loyalists as Communists. Also, the evangelistic aspects of the Catholic religion have led the Church to seek new converts among Negroes.[45] In the South, the political impact of the Church's traditional freedom from racism is heightened by official declarations in opposition to segregation. However, the tensions between Protestants and Catholics become most severe over those questions of a fundamentally religious nature which the Catholic Church has, of necessity, introduced into the political arena. The Church prefers that its members refrain from reading certain books and seeing certain types of motion pictures, but it discovers that Catholics adopt the ways of the majority, and thus has sought legislation to insulate Catholics or has tried to prevent the passage of legislation which conflicts with Catholic dogma.

Many such issues arise at the state and local level where Catholic

---

[44] Rose, *op. cit.*, p. 58.

[45] Jesse Bernard, *American Community Behavior* (New York: Holt, Rinehart, & Winston, Inc., 1949), p. 253.

political power has usually been most impressive. In the days of the urban "bosses" and "machines," the Irish dominated the politics of many cities, but the passing of the urban machines has reduced this Catholic influence to some degree. For instance, in New York the issue of the Sunday closing laws has activated politico-religious activities. The initial attack on the law was begun by the Jewish organizations. After many unsuccessful attempts to have the Sunday closing law modified by the state legislature, the efforts were concentrated in the New York City Council. This required enabling home rule legislation and a two-thirds majority of each house in the State Legislature. As pressure for the passage of a home rule resolution gained in momentum, the Chancery Office of the New York Archdiocese released a statement opposing the resolution and thus declaring opposition to many of the Protestant churches and the Joint Committee for a Fair Sabbath Law (Jewish). The vote in the City Council reflected these religious tensions. The vote was fourteen to seven in favor of the resolution, with the eleven Jewish Councilmen and the three Protestant Councilmen making up the majority. Significantly, seven out of eight Irish Catholic Councilmen voted against the resolution but the three Italian Catholics abstained.[46]

This incident reflects both decline of influence and internal cleavages, the latter problem being endemic to all political organizations irrespective of the formal distribution of authority. Will Maslow, Executive Director and General Counsel of the American Jewish Congress, observes that "this tactical victory was particularly significant because to the writer's knowledge it was the first time in his generation that any legislative measure opposed by the Catholic Church had ever been approved in New York or Albany." [47] In addition to the decline of the machine, we must not overlook the possibility that second or third generation immigrants may look less to the Church for guidance and, in reaction to political pressures by the Catholic Church, the crystallization of Protestant opposition. However, the lack of cohesion among Protestant denominations and the lack of centralization which characterizes most Protestant

---

[46] Will Maslow, "The Legal Defense of Religious Liberty—The Strategy and Tactics of the American Jewish Congress" (Paper presented to the American Political Science Association Meeting, Sept., 1961), p. 20.

[47] *Ibid.*

churches make it unlikely that Protestants will use the church as a political instrument. The question of federal aid to education illustrates this point. Although the use of federal funds for education involves broader problems, the problem of public expenditures for parochial schools has contributed to Catholic-Protestant tensions, especially since the Kennedy administration pressed vigorously for federal support of education. The Catholic Church, and in this case the National Catholic Educational Association, has said that all schools, whether religious or public, should be supported by public tax funds. The opposition to this point of view, though often unorganized, has come from many Protestant religious circles. Organized Jewish groups and ideologically based associations like the American Civil Liberties Union have drawn the lines of battle more clearly.

THE JEWS

The Jews stand in sharp contrast to the Catholics on two counts. First, the church and religion are not strongly emphasized in Jewish life and, second, the Jewish religion is split into orthodox, conservative, and reformed branches. These factors contribute to a weak hierarchical structure of Jewish religious life and thus make it inevitable that the expression of Jewish political values be undertaken by voluntary associations. Also, discrimination against Jews has been based not only upon their status as a religious minority, but also on the basis of ethnic or racial characteristics. In fact, in contemporary American life, the tendency toward anti-Semitism has been almost wholly divorced from religious objections and has rested upon a stereotype built upon presumed cultural characteristics. Discrimination against Jews had been both brutally direct and subtle. Social discrimination, such as the exclusion of Jews from exclusive clubs, occupational discrimination, the operation of the "quota system" in colleges and graduate schools, and occasional discrimination against Jews in the buying and selling of real estate attest to the persistence of anti-Semitism.

Anti-Semitism, like other patterns of discrimination, started slowly and reached its peak in correlation with Jewish immigration. Jewish immigration spurted upwards in the 1880's and continued to increase until World War I, after which a policy of restriction was followed. Accordingly, World War I represents a high point in anti-Semitism. One measure of anti-Semitism may be found in A. L. Severson's study of discriminatory want ads. Ads specifically excluding Jews rose from less than 1 per cent in 1911 to 4 per cent in 1921 and finally to slightly over 13 per cent in 1926.[48] It was during this period that the first Jewish defense organization came into existence. The American Jewish Committee was a small organization of wealthy Jews who were not recent immigrants. Its goal was to resist anti-Semitism by the use of restrained and localized action. The Anti-Defamation League of B'nai B'rith came shortly after to serve as the political branch of a well-established fraternity. The A.D.L. was more of a mass organization and has been more inclined toward more general exposure of discrimination. Rose believes that the A.D.L. has been the most effective of the Jewish organizations and has served to increase group identification. He remarks: "when Jews meet anti-Semitism, and in so far as they look to a national organization to aid them, they probably think first of the A.D.L." [49] A third organization, by far the most militant, is the American Jewish Congress, begun in 1918 as a "democratically elected parliamentary assembly representing all American Jews." [50] Its membership was primarily the newer immigrants and a partial reason for its creation was opposition to the more elitist American Jewish Committee. Its militancy is expressed in its passionate defense of Zionism and its reliance upon direct lobbying techniques in efforts to secure governmental prohibitions against racial and religious discrimination. Initially, the American Jewish Congress proposed to obtain treaty provisions at the Versailles conference protecting the rights of Jews in the defeated countries and to generate support for a Jewish state in Palestine, the latter goal being realized many years later. During the 1930's anti-Semitism increased after a brief drop, according to Severson's statistics, and was expanded into political forms by means of organized groups using anti-Semitism in efforts to achieve political power. Donald Strong accounted for one hundred and twenty-one organizations disseminating anti-Jewish literature between 1933 and 1940. The growth of such organizations seemed to be tied in with the increas-

---

[48] A. L. Severson, "Nationality and Religion in Newspaper Ads," *American Journal of Sociology*, XLIV (Jan. 1939), 545.
[49] Rose, *op. cit.*, p. 198.
[50] Maslow, *op. cit.*, p. 1.

ing power of Nazi Germany, for prior to 1933 only five anti-Semitic associations were in operation.[51] This new type of threat was combated under the energetic leadership of the American Jewish Congress whose usual militant posture plunged it actively into resistance.

The initial response to organized anti-Semitism by Jewish groups was vigorous, but more enduring has been the articulation of goals designed to insure the preservation of Jewish cultural values. While the Anti-Defamation League continues to propagandize against discrimination and anti-Semitism, the American Jewish Congress has expanded its interests particularly with respect to religious liberty. The A.J.C.'s Committee on Social Action is actively engaged in winning support for the position that "religious liberty is best preserved when government remains strictly and severely aloof from all religious affairs." [52] This belief is expressed in the A.J.C.'s resistance to the releasing of children for religious instruction, recitation of prayers in class, nuns teaching in their religious attire, and many other similar examples. Of course, church-state controversies are not confined to public schools, as is illustrated by the A.J.C.'s opposition to the inclusion of religious questions in the census. About 75 per cent of the Jewish population, estimated in 1959 as 5,367,000, is concentrated in large metropolitan areas and, to meet the needs of this population, nearly every large city in the country has some type of Jewish organization, usually called a Jewish Community Council or Jewish Community Relations Council. The function of these organizations is "to deal with problems of anti-Semitism and community relations and to coordinate the network of Jewish charitable, religious, educational and social welfare agencies." [53] Also represented on such councils are representatives of the national organizations. The national organizations operate through the local groups primarily on questions of anti-Semitism, and the initiative for action frequently begins at the local level. The local association is more directly involved in the affairs of the community and is sensitive to the problem of establishing workable relationships with

---

[51] Donald S. Strong, *Organized Anti-Semitism in America* (Washington, D.C.: American Council on Public Affairs, 1941), pp. 146-147.

[52] Maslow, *op. cit.*, p. 6.

[53] *Ibid.*, p. 6. *See also* Solomon Sutker, "The Role of Social Clubs in the Atlanta Jewish Community," in Sklare, *op. cit.*, pp. 262-270.

majority portions of the population. For example, when a question of beginning legal action to prohibit the performance of a nativity play in the public schools is being debated, the community council may feel that, if the litigant is known to be a Jew or if his case is supported by a Jewish organization, the pattern of relationships between Jews and Christians may be upset. The American Jewish Congress, not so closely identified with a particular locale, is usually more anxious to begin action but cannot risk disruption of the Jewish community by moving without prior discussions with local leaders through the community councils. As in any political organization, a major part of the pressure process is internal. The A.J.C. must persuade its clientele that a particular course of action will have beneficial consequences sufficient to offset the possibility that community relations will be damaged.

On national issues the same necessity for achieving minimal cohesion exists. Since none of the national organizations is in a position to attempt solidification, several "umbrella" organizations undertake the task.[54] The Synagogue Council of America is composed of the rabbinical and congregational bodies of the three branches of Judaism, and the National Community Relations Advisory Council serves as a coordinating mechanism for the national Jewish organizations and the local community councils. These two organizations include approximately 80 per cent of the organized Jewish community. The two inclusive organizations work together through joint committees such as the Joint Advisory Committee on Religion and Public Schools. This committee, with its legal work prepared by the American Jewish Congress, advises local organizations and undertakes direct action at the national level as, for example, the filing of an *amicus curiae* brief in the McCollum case or the testimony in Congress against the proposed constitutional amendment declaring the country as Christian. Yet such formal devices will never achieve total mobilization for there will always be internal conflicts. The Anti-Defamation League and the American Jewish Committee have withdrawn from the National Community Relations Council. These organizations have been less rigid in their approach to church-state relations and have usually favored, for example, joint Christmas-Chanukah celebrations, a practice strenuously opposed by the American Jewish Congress. Also, local-national

---

[54] Maslow, *op. cit.,* p. 6.

conflict occasionally erupts. When the American Jewish Congress challenged the New York Sunday closing law as applied to a kosher butcher shop which closed on Saturday, both the local kosher butchers association and the kosher butchers workers union filed briefs defending the statute. Examples of such conflict occur with such frequency that the problem of cohesion can be delineated as crucial in the influence process. In order to focus upon external problems, internal disunity must be reduced beneath the level of distraction, a task which occupies a substantial portion of the efforts of the leadership.[55]

NEGROES

The Negro minority, which constitutes 10 per cent of the American population, is both the oldest and most consistently discriminated against of all minority groups. The visible physical characteristics and slave ancestry of Negroes might be considered as two basic factors in explaining why they have retained minority status for so long. From the beginning of slavery in the early seventeenth century until the defeat of the Confederate States of America, there was virtually no opportunity for group identification and protest activity. The slaves were not allowed to communicate and few were even given the opportunity to learn to read. Although there were sporadic outbursts of a revolutionary fervor, the group life of the Negro was too restricted for cohesive action. As Robin Williams has suggested, "militancy, except for sporadic and short-lived uprisings, is not characteristic of the most deprived and oppressed groups, but rather of those who have gained considerable rights so that they are able realistically to hope for more." [56]

Williams states further that "a militant reaction from a minority group is most likely when (a) the group's position is rapidly improving, or (b) when it is rapidly deteriorating, especially when this follows a period of improvement." [57] Such was the situation giving birth to the first organized Negro protests. The freedom of Reconstruction gave them new opportunities for political participation but the militant protests of the Reconstruction period were sub-

---

[55] Truman, *The Governmental Process*, p. 156.
[56] Robin M. Williams, Jr., *The Reduction of Intergroup Tensions* (New York: Social Science Research Council, 1947), p. 61.
[57] *Ibid.*

merged by vigorous white southern countermovements following the removal of federal troops. By the 1890's white supremacy was firmly established as a way of life. The white South believed that it was possible and desirable to return the Negroes to their original status and, with the aid of secret societies and the tacit support of the federal government, the rule of Jim Crow dominated. Protest movements could not survive such an assault and were replaced by "accommodation." Myrdal describes the leadership of Booker T. Washington as typical of the period of accommodation in that it was "realistic." [58] As leader of a conciliatory school of thought, he was willing to sacrifice social and political equality, even to the extent of accepting inequalities in justice.[59] It is doubtful that more could have been accomplished under the circumstances, and Washington did mold together a basis of support in the white community which would probably have been lost by more vigorous methods.

However, dependence upon the benevolence of whites could not obliterate the fact that "every Negro has some sort of conflict with the white world." [60] It was inevitable that a reaction against Washington's leadership would occur and that this reaction would take the form of protest. Led by W. E. B. Du Bois, a small group of Negro intellectuals demanded full social and political equality and, hopefully, cultural assimilation. The "Niagara Movement" (so called because the first meeting of the leaders of the reaction met at Niagara Falls in 1905) intended not only to develop more vigorous forms of political activity, but also to replace Washington's compromising policies as the dominant mode of the Negro community. Although this movement lasted only five years, it merged with the National Association for the Advancement of Colored People four years later.

From the beginning of its organizational life, the NAACP has exhibited many of the qualities typifying it at its inception. The initiative for the organization came from white abolitionists such as Oswald Garrison Villard and, for many years, a substantial portion of leadership positions was filled by whites. Gradually, while retain-

---

[58] Gunnar Myrdal, *An American Dilemma* (New York: Harper & Row, Publishers, 1944), pp. 720-735.

[59] Booker T. Washington, *Up From Slavery* (Garden City, N.Y.: Doubleday & Company, Inc., 1905).

[60] Myrdal, *op. cit.*, p. 720

ing its interracial distribution at the branch level, the NAACP national leadership has become primarily the responsibility of Negroes. However, the organization has had primary attraction, not for the Negro masses, but for the "talented tenth"—the minority of upper class, educated Negroes. The militancy of Du Bois did not appeal to this type of membership which, according to Lewin's "periphery theory," would desire to achieve status within the society at large. To achieve such status, it is necessary to reduce identification with the low-status minority group. Lewin states that:

> In a minority group, individual members who are economically successful, or who have distinguished themselves in their professions, usually gain a high degree of acceptance by the majority group. This places them culturally at the periphery of the underprivileged group and makes them more likely to be "marginal" persons. They frequently have a negative balance and are particularly eager to have their "good connections" not endangered by too close a contact with those sections of the underprivileged group which are not acceptable to the majority.[61]

The elitist type of NAACP membership has behaved in a manner generally within the limits of Lewin's description of the peripheral leader. Although its rank and file membership has expanded and hence shifted to some extent from the elite to the "common Negroes," it is still committed to the avoidance of any form of protest other than the pursuit of civil rights through legal action. Thus Roy Wilkins, head of the NAACP, has said that the organization "would prefer using legal action as a last resort in the many situations which will arise in hundreds of communities."[62]

Largely avoiding participation in mass protest movements such as the March on Washington Movement (which ultimately forced President Roosevelt to establish a Fair Employment Practices Commission during World War II) has, of course, worked to the advantage of the NAACP in many instances.[63] By pursuing a persistent policy of hammering away at restrictions, the NAACP can claim such notable victories as the abolition of white primaries, restrictive covenants, and segregation in public schools. The success of the

---

[61] Kurt Lewin, *Resolving Social Conflicts* (New York: Harper & Row, Publishers, 1948), pp. 195-196.

[62] Roy Wilkins, "The Role of the NAACP in the Desegregation Process," *Social Problems*, II (Apr. 1955), 201.

[63] Herbert Garfinkle, *When Negroes March* (New York: The Free Press of Glencoe, Inc., 1959).

NAACP in the 1954 *Brown* v. *Board of Education* decision marked the zenith of NAACP popularity with the Negro community but also brought about the end of an era. The decision seemed to serve as a stimulant for the beginnings of more militant, extralegal forms of protest such as the sit-in demonstrations. It is indeed a paradox that, by the use of legal tactics, the NAACP contributed to a more militant protest which has seriously damaged the prestige of the organization. While the NAACP has been stereotyped by many southern whites as a radical organization, the surge of more direct protest movements suggested that ". . . to many Negroes, the way of the NAACP is too slow, too expensive and too uncertain. . . . Negroes cannot understand why they must spend time and money again and again to have the courts secure them privileges that all other Americans—and many resident aliens—take for granted." [64]

Reactions against the dominant conservatism of Negro leadership are not new. In addition to the March on Washington Movement, the "black nationalism" of the post-World War I Universal Negro Improvement Association and the Black Muslims of today reflect the most extreme forms of this reaction. However, this type of ultra-militant movement is no real threat to the NAACP because its goals are sufficiently extreme as to make them impossible to achieve. More serious to dominant leadership is the growth of localized spontaneous action, such as the sit-ins, and the rise of competing organizations to coordinate these efforts. There is much evidence to suggest that the NAACP had nothing to do with these student demonstrations. One NAACP official is quoted as saying "these demonstrations are not something we planned. . . . The students moved on their own. We didn't know what was going on until it happened." [65]

---

[64] C. Eric Lincoln, *The Black Muslims in America* (Boston: Beacon Press, 1961), p. 146.

[65] Louis E. Lomax, "The Negro Revolt Against 'The Negro Leaders,'" *Harpers Magazine* (June 1960), 43. *See also* Lomax, *The Negro Revolt* (New York: Harper & Row, Publishers, 1962). The following sources are useful in understanding shifts in Negro leadership at the local level: M. Elaine Burgess, *Negro Leadership in a Southern City* (Chapel Hill: University of North Carolina Press, 1962); Lewis M. Killian and Charles U. Smith, "Negro Protest Leaders in a Southern Community," *Social Forces*, XXXVIII (Mar. 1960), 253-257; Tilman C. Cothran and William Phillips, Jr., "Negro Leadership in a Crisis Situation," *Phylon*, XXII (Summer, 1961), 107-118.

Although the NAACP has supported the sit-ins and freedom rides, organizations such as Martin Luther King's Southern Christian Leadership Conference, the Congress on Racial Equality, and the Student Non-Violent Coordinating Committee have been more intimately associated with the rising protests and, while NAACP membership is large but declining, the membership of these organizations is increasing rapidly. Much of the impetus for protest, as opposed to accommodation, has come from the local Negro communities, and coordination of the various movements has been accomplished by the national organizations. The NAACP, which, like the American Jewish Congress, allows local branches to assume the role of initiator, has consequently been faced by an increasing interest in mass protest on the part of its branches. Whereas the local Jewish organizations frequently have to be prodded because of their reluctance to incur hostility, the pattern is reversed in the NAACP. The low status group, being less assimilated into the majority, has little to gain from quiescence, and has responded to local conditions of discrimination more quickly than have the national organizations. In many cases, local NAACP branches have become less compromising in response to the competition of other organizations, but in other cases, the total leadership of the local Negro community has undergone a shift from accommodation to protest orientation.

In Little Rock and Chicago, for example, the NAACP leaders have been at the vanguard of protest. In the areas where there has been a change in leadership, there has been a corresponding shift in the basis of leadership. Whereas the accommodating leaders held positions of influence because they were acceptable to whites, the communication between whites and the protest leaders is not well established. In Chicago, as the militant NAACP has become "identified with Negro protest and explosive issues such as school integration, [it] has become suspect in the eyes of influential white businessmen and civic leaders." [66] The Chicago experience seems typical of the pattern of shifting goals in Negro organizations. There is pressure from the rank and file upon the "active minority" at the top of the NAACP hierarchy and, in turn, there have been some efforts to smother local leadership. Also, there is some pressure

---

[66] James Q. Wilson, *Negro Politics* (New York: The Free Press of Glencoe, Inc., 1960), p. 138.

from the sections of the Negro community which have a "vested interest" in segregation. For example, Negro restaurants and other businesses such as insurance companies would have to compete on a larger scale if segregation were eliminated.[67] Thus the NAACP leadership is adjusting to cross-pressures from varying sources but, being deeply rooted in traditions of moderation, is perhaps changing too slowly to avoid the rise to prominence of competitors.

Ideological Groups

Classification of interest groups is always a difficult task, especially when one recognizes that any typology based on goals, for example, may be refuted by another typology based on organizational structure. In this section, we focus on what is termed the "ideological group." Social scientists have recognized that interest group politics, as a conceptual device, does not require that we assume that all groups function to achieve some tangible interest of immediate benefit for its members. A certain type of interest group may advocate long-range goals which, if the welfare of its participants is taken into account, have no relation to individual aspirations. Samuel Eldersveld, drawing upon the ideas of Robert C. Angell, Ralph H. Turner, and Lewis M. Killian, suggests a contrast between the "ideological 'struggle group'" and the "expediency-oriented 'control movement'" based upon the existence of interests whose objectives are directed toward societal improvement rather than subgroup gratification.[68]

It should be clear, however, that such a categorization does not attempt to distinguish among groups according to the existence, or lack of existence, of "self-interest." Obviously, the members of an ideological group perceive the group's particular struggle as one of crucial importance and are able to identify the successful

[67] E. Franklin Frazier, "The Negro's Vested Interest in Segregation," in Arnold Rose, ed., *Race Prejudice and Discrimination* (New York: Alfred A. Knopf, Inc., 1951), pp. 332-339.

[68] Samuel J. Eldersveld, "American Interest Groups: A Survey of Research and Some Implications for Theory and Method," in Henry W. Ehrmann, ed., *Interest Groups on Four Continents* (Pittsburgh: University of Pittsburgh Press, 1958), p. 181.

*c*ulmination of the struggle in terms of personal satisfaction. This might be considered the attitude of the members of the Americans for Democratic Action, Committee for Constitutional Government, United World Federalists, or John Birch Society. Thus, an official of the Americans for Democratic Action, in drawing a distinction between his organization and those organizations speaking for "private or commercial interests," explained that "our competition is in the realm of ideas." [69] However, different ideas attract different types of people. It is therefore to be expected that the membership in an ideological group will be typified by certain class, educational, or income levels. Also, an ideological group's principles may fit nicely into the stream of ideas espoused by an economic association. Thus, the dedication of the Committee for Constitutional Government to the goals of fighting "for economic freedom as against encroaching big government . . . for lower taxes, for reducing the number of Federal employees by 600,000, for curbing the power of labor monopolies, and for restoring equality before the law to all citizens, and for ending confiscatory upper-bracket taxation, so that industry can obtain more capital to provide better tools, a higher scale of living, and more remunerative jobs for oncoming youth" [70] would make the organization a useful ally for the National Association of Manufacturers. Similarly, the Americans for Democratic Action, by advocating "the protection of civil liberties, enactment of FEPC, repeal of the Taft-Hartley Act, and a return to the Wagner Act . . . ," gains the support of labor and minority groups.[71]

THE NEW AMERICAN RIGHT AND STATUS POLITICS

This mixing of the activities of groups "concerned with the satisfaction of an interest" and those interested in the "propagation of

---

[69] House Select Committee on Lobbying Activities, *Hearings,* Americans for Democratic Action, 81st Cong., 2d. sess., 1950 (Washington, D.C.: Government Printing Office, 1950), 3, 4.

[70] House Select Committee on Lobbying Activities, *Hearings,* Committee for Constitutional Government, 81st Cong., 2d. sess., 1950 (Washington, D.C.: Government Printing Office, 1950), p. 63.

[71] House Select Committee on Lobbying Activities, *Hearings,* Americans for Democratic Action (Washington, D.C.: Government Printing Office, 1950), p. 5.

faiths or evocation of loyalties" is well illustrated by what has come to be known as the "radical right." [72] In interpreting this movement, the suggestion of a distinction between "interest politics" and "status politics" has been offered, principally by Hofstadter, Lipset, Bell, and Gussfield.[73] Hofstadter explains the distinction in this way. "We have, at all times, two kinds of processes going on in inextricable connection with each other: *interest politics*, the clash of material aims and needs among various groups and blocs; and *status politics*, the clash of various projective rationalizations arising from status aspirations and other personal motives." [74] If we agree that interest politics are conducted entirely in the area of tangible rewards, then there would be no doubt that we could not account for much of political life by using such a conceptual scheme. As Gusfield states, "the strength of such movements as Progressivism, McCarthyism or Temperance are not easily explained by the appearance of economic discontents." [75] It would seem, however, that such a distinction places too narrow a connotation upon the word "interest." It is true that economic determinism has characterized *some* of the traditional interest group studies, but there has always been the recognition that supposedly "irrational" or symbolic satisfaction fulfills the needs of many of the participants in a political struggle.

The emergence of the radical right in the 1950's is hardly a unique experience in the American political system. From the nativistic "Know-Nothing" Party of the 1840's, through the Populist Party, the Ku Klux Klan, to the current radical right, there is similarity both in espoused goals and in the social backgrounds of the supporters of these movements. Essentially, while the scapegoat, or symbol toward which hostility is expressed, has varied, the *conspiratorial* outlook has remained intact. Thus, the strong anti-

---

[72] This distinction on the basis of goals is made in Harold Lasswell and Abraham Kaplan, *Power and Society* (New Haven: Yale University Press, 1950), p. 40.

[73] Daniel Bell, ed., *The New American Right* (New York: Criterion Books, 1955). Joseph R. Gussfield, "A Dramaturgical Approach to Status Politics" (unpublished mimeograph). *See also* Bell, ed., *The Radical Right* (Garden City, N.Y.: Doubleday & Company, Inc., 1963). This is an updated version of the earlier *The New American Right.*

[74] Richard Hofstadter, "The Pseudo-Conservative Revolt," in Bell, *The New American Right*, p. 43.

[75] Gussfield, *op. cit.*, p. 2.

Semitism and anti-intellectual aura of the Populist movement found
contemporary expression in the hostility of the McCarthy movement
toward the "Ivy League," symbolizing the sophistication associated
with the Eastern seaboard.[76] Westin, Trow, and Lipset, have examined the course of extremist movement, both of the left and
right, and concluded that the source of strength has usually been
frustrated fringes of the middle class.[77] Generally, the less educated
lower strata of the middle class has responded to the rapid changes
of a complex society with demands for a return to an idealized version of America before the deluge—that is, before the growth of
bigness, whatever its form. Trow found that support for McCarthy,
for example, was positively correlated with fear of both large labor
unions and giant corporations. He notes that McCarthy expressed
for these people ". . . their fear and mistrust of bigness, and the
slick and subversive ideas that come out of the cities and the big
institutions to erode old ways and faiths."[78]

Organizationally, the extremist attitude is difficult to express. The
conspiratorial outlook underlying such an organization seems to
infect the participants to such a degree that even their associates
are viewed with suspicion. Structurally, the extremist movement is
characterized by the delegation of total formal control to the personality who symbolizes group aspirations. The leader who is unwilling to do less than nearly everything required of an organization cannot afford to permit diffusion of authority for fear of sowing
the seeds of infiltration and subversion.[79] These characteristics are
well substantiated by the organizational apparatus of the extreme
right, such as the John Birch Society. The Society, in Westin's
words, represents a "nihilistic plea for the repeal of industrialism

[76] Victor C. Ferkiss, "Populist Influences in American Fascism," *Western Political Quarterly*, X (June 1957), 350-373.

[77] Alan F. Westin, "The John Birch Society: Fundamentalism on the Right," *Commentary*, XXXII (August 1961), 93-104; Martin Trow, "Small Business-men, Political Tolerance, and McCarthy," *American Journal of Sociology*, LVIV (Nov. 1958), 270-281; Seymour Martin Lipset, "The Sources of the 'Radical Right,'" in Bell, *The New American Right*, pp. 166-233. *See also* Lipset, *Political Man* (Garden City, N.Y.: Doubleday and Company, Inc., 1960), pp. 134-139.

[78] Trow, *op. cit.*, p. 278.

[79] Edward A. Shils, "Authoritarianism 'Right' and 'Left,'" in S. Sidney Ulmer, ed., *Introductory Readings in Political Behavior* (Chicago: Rand McNally Company, 1961), p. 30.

and the abolition of international politics." [80] Its image of the surrounding environment is totally conspiratorial—so conspiratorial that it is reluctant to trust any government institution, voluntary association, religious institution, the mass media, or the schools or courts to be free of Communist infiltration. According to the *Blue Book,* the official statement of the posture of the Society, the Communists are "taking us over by a process so gradual and insidious that Soviet rule is slipped over so far on the American people, before they ever realize it is happening, that they can no longer resist the Communist conspiracy as free citizens, but can resist the Communist conspiracy only by themselves becoming conspirators against the established government." [81]

Since most of the institutions of the society are not to be relied upon, there is nothing to be achieved unless we contemplate a form of action more basic than the mere election to public office of individuals sympathetic with the goals of the Society. The political system, and especially politicians, are only of ephemeral value. Robert Welch, founder of the John Birch Society, writes "I am thoroughly convinced . . . that we cannot count on politicians, political leadership, or even political action except as part of something much deeper and broader, to save us." [82] In rejecting the normal "playing the political game," the Society operates under a more authoritarian structure than most of the interest groups whose goals are more limited. This is not to deny the role of the minority in all organizations, nor to deny that internal conflict is always present, but to suggest that, in the extremist organization, the role of the leader is more pronounced. The Society is described as an "organic entity" which is loyal to, and under the direction of, a "dynamic personal leader." Welch often speaks of the desirability of the "hardboiled, dictatorial, and dynamic boss"—the person who, although not necessarily desirous of undertaking the strenuous task of substantial revision, is placed in the position of being the most qualified candidate for the job by reason of the seriousness of the circumstances: "It is the imminence and the horror of this danger which drives me to so desperate a course as to offer myself as a personal leader in this fight, and to ask you to follow that leader-

---

[80] Westin, *op. cit.,* 95.
[81] *The Blue Book of the John Birch Society* (Fifth Printing, 1961), p. 29.
[82] *Ibid.,* p. 121.

ship. It is not because I want so frightening a responsibility. . . .
It is simply that, under the pressures of time and the exigencies of
our need, you have no other choice, and neither do I." [83] Thus the
founder of the John Birch Society describes himself in terms similar
to the "Fascist agitators" examined by Lowenthal and Guterman.
They write of this type of leader for whom . . . "forces stronger
and more imperious than his own will push him to leadership." [84]

With its remote objectives likely to be achieved only by dedicated fanaticism, there is no room for dissenters. The Society is
conceived to be a monolithic body which will operate under "completely authoritative control at all levels." Welch makes dedication
fundamental by saying "those members who cease to feel the
necessary degree of loyalty can either resign or will be put out
before they build up any splintering following of their own inside
the Society. . . . Whenever differences of opinion become translated into a lack of loyal support, we shall have short cuts for
eliminating both without going through any congress of so-called
democratic processes. *Otherwise, Communist infiltrators could bog
us down in interminable disagreements, schisms, and feuds before
we ever became seriously effective."* [85]

By establishing rigid patterns of recruitment and stimulating in-
tensification of involvement, the Society has been able to keep internal conflict at a minimum. Structurally, the flow of communication descends from the top to the bottom. Its local chapters are
kept small, usually made up of from ten to twenty members, and
each chapter is assigned a leader from the national headquarters
in Belmont, Massachusetts. Above the chapter leaders are coordina-
tors, who also are expected to keep "strict and careful control on
what every chapter is doing, and even every member of every
chapter so far as the work of the John Birch Society is concerned." [86]
The content of the downward communications flow is concerned
with the undertaking of specific activities by local chapters. In contrast, the upward flow of communications consists of "members'
monthly memos," a device whereby each member reports on his or

---

[83] *Ibid.*, pp. 116, 117, 170.

[84] Leo Lowenthal and Norbert Guterman, "Self Portrait of the Fascist Agitator," in Alvin W. Gouldner, ed., *Studies in Leadership* (New York: Harper
& Row, Publishers, 1950), p. 87.

[85] *The Blue Book of the John Birch Society*, pp. 161-162.

[86] *Ibid.*, p. 165.

her activities to the national headquarters.[87] Thus, a careful eye is kept on the members of the organization in keeping with the authoritarian structure on which it was founded. In a sense, then, the participants in the Society are not typical of the members of a voluntary association in that their function is that of "agent." The agent is expected to perform in a manner satisfactory to his immediate superiors or be expelled.[88] The goals of the organization are basically different from those of the "normal" pressure group. In seeking a total revision of the society, rather than piecemeal alterations in some aspect of the society which are perceived as harmful, the extremist group feels none of the need to conform to societal mores.

The demand that an organization be "democratic" in appearance though not in reality, suggested by David Truman as an example of environmental influence on the behavior of interest groups, would not affect an organization whose goals are abstract enough to permit perception of the total environment as being a conspiracy. Differing in goals and structure from the more restrained type of interest group, the organizations committed to radical change can also be expected to differ in their goal-reaching techniques.

The general distinction, drawn from the anxieties expressed in the extremist organizations' desire to remain aloof from the political game, tends to break down in actual practice. Whereas a long-term goal might be a total revision of the society, the firmly institutionalized structure of American politics makes it necessary to participate at least minimally through existing agencies or lose. Hence the Birch Society has on occasion sought to place members or those supported by the Society in official positions within political parties, such as the Republican Party in California. It is nevertheless true that organizations with more limited aspirations participate on a much more sustained basis. We therefore turn our attention to the techniques regularly employed by interest groups as they operate within the network of the established political structure.

---

[87] Westin, op. cit., 99.

[88] See Philip Selznick, The Organizational Weapon (New York: McGraw-Hill Book Company, Inc., 1952) for a discussion of the role of the agent.

The Group, Its

VIII

Membership,

and the Public

A popular conception of lobbying techniques is that, for the most part, lobbyists indulge in providing elaborate entertainment for legislators, offering bribes, and, if all else fails, threatening retaliation by defeating the recalcitrant legislator in his next effort at re-election. This notion of the unscrupulous lobbyist is almost entirely without foundation. What may have been true of days gone by has been made impossible by, among other things, the rapid development of the mass communications media. Indeed, instead of devoting most of their efforts exclusively toward cultivating direct channels of access to governmental decision makers, it has become a steady trend for interest groups to expend more of their energy and resources in the hopes of creating a more generally favorable climate of opinion in the society as a whole. Presumably, the goal of an interest group would be not to influence a wider public but rather to use widespread support in order to extract favorable reactions from those in a position to make authoritative decisions. Further, all interest groups do not rely on public relations techniques to the same extent. In some instances, the cause of a particular group is furthered by the avoidance of publicity and the utilization of the advantage of surprise. The Army, for example, in seeking to establish military control over the creation of atomic energy, worked in absolute secrecy in close cooperation with the War Department to draft legislation before the atomic scientists, who were anxious to impose civilian control, were even aware that legislation was being contemplated. Consequently, when a bill assuring military control was introduced in the House, those who opposed the legislation had to work at a feverish pace to try to recoup what had been lost because of lack of access to information about the opposition's activities.[1]

Public Relations: Aspirations and Effects

The use of extensive public relations may also vary considerably according to the degree to which a group is subjected to unusually hostile publicity. Thus, the AFL-CIO spent more than a million dollars to try to counter the unfavorable image which it believed organized labor was creating due to the exposure by the McClellan Committee of some rather unsavory aspects of the labor movement. Finally, one might suspect that the use of mass propaganda might vary with the size of the organization. Key has suggested that smaller groups, such as business organizations, would be more attracted to extensive reliance upon public relations since "they command directly the support of only a few people, and they can readily subscribe to the doctrine that they must carry their cause by the generous support of propaganda to shape the opinions of the general public." [2] However, Lester Milbrath's research based upon interviews with lobbyists reveals that mass membership organizations, particularly farm and labor, rated public relations campaigns

---

[1] Byron S. Miller, "A Law Is Passed—The Atomic Energy Act of 1946," *University of Chicago Law Review*, XV (Summer, 1948), 804. *See also* Richard G. Hewlett and Oscar E. Anderson, Jr., *The New World, 1939/1956* (University Park, Pa.: The Pennsylvania State University Press, 1962), Vol. 1, 422.

[2] V. O. Key, Jr., *Public Opinion and American Democracy* (New York: Alfred A. Knopf, Inc., 1961), p. 515.

highest in comparison with other groups.[3] Since these mass organizations also ranked letter-writing campaigns higher than other types of groups, Milbrath suggests that the assumption of the lobbyist from the large organization that he has a greater potential audience produces the higher rating. The obvious assumption is that the mass membership organizations apparently look upon public relations as a device to mobilize *membership* behind the position of the organization, while the smaller organizations are aiming toward "general" public opinion. As Monypenny argues, the smaller group can expect more internal cohesion than the larger group, and hence would expend more of its energy outward.[4] Indeed, business groups such as the National Association of Manufacturers, place primary reliance upon public relations.[5]

If we consider the techniques of mass propaganda, we should not be victimized by the vast amount of attention given to the idea that private groups can control or even shape opinions. Although the effects of a public relations campaign are difficult to measure, a body of firm generalizations developed in the social sciences state that it is very likely that the consequences of propaganda efforts are negligible. It is one thing to sell a particular brand of soap through advertising; it is quite another matter to sell a candidate or a legislative proposal by the same techniques. In the case of soap, most Americans are sufficiently convinced that personal cleanliness is a desirable attribute; the particular brand they use is of no great importance. On the other hand, propaganda which deals with more complex situations comes into contact with more deeply rooted values.[6] In the case of ethnic prejudices, for example, propaganda would not reshape basic attitudes to any appreciable extent. Further, the attempts of organized labor to show that "union workers are

---

[3] Lester Milbrath, "Lobbying as a Communications Process," *Public Opinion Quarterly*, XXIV (Spring, 1960), 45.

[4] Phillip Monypenny, "Political Science and the Study of Groups: Notes to Guide a Research Project," *Western Political Quarterly*, VII (June 1954), 197.

[5] Joseph G. La Palombara, "Pressure, Propaganda, and Political Action in the Election of 1950," *Journal of Politics*, XIV (May 1952), 305.

[6] Paul Lazarsfeld and Robert K. Merton, "Mass Communication, Popular Taste and Organized Social Action," in Lyman Bryson, ed., *The Communication of Ideas* (New York: Institute for Religious and Social Studies, 1948), pp. 113-118. *See also* Joseph T. Klapper, *The Effects of Mass Communication* (New York: The Free Press of Glencoe, Inc., 1960), pp. 12-97.

nice people" would have little impact unless the recipients of the propaganda were already inclined to accept this premise.[7] It is the function of propaganda, whether recognized by practitioners of the art or not, to mobilize, reinforce, or channel pre-existing, but possibly latent, attitudes. It is interesting to note Milbrath's comments upon the lobbyists' perception of the effect of propaganda in view of these conclusions. Some lobbyists, while they were not convinced that the message of their organization was penetrating very deeply, rationalized that governmental decision makers might believe that a particular campaign was persuasive and might possibly alter their position in order to conform to an expected reaction from the "outside world."[8]

PROPAGANDA TECHNIQUES

Generally, the propaganda campaigns of organized groups are of two types: defensive efforts to ward off some immediate threat, such as the campaign of the American Medical Association to defeat the King-Anderson bill; and generalized, long-range programs to create a favorable image of the organization without reference to any immediate objectives.[9] In both types of campaigns there are similarities, one of the most obvious being the use of symbols. If the group is trying to establish its legitimacy, or its conformity to generally held societal norms, it will utilize "good" symbols. Organized labor, to illustrate, seeks to create an association of the words "labor" and "America," an identification of unions with "freedom" and "neighbors." The AFL-CIO Industrial Union Department's brochure entitled "The All Union Family" describes a family as living at "99 Shady Lane, Anytown, U.S.A." The members of the union family are "Mr. and Mrs. John Q. America and their two wonderful kids."[10] Labor, which we have described essentially as a protest movement, has to try to integrate itself more fully into the mainstream of American life. Its program is, of course,

---

[7] Gerald Pomper, "The Public Relations of Organized Labor," *Public Opinion Quarterly,* XXIII (Winter, 1960), 487.

[8] Milbrath, *op. cit.,* 45.

[9] Adapted from the suggestion of S. E. Finer in Henry W. Ehrman, ed., *Interest Groups on Four Continents* (Pittsburgh: University of Pittsburgh Press, 1958), p. 251.

[10] Pomper, *op. cit.,* 488. *See also* AFL-CIO, Industrial Union Department, "Mr. and Mrs. America: The All Union Family," p. 3.

long-term. It begins with the assumption that labor has to carve out a niche for itself and, in so doing, faces an uphill struggle. Attention has already been given to the absence of unions as a discernible part of the mass, or popular, culture. By contrast, an association such as the American Bar Association, whose membership operates with less of a handicap, sees its job to be one of *restoring* confidence.

If the goals of an organization are to prevent the establishment of a program judged to be detrimental to its organizational interests, the technique is to identify the proponents of the program with "evil" symbols. No symbol is more exhausted by constant usage than the old reliable, "socialism." This symbol, made famous by its repeated use by the American Medical Association, has become almost standard in the operating procedure of nearly all organizations whose objectives can, without a thoroughly implausible stretching of the imagination, be associated with free enterprise. Real estate organizations, such as the National Association of Real Estate Boards and National Association of Home Builders, played heavily upon the theme of socialism in their efforts to defeat public housing legislation. Electing to concentrate propaganda dissemination at the local level, where the impact of public housing would be apparent, the Realtors' Washington Committee (which served as coordinator) distributed "kits" to local realtors which spelled out in some detail the approach to be taken. The advice was to equate public housing with "statism," "socialism," or any other "scarism," and "wherever possible stir up religious and racial prejudice." [11]

These instructions did result in advertisements in local papers stressing the drastically simplified alternative: "Do you believe in socialism? No! Is public housing socialism? Yes!" [12] However, there were organizations equally concerned with supporting public housing. If there had been little counterpropaganda there would have been, theoretically, a greater possibility that the symbolism of the realtors could have effected at least a mobilization of opposition. Monopolization of media for the promulgation of specified objec-

[11] Lee F. Johnson, "Housing: A 1950 Tragedy," *The Survey*, December 1950, p. 553. *See also* House Select Committee on Lobbying Activities, *Hearings*, Housing Lobby, 81st Cong., 2d. sess., 1950 (Washington, D.C.: Government Printing Office, 1950).

[12] House Select Committee on Lobbying Activities, *Hearings*, Housing Lobby, p. 370.

tives is a rarity, and, with the existence of opposing propaganda, the probable result of the entire effort was neutralization.[13]

Organizations using propaganda techniques often feel that they can do a more effective job if some other organization, not directly identifiable with the primary antagonist, can be persuaded to do most of the arguing. Key notes that ". . . any group that feels itself to be in the doghouse will tend to hide behind false fronts when it propagandizes the public." [14] The exact rationale for this assumption is difficult to locate. Perhaps the most readily understandable explanation is the fear that a public relations campaign might succeed in stimulating opposition which then could be transferred to the source of the propaganda. The extent to which this occurs is, like the effects of public relations activities, difficult to ascertain. However, Stokes' analysis of the 1958 right to work referendum in Ohio is suggestive of the possibilities of unanticipated consequences in propaganda campaigns. Stokes notes that the beginning of the campaign found little more than half of the electorate even familiar with the issue, with about half of this aware group in favor of adoption of a right to work law. However, as the efforts for and against the law grew more intense, awareness spread to three-quarters of the electorate. As interest spread, support for right to work held firm only in the business community. In every other segment of the population, right to work declined in popularity until, at the conclusion of the campaign, only businessmen gave majority approval. What was the basic contributing factor to this growth of opposition? Stokes offers the following explanation:

> . . . the primary source of the rising tide against right to work was the connection the public drew between the issue and the recession. Responsibility for the economic distress of 1957-1958 was not at first charged to the business community. The recession *had* reinforced the public's belief that the Republicans, as the party of business, would not prevent unemployment. But it was not until right to work was brought before the public that the economic distress was given a forceful political translation. To many people in Ohio, placing right to work on the ballot looked like an effort by business to kick the working man when he was down. With this idea planted in the public's mind, labor was able to rally the

---

[13] Lazarsfeld and Merton, *op. cit.*, p. 115.

[14] Key, *op. cit.*, p. 517.

opposition to the issue successfully, leaving business isolated in support of the law.[15]

The Ohio experience suggests that the more business propagandized, the more it became identified with circumstances over which it had no control. Perhaps, then, there is wisdom in the use of "front groups."

The American Bar Association has stated that ". . . the most effective way to tell the lawyer's story is to have someone else tell it." [16] In this case, the lawyers have a ready-made proponent in insurance companies and related financial institutions. Lawyers, as the ABA observes, "are in a position to control the appointment of many fiduciaries—executors, trustees, escrow agents and the like [and] are in a position to advise a client that he should have more insurance because of estate and inheritance tax problems, and may even recommend an insurance company if requested to do so by a client." [17]

Whether or not as a result of this none too subtle suggestion, the organized bar has enjoyed the cooperation of banks and insurance companies ranging from the very large, such as John Hancock and the Guaranty Trust Company of New York, to the smaller local institutions of considerable regional prestige. Other groups are less fortunate and have to resort to the deliberate creation of auxiliary organizations. The railroad interests in Pennsylvania, in opposing a law to raise the long haul truck weight limit, not only used established associations like the Pennsylvania State Grange to disseminate their literature, but also relied upon some very obvious artificial fronts. One of the public relations specialists directing the railroads program was quoted as saying: "Of course we release some stories under direct attribution, but they will be of less propaganda value than those we can generate from motorists, property owners, tax payers, farmers or women's groups. In sum, we not only have to create publicity ideas; we also have to go out into the field and

---

[15] Donald E. Stokes, *Voting Research and the Businessman in Politics* (Ann Arbor: The Foundation for Research on Human Behavior, 1960), p. 23. Similar examples of the negative consequences of organization support would be labor or NAACP endorsement in the South.

[16] American Bar Association, Standing Committee on Public Relations, *op. cit.*, p. 61.

[17] *Ibid.*, pp. 61-62.

create the groups and occasions so that these ideas will become realities." [18]

This technique is different from the alliance formation operations often indulged in by groups with similar aspirations, such as the American Jewish Congress and the National Association for the Advancement of Colored People.[19] It also differs from the more direct infiltration methods of the John Birch Society. The Society does seek to establish fronts, but also hopes to infiltrate established community organizations without incurring overt identification. This semisecret association would be less inclined to rely on the shotgun type propaganda effort in the expectation that it would be able to exert a more subtle influence upon opinion leaders within a community. Most of its activity is local, although coordinated from its national headquarters. Loss of the element of secrecy—the ability to catch an opponent by surprise—might also mean public disapproval and loss of support.[20]

Pressure Groups and Elections: Myths and Realities of Group Voting

Many of the propaganda activities of organized groups become most intense when they are given personification by means of the electoral process. This is the time when nonmember opinion is more easily accessible to the pleadings of organizations, and it is also the time when membership opinion might be more readily unified. Interest groups also reason that, if the "right" man can be elected, their task of persuasion will be simplified. Finally, we cannot neglect the most widely publicized aspect of electoral activity by interest groups—the threat of retaliation against a candidate for public office whose record is displeasing. When the NAM declares "we have endeavored . . . to elect congressmen whom we have

---

[18] Robert Bendiner, "The Engineering of Consent–A Case Study," *The Reporter*, Aug. 11, 1955, p. 17.

[19] Senate Committee on the Judiciary, *Hearings*, Civil Rights, 86th Cong., 1st sess., 1959 (Washington, D.C.: Government Printing Office, 1959), pp. 1527-1571.

[20] Westin, *op. cit.*, 306.

known to possess the courage of their convictions . . . and who
fearlessly oppose the legislation we have been opposing" and countless other organizations inform legislators that their record will be
remembered in November, the student of group politics might indeed tremble at such awesome displays of power.[21] However, as in
the case of public relations campaigns, the hard facts of political
life do not coincide with a simplified model of human motivations.

It is beyond the abilities of an organized group to guarantee,
with any degree of certainty, that its members will automatically
respond to the suggestions of the leaders. It is, however, true that
group affiliations are an important variable in the reaching of an
electoral decision. We know that, with varying degrees of consistency, people with similar group memberships tend to vote as
a unit or, to use an expression popular among southern politicians,
a "bloc." Jews, Negroes, Catholics, and members of labor unions
are predominately Democratic in preference; professional or managerial people are more inclined to identify with the Republican
Party.[22] Yet it would hardly be accurate to assume that relatively
consistent voting patterns can be equated with a simple delivery of
a group's votes by leaders of organizations formally representing
that group. Few groups will fail to reveal a minority who do not
conform to the preponderant group mood. The basic exception to
this statement is the Jews. Unlike most ethnic groups, the pro-
Democratic inclinations of the Jews do not vary with class or status
lines within the group. Wealthier and more educated Jews are, if
anything, more Democratic than lower income Jews.[23] However,
with Catholics and Negroes, such homogeneity is lacking. While
Negroes have been principally Democratic, there has been some
defection of Negro leadership to the Republican Party. Catholics
are slightly more Democratic than the total population, but, when
the voting of Catholics is compared with Protestants of similar

[21] Quoted in La Palombara, *op. cit.*, 306.
[22] Angus Campbell and Homer C. Cooper, *Group Differences in Attitudes
and Votes* (University of Michigan: Survey Research Center, 1956), pp. 19-
37.
[23] Lawrence Fuchs, "American Jews and the Presidential Vote," *American
Political Science Review*, XLIX (June 1955), 355. See also Fuchs, *The Political
Behavior of American Jews* (New York: The Free Press of Glencoe, Inc.,
1956).

social and economic circumstances, the Democratic bias tends to disappear.[24]

Intragroup differences become greater if we consider not merely voting but also attitudes. Again the Jews exhibit a strong awareness of group-oriented political goals. There are apparently well defined standards on contemporary questions, stemming from the application of traditional Jewish values to current problems. Fuchs notes that "no matter what criteria have been used to define liberalism and conservatism, Jews have invariably been rated overwhelmingly more liberal than Christians." [25] Catholics, while responding to group norms on some issues, do not seem to have developed a unique position on most political problems. In the case of the Negroes, there is conspicuous absence of any distinct combination of attitudes beyond the vote. Negroes are less politically involved and considerably less sophisticated than other ethnic groups and are therefore less likely to respond cohesively on the basis of a commonly perceived external stimulus.[26]

These differences suggest that there should be a distinction between examples of people with the same backgrounds and environments taking a position in response to the overt political "line" of a group, and situations in which people of similar circumstances react in the same way independent of actual group pressure.[27] The latter case is probably the rule. Individual values, to the extent that they reflect group norms, are sufficiently established to resist any sudden or capricious reversal of position by a formal organization. It would be absurd to suppose that the American Jewish Congress, if for some reason it chose to do so, could hope to accomplish even the slightest reduction of the Democratic leanings of the Jewish community. On the other hand, it is not always necessary for an organization to inform its clientele of the need for activity to redress a wrong. As Stokes says, ". . . wheat farmers may respond in unison to a drop in the price of their crop, without needing a

---

[24] Stokes, *op. cit.*, p. 18. See also Angus Campbell, Philip E. Converse, Warren E. Miller, and Donald E. Stokes, *The American Voter* (New York: John Wiley and Sons, Inc., 1960), p. 302.

[25] Fuchs, "American Jews and the Presidential Vote," *op. cit.*, 392.

[26] Campbell and Cooper, *op. cit.*, pp. 99-100.

[27] Stokes, *op. cit.*, p. 15.

farm organization to tell them that their pocketbook nerve has been touched." [28]

Having examined limitations upon the electoral activity of political associations, we can now approach their electoral techniques with greater perspective. Pressure groups seek to achieve the election of favorable candidates by two basic methods: financial contributions and voter mobilization. In spite of the frequently cited folksaying that "money talks," lobbyists do not put much stock in this technique as a means of establishing a channel of communication with a politician.[29] Naturally, contributions flow into the campaign chests of candidates whose public record or personal inclinations coincide with the views of the contributing group. Most of labor's contributions go to Democratic candidates and most corporate contributions are made to Republicans. Heard points out that the two sources of contributions balanced approximately equally in 1956.[30] In some cases, where an organization takes part in electoral activity only sporadically, its campaign contributions will be more carefully placed. Thus, while the AFL-CIO's Committee on Political Education ranks candidates on the basis of their votes on a series of issues, and makes contributions accordingly, the American Medical Association's Political Action Committee, organized in 1961, concerned itself only with the defeat of the King-Anderson Bill. Labor's money is usually sent into every state where a favorable candidate is contesting an election, while the AMA's contributions went into far fewer campaigns. Contributions were offered to the five Democratic and three Republican members of the House Ways and Means Committee who were regarded as doubtful on the medicare issue.

Regardless of the way money is spent, one cannot argue that the candidate who has the most money will invariably win, although this argument was once fashionable. There are, of course, basic campaign costs to be met, and the organization which provides

---

[28] *Ibid.*

[29] Milbrath, *op. cit.*, 50.

[30] Alexander Heard, *The Costs of Democracy* (Chapel Hill: University of North Carolina Press, 1960), p. 196.

money for the distribution of literature, appeals through mass media, and the various types of appeal to the voters might hope to gain the favor of the recipient of such funds. Perhaps more important to a candidate's campaign is the willingness of an organization to undertake a sustained effort to increase the voting of people who are in agreement with the candidate's position. The very large organizations, such as the AFL-CIO, that like to think they have substantial strength at the polls, engage quite heavily in the publication of voting records and personal solicitation of votes among their own members. But the smaller organizations, such as business or professional groups, can make no claims of a deliverable body of voters and can only offer their services as proselytizers of a larger public. However, while the target of the efforts of the two types of groups varies, their techniques are similar. There is general recognition of the very basic fact that, while the nonpersonal appeals of mass communication should not be neglected, success will depend more upon informal and personal contacts. Examples drawn from divergent sources will illustrate this technique.

Studies of United Automobile Workers Unions in Detroit and Chicago note that the leadership of both unions is actively engaged in the support of Democratic candidates through personal contacts with members. In Chicago, the local union president spent considerable amounts of time in supplementing an organizational postcard campaign. Each member of the union was given one of these cards by leadership within the place of employment and "if you got one of these Poles or Bohunks who couldn't read or write, we'd get somebody to do it for them and make them sign their X [indicating a pledge of support] on it." [31] In Detroit, similar efforts were more coordinated. The membership of the union was divided according to congressional district, and neighborhood meetings were sponsored, giving workers the opportunity to discuss the issues. At the plants, "lists of endorsed slates are passed out to the workers, and lunch hour and coffee breaks at election time are punctuated with political discussion." [32] Although both unions were equally vociferous in their efforts, the results were not the same. The majority of

---

[31] Harold Wilensky, "The Labor Vote: A Local Union's Impact on the Political Conduct of Its Members," *Social Forces,* XXXV (Dec. 1956), 114.

[32] Nicholas A. Masters, "The Politics of Union Endorsement of Candidates in the Detroit Area," *Midwest Journal of Political Science,* I (Aug. 1957), 146.

Detroit union members "trust the voting recommendations of labor groups," but in Chicago there is greater distrust and apathy.[33] What explains this difference? We know that the more active members of an organization tend to conform more readily to group norms.[34] The Detroit union has developed an elaborate plan of formal endorsement of candidates in which the individual member, while not participating directly, does not necessarily feel that a candidate is being "shoved down his throat." Further, there is very close collaboration between the union and the state Democratic party. This proximity between the union and the political process enables the organization to establish a "natural" connection with politics. The establishing of union membership is frequently an automatic process, and since there is an inclination of union members to look upon political activity as a secondary aspect of the union's proper sphere of activities, the methods of the Detroit union are a good remedy for this situation. However, the Detroit case is hardly typical.

What of the smaller organization that must work with nonmember opinions? Even if their own members are ready and willing to toe the mark, this is of little consequence. However, if the organization or its members enjoy considerable community prestige, a candidate may believe that his campaign will be augmented by its participation. In political contests in which the issue of compulsory health insurance is being debated, various "medical arts committees" have arranged for doctors to write personal letters urging their patients' opposition to "forces at work in this nation today which replace the health and medical care you have always enjoyed under the truly American system of private medicine."[35] In most cases, such letters urged the patient to vote for lists of endorsed candidates who, according to the physicians, could be expected to vote "right" if elected. In Ohio, a small group of trade

[33] Harold L. Sheppard and Nicholas A. Masters, "The Political Attitudes and Preferences of Union Members: The Case of the Detroit Auto Workers," *American Political Science Review,* LIII (June 1959) 447. *See also* Arthur Kornhauser, Harold L. Sheppard, and Albert J. Mayer, *When Labor Votes: A Study of Auto Workers* (New Hyde Park, New York: University Books, 1956).

[34] James G. March, "Group Norms and the Active Minority," *American Sociological Review,* XVIV (Dec. 1954), 733-741. *See also* Campbell, Converse, Miller, and Stokes, *op. cit.,* p. 311.

[35] "New Power at the Polls," *Medical Economics,* Jan. 1951, p. 77.

association executives, using virtually no publicity, worked on behalf of the candidacy of Senator Robert Taft by singling out
opinion leaders in every county of the state. Each of these local
influentials was urged to arrange meetings, to register Taft supporters and get them to the polls, and to have voters visited by
members of their professions.[36] These programs roughly parallel
the standard political party operations. To attribute unusual success
to them would be to overlook the many other variables contributing
to victory or defeat. In Ohio, for example, the substitution of the
office-block for the party column ballot was estimated by Taft to
have been responsible for more than one-fourth of his majority.[37]
The fact that physicians in Florida supported George Smathers in
his successful attempt to unseat Senator Claude Pepper in the
1950 Democratic primaries can hardly be regarded as any sort of
first cause. The threat of an organization that it will punish politicians for poor voting records simply cannot be made good.[38]

A CONCLUDING EVALUATION

A more plausible assessment of the role of pressure groups in the
electoral process can be made if we consider them as allies of the
regular political organizations. The cooperation between the AFL-
CIO and the Democratic party well illustrates the nature of this
alliance. Labor support is not a unified and reliable basis of support
for the Democratic party. E. E. Schattschneider estimates that the
Democrats can be expected to get about 5,600,000 votes from among
the membership of the AFL-CIO, which is about one-third of the
total membership.[39] While this is not a great many votes in a Presidential election, for example, some consideration should be given
to the geographical distribution of these votes. Nicholas Masters,
drawing our attention to the tiny smattering of votes that meant
victory for Kennedy, maintains that labor support has become crucial in the urban areas of states having large electoral votes. Candi-

---

[36] La Palombara, *op. cit.*, 303-325.

[37] V. O. Key, Jr., *Politics, Parties, and Pressure Groups* (New York: Thomas
Y. Crowell Company, 1958), p. 694.

[38] V. O. Key, Jr., "The Veterans and the House of Representatives: A Study
of a Pressure Group and Electoral Mortality," *Journal of Politics,* V (Feb.
1943), 27-40.

[39] E. E. Schattschneider, *The Semisovereign People* (New York: Holt, Rinehart & Winston, 1960), p. 50.

dates in these areas of labor concentration need the active support
of unions, not because union leaders control a bloc of votes, but
because they may be able to increase the magnitude of urban
majorities for the Democrats.[40] However, this does not mean that
the Democratic party is in a position of dependence for ". . . the
AFL-CIO must remain Democratic in order to maintain a strong
and viable bargaining position in politics." [41] If one tries to assess
the relative dependence of the two organizations upon each other,
a good beginning can be made with Key's labeling of the pressure
group as the "junior partner." [42] If the pressure group has no choice
but to support party candidates, then the party clearly assumes
the position of dominance. Schattschneider's argument that "the
pressure system is much too small to play the role sometimes assigned to it" in the electoral process is based upon the argument
that no pressure group could win an election by itself and that
"there is no political substitute for victory in an election." [43] In view
of these arguments and those presented in this text, there is much
to be gained from examining the activities of pressure groups in
the governmental arena itself, if for no other reason except that, by
a simple process of elimination, this must be the place where group
influence is greatest.

---

[40] Nicholas A. Masters, "Organized Labor as a Base of Support for the
Democratic Party," *Law and Contemporary Problems,* XXVII (Spring, 1962),
255.

[41] *Ibid.,* 256.

[42] Key, *Public Opinion and American Democracy,* 524.

[43] Schattschneider, *op. cit.,* p. 58.

The Representation

IX

of Interests

Through Legislation

In examining the legislative process we need at the outset some understanding of the role of the legislature and legislators in establishing a basic pattern of order for the society.[1] It would hardly be plausible to assume that the group conflict inherent in a changing society can resolve itself automatically. Recalling for the moment Easton's idea of the study of politics constituting the "authoritative allocation of values," we can assign to the legislature the function of providing competitive demands with a tentative decision of victory or defeat.[2] The conflicting demands of groups will gravitate toward the formal institutions of government, for it is only within such institutions that demands can be transformed into legally binding mandates. The legislature, however, is not the sole

---

[1] See Roland Young, *The American Congress* (New York: Harper & Row, Publishers, 1958), pp. 1-17 for a theoretical statement of the role of the legislature.

[2] David Easton, *The Political System* (New York: Alfred A. Knopf, Inc., 1953), pp. 129-134.

arbiter of disputes. Other governmental institutions—administrative agencies and courts—perform the same function; indeed some would say that these institutions have gradually assumed more responsibility in the formation of public policy, while the legislature's role in this area has diminished in significance. It is not our task to attempt an evaluaton of the importance of legislative assemblies in the total policy formation process but rather to explore the process whereby laws are made.

The Legislative System

The best theoretical introduction to this process can be gleaned from Easton's concept of the political system, as applied by Wahlke, Eulau, Buchanan, and Ferguson in *The Legislative System*.[3] A system, in Easton's thought, is simply a set of interrelated activities, and a political system consists of those activities which can be analytically, if not actually, isolated from the totality of social activity. The political system is essentially a conversion process, a means of turning "inputs" into "outputs." In Easton's words:

> Presumably, if we select political systems for special study, we do so because we believe that they have characteristically important consequences for society, namely, authoritative decisions. These consequences I shall call outputs. . . . Unless a system is approaching a state of entropy . . . it must have continuing inputs to keep it going. Without inputs the system can do no work; without outputs we cannot identify the work done by the system. The specific research task in this connection would be to identify the inputs and the forces that shape and change them, to trace the process through which they are transformed into outputs, to describe the general conditions under which such processes can be maintained, and to establish a relationship between outputs and succeeding inputs of the system.[4]

When we speak of a legislative system, we use these same concepts in a narrower way. The legislature can be described as an autonomous system within its own set of inputs (political parties, interest

---

[3] John C. Wahlke, Heinz Eulau, William Buchanan, and Leroy Ferguson, *The Legislative System* (New York: John Wiley and Sons, Inc., 1962).

[4] Easton, "An Approach to the Analysis of Political Systems," *World Politics,* IX (1956-1957), 385-386.

groups, constituencies, and administrative agencies) which it transforms into decisions or outputs. Notice that interest groups are only a part of the total set of demands, and the importance of this particular source of demands is not a constant. The importance of interest groups might vary from issue to issue, or from institution to institution.

THE LEGISLATURE AS AN INSTITUTION

Obviously, then, the conversion process is not to be understood solely by locating and assessing the extent and intensity of interest group demands. The legislature is an institution not only in the commonly understood sense that it has a physical home, officers, and formal rules of procedure, but also because it has a recognized normative pattern.[5] This means that the legislature has developed into a self-sufficient system. Its norms are supported by sanctions which the members accept. We cannot study the legislature entirely by means of understanding external pressures upon it; we must also inquire into patterns of internalized pressure, described by Matthews as "folkways." [6] While the institutional norms of the legislature are worthy of study in their own right, they are most significant for our purpose because they interact with external pressures and thus play a part in the conversion or decision-making process. Latham has written that "the legislature referees the group struggle, ratifies the victories of the successful coalitions, and records the terms of the surrenders, compromises, and conquests in the form of statutes." [7] On the other hand, Burns once described legislators as little more than elected lobbyists.[8] How can one referee if he is committed to the values of one of the participants? One way to reconcile these opposing points of view is to avoid the use of "either-or" language. Latham does not intend to suggest that the

[5] Vernon Van Dyke, *Political Science: A Philosophical Analysis* (Stanford: Stanford University Press, 1960), pp. 135-137.

[6] Donald Matthews, "The Folkways of the United States Senate: Conformity to Group Norms and Legislative Effectiveness," *American Political Science Review*, LIII (Dec. 1959), 1064-1089. *See also* Matthews, *U.S. Senators and Their World* (Chapel Hill: The University of North Carolina Press, 1960), pp. 92-117.

[7] Earl Latham, *The Group Basis of Politics* (Ithaca, N.Y.: Cornell University Press, 1952), p. 35.

[8] James Burns, *Congress on Trial* (New York: Harper & Row, Publishers, 1949), p. 18.

legislature is a dormant *tabula rasa* which merely approves previously reached decisions: "the legislature does not play the inert part of cash register, ringing up additions and withdrawals of strength, a mindless balance pointing and marking the weight and distribution of power among the contending groups." [9] Still less can the legislative system be understood as being made up of philosopher kings who distill private interest into public good.

THE LEGISLATOR'S DEFINITION OF THE SITUATION

There is no objective standard by which to measure legislative performances, and it is far more fruitful to rely upon the legislator's perception of his role or "definition of the situation." Members of legislatures fill a status to which certain expectations have been attached. All of the expectations do not originate with a single source, and the role played by each legislator can be understood as a sum of the total pattern of expectations. The legislator is expected to perform in a certain way by his colleagues, his constituents, and formal organizations, to name a few. The expectations may reinforce each other or they may conflict. Each legislator is a formal or informal member of many other groups. In addition, a legislator possesses individual ecological characteristics, which, to an extent not yet totally determined, are reflected by his particular personality. All of these variables help to determine how a legislator will interpret the demands of an interest group, and the reaction of a legislator to group pressure is a critical factor in determining the influence of a group.

Formal Structure: The Committees

The importance of formal structure in the legislative process is that it provides part of the framework in which group conflicts can be resolved; it has "restraining and channeling effects." [10] By far the most easily identifiable aspect of the formal structure of the American legislature is the committee system. George B. Galloway notes that the "operation of the committee system is recognized as

[9] Latham, *op. cit.*, p. 37.
[10] Norman Meller, "Legislative Behavior Research," *Western Political Quarterly*, XIII (Mar. 1960), 131-153.

the heart of congressional activity . . . these miniature legislatures have acquired such power and prestige over the years that they are largely autonomous in the House itself which created them and whose agents they are supposed to be." [11] Matthews says much the same about the Senate, while the Committee on American Legislatures of the American Political Science Association finds the committee system dominant in the state legislative process.[12] While the committee might not make the final decision, it is here that a potential law comes in for its first public scrutiny, where the compromises and subtle variations upon the *quid pro quo* are agreed upon.

GROUP STAKES IN COMMITTEE ASSIGNMENTS

The relations between interest groups and committees may develop a certain degree of stability due to the fact that most committees are "stacked" with legislators whose constituencies are most concerned with the work of the committee. For example, both the House and Senate Agriculture Committees are manned by farmers, or legislators from constituencies with vital interest in farming. This does not insure that the demands of interest groups and the preferences of legislators will always be harmonious, for each particular interest will have several organizations competing for the right to speak authoritatively. Consequently, organized groups take considerable interest in the process of committee assignments. While overt participation in the assigning of committee positions is rare, organizations have clearly articulated "expectations" as to the kinds of legislators who should be appointed. Masters discovered that "Democrats attempt to placate organized labor by placing pro-labor representatives on the Education and Labor Committee, while Republicans attempt to satisfy the National Association of Manufacturers by appointing pro-business members to the same committee." [13]

In addition, the operation of the seniority system serves to limit

---

[11] George B. Galloway, *History of the House of Representatives* (New York: Thomas Y. Crowell Company, 1961), p. 95.

[12] Matthews, *U.S. Senators and Their World*, pp. 147-175. Belle Zeller, ed., *American State Legislatures* (New York: Thomas Y. Crowell Company, 1954), pp. 95-102. Exceptions to the conclusions reached in *American State Legislatures* will be offered later in the chapter.

[13] Nicholas A. Masters, "House Committee Assignments," *American Political Science Review*, LV (June 1961), 355.

the rapport between interest group and committee. Seniority is particularly troublesome for organized labor. Since the seniority system works to the advantage of Southerners from safe districts, labor has had a difficult time working with the chairmen of the House Education and Labor Committee. According to Masters, the Democrats seek to appoint either Southerners or members who can afford to take a forthright pro-labor stand, while Republicans, having closer connections with management, try to appoint Congressmen whose pro-management bias will not diminish their chances of re-election.[14] The make-up of this committee as a factor in the strategy of interest groups is illuminated by the case of the 1955 legislative campaign for raising the federal minimum wage. Various unions had formed the Joint Minimum Wage Committee to direct an extensive effort to achieve an increase in the minimum wage from 75 cents to —at the least—90 cents. After a series of preparatory operations, the Joint Committee turned to the task of guiding a bill through Congress. The first obstacle was the House Committee on Education and Labor, chaired by Graham Barden of North Carolina. Gus Tyler, director of the Political Department of the International Ladies Garment Workers' Union, saw Barden as the "key problem" and commented that "it appeared to the press that the real struggle in Washington on minimum wages was between organized labor and Barden." [15]

Most successful lobbyists are sophisticated enough to realize that the committee hearings, and the testimony presented therein, are of doubtful value in the communication of influence. Most legislators have already made up their minds and little can be done to cause a sudden change of heart. Tyler says of Barden that his "philosophy on federal minimum-wage law was a matter of public record. In open hearings before his committee, Barden announced that 'everybody knows that minimum-wage legislation is basically counter to our democratic form of government and to our competitive economy.' This philosophy was not something invented in 1955. Barden had espoused and fought for this point of view over many years in Congress, where his seniority had earned him a top post on the

---

[14] *Ibid.*, 354.

[15] Gus Tyler, *A Legislative Campaign for a Federal Minimum Wage*, Eagleton Foundation Case Studies in Practical Politics (Holt, Rinehart & Winston, Inc., 1959), p. 3.

labor committee." [16] The significance attached to the hostility of a committee chairman is not exaggerated. The chairman has the authority to call hearings, or not to call hearings and thus kill a bill; he controls the committee's agenda, appoints subcommittee chairmen and most staff members. Interest groups whose values conflict with those of committee chairmen had better devise a scheme whereby the chairman can be circumvented.

COMMITTEE POWER AND GROUP STRATEGY

The bicameral nature of the legislature can be of great advantage in overcoming the influence of a hostile chairman. Since legislation must clear both houses of Congress, it is possible in some cases for an interest group to generate or mobilize enough support in the corresponding committee of the opposite house so that the bill is at least given some measure of momentum to start it on its legislative history. The proponents of the 1955 minimum wage law thus sought to get the bill moving in the Senate in the hope that "if the Senate passed the bill, this would favorably influence the behavior of the House and its key committee." [17] In a similar fashion, the atomic scientists who lobbied for civilian control of atomic energy in 1945 were given relief from the determined opposition of Congressman May, chairman of the House Military Affairs Committee, when the Senate voted to establish a Special Committee on Atomic Energy. Whereas the House Military Affairs Committee had opened and closed hearings on a bill to establish military control in one day, the Senate Committee spent four weeks taking testimony, thus giving the scientists critically needed time to evaluate their position.[18]

What, then, is the function of the committee hearing? If the decisions have been or will be made elsewhere (whether in the executive sessions of committees or perhaps outside the formal boundaries of the legislature), why is so much attention fastened to the hearings? There are many speculations, each of which may contribute something to our understanding of the problem. Truman suggests that the hearings serve as "safety valves" for the release of tension built up during the period prior to the opening of the formal hear-

---

[16] *Ibid.*

[17] *Ibid.*

[18] Byron S. Miller, "A Law Is Passed—The Atomic Energy Act of 1946," *University of Chicago Law Review,* XV (1947-1948), 804.

ings.[19] This idea has some merit, for it is true that crystallization, or "choosing up sides," is facilitated during the hearings. Legislators and lobbyists have the opportunity to arrive at some rough estimate of the intensity of support or opposition and to locate the various coalitions which invariably have been formed. In addition, if the hearings are given good press coverage, there is the opportunity for an interest group to pick up some inexpensive publicity. While this is of limited value in influencing the outcome of the legislation, widely publicized testimony at least gives the lobbyist the opportunity to demonstrate to his organization that he is doing his job properly. Finally, it is possible that the lobbyist can "prove his worth" during hearings. If he displays familiarity with the issues, presents his testimony without seeking to evade difficult questions, and appears willing to listen to the suggestions and comments of legislators, he may be able to establish contact with one or more of these legislators on a more personal basis and thus improve his chances of influence in the future. Hearings are a ritual—a "large verbal orchestration" in the words of Representative Clem Miller— but the artificial nature of the hearing with regard to actual decision-making should not mask its more subtle functions.[20]

Since the members of congressional committees have life or death power over the outcome of legislation, access to these members is a key part of the strategy of the lobbyist. However, this does not necessarily mean that the point of initiative rests entirely in the committee. At the state level, Steiner and Gove have indicated that "as an independent determinant of the fate of legislative proposals, the standing committee is of scant importance." [21] In this study of the Illinois legislature, the authors argue that the committees will abide by a decision reached outside the legislature if all the groups which are concerned with the issue have been involved in this informal negotiation process. While Illinois is admittedly an exception to the rule, the significance of the resolution of group conflict *before* the commencing of the formal legislative process should not be overlooked. Here, the legislators do not referee, they ratify.

---

[19] David Truman, *The Governmental Process* (New York: Alfred A. Knopf, Inc., 1951), p. 372.

[20] John W. Baker, ed., *Member of the House* (New York: Charles Scribner's Sons, 1962), p. 8.

[21] Gilbert Y. Steiner and Samuel K. Gove, *Legislative Politics in Illinois* (Urbana: University of Illinois Press, 1960), p. 82.

In corroboration of Steiner and Gove, the author investigated the conflict over the regulation of milk prices in the Florida legislature.[22] The issue was whether or not to amend the milk control law to allow for more flexible and discretionary setting of prices by the Florida Milk Commission. In their course through the legislature, any amendments to the law would have to be passed on by the House Public Health Committee. All participants in the struggle agreed that this committee would never report out the amendments until it was given evidence that the dominant interest group, the Florida Dairy Products Association, had given its approval. The Florida Milk Commission and its ally the Florida Dairy Farmers Federation did not have to persuade the legislative committee; they had to persuade the interested organizations. To achieve this goal, a series of meetings were arranged in the offices of the Florida Milk Commission, and, after a series of negotiations and compromises, united industry support was achieved. Only at this point did the Public Health Committee, which had simply been waiting for the verdict of the interest groups, report out the amendments; the substance of these amendments exactly paralleled the statements of the milk industry speaking through its organizations. The crucial decision was reached without the involvement of legislators. After the interest groups agreed, legislative approval was no more than a formality.

Parties and the Formation of Policy

Some of these examples cited above make it clear that in some cases the initiative for the beginning of the chain of circumstances that eventually culminate in a law rests deep in the fabric of the society. In keeping with the ideas inherent in the concept of the political system, we can generalize to some extent and say that a legislative body *reacts* to demands originating in the larger environment. It is exceedingly difficult to trace a specific policy back to its origin, and most studies which attempt to do so actually begin

[22] Harmon Zeigler, *The Florida Milk Commission Changes Minimum Prices* (New York: The Inter-University Case Program, 1963). For conclusions similar to the above *see* Oliver Garceau and Corrine Silverman, "A Pressure Group and the Pressured: A Case Report," *American Political Science Review,* XLVII (Sept. 1954), 675.

when the demands become visible. Blaisdell has hit upon this point very nicely in his analysis of the origins of public policy. He argues that "the laws which Congress enacts originate in most cases with the informal agencies, that is, the outside pressure groups." While this would seem to be a clear-cut answer to the question, Blaisdell is careful to explain that these "informal agencies" may be both primary and secondary originators of policy. By the time an issue reaches the level of visibility, there will be an array of interest groups distributed on both sides of the question. However, "we can never be certain that our research has produced the real originator." [23] Where did the pressure for a civil rights act begin? Perhaps it began with the Emancipation Proclamation, perhaps earlier. At any rate, it is unnecessary to belabor the point, for it should not be too unreasonable to suggest that, while we do not know the exact point at which a demand originates, we do know demands come to the attention of legislatures through the mechanism of group interpretation and articulation.

We have seen that, when the demands become stated in formal terms before legislative bodies, the institutional framework of these assemblies channels or distorts the flow of pressure. The committee system can thus be understood as part of an institutional framework which can, to some extent, control the success of particular sets of demands. A second part of the institutional framework which should be considered is the party system. As stated earlier, the parties function less as formulators of public policy and more as leadership recruitment and consensus building mechanisms. In the recruitment, or electoral phase of the political process, the party seems to outweigh the interest group in importance. The system is so constructed that the only way an electoral victory can be achieved is through the party. While it would be an oversimplification to say that the positions of parties and interest groups are reversed in the legislative process, it is certainly true that the role of the party is diminished considerably. In the national Congress, the machinery of the parties operates most efficiently at the organizational phase of activity, not at the policy formation phase. Neither party spends much of its time trying to discipline recalcitrant members, although the formal mechanisms for such discipline are

[23] Donald C. Blaisdell, *American Democracy Under Pressure* (New York: The Ronald Press Company, 1957), pp. 218, 221.

not absent. For policy formation purposes, the power of the party is diffused and not suited to achieving unity of purpose. Ranney and Kendall write that "the power of the congressional majority is highly fragmented, so that bits and pieces of it are lodged in floor leaders, standing committees, committee chairmen, presiding officers and rules committees, among whom there may be countless differences of opinion and emphasis. . . ." [24]

PARTY INFLUENCE ON VOTING

Given the fact that the congressional party is poorly constructed for the planning and promulgation of policy, there is still the matter of the party as an influence upon the voting behavior of a legislator. At the moment in time in which a legislator votes "yea or "nay," what role did the party play?

This question can be answered only by inference. McDonald's statement that "the ideal way to assess the nature and role of party influence would be to get a machine that would look into a person's mind as he was making it up and sort out and measure all of the various considerations that went into the final result" sums up well the inferential nature of this analysis.[25] The most frequently used technique, roll call analysis, enables us to describe the degree to which members of parties vote together and the composition of deviating blocs, but it too is limited. The casting of a vote is only the final phase of the legislative process. Heinz Eulau notes that "a legislator's conduct in the final voting provides little basis for inferences about his behavior at other stages of the legislative process." [26] While he may vote with the party, he may also have engaged in negotiations with pressure groups, argued for compromises during the committee stages of a bill, or sought to have the bill made more compatible with his personal philosophy. Nevertheless, we turn to roll call votes for some fundamental data about the importance of the party.

From the vast amount of research conducted by means of roll call analysis, there seems to be no question that party influence is dis-

---

[24] Austin Ranney and Willmoore Kendall, *Democracy and the American Party System* (New York: Harcourt, Brace & World, 1956), p. 397.

[25] Neil A. McDonald, *The Study of Political Parties* (Garden City, N.Y.: Doubleday and Company, Inc., 1955), p. 70.

[26] Wahlke *et al.*, *The Legislative System*, p. 239.

cernible in voting behavior. Less clear, however, are questions of
the conditions under which party influence will be strong or weak,
and what kinds of legislators seem to respond more quickly to party
pressures. Neither party comes very close to the ideal of some political scientists that they should be "responsible," that is, formulate
opposing programs and vote strictly according to the dictates of
the party leadership.[27] Both parties are made up of legislators whose
ideological commitments range widely across a continuum from
"liberal" to "conservative," no matter how these terms are defined;
neither party is wholly committed to a specific set of values. However, the lack of total unanimity should not serve to conceal the
fact that ". . . the ideological center of gravity of the two parties
is different; the Democrats' is toward the 'Left' and the Republicans'
is toward the 'Right' of the abbreviated American political spectrum." [28]

Support for the above description of congressional parties can be
gathered from Julius Turner's classic description of party and constituency pressures, Robert Dahl's study of party voting and foreign
policy and David Truman's analysis of the eighty-first Congress.[29]
Dahl reports that "the Republicans were, at least until 1943, overwhelmingly the party of 'isolation,' whereas the persistent tendency
of the Democrats was to support 'internationalist' efforts." [30] Dahl's
conclusion is based upon the examination of a single set of related
issues through time and does not take into account the disunities
which may have made intraparty conflict more discernible over a
broader range of issues. Turner's approach anticipated Truman's in
that Turner categorized issues according to the extent of party
cleavage. His findings may be summarized as follows: The parties
displayed sharp, consistent cleavage on questions of tariff, govern-

[27] The most articulate statement of this position is given in Committee on
Political Parties, American Political Science Association, *Toward a More Responsible Two-Party System* (New York: Holt, Rinehart & Winston, Inc.,
1950). *See also* Austin Ranney, *The Doctrine of Responsible Party Government* (Urbana: University of Illinois Press, 1954).

[28] Matthews, *op. cit.*, p. 119.

[29] Julius Turner, *Party and Constituency: Pressures on Congress* (Baltimore:
The Johns Hopkins University Press, 1951); Robert Dahl, *Congress and Foreign
Policy* (New York: Harcourt, Brace & World, 1950); David B. Truman, *The
Congressional Party: A Case Study* (New York: John Wiley and Sons, Inc.,
1959).

[30] Dahl, *op. cit.*, p. 190.

ment action ("that is, issues involving government action in fields traditionally reserved for private institutions, such as public power, crop insurance, or disaster relief"), social welfare and labor legislation, and farm legislation. They were divided, but only moderately, on questions of government regulation, Negro rights, and immigration problems. On all other issues the parties were either divided, but inconsistent in the basis of their division, or quite similar in their positions. Turner was interested in finding out the conditions which were most contributory to party loyalty. Not surprisingly, he suggested that, when the group pressures of a legislator's geographical area and the stated position of his party are complementary, ". . . independent action on the part of a congressman . . . was a rare event." [31]

PARTY VS. CONSTITUENCY

An example of the consequences of conflicting pressures when groups in the constituency oppose the legislator's party can be found in the "tariff revolution." It will be recalled that Turner listed tariff questions as productive of sharp and consistent cleavages between the parties. Since 1944, the last year studied by Turner, the cleavages have been blurred considerably as the southern Democrats—traditional defenders of free trade since the days of John C. Calhoun—have become more protectionist in their attitudes. What interests us is that these protectionist sentiments have grown as the textile industry has extended from New England into the deep south. In 1951, the first evidence of the breakdown of party loyalty on tariff questions occurred as the House considered a three year extension of the Reciprocal Trade Program. On the matter of a "peril point" amendment (requiring the Tariff Commission to apprise the President of the minimum duties required to protect domestic industries), the southern Democrats defected from their party and the amendment was adopted. Since then, the once prominent partisan voting patterns have been replaced by bipartisan coalitions, with the southern Democrats and a majority of the Republicans forming the protectionist bloc and the central states Republicans and the majority of Democrats forming the opposition. On the basis of this evidence, Watson concludes that ". . . the evolution in party voting may be traced directly to certain

---

[31] Turner, *op. cit.*, pp. 164-179.

economic changes which have occurred in recent years in various regions of the country." [32]

The declining role of the party in trade expansion does not support Turner's contention that, in cases of constituency-party conflict, the party is more often influential than is the constituency. However, this is a single example, and concerns a section of the country whose deviation from the Democratic party is expected in other policy areas, thus perhaps easing the transition from loyalty to defection.

SOURCES OF CLEAVAGE IN LEGISLATIVE PARTIES

Truman gives us a clearer picture of the pattern of cleavage in both parties. In the Senate, he finds the Democrats consistently divided on questions of civil rights, labor, and internal security, while the Republicans were "relatively united." Greatest Republican disunity occurred over the issues of agriculture, foreign policy, and public works. Truman notes the greater agreement among Democrats on votes relating to presidential appointments, foreign policy, and public housing, but is inclined to attribute this unity to the importance of the White House in the affairs of the majority party rather than to factors inherent in the structure or values of the party in itself. These last issues were vital parts of the Administration's legislative program. Neither party showed much consistency on agricultural matters which "normally reflect a maximum of trading between regions and among the representatives of constituencies in which particular commodities are important. . . ." In the House, Truman finds similar sources of cleavage within the parties; Democrats divide on civil rights, internal security, and labor, but Republicans do not. [33]

By analyzing the distribution of votes in the low-cohesion category, Truman is able to conclude that the cleavages within the parties are not random, the result of chance or personal idiosyncrasies, but rather are stable and indicative of a "marked consistency of underlying attitude." In both houses of Congress, the Democratic party divides into two clearly discernible factions whose common denominator is sectional. Speaking of the House, Truman observes

---

[32] Richard A. Watson, "The Tariff Revolution: A Study of Shifting Party Attitudes," *Journal of Politics,* XVIII (Nov. 1956), 698.

[33] Truman, *op. cit.,* pp. 50, 150.

that "the familiar North-South division was again the dominant characteristic, and it is evident . . . that deviation from the party majority and coalition with the Republican opposition were peculiarly characteristic of Southern representatives but by no means of all Democrats from the South." Sectional divisions were not quite so uniform among Republicans as among the Democrats, but were still very obviously a part of the voting pattern. Especially on foreign affairs, the Republicans displayed factional voting tendencies on an East versus West basis.[34]

These data suggest that, although there is good evidence that there are identifiable differences between the parties, the congressional party is a "segmental group." [35] The party controls a restricted or limited portion of the legislator's total behavior. Other portions of this behavior are given cues from other groups within the larger environment, and, depending upon "circumstances" (i.e., the nature of the issue, the perceived reaction in the constituency, the intensity of interest group demands, etc.), the party may increase or decline in importance. It is therefore difficult to categorize sources of influence, particularly since party identification may govern the reaction of the legislator to other sets of demands. For example, Matthews notes that while there is a tendency for senators from the same state to vote the same way (suggesting the dominance of constituency pressures), this occurence is most frequent when the senators are from the same party and less frequent when they are from different parties. Matthews thus infers that ". . . a senator's political party affiliation influences which groups in his constituency he chooses to 'represent,' since he cannot possibly represent them all." [36] This comment leads to speculation about the make-up of the

---

[34] *Ibid.*, pp. 167, 179. *See also* George L. Grassmuck, *Sectional Biases in Congress on Foreign Policy* (Baltimore: The Johns Hopkins University Press, 1951).

[35] The phrase "segmental group" is borrowed from Robert K. Merton, *Social Theory and Social Structure* (New York: The Free Press of Glencoe, Inc., 1957), p. 311.

[36] Matthews, *op. cit.*, p. 233. *See also* J. Roland Pennock, "Party and Constituency in Postwar Agricultural Price-Support Legislation," *Journal of Politics,* XVIII (May 1956), 167-210; Samuel P. Huntington, "A Revised Theory of American Party Politics," *American Political Science Review,* XLIV (Sept. 1950), 669-677; Duncan MacRae, Jr., "The Relation Between Roll Call Votes and Constituencies in the Massachusetts House of Representatives," *American Political Science Review,* XLVI (Dec. 1952), 1046-1055; Thomas R. Dye, "A Comparison of Constituency Influences in the Upper and Lower Chambers of

constituency itself. Senators represent a large area which is in most cases more heterogeneous than the average congressional district. In the case of smaller districts, particularly those with a single dominant economic interest, the freedom of the legislator may be considerably less. If the district is characterized by divergent interests there is a greater possibility of close elections and perhaps the necessity of more attention to the climate of opinion or overt demands originating at the local level.

LOBBYING STRATEGY AND PARTY STRUCTURE

It is sometimes argued that the fluid nature of congressional parties and their inability to develop and adhere to a specific set of legislative proposals creates a vacuum which can be filled only by "outside" sources, that is, interest groups.[37] This does not seem to be a correct assumption, since it depends for its validity upon the party being the *only* source of internal pressure, a point which has been proved false by studies of the informal patterns of interpersonal relations within legislative bodies. Interest group leaders must achieve access to decision makers of both parties, since the informal structure of power in legislative bodies *may* cut across party lines. Generally, the informal structure of power seems to correspond to the "real" structure of power, so that formal leaders, whose position of leadership is assigned by the party, are usually the legislators considered to be most influential. While the similar ideological characteristics of lobbyists and legislators of compatible persuasion make it inevitable that some drift toward partisanship on the part of interest groups will occur, lobbyists try to avoid strong partisan attachment on the assumption that, in the House or Senate, it is necessary to cooperate with leaders of both parties no matter which is in the majority. Activity on behalf of one of the major parties is not a typical part of the career patterns of lobbyists in Washington and most believe that political parties have little to do with the

---

a State Legislature," *Western Political Quarterly*, XIV (June 1961), 473-480; Lewis Dexter, "The Representative and His District," *Human Organization*, XVI (Spring, 1956), 2-13; Charles O. Jones, "Representation in Congress: The Case of the House Agriculture Committee," *American Political Science Review*, LV (June 1961), 358-367.

[37] See E. E. Schattschneider, *Party Government* (New York: Holt, Rinehart & Winston, Inc., 1942) and *The Struggle for Party Government* (College Park, Md.: Program in American Civilization, University of Maryland, 1948).

formation of public policy.[38] For example, during the 1961 controversy over enlarging the House Rules Committee to reduce the influence of southern Democrats not in sympathy with the program of the President, interest groups whose ideological preferences might be described as "Republican" such as the National Association of Manufacturers, Chamber of Commerce, American Medical Association, and American Farm Bureau Federation were engaged in a series of strategy meetings with the Democratic chairman of the Rules Committee, Howard Smith of Virginia.[39]

In legislative systems characterized by firm party lines we find that there is a greater tendency toward open partisanship on the part of interest groups. Lockard's survey of the legislative process in New England reveals that there are two patterns of pressure group activity, each pattern apparently being a function of the cohesion of the political parties.[40] In one-party states, interest groups play a major role in the determination of legislative policy. In Maine, for example, the legislative process is oriented around the policy recommendations of the "big three" economic interests, power, timber, and manufacturing. However, in Massachusetts, Connecticut, and Rhode Island, where the parties are more competitive and cohesive, "the party organization sits astride the channels through which all legislation must flow, a fact to which the pressure group must accommodate itself." This means that interest groups tend to develop permanent and stable webs of interaction with the parties to the extent that they are actually little more than auxiliary sections of the parties. In Massachusetts, the relations between interest groups and parties are considerably more intimate than is the case on the national level. Lockard writes:

> Farm groups on the national level have not aligned themselves with either party, but in Massachusetts they are with the Republicans. Labor nationally is more sympathetic to the Democratic party and is much more helpful to it, but it maintains cordial

---

[38] Lester Milbrath, "The Political Party Activity of Washington Lobbyists," *Journal of Politics*, XV (May 1958), 345.

[39] Richard L. Lyons, "Pressure Rises as House Moves to Vote on Rules," *Washington Post*, Jan. 31, 1961. Cited in Nelson W. Polsby, "Two Strategies of Influence in the House of Representatives: Choosing a Majority Leader, 1962" (Paper presented to the 1962 annual meeting of the American Political Science Association).

[40] Duane Lockard, *New England State Politics* (Princeton: Princeton University Press, 1959).

relations with many Republicans and does not move into the inner councils of the Democratic party to the extent that it does in Massachusetts. In some areas the Democratic party in Massachusetts will leave to labor almost the whole job of campaigning for state candidates, and in many campaigns the money labor gives is a very crucial factor in the Democratic effort.[41]

Such "built-in access" has obvious consequences for lobbying techniques. In the national legislative process, lobbyists place a great amount of emphasis upon personal contacts with individual legislators and devote a substantial portion of their energy toward the goal of establishing "connections." In a strong two-party state such as Connecticut, very little time is spent by lobbyists in direct contact with legislators. Much of their efforts are aimed at influencing the decision of the party made at its caucus, party leadership thus absorbing the brunt of the pressure. A strong party system does not reduce the amount of pressure, as its proponents occasionally argue, but rather it channels the pressure toward holders of formal party office. While such a system may give an interest group an advantage when its particular party is in the majority, it would have adverse consequences when the opposition gained control of the legislature.

LOBBYING TECHNIQUES: SKILLFUL AND INEPT

Since lobbying techniques vary to some extent with the arena in which the pressure activity is to be conducted, it will suffice to describe some techniques which seem to hold true for the lobbying process in general. In lobbying, as in any other profession, there are successes and failures. In fact, it is hard to avoid making the comment that a great many of the droves of lobbyists swarming around Capitol Hill really accomplish little but convince their own membership that the flow of dues should continue. Literature produced by these organizations is devoted to an internal selling job, and an ever-expanding membership is often the basic goal in the

---

[41] *Ibid.*, p. 163. For descriptions of the role of the party in other state legislatures *see* Malcom E. Jewell, "Party Voting in American State Legislatures," *American Political Science Review*, XLIX (Sept. 1955), 773-791; William J. Keefe, "Party Government and Lawmaking in the Illinois General Assembly," *Northwestern University Law Review*, XLVII (Mar.-Apr. 1952), 55-71; Keefe, "Parties, Partisanship, and Public Policy in the Pennsylvania Legislature," *American Political Science Review*, XLVIII (June 1954), 450-464.

---

mind of the lobbyist. Many of these groups have no contact with the legislative process except at formal hearings of committees, and they are treated with patient tolerance by veteran legislators who have developed a good knowledge of the relative merits of interest groups. Often the testimony of such groups is saturated with clichés and is of limited value as a source of information. Occasionally, some lobbyists will resort to a form of misrepresentation which seems to indicate a belief that legislators can be fooled rather easily. The following comment illustrates this kind of "pressure": "I believe our case opposing the extension of rent control would be helped tremendously if we could parade in a few small property owners from around the country, a little bedraggled and run-down-at-the-heels-looking, who could get their story over to Congress that the small man who owns a little property is taking one hell of a beating." [42]

On the other hand, there are a number of expert lobbyists who know the vagaries of the legislative process and are adept at getting along with politicians. Many of these lobbyists are lawyers with a background in government service. Samuel Patterson provides a cogent description of this kind of lobbyist, whom he labels as a "contact man."

> He is the legislative representative who conceives his job to be that of making crucial contacts with the members of the legislative group. He devotes his time and energies to walking legislative halls, visiting legislators, collaring them in the halls, establishing relationships with administrative assistants and others of the congressman's staff, cultivating key legislators on a friendship basis, and developing contacts on the staffs of critical legislative committees. [43]

THE IMPORTANCE OF LEGISLATIVE SYMPATHY

The creation of the situation in which the contact man is successful depends to some degree upon his own particular skills. However, it is probable that the success of the contact man depends more upon the degree to which the legislators agree with the professed

---

[42] House Select Committee on Lobbying Activities, *General Interim Report*, 81st Cong., 2d sess., 1950 (Washington, D.C.: Government Printing Office, 1950).

[43] Samuel C. Patterson, "The Role of the Labor Lobbyist" (Paper presented to the 1962 annual meeting of the American Political Science Association), p. 11.

ideals of the group for whom the lobbyist is speaking, and this in turn depends more upon the personal ideology of the legislator rather than upon the ability of the lobbyist to manipulate or persuade. If the legislator and lobbyist have similar goals, then it is quite possible that the notion of "pressure" will be foreign to both. Rather than being aware that he is the object of an attempt at influence, the legislator will probably regard any personal solicitation as the "legitimate" expression of a sound point of view.[44] On the other hand, contact between lobbyist and legislator who are working toward conflicting goals will probably be defined as an attempt at pressure, hence most senators name the organizations with whom they disagree as the most powerful and influential.[45] Frequently, such organizations are presumed to have certain legislators "in their pockets," meaning that these legislators will do the bidding of the organization once its position has been clarified. The often heard phrase, "all it takes is a phone call," reflects the sinister perception of the relationship between the group identified as influential and the legislators upon whom its influence can be exercised. Actually, such a relationship is not one of power, in the sense that power describes a situation in which one actor can secure compliance from another whether or not such compliance is given voluntarily. Rather, the relationship is most likely to develop when the interest group has a sufficiently broad or permanent set of objectives to keep it constantly involved in the affairs of the legislature. The "big four" interest groups, farm, labor, business, and professional, would fall into this category; and, since most American politicians come from the same groups, the development of friendship patterns should be expected to be strongest between legislators and representatives of these organizations. Teune's study of the Indiana legislature, which records the correlation between the occupational affiliation of the legislator with attitudes toward specific interest groups, finds that the clearest relationship is that of sympathetic identification between legislators and lobbyists from the same occupational category. Thus, legislators whose occupation is farming ranked the Farm Bureau first in order of agreement with organizational goals; businessmen tended to agree with the goals of busi-

---

[44] Frank Bonilla, "When Is Petition 'Pressure'?," *Public Opinion Quarterly*, XX (Spring, 1956), 46-48.

[45] Matthews, *op. cit.*, pp. 177-178.

ness groups, and so on. In addition to the expected hostility between business and labor, an interesting finding is the degree to which professional associations are given a high rank in agreement. Of course the professional groups provide the largest number of political decision makers, but it is still somewhat remarkable that even labor legislative candidates are more favorably disposed toward professional groups than they are toward labor unions.[46]

The Indiana study also provides useful comparison with Matthews' description of senators' attitudes toward lobbyists, referred to earlier in the chapter. Indiana legislators showed striking agreement as to the most effective interest groups, even though they differed widely on agreement with the goals of these groups. In fact, there is a definite tendency for legislators who agree with a group's goals to score that group somewhat higher in legislative effectiveness than groups with whom they disagree. Democrats ranked the AFL-CIO more effective than the Farm Bureau, while the order is reversed with the Republicans. However, the question which elicited this response was phrased so as to equate effectiveness with the group's skill in presenting its case before the legislature. When the question was phrased to include the word "powerful," a different set of rankings was obtained. In this case, members who disagreed with the policies of the group were more likely to name that group as powerful.[47]

As a final note to this section, caution should be taken lest we drift into some form of determinism by the automatic assumption that access to sympathetic legislators is simply a function of overlapping group affiliation. Legislators need not look upon themselves as governmental spokesmen for interest groups whose aspirations they share. The authors of *The Legislative System* have developed a typology of legislators' role orientations toward pressure groups consisting of three categories: facilitators, neutrals, and resistors. By relating these roles with the group identification of legislators (pro-business, pro-labor, and economic neutrals), the authors were able to conclude that the role of facilitator is most apparent among

---

[46] Henry Teune, "Occupational Affiliation and Attitudes Towards Interest Groups" (Paper presented to the 1962 annual meeting of the American Political Science Association).

[47] Kenneth Janda, Henry Teune, Melvin Kahn, and Wayne Francis, *Legislative Politics in Indiana* (Indiana University: Bureau of Government Research, n.d.), pp. 18-19.

the neutrals. Those legislators who are not personally involved in the attainment of interest group goals are most likely to be open to the representations of any group which they believe to have a legitimate claim. These facilitators have had longer legislative service and are more socialized toward the "legislative way of life" than younger colleagues whose basic identifications may be with external groups.[48] Bentley's famous comment, that, when we say a person is reasoning on a question of public policy we are actually saying that he belongs to two groups which are clashing, does not necessarily mean that the "clashing groups" are formally organized interest groups.[49] The legislature itself is a group which imposes norms upon its members.

MOBILIZATION OF SUPPORT

Recognition of the "independent" nature of some legislators has led to a conceptualization of the influence process as reciprocal. Lobbyists may influence legislators but may also be influenced themselves. The influence process is clearly not one of a one-way power relationship in which the side with the greatest amount of support invariably wins; and for that matter there is no agreement upon what attributes are necessary for an interest group to be classified as "powerful." Key has come to believe that the threat of electoral retaliation is not to be regarded as a source of power, yet interviews with state legislators indicate that they consider the electoral influence of interest groups as genuine.[50] As a source of power, the willingness of a group to provide helpful services, such as information and research, does not count for much. However, such nonthreatening acts as serving as a source of expert knowledge become much more crucial when the vague notion of power is put aside and the legislator is asked to give his reasons for listening to the claims of a particular group; "pressure groups are most welcome

---

[48] Wahlke *et al., The Legislative System*, p. 341. *See also* Duncan MacRae, Jr., and Edith K. MacRae, "Legislators' Social Status and Their Vote," *American Journal of Sociology*, LXVI (May 1961), 603.

[49] Arthur Bentley, *The Process of Government* (San Antonio, Texas: The Principia Press of Trinity University, 1908).

[50] V. O. Key, Jr., "The Veterans and the House of Representatives: A Study of a Pressure Group and Electoral Mortality," *Journal of Politics*, V (Feb. 1943), 27-40. *See also* Key, *Public Opinion and American Democracy* (New York: Alfred A. Knopf, Inc., 1961), pp. 521-524.

in the legislative arena when they go beyond a mere assertion of demands and interests and present information and data which help legislators work out compromises and adjustments among the most insistent demands of groups on the basis of some vague conception of the public interest against which particular claims can be judged." [51] Legislators do not like to be "pressured," and, while they operate upon the assumption that interest groups are powerful, they react to specific group claims more on the basis of usefulness.

Perhaps it is because of these reasons that many of the techniques which pressure groups regularly employ are of doubtful impact. A case in point is the stimulation by an interest group of a deluge of letters or telegrams designed to show the legislator that there is a great amount of popular interest in his decision. This technique is most favored by organizations with a large membership. Unfortunately for the groups which seek to organize letter-writing campaigns, the mark of their organizational efforts is almost invariably present in the letters. While legislators give their mail serious consideration, generally they are not receptive to letters whose actual origin may have been with a constituent but whose wording bears close resemblance to thousands of others. Dexter writes that "it is almost impossible to organize a letter writing campaign so skillfully that an experienced mail clerk does not spot it at once as simulated and even identify its source." [52] The methods whereby such letters are obtained vary considerably in subtlety. In some instances sample letters are prepared, resulting in the legislator receiving communications whose nearly identical wording leaves no doubt as to origin. Other interest groups prefer to leave more to the imagination of the writer and emphatically urge that the letter be phrased in one's own words. Even in these cases the group must make known to the potential writer the basic facts about the particular issue, making it quite likely that the language of the letter writer and the official statements of the group will not vary appreciably. Variations upon the letter-writing theme are many. Some organizations submit ballots to their members and deposit the results in the offices of legislators, offering the ballots as evi-

---

[51] Wahlke *et al., op. cit.,* pp. 338-339. *See also* Janda *et al., op. cit.,* p. 19.
[52] Lewis A. Dexter, "What Do Congressmen Hear: The Mail," *Public Opinion Quarterly,* XX (Spring, 1956), 20.

dence of "genuine" as opposed to organizationally inspired sentiments. Most mail of this kind is sorted out by an administrative
assistant before it ever reaches the desk of the legislator, and if it
does happen to reach his desk the chances are good that its time
of arrival, in addition to its origin, will make it ineffective. Frequently, mass produced mail arrives after the bill which is being
supported or opposed is out of committee and scheduled for debate,
when the opinions of a single legislator are diminished in importance.

Considered singly, the letter-writing campaign is probably the
least effective and most relied upon lobbying technique. Its extensive use results from the fact that many pressure groups simply do
not have the resources necessary to engage in more elaborate techniques. Creating the impression of constituency pressure need not
be attempted only through the mails. Since a legislator's view of his
constituency may in reality be concentrated toward the individuals
or organizations which have been unusually active in his behalf, it
is frequently of greater benefit for an interest group to arrange for
these politically active individuals to contact the legislator. An
example of this technique is afforded by the American Cotton
Manufacturers Institute in its efforts to have quotas applied to
Japanese textile imports. While cotton manufacturers in New England were relatively united in their desire to reduce the effects of
cheap textile imports, manufacturers in the South were not so
vociferous. There had occurred some migration of the textile industry from New England to the South, but the traditional values
of the "cotton bloc" were not entirely overcome. Accustomed to
supporting a free trade program which would benefit cotton farmers
rather than manufacturers (Japan is the largest consumer of American raw cotton), southern legislators were only gradually adopting
a more protectionist position. In order to dramatize the necessity
for strong protectionist support in the South, the American Cotton
Manufacturers Institute devoted space in the *Textile World* to a
southern audience. Manufacturers were urged to oppose congressmen who refused to abandon their free-trade views by appeals of
which the following is typical: "If your wife comes home with an
armful of Japanese textile goods at a time when your mill is running
half-time, remember whom you voted for in the last election and

why." [53] The first evidence of increasing awareness, whether or not it was due to the public relations activities described above, was the passage of laws by the legislatures of South Carolina and Alabama requiring retailers who sold Japanese textile to exhibit a sign saying "Japanese textiles sold here." In the sessions following the efforts of the American Cotton Manufacturers Institute, legislation creating import quotas was repeatedly introduced, with sponsorship usually including both New England and southern congressmen. The support for quota legislation reached its peak in the Eighty-fourth Congress, during which an amendment to the Mutual Security Act establishing a quota system failed by only two votes. In order to avoid the eventual passage of such legislation, the executive branch began negotiations with Japan for the establishment of quotas.

This example illustrates the basic effect of carefully planned lobbying, the maximization of the possibility of victory by mobilization of sympathetic legislators. Had the economic structure of the South not shifted, the activities of those interested in limiting Japanese imports would in all probability have come to nought. As is true in most other forms of communication, conversion in the lobbying process is rare.

The techniques of interest groups in the legislative process vary not only with the situation, but with the structure of the group. In the Japanese textile quota struggle, directly contacting congressmen would have been of little use until some groundwork could be laid at the grass roots level. Much the same sort of effort was made by the AFL-CIO Joint Minimum Wage Committee in its efforts to increase the minimum wage to $1.25 in 1959; but in labor reform legislation controversy generated by the hearings of the Select Committee on Improper Practices in the Labor-Management Relations Field, the AFL-CIO relied mainly on a few experienced lobbyists whose job was to make direct contact with congressmen. Patterson reports that the strategy was based upon "*rapport* with, and promises from House and Senate Democratic leaders, and particularly the effectiveness and prestige of Senator Kennedy. It hinged on congressional understanding of the problems and complexities of organized labor, without planning for a campaign to

---

[53] *Textile World*, Feb., 1955, p. 51.

engender widespread public support for sympathetic treatment." [54]
The AFL-CIO was adjusting its strategies to what it believed to be
the exigencies of the situation, but many groups never vary their
techniques to any appreciable degree and this seems to be a function of their structural characteristics. Cohen's study of the Japanese
peace settlement indicates that two kinds of groups were observable:
those which served "specific and relatively tangible interests," and
those which "cater to more general and intangible interests." Cohen
found that the organizations representing tangible interests used a
wide variety of methods consisting of indirect and direct communication, but the organizations whose goals were intangible relied heavily on explanatory articles. Further, the more specific the
goals of the organization, the more likely it was to react quickly to
the changing developments in the legislative process, giving such
groups a considerable advantage in timing of communications. The
smaller groups with clear objectives were more maneuverable and
less incumbered by the need to keep a large membership educated
in its goals.[55]

Interest Groups and Foreign Policy

To summarize briefly the development of the argument up to
this point, we might say that the influence of interest groups in the
legislative process depends more on the harmony of values between
the group and the legislators than it does on the ability of a group
to wield its "power" either through skillful techniques or presumed
electoral influence. As a concluding note, some consideration will
be given to the role of interest groups in the foreign policy process.
One of the basic claims which an interest group may use to gain
a hearing is its role as legitimate spokesman for a segment of public opinion. In making foreign policy, the situation is more complex
than in domestic policy because decision makers are exposed to
demands originating from outside the normal boundaries of domestic
politics. This is not to say that foreign policy is unique, since, in
many cases such as the Japanese textile import quota controversy,

---

[54] Patterson, *op. cit.*, p. 21.
[55] Bernard C. Cohen, "Political Communication on the Japanese Peace Settlement," *Public Opinion Quarterly*, XX (Spring, 1956), 32-33.

domestic and foreign policies are inextricably intertwined. While it is probably safe to assume that interest groups are less active in the foreign than in the domestic policy formation process, the interrelationship between the two means that, when domestic organizations are affected by foreign policy decisions or planned decisions, they will react to safeguard their position. Cohen's *The Influence of Non-Governmental Groups on Foreign Policy-Making* supports this argument in his catalogue of effective groups. He concludes that the most influential groups in the foreign policy process are those with a clear economic stake in the outcome of a decision rather than those with an ideological commitment to a principle, such as disarmament.[56] He finds, for example, that the most powerful group in the making of the Japanese peace treaty was the West Coast fishing industry, represented organizationally by the Pacific Fisheries Conference. While the State Department held firm against the demands of other businesses to have private claims represented in the final settlement, it responded to the West Coast fishing industry's demands that its fishing preserves not be entered by Japan. Cohen believes that at least part of this strength stemmed from the strength of the industry in three West Coast states, and the determination of senators from the area that this vital industry be protected if a treaty was to be approved.[57] However, of at least equal weight is the recognition of the legitimacy of the objectives of the Pacific Fisheries Conference. Legitimacy would also mean that the demands of a group do not conflict with a legislator's perception of foreign policy objectives, no matter how intense his actual or virtual identification with the values of the claimant organization.

Ethnic groups are perhaps more consistently concerned with foreign policy than economic interest, but each ethnic group becomes aroused to activity only when the interests of the nation of origin are under consideration. Generally the consensus is that they are less effective than business groups. Certainly the perception of issues and candidates during elections is distorted by ethnic loyalties, and legislators from districts with high ethnic homogeniety may be expected to reflect the values of the particular ethnic

---

[56] Cohen, *The Influence of Non-Governmental Groups on Foreign Policy-Making* (Boston: The World Peace Foundation, 1959), p. 15.

[57] Cohen, *The Political Process and Foreign Policy* (Princeton: Princeton University Press, 1957), p. 218.

minority without the necessity of overt pressure. However, since ethnic groups do not vote in cohesive blocs the effectiveness again depends on shared values. Since the ethnic loyalties of any particular group are infrequently stimulated by the foreign policy process, as in the case of the Jews and policy toward Israel, their impact will vary with the intensity of the stimulation of ethnic identifications. The fact that the organizations maintained by most ethnic groups are in firm support of America in its struggle with Russia contributes to the prestige of these interests when they press their claims, even though these claims may have no relation to our policy toward the Communist nations.[58]

Conclusion

The role of interest groups is that of articulating demands and placing them within the context of institutional decision-making. They are important not solely because they are occasionally able to achieve their goals at the expense of other and competing values, but also because they provide organizational representation for the opinions of the fluid publics which help to form the environment surrounding the legislature. Since interest groups do not monopolize the communication of demands to the legislature, it is not likely that effects of lobbying are as great as lobbyists themselves or journalistic writers seem to believe. The effective lobbying organization is hard to describe, since success is not singly dependent upon the techniques or goals of a particular interest. Those groups which are recognized by legislators as serving a representative function for a legitimate public will be more effective than those that are not; those groups whose goals do not conflict with legislators' perceptions of the public interest will be more effective than groups whose goals do conflict with such perceptions. Within this context, the skillful or inept tactics of lobbyists are given their limits.

---

[58] Franklin L. Burdette, "Influence of Noncongressional Pressures on Foreign Policy," *Annals of the American Academy of Political and Social Science,* Sept. 1953, pp. 93-94. *See also* Lawrence H. Fuchs, "Minority Groups and Foreign Policy," *Political Science Quarterly,* LXXIV (June 1959), 161-175, and Louis L. Gerson, "Immigrant Groups and American Foreign Policy," in George L. Anderson, ed., *Issues and Conflicts* (Lawrence: University of Kansas Press, 1959), pp. 171-192.

Administrative
X Policy-Making
Under Pressure

The process of adjustment and compromise among conflicting demands which is undertaken by the legislature is continued by administrative agencies. Early students of administration were committed to the idea that "politics" ended with the passage of legislation, and that the administrative process consisted of the automatic enforcement of the legislative mandate. Such assumptions have long been abandoned, and administration has come to be regarded as an extension of the struggle which began in the legislature.[1] It is indisputable that the administrative process does have certain differentiating features; such as alterations in techniques of influence by interest groups and perceptions of the environment by administrators which differ from the perceptions of legislators. But it is

---

[1] Dwight Waldo, *The Study of Public Administration* (Garden City, N.Y.: Doubleday and Company, 1955), p. 41. *See also* Martin Landau, "The Concept of Decision-Making in the 'Field' of Public Administration," in Sidney Malick and Edward H. Van Ness, eds., *Concepts and Issues in Administrative Behavior* (Englewood Cliffs, N.J.: Prentice-Hall, Inc., 1962), pp. 16-18.

clearly untenable that administrators differ from legislators in that the nature of administrative tasks is so restricted that their only concerns are with efficiency. As governments become more intensely involved in the control or guidance of the nation's economic system, the complex nature of the ensuing decisions requires that administrative agencies assume much of the burden. The legislatures, faced with a multiplicity of problem-solving situations, can undertake only a general statutory suggestion of the direction of public policy. Very often decisions which may be interpreted by a group as having life or death consequences are made in the relatively secretive atmosphere surrounding administrative agencies, far from the glare of public scrutiny which permeates the legislative process. Therefore, groups hoping to influence public policy often exhibit strong interest in the establishment of administrative agencies responsible for policy in the areas of the groups' concern.

How Agencies Begin

The creation of administrative agencies is primarily a legislative function. The conditions existing at the time of the establishment of a new agency may vary considerably according to the degree of controversy, the quantity of interest-group activity, the organizational apparatus of the groups involved, and the intensity of the demands for or against the proposed agency. The establishment of the first clientele agencies such as the Department of Commerce and the Department of Agriculture was undertaken in an atmosphere of relative calm.[2] The agencies were originally designed to provide services to specified segments of the economic population without much regulation. Opposition was minimal and organizationally it was practically non-existent. In contrast, the National Labor Relations Board and the Interstate Commerce Commission were created over the vigorous and organizationally articulated objections of interest groups whose economic stability was seen as

---

[2] John A. Vieg, "The Growth of Public Administration," in Fritz Morstein Marx, ed., *Elements of Public Administration* (Englewood Cliffs, N.J.: Prentice-Hall, Inc., 1961), pp. 14-15; John M. Gaus and Leon O. Wolcott, *Public Administration and the United States Department of Agriculture* (Chicago: Public Administration Service, 1940), pp. 1-87.

threatened. These agencies were given extensive regulatory authority over economic interest which had no desire to be regulated. Under these circumstances, the job of administration was begun in an atmosphere of hostility and resistance. Administrators had to cope with organizations whose fundamental objectives were either the abolition of the agency or the reduction of its authority to the point of impotence. Administrative agencies seek to survive, and in order to do this it is necessary to reduce external opposition as much as possible. This frequently means the adjustment of programs to the desires of the regulated interests.[3] Cooperation between "bureaucrats and businessmen," or the establishment of satisfactory relationships with clientele groups, is the subject of this chapter.

THE CASE OF THE FLORIDA MILK COMMISSION [4]

In some cases, regulatory agencies begin their activities as a result of the desires of economic groups that the government "do something" to eliminate an unsatisfactory competitive situation. This is particularly true when the entire economy, or at least a portion of the economy, is suffering from chronic depression. For example, the Florida Milk Commission was created in 1933 as a result of the youthful commercial structure of the milk industry in that state. Faced with a substantial reduction in consumer buying power, and with competition from milk imports from more established dairy states, the milk industry began to engage in price wars. A drop in prices by one distributor was met by a corresponding drop by competitors and eventually prices fell so low that below-cost selling became prevalent. The milk industry was organized into trade associations, but they were unable to negotiate a truce privately. Finally the industry urged the state government to undertake the responsibility of establishing the exact price to be paid to dairy farmers for milk and the minimum prices at which milk could be sold wholesale and retail. The legislature, in response to this re-

---

[3] On this topic William R. Dill notes that "as an organization begins to function, its founders and sponsors are apt to be more sensitive to environmental inputs and more anxious to seek them out than they will be at most later stages of the organization's history." *See* "The Impact of Environment on Organizational Development," in Malick and Van Ness, *op. cit.*, p. 101.

[4] All comments on this agency are drawn from the author's *The Florida Milk Commission Changes Minimum Prices* (New York: The Inter-University Case Program, 1963).

quest, and in the absence of any discernible opposition, established a Milk Control Board which became the independent Florida Milk Commission in 1939. The Commission was responsible for the supervision and regulation of all economic levels of the milk industry—production, transportation, delivery, and sale. To carry out its tasks, the Commission was given statutory powers not only to set prices but also to issue licenses, which were required of all dealers for the purchase, sale, or distribution of milk.

This commission, as is true of any government organization, originated because some persons believed that a new agency was necessary for the achievement of a goal. The structure of the new Milk Commission reflected quite accurately the desires of its advocates and the restricted nature of the interest in milk regulation. Discussion was confined to the milk industry itself and never reached the level of broader public discussion. Consequently the law placed the regulated clientele in a position to control the operations of the Milk Commission. Rather than providing compulsory regulation, the law allowed producers in various marketing districts to petition both for control or for withdrawal of control. Further, the Commission was financed by taxes upon the industry rather than legislative appropriation. Finally, its membership consisted of persons with a professional interest in the Commission.

Agency-Clientele Relationships

The clientele of an agency—"groups whose interests [are] strongly affected by an agency's activities [and provide] the principal sources of political support and opposition"—may have great impact on the way the agency's programs are enforced.[5] If the clientele of the agency is large and heterogeneous, the agency will function in a climate of greater potential conflict than if the clientele is limited and relatively united. The establishment of communications will be relatively simple in the latter case. The agency, in reaching its decisions, will have access to a limited amount of information from a single point of view. The regulated interests, in presenting argu-

[5] This definition is from Herbert A. Simon, Donald W. Smithburg, and Victor A. Thompson, *Public Administration* (New York: Alfred A. Knopf, Inc., 1950), p. 461.

ments, will not have to compete with opposing interests. Consequently, the fewer the number of interests in the clientele of an agency, the more influential each is likely to be.[6] Attention has been given by students of administration, notably Selznick and Bernstein, to the process whereby an administrative agency gradually abandons its original crusading spirit and becomes, in a sense, the captive of the clientele.[7] This situation arises either when one of the regulated groups is dominant from the beginning, or when the political support of competing groups evaporates. The agency "becomes a protector of the *status quo* and uses its public powers to maintain the interest of the regulated. . . . Although an agency in this situation stresses its role of mediator and judge among conflicting group interests, its actual role is that of advocate and partisan." [8] Selznick refers to this process of accommodation as "cooptation," which he defines as "the process of absorbing new elements into the leadership of policy-determining structure of an organization as a means of averting threats to its stability or existence." [9] Selznick uses the relationship between the Tennessee Valley Authority and powerful groups within the valley to illustrate cooptation. In this case the clients of the agency had values which conflicted with the stated goals of the agency. In order to elicit the support of local groups, the TVA abandoned its policy of using public ownership of land as a conservation measure and thus altered its goals in exchange for support.

"AUTOMATIC" COOPTATION

In the case of the Florida Milk Commission, the identification of interests between regulators and regulated was immediate, and cooptation was automatic. A single-interest group, the Florida Dairy Association, presented a united, industrywide front in defense of the activities of the Commission, and kept a close eye on the Commission itself to make certain that all its members were informed of industry problems. By including both dairy farmers and milk dis-

---

[6] Murray Edelman, "Governmental Organization and Public Policy," *Public Administration Review*, XII (Autumn, 1952), 278.

[7] Philip Selznick, *TVA and the Grass Roots* (Berkeley: University of California Press, 1949); Marver Bernstein, *Regulating Business by Independent Commission* (Princeton: Princeton University Press, 1955).

[8] Bernstein, *op. cit.*, pp. 270-271.

[9] Selznick, *op. cit.*, p. 13.

tributors within its membership, the Florida Dairy Association contained the potentiality of disunion. However, no stresses upon the organization in the form of opposing interests existed. Also, the distributors were able to affect the farmers adversely through private action. The development of specialized dairy farms brought with it dependency of the farmer upon the continuation of satisfactory relations with a single large distributor who could afford to handle his entire supply of milk. Since milk is a highly perishable product, needing to be marketed immediately, the contract between farmer and distributor was of crucial importance. By maintaining its role as sole spokesman for the milk industry, the Florida Dairy Association established clear access to the administrative decision-making machinery. Representatives of the industry served on the Commission and, although they were appointed by the governor, it became accepted practice for the industry to recommend a slate of acceptable appointments, leaving the governor the choice of a final selection. The Commission established a price-fixing system acceptable to the industry and continued to regard the Florida Dairy Association as its principal source of information. An officer of the organization underscored the intimacy of governmental agency and interest group by declaring "I have had to give so much thought to the Milk Commission . . . that I possibly think I am on the Milk Commission staff."

ACCESS AND LACK OF ACCESS:
THE STATE DEPARTMENT
AND AMERICAN TEXTILE MANUFACTURERS

A roughly analogous situation would be the cooperation between the National Rivers and Harbors Congress and the Corps of Engineers. In these cases of almost total harmony of interests between the government organization and the interest group, the regulated clientele actually acquires a beachhead within the institutions of government. Groups enjoying this relationship have a distinct advantage over groups which face the obstacle of lack of access. The cooperation between railroads and the Interstate Commerce Commission against the interests of trucks and water carriers has left these latter groups in a difficult position. Similarly, the American Cotton Manufacturers Institute, in seeking to accomplish a reversal of the Department of State decision with regard to the importing of Japanese textiles, had to cope with an agency which did not include any portion of the business community in its clientele. The Department of State provides an example of a government organization whose responsibility cannot be traced to one or several interest groups.[10] Its function, that of conducting the foreign relations of the nation, orients its personnel more in the direction of external pressures. This is not to say that domestic interest groups are not concerned with foreign affairs, either as a result of the impact of a given policy upon the economic security of a group or as a result of ideological commitment to various causes which may be furthered or retarded by Department of State decisions. However, it is quite likely that the "position of the State Department renders it immune to the influence of such pressure groups, and its contacts with these associations are of little significance in the administration of the department's work." [11]

The Department of State does have formal mechanisms for taking the views of interest groups into account. The Bureau of Public Affairs has its Public Opinion Studies Staff which analyzes the public opinions of private groups; and the Office of Public Services (a section of the Bureau of Public Affairs) has an Organizational Liaison Staff to handle relations with interest groups at more subtle levels of communication. The publications analyzed by the Public Opinion Studies Staff are the products of six broad types of interests: international relations, economic, men's, women's, veterans, and religious organizations. Included within this spectrum would be the American Farm Bureau Federation, American Legion, the various pacifist, religious, and nationalistic groups which regularly review State Department policy.[12]

Yet while the American Farm Bureau Federation is very influential in the affairs of the Department of Agriculture, and while the American Legion has come close to total domination of the Veterans Administration, neither of these organizations can muster much

---

[10] For explorations in the decision-making process within the Department of State *see* Robert Ellsworth Elder, *The Policy Machine* (Syracuse: Syracuse University Press, 1960), Bernard C. Cohen, *The Political Process and Foreign Policy* (Princeton: Princeton University Press, 1957), and E. Pendleton Herring, *Public Administration and the Public Interest* (New York: McGraw-Hill Book Company, Inc., 1936), pp. 69-88.

[11] Herring, *op. cit.,* p. 77.

[12] Elder, *op. cit.,* pp. 140-144.

influence with the Department of State. This is suggestive of Riesman's "veto groups," each group having considerable influence in its own unique area of activities, but virtually no influence when ventures into other policy areas are undertaken.[13] The American Cotton Manufacturers Institute discovered the importance of clientele relationships when it encountered a stubborn State Department commitment to the expansion of trade with Japan. State Department policy in this area was based on the following assumptions: (1) Japan is basic to the Pacific defense system and must not be allowed to drift into the Communist orbit, (2) Japan's economic position requires that it rely heavily on imports, (3) there is increasing pressure on Japanese policy makers to extend market relations with Communist China. In order to enable the Japanese government to resist these internal pressures, the State Department took steps to improve the international flow of Japanese goods. Largely as a result of United States pressure, Japan was admitted to the General Agreement on Tariffs and Trade in 1955 and shortly thereafter the United States and Japan entered into a bilateral agreement under which tariff concessions were granted to two hundred and eighty-six items.[14] The American textile industry was opposed to the admission of Japan to GATT, and its anxiety that foreign competition destroy an already depressed industry increased with the bilateral agreement.

The manner in which such agreements are negotiated left the textile interest little hope of influencing a reversal of American policy. Under the original trade agreements legislation of 1934, the President was given the authority to negotiate bilateral agreements after consulting with the major executive departments concerned. To facilitate this process, President Roosevelt organized the Trade Agreements Committee consisting of all executive departments involved with foreign trade. In fact, the Trade Agreements Committee became dominated by the State Department in the Eisenhower administration, partially as a result of President Eisenhower's inclination to delegate final authority over foreign policy to his

---

[13] David Riesman, *The Lonely Crowd* (Garden City, N.Y.: Doubleday and Company, Inc., 1955), pp. 244-251.

[14] U.S. Department of State, "Analysis of Protocol for Accession of Japanese-General Agreements on Tariffs and Trade," *Commercial Policy Series No. 150* (Washington, D.C.: Government Printing Office, 1955).

Secretary of State, John Foster Dulles. Hence the negotiations for the bilateral agreement with Japan had been handled exclusively by the State Department. A brief survey of the publications of textile manufacturers clearly demonstrates their belief that the State Department was not only indifferent to their problem but hostile to their interest. The attitude of indifference was inferred from the Congressional testimony of Secretary of State Dulles. Consider for example his testimony before the House Ways and Means Committee: "Let me confess . . . that I am not an expert on tariff matters. . . . I do know something about the foreign relations of the United States. Our foreign policy, as I have put it in capsule form, is to enable the people to enjoy the blessings of liberty in peace. I am convinced that this result cannot be achieved without a cooperative trade relations." [15] This statement provides a good illustration of the conflict between the textile interest and the State Department and also describes the natural consequences of organizations which are not a part of the clientele of an agency to influence its decisions. The textile industry complained that here the State Department "can give away the whole textile market, shut down every mill in the United States. . . . They still have done their job successfully if they keep Japan away from the Communists." [16]

Techniques of Influence

Without access to administrative machinery it is very difficult for interest groups to influence decisions. If it is true that competition among interests tends to decrease the chances of success of any one of these interests, it is also likely that groups that are unable to concentrate upon any single agency, but must divide their activities among several agencies, are at a disadvantage. Consequently, most interest groups find it highly desirable to operate within the control of a single government body. Sayre and Kaufman's analysis of interest groups in New York City reveals that these groups are highly specialized in their activities, even though some have a broad range of interest. The authors discern four types of groups con-

---

[15] House Ways and Means Committee, *Hearings* on H.R.1, 84th Cong., 2d. sess., 1956 (Washington, D.C.: Government Printing Office, 1956), p. 114.
[16] *Textile World,* Feb. 1955, p. 65.

cerned with government activity: those with "broad interests and a record of participation in governmental decision making" (civic associations); those with a "relatively narrower scope of interest and a high rate of participation" (i.e., health and medical groups); those with a "narrow range of interest and low or intermittent participation" (*ad hoc* groups such as anti-fluoridation associations); and those with "broad interest and low participation." There are very few groups in this final category.[17] The first two categories of groups are the only ones capable of developing close relations with government agencies, since the *ad hoc* groups pass from the scene when the particular issue which brought them into being has been resolved.

Concentration of Energy

Civic groups, typifying the type of association with broad interests and constant participation, concern themselves primarily with the *process* of decision-making rather than with its consequences. This means that they are theoretically interested in all governmental structures irrespective of the particular area of responsibility. In fact, the civic groups find themselves involved with "overhead" agencies and the Mayor's office. Naturally, those groups with more specialized interests are able to locate the one agency with authority over their unique area of public policy. This means that all the interest groups cultivate stable interaction with one agency. As the group and the administrative agency continue to interact, each develops specialized knowledge which may be of mutual benefit. For example, retail merchants may seek the advice of the traffic engineer's office on traffic problems; in turn the traffic engineer's office may turn to the retail merchants association for support in the event one of its programs is encountering stiff opposition. Concerning this type of relationship, Sayre and Kaufman write:

> In some particular segment of officialdom, leaders of each group are usually received whenever they request an audience, their advice considered seriously when offered and often incorporated in official decisions, their views canvassed when not volunteered. In

---

[17] Wallace S. Sayre and Herbert Kaufman, *Governing New York City* (New York: Russell Sage Foundation, 1960), pp. 77, 481-482.

a manner of speaking, many group leaders become intimate parts of the city's machinery of governmental decision in certain spheres. They are nongovernmental in the sense that they cannot *promulgate* binding orders and rules the way officeholders clothed with public authority can, but they often have as much to say about what office-holders promulgate as the officeholders themselves, let alone the parties and other contestants for political prizes. Officeholders feel compelled to cooperate with them because they have so much influence, knowledge, and interest. Out of this official acceptance grows an integration of portions of government with relevant non-governmental groups.[18]

SECURING "GOOD" APPOINTMENTS

As was the case with legislative influence, the criteria of effec-tiveness appears to rest upon the acceptance of the interest group by the governmental decision maker as a legitimate agent for the representation of the opinion of a public. As we have seen, this process may be gradual or sudden, depending upon the goals of the agency, the perception by government administrators of their duties, and the amount of support which the agency is able to generate for its policies.[19] Ideally, one sure way to guarantee close ties with an agency is for the interest group to play a part in the selection of its personnel. Generally unsuccessful in their efforts to influence the electoral process, interest groups have had more luck in the appoint-ment of administrative personnel. The acknowledgment that the interest group and the government agency will work together in a common area of interest of less concern to a more general public perhaps establishes more credibility. At any rate, there are far fewer targets of influence than is the case in the electoral process. High level national appointments, such as those to the positions of Secre-tary of Agriculture, Commerce, or Labor, are made by the President after consultation with the interest groups representing the clientele

---

[18] *Ibid.*, p. 511.

[19] With regard to the regulation of business, Robert E. Lane has suggested that there are sources of friction "rooted more in the nature of the respective occupations of businessmen and bureaucrats, in their social milieux, and in the perspectives granted them by their tasks." These sources, which he lists as differential standards of evaluation, and differential reference groups, operate without the conscious control of either party. They would therefore counteract the tendency toward identification between administrators and businessmen. *See The Regulation of Businessmen* (New Haven: Yale Uni-versity Press, 1954), pp. 72-88.

of these agencies. Of course the degree to which the President chooses to accept their advice depends on the extent to which he agrees with their goals and the record of these groups in political support of the President's party.

During the Eisenhower administration, the business and conservative farm organizations had more to say about appointments than they had during the previous Democratic administrations.[20] For example, the Department of Agriculture, which under Secretary Brannan had identified with the National Farmers Union, became much more accessible to the American Farm Bureau Federation when the Republicans captured the White House in 1952. Prominent appointments to the Department of Agriculture were closely identified with the Farm Bureau or the land grant colleges; and at the state level the committees serving the Commodity Stabilization Service and the Agricultural Stabilization and Conservation Committee were selected from the recommendations of the land grant colleges and the Farm Bureaus. Consequently most appointees were large commercial farmers typical of the Farm Bureau membership rather than family type farmers.[21]

Efforts to influence appointments to independent regulatory agencies have been characteristic of interest groups since the creation of the first of these bodies, the Interstate Commerce Commission, in 1887. While there was considerable disagreement among public administration specialists about the meaning of the word "independence"—some arguing for institutional guarantees against domination by the chief executive, others believing that independence should also extend to freedom from control by centers of economic or political power—interest groups have generally been accorded the right to participate in the appointment process by government decision makers. The case of Leland Olds, former chairman of the Federal Power Commission, illustrates this point.[22]

---

[20] Herbert Miles Somers, "The Federal Bureaucracy and the Change of Administrations," *American Political Science Review*, XLVIII (Mar. 1954), 131-151.

[21] Charles M. Hardin, "The Republican Department of Agriculture—A Political Interpretation," *Journal of Farm Economics*, XXXVI (May 1954), 210-227.

[22] This account is drawn from Joseph P. Harris, "The Senatorial Rejection of Leland Olds: A Case Study," *American Political Science Review*, XLV (Sept. 1951), 674-692.

Olds was a vigorous believer in the necessity of regulation of natural gas rates, a position which created organized hostility from the oil and natural gas producers who fought steadfastly against his reappointment. These interests were supported by Senators Kerr and Johnson and other congressmen from oil and gas producing states. In contrast, Olds was defended primarily by poorly organized consumers groups, the Americans for Democratic Action, various co-operative associations, and the National Grange. Olds' appointment had to be approved by the Senate Interstate and Foreign Commerce Committee; the subcommittee which would hold the hearings was chaired by Lyndon Johnson of Texas. The appointment was inextricably intwined in the controversy over the Kerr bill, a bill which the gas and oil industry had been trying to steer through Congress in an effort to amend the Natural Gas Act of 1938 in such a way as to remove the possibility of federal regulation. Serving as chairman of the Federal Power Commission, Olds had been a constant opponent of the Kerr bill and similar legislation. In fact, he had testified against the legislation only three months before his reappointment was scheduled to come before the Interstate and Foreign Commerce Committee. Unable to achieve official confirmation of their point of view either through the courts or through the legislature, the natural gas interests devoted their energies to finding a commission more amenable to their suggestions: "if Mr. Olds could be rejected and a person who was sympathetic to the industry's point of view appointed, the way would be paved to secure the enactment of desired amendments to the Natural Gas Act to remove federal regulation of the field price of gas." [23] This attitude was expressed by a representative of the Ohio Oil and Gas Association when he claimed that if Olds were reappointed "we face but one destiny—full extinction. . . . We deeply feel that the retention of Mr. Olds as a member of the FPC is a full threat to the free-enterprise system of this life in these United States." [24] Although President Truman made clear his unqualified support of Olds, the committee voted against confirmation. Before the confirmation came before the Senate, Truman commenced his support of Olds, by requesting that the Democratic National Chairman send telegrams to

---

[23] *Ibid.*, 680.

[24] Statement of Russell B. Brown, General Counsel of the Independent Petroleum Association of America, quoted *ibid.*, 686.

the state chairmen suggesting that they urge the senators from their states to vote for confirmation, but this effort failed. Without attributing the result directly to the removal of Olds, it is worthy of mention that the Federal Power Commission ruled two years later that the regulation of natural gas prices was beyond its jurisdiction.

In this case the victory of the regulated clientele was won over Presidential opposition by means of access to the legislative body, which was required by law to approve the appointment. If the chief executive agrees with the aspirations of a group to be relieved of the burden of regulation, the task is made easier. During the Eisenhower administration, business and management groups which had been unable to gain much influence in the appointive process during the Roosevelt and Truman years found themselves in a position to offer advice on prospective appointments at the innermost circles of the government. The influence of the Farm Bureau in the Department of Agriculture has been touched upon; the Chamber of Commerce and the National Association of Manufacturers appeared to have been equally successful in seeking to affect the performance of the National Labor Relations Board through the appointive process. Long smarting under what they considered the pro-labor bias of the NLRB, management groups urged the President to use his power of appointment to achieve a "good" board. A combination of expirations of terms and resignations, coupled with the business-oriented attitude of Eisenhower's advisors, made 1953 a crucial year for the NLRB. In contrast to years of urging the abolition of the NLRB or at least reduction of its powers, the NAM in 1954 seemed satisfied:

> As an over-all appraisal it can be fairly said that the Board, with few exceptions, has followed a course of administration designed to give full faith and credit to the intent of Congress when the Taft-Hartley Act was put on the statute books.

> Though the language of Taft-Hartley has remained unchanged, its interpretation by the Labor Board has not. On numerous and important issues the new Board, a majority of whose members have been appointed by President Eisenhower, has overturned established rulings, and has given the Act a new, and almost always anti-labor meaning. Indeed the Eisenhower appointees seem to have taken office with that end consciously in mind. . . . They seem to have proceeded on the assumption that since they were appointed by a new administration, they had a license to overhaul

any or all of the Board's policies. They have proceeded to imbue the Board with the employer-oriented interests of the new Administration.[25]

Agency Influence on Interest Groups

The power of the chief executive to appoint administrative personnel certainly earmarks him as the object of group pressure. It should not be assumed, however, that the chief executive is a helpless pawn at the mercy of the most effectively organized groups. In Florida, Governor LeRoy Collins elected to use his office to resist the tendency of the Florida Milk Commission to regulate in the interests of the milk industry by appointing a chairman who did not believe in any form of regulation. The man he selected was considered by the Florida Dairy Association to be totally unfamiliar with the problems of milk marketing and even to be an enemy of the trade association itself. The Florida Dairy Association had supported Collins in his contests for Governor and were inclined to regard him as friendly. When the members of the Association heard of Collins' intention, they sought a conference in the hope of changing his mind, and were supported by the Florida Farm Bureau and the state Chamber of Commerce. A conference was arranged, but only after the appointment had been made. While the reaction of the organized clientele of the Milk Commission was extremely hostile, support for the Governor was limited to a few urban papers and some temporary and hastily organized consumer groups. Collins was sacrificing trade association support for what he believed to be a broad but unarticulated public sympathy.

IDENTIFICATION WITH CLIENTELE

Administrative decision makers, like their legislative counterparts, do not have their total pattern of activity defined by the interest groups in the immediate environment. Again, the overextension of the Bentleyan thesis that governmental institutions are no more than reflections of dominant combinations of interests in the com-

---

[25] *N.A.M. Law Digest*, Dec., 1954, p. 1., quoted in Seymour Scher, "Regulatory Agency Control through Appointments: The Case of the Eisenhower Administration and the NLRB," *Journal of Politics*, XXIII (Nov. 1961), 687.

munity is rejected.[26] Fainsod's comments on the nature of the
regulatory process, stressing the ability of government agencies to
do more than accede to the demands of clientele groups, deserve
inclusion at some length:

> In stressing the limits which environmental pressures impose on
> the uses to which these instruments [regulatory agencies] are put,
> there is a tendency to underestimate the independent creative force
> and manipulative power which the wielders of these instruments
> acquire by virtue of their special competence or their strategic
> position in the regulatory hierarchy. The strategy by which regula-
> tory agencies develop ability to resist or guide pressures has been
> relatively little explored. Yet it is obvious that, within limits, such
> power exists. The regulatory agency itself is capable of generating
> a certain amount of independent power to change its environment.
> . . . In the process of exercising their discretionary power, regula-
> tory agencies are often in a position to create some pressures and
> to extinguish others, to stir dormant parties in interest into activity
> and to anesthetize others, to mobilize groups to come to their
> support and to penalize opposition. Investigation may deflate pre-
> tensions and reveal divisions and minorities within groups which
> are spoken for as units. The impact of the articulate may be softened
> by the gentle ministrations of discreet inquiry. The manipulative
> power of regulatory agencies may be utilized to maintain an exist-
> ing equilibrium of interests; it can be used to tilt the scale and
> create a new equilibrium.[27]

One of the most frequently cited reasons for the inability of administrators to perform in the manner suggested by Fainsod is the
gradual identification between the administrator and the regulated
clientele.[28] This is not so much a matter of overt pressure or threats

---

[26] Leading interpreters of Bentley, such as David Truman, have been careful
to avoid this pitfall. *See* Truman, *The Governmental Process* (New York:
Alfred A. Knopf, Inc., 1951), pp. 446-450.

[27] Merle Fainsod, "Some Reflections on the Nature of the Regulatory
Process," in C. J. Friedrich and Edward S. Mason, eds., *Public Policy* (Cambridge: Harvard University Press, 1940), pp. 299-320.

[28] Lane has suggested that specialized personnel in both business and government will develop more identification but that more generalized managerial
personnel are less prone to do so because of different reference group identification. *See op. cit.,* p. 87. *See also* Reinhard Bendix, *Higher Civil Servants
in American Society* (Boulder: University of Colorado Press, 1949) and Morris
Janowitz and William Delany, "The Bureaucrat and the Public: A Study of
Informal Perspectives," *Administrative Science Quarterly,* II (Sept. 1957),
141-162. This later study finds that the place of the government employee in
the structure of his organization is contributory to his perception of the
environment.

made to the administrator but rather a consequence of administrators being "thrown into a constant association with the people they are supposed to regulate." [29] In the day-by-day performance of their tasks, administrators see very little of the more general public support which accompanied the establishment of the agency. The only people who are likely to come to the attention of administrators are those whose problems are uniquely a part of the administrative environment. Consequently there is the tendency to look upon others as "outsiders." Under such circumstances it is not surprising that the administrator's perception of the public interest is in reality defined by the interests of the regulated parties. Such a situation is most likely to occur when the environment of the agency is dominated by a single interest because the administrator will not be exposed to any appreciable extent to competing sources of information. Edelman notes that "the most effective way to make a public official act as an interest wishes him to is to assure by institutional means that he will become thoroughly acquainted with its problems as the adherents of the interest see them." [30]

As we have seen, interests tend to concentrate their efforts at one or a few agencies. Within each agency, there are usually attempts to carve out subordinate units to deal with the exclusive problems of a narrow interest; this frequently confuses efforts at reorganization. Thus the National War Labor Board, which had jurisdiction over wage stabilization for most of American industry and labor during World War II, came to be subdivided into boards to deal with stabilization problems for only a few industries. It was found that these smaller boards were more malleable in yielding to demands for wage increases than the national board because these industry boards were able to give undivided attention to the concerns of particular industries in a manner that the larger national board could not duplicate. Commissioners working on these industry boards "became an effective part of the industry and labor interests simply because it was their job to know the problems of the industry thoroughly." [31]

[29] Statement of Senator Aiken of Vermont before the Senate Committee on Labor and Public Welfare, *Hearings, Establishment of a Commission on Ethics in Government*, 82d. Cong., 1st sess., 1951, p. 213. Cited in Bernstein, *Reg. Bus. by Ind. Comm.*, p. 158.

[30] Edelman, *op. cit.*, p. 279.

[31] *Ibid.*

SEEKING INDEPENDENCE: PUBLICITY

It follows from the above remarks that there is the possibility of institutional isolation of administrators from pressure by broadening the scope of responsibility to include diverse and competing interests. This will embroil the agency in organizational disputes that are of unusual interest to regulated groups. However, there are tactics of resistance that do not necessarily involve alterations in institutional arrangements. One of the most frequently used devices is agency publicity. In seeking to guarantee that the continued existence of an agency will depend upon an alliance with clientele groups, these groups will normally seek to keep the operations of the agency as far from public awareness as possible. This, in turn, will reduce the possibility of the agency recruiting strength from more general public support and developing alternative reservoirs of political strength. To counteract the desire for secrecy, administrative agencies may use carefully executed public relations and propaganda programs. Thus Simon notes that "community satisfaction with the services of the Forest Service, and community understanding of those services, brought about partly by the public relations activities of the district forest ranger, have created sufficient support to keep the Forest Service in the Department of Agriculture in spite of constant pressure from the conflicting interests of stock grangers and lumbermen to transfer it to the Department of the Interior where those interests have considerably more influence." [32]

THE REDUCTION OF CLIENTELE HOMOGENEITY

Another bit of strategy which can be used by administrators is the reduction of monopoly in the environment. Some interests which appear to be monolithic actually contain the seeds of discontent. If the agency can create and nourish competition by contributing to the bifurcation of an interest, its independence from that interest will be enhanced. The experience of the Florida Milk Commission serves to illustrate this point. From its creation in 1934 until the early 1950's, the Commission operated beneath the level of public awareness. Although public hearings were held, little mention of

[32] Simon *et al.*, *Pub. Admin.*, pp. 415-416.

its activities was made in the press. Since no public funds were involved, the State Legislature tended to approve routinely any Commission recommendations. No legislation seriously altering the functions of the Commission ever reached the floor of either the Senate or House of Representatives, and only rarely were such bills introduced. In the early 1950's the operations of the Commission became the subject of some public controversy. Occasional complaints that the Commission was dominated by the industry trade association, the Florida Dairy Association, were expressed by temporary and hastily organized consumers' groups. The activities of the Milk Commission were brought sharply to the public attention during the 1954 primary for governor when one of the candidates campaigned on a platform calling for the abolition of the Milk Commission. This candidate, Brailey Odham, was opposed vigorously by the Florida Dairy Association and ran last in a field of three. However, he was subsequently appointed Chairman of the Milk Commission. Joined by others who believed that the Commission should not set milk prices, Odham faced the united opposition of the Florida Dairy Association which insisted that prices should be set to avoid price wars.

During this time, the Commission had agreed to abandon all price controls above the producer level for one year. This meant that, while the milk prices offered by dairies to farmers were set, prices at wholesale and retail levels were allowed to fluctuate. In this climate, differences of opinion between farmer and distributor members of the Florida Dairy Association began to appear. In the past, farmers had supported the regulation of prices at all levels. Now some of these farmers began to express the desire for an organization, independent of the dairies, which would support the efforts of the Commission to remove controls permanently. The new members of the Commission began a campaign of persuasion, both inside and outside of the Commission, designed to take advantage of the emerging industry discord. They urged farmers to think in terms of their own interests and tried to persuade them to attend Commission meetings. At the same time, farmers were assured that the Commission would never oppose price controls at the producer level. In addition to encouraging farmers, the Commission took concrete action which could be interpreted as antagonistic to dairies. It ordered price controls extended at the producer level to surplus milk, ordered a revision in the prices charged to farmers for hauling milk, and began an investigation of possible rebating practices between dairies and retailers.

This concern for producer interests enhanced a growing cleavage within the Florida Dairy Association. In its hearings, the Commission began to see a rising independence on the part of producers. In the past the testimony of dairy farmers had not deviated from that of distributors. Now local producer groups began to declare publicly in support of the program of scrutinizing the activities of dairies. While these dairies were seeking a return to controls, some producers appeared to be satisfied with the Commission's policies. Operating under a Commission which they thought was not easily influenced by the distributors, some of the younger producers began to work for the formation of a separate, statewide organization. These efforts were consummated with the creation of the Florida Dairy Farmers Federation in 1958. The new members of the Commission were delighted with this development. Now there was an interest group in existence which was competitive with the Florida Dairy Association. The environment was no longer dominated by a single organization as it had been for so long. To insure the continued existence of the new and friendly group, the Commission passed new orders providing for a measure of economic independence for farmers. Distributors had provided for a "dues check-off plan" by which producer organization dues were automatically deducted when the farmer was paid for his milk. Producers affiliated with the new Florida Dairy Farmers Federation were being denied this convenience, so the Commission passed an order providing that any producer group meeting certain standards could qualify for dues check-off. The Commission also tried, against distributor opposition, to institute a "just cause" order providing that a contract between producer and distributor could not be terminated without Commission approval. The Commission was thus developing an alternate source of information in the expectation that the agency would no longer have to cope with united, industrywide opposition to its programs. The Florida Dairy Association, so long the defender of the Commission, now was discouraged by what it saw as a new bias. The agency had, as Fainsod suggests, created a new equilibrium.

Organization and Reorganization

Interest groups are concerned not only with the substance of policy but also with the structure of administrative agencies, which, it is assumed, is related to policy decisions: "it is . . . widely believed that a change in the location of an executive agency within the administrative branch will seriously affect the ability of outside groups to influence the substance of policy as administered by the agency."[33] Even if there is no contemplation of a change in policy to accompany reorganization, agencies and their clientele are extremely suspicious of changes which might alter the established pattern of relationships and hence render the clientele less in control of policy. The ability of an agency to survive is dependent upon the establishment of support in the community of interests to which it is responsible.[34] We have described some of the informal means whereby this is accomplished. On a more formal level, the establishment of advisory committees, whether by legislative statute or administrative decree, can serve to give interest groups favored access.[35] Proposals which suggest disequilibrium in these relationships are therefore to be construed as a threat by the affected groups and agencies.

SOME EXAMPLES OF REORGANIZATION

Quite often proposals for reorganization come from groups who have lost or cannot achieve access to an agency that has responsibility for policy in the area of the group's concern, and these pro-

---

[33] Francis E. Rourke, "The Politics of Administrative Organization: A Case History," *Journal of Politics*, XIX (Aug. 1957), 461.

[34] Oliver Garceau's study of public libraries is a useful illumination of this idea. He found that, while the library has no natural enemies, it also has no reliable supporters. Although libraries try to remedy this situation by creating groups such as the Friends of the Library, they still "float along helplessly." Garceau notes that the library's clientele is "a minority of individual consumers" who are not motivated to form support groups. *See The Public Library in the Political Process* (New York: Columbia University Press, 1949), p. 135.

[35] The definitive work on the function of advisory committees is Avery Leiserson, *Administrative Regulation* (Chicago: University of Chicago Press, 1942).

posals are resisted by groups who view their relationships with the agency as satisfactory. Such recommendations very often are phrased in language reflecting the standard canons of public administrations, such as the reduction of overlapping functions to reduce the burden of executive control and to insure economical operation. However, such abstract values are not without their political implications. For example, the Hoover Commission recommended that the Department of Agriculture's Soil Conservation Service be abolished and most of its functions be assigned to the Extension Service, a goal long sought by the American Farm Bureau Federation which has extremely close ties with the Extension Service.[36] Again, the proposals that the functions of the Interstate Commerce Commission be assigned to an administrator directly responsible to the President have been opposed by railroads which have benefited by the independent status of the agency. Textile manufacturers, confronted by the President's frequent rejections of the Tariff Commission's recommendations, have sought through legislation to make the Commission's decisions final rather than advisory. During World War II, organized medicine began to attack the Emergency Maternal and Infant Care program of the Children's Bureau and urged its transfer from the Department of Labor to the U.S. Public Health Service, "considered by the AMA to be a more 'controllable' body." [37]

STABILITY IN RELATIONSHIPS AND RESISTANCE TO CHANGE

These examples—drawn from the hundreds that could be given— reflect concern over maintenance of what Truman calls the "inflexibility of the established web." [38] This set of relationships, which includes the interest group, "its" agency, and the legislative committees or subcommittees that are charged with the responsibility of supervising the activities of the agency, may provide the most powerful weapon in the arsenal of interest groups.[39] Administrative

---

[36] Grant McConnell, *The Decline of Agrarian Democracy* (Berkeley: University of California Press, 1959), p. 136.

[37] E. Drexel Godfrey, Jr., *The Transfer of the Children's Bureau* (Committee on Public Administration Cases, 1949, Mimeograph), p. 5.

[38] Truman, *op. cit.*, p. 467.

[39] Avery Leiserson, "Political Limitations on Executive Reorganization," *American Political Science Review*, XLI (Feb. 1947), 79. *See also* J. Leiper Freeman, *The Political Process: Executive Bureau—Legislative Committee Relations* (Garden City, N.Y.: Doubleday and Company, Inc., 1955).

politics is often more circumspect than legislative politics, and techniques of influence less flamboyant. Considerable security for the interest group can be derived from the knowledge that, through the ebb and flow of legislative victories and reverses, its support within the administrative web remains unchanged. Laws are not necessarily productive of the reallocation of values suggested by their language. The actual or operational meaning of statutes may be found in the day-by-day administration of these statutes; and in this process of administration, groups which appear to have lost in the legislative arena may be successful in minimizing the effects of the law.[40] The techniques used by interest groups in the legislative process have little value and are rarely employed by those who are part of the established web. To illustrate, in spite of the great amount of legislative effort to distribute defense contracts to small firms, the stubborn resistance of the Department of Defense and its few prime contractors has ridden out this legislative activity and, in fact, there have been no basic changes in contract allocation since World War II. Although modifications in administrative structure do not automatically mean that the pattern will be disrupted and a new balance of interests created, the exchange of a proven relation of influence for a situation in which there is at least the risk of reduction in power is a gamble that few interest groups are willing to make.

---

[40] Murray Edelman, "Symbols and Political Quiescence," *American Political Science Review*, LIV (Sept. 1960), 695-704.

The Judicial Process:

XI   Conflict Under
Carefully Defined Rules[*]

The study of politics as a process whereby authoritative decisions are made which operate to the advantage of some groups and to the disadvantage of others runs into a stubborn roadblock when the judicial branch of government comes under consideration. The gradual abandonment of traditional or legalistic approaches that has taken place in studies of legislation and, with some resistance, administration, has not proceeded with much speed to the judiciary.[1] From the point of view of research, the reluctance of scholars to place the judicial within the general political process is perhaps more a reflection of a popular belief system than the result of in-

---

* This phrase is taken from Will Maslow, "The Use of the Law in the Struggle for Equality," *Social Research*, XXII (Autumn, 1955), 308.

[1] Notable exceptions to this statement are Jack W. Peltason, *Federal Courts in the Political Process* (Garden City, N.Y.: Doubleday and Company, Inc., 1955), Glendon Schubert, *Quantitative Analysis of Judicial Behavior* (New York: The Free Press of Glencoe, Inc., 1959), Schubert, *Constitutional Politics* (New York: Holt, Rinehart & Winston, Inc., 1960), and John R. Schmidhauser, *The Supreme Court* (New York: Holt, Rinehart & Winston, Inc., 1960).

adequate methodology or inaccessibility of materials. While it is true that the courts deliberate and make decisions in an atmosphere more secretive than other governmental bodies, recent research has demonstrated that this seclusion is no real handicap. However, the judiciary branch and especially the United States Supreme Court occupies a position in our belief structure unlike that of any other agency of government. Lerner comments upon this unique status:

> Talk to the men on the street, the men in the mines and factories and steel mills and real-estate offices and filling stations, dig into their minds and even below the threshold of their consciousness, and you will find in the main that the Constitution and Supreme Court are symbols of an ancient sureness and comforting stability.[2]

Judges and Politics

What Lerner suggests is that the judiciary is not looked upon as being "political" but is somehow regarded as a purely "legal" body which functions to discover permanent truths. It is indeed paradoxical that America with its doctrine of judicial review has placed the court at the center of the policy-making process while persisting in the belief that judges are above politics.[3] Since the courts can refuse to uphold legislation which they construe to be unconstitutional, interests which cannot achieve their goals in one arena are given another chance. In such a situation, it is impossible for judges to be "above politics" simply because the decisions they reach are political. The decisions confirm benefits upon groups of people while impeding the aspirations of others.[4] Thus the political nature of the judiciary is not solely a function of the biases or group affiliations of judges but is rather inherent in the structure of the governmental system. Coupled with the clearly supportable assumption that the values of judges are a fundamental ingredient in the process of judicial decision-making, the institutional role of courts

---

[2] Max Lerner, *Ideas for the Ice Age* (New York: The Viking Press, Inc., 1941), p. 232.

[3] Fred V. Cahill, Jr., *Judicial Legislation* (New York: The Ronald Press Company, 1952), p. 7.

[4] Lewis A. Froman, *People and Politics* (Englewood Cliffs, N.J.: Prentice-Hall, Inc., 1962), pp. 89-93.

in the governmental system makes these bodies central to the political process. The neutrality of judges is part of our myth system, but has never been characteristic of the actual decision-making process.

Arthur Bentley correctly assessed the nature of judicial politics:

> It is possible to take a Supreme Court decision, in which nothing appears on the surface but finespun points of law, and cut through all the dialectic till we get down to the actual groups of men underlying the decisions and producing the decisions through the differentiated activity of the justices.[5]

The activity of the Supreme Court in outlawing segregation in public schools brought home to many people the role of interest groups in the formulation of judicial policy and perhaps, as Dahl suggests, the intense criticism leveled at the Court as a result of these decisions arises from dismay that the Court had forsaken its role as infallible finder of truth and gotten involved in "politics." [6] Of course one does not have to look at only the recent history of the Court to find examples in support of Bentley's thesis. Those scholars skilled at tracing periods in the development of the Supreme Court's interpretation of the Constitution have little trouble in refuting the myth of neutrality. For example, Miller and Howell have noted three distinct eras of constitutional interpretation: (1) from the establishment of the Supreme Court until the Civil War, when the Court sought to create and maintain a strong national union; (2) from about 1870 to 1937, when the basic drive of the Court was toward establishing a favorable climate for business by protecting it against governmental interference; (3) from 1937 until the present, when individual liberties and personal freedoms assumed more prominence than they had in either of the two previous periods.[7] In each of these periods the judges were required to choose among competing alternative choices of public policy without recourse to precedent. Even in the interpretation of precedent there can be no neutrality, for the values of the judge will color and

---

[5] Arthur F. Bentley, *The Process of Government* (San Antonio, Texas: The Principia Press of Trinity University, 1908), p. 205.

[6] Robert A. Dahl, "Decision-Making in a Democracy: The Supreme Court as a National Policy-Maker," *Journal of Public Law,* VI (Fall, 1957), 279.

[7] Arthur S. Miller and Ronald F. Howell, "The Myth of Neutrality in Constitutional Adjudication," *University of Chicago Law Review,* XXVII (Summer, 1960), 672.

shape what he reads.[8] It is useful also to realize that the precedents were established by prior courts, each with its own particular combination of values. Some of the leading decisions of the first part of the nineteenth century, which were woven by future justices into the fabric of the law, are primarily essays in political philosophy with only peripheral reference to the actual legal issue before the Court. John Marshall's opinion in *McCulloch* v. *Maryland* is a clear example of this technique.[9]

JUDICIAL RESPONSE TO CRITICISM

In view of this evidence, it is instructive to consider what is perhaps the most articulate cornerstone of the myth that judges merely "discover" law. In *U.S.* v. *Butler* former Justice Owen J. Roberts defined the duty of the Court: "When an act of Congress is appropriately challenged in the Courts as not conforming to the constitutional mandate, the judicial branch of the government has only one duty; to lay the Article of the Constitution which is invoked beside the statute which is challenged and to decide whether the latter squares with the former." [10] Roberts was thus suggesting that the Supreme Court justice is capable of absolute detachment and objectivity and is totally uninfluenced by his social background, his identification with social or economic interests. One of Roberts' colleagues, Justice George Sutherland, defined his function similarly by saying that "the meaning of the Constitution does not change with the ebb and flow of economic events." [11] In this case, *Adkins* v. *Childrens Hospital,* Sutherland held the Minimum Wage Act of 1918 to be a violation of the Fifth Amendment which he held to be protective of "freedom of contract." However, the Fifth Amendment makes no mention of such a freedom. The idea of freedom of contract was first given explicit notice in *Allgeyer* v. *Louisiana,* a Fourteenth Amendment case in which the Court

---

[8] *See* the following works of Stuart S. Nagel for development of this point: "Political Party Affiliation and Judges' Decisions," *American Political Science Review,* LV (Dec. 1961), 843-850; "Ethnic Affiliations and Judicial Propensities," *Journal of Politics,* XXIV (Feb. 1962), 92-110; and "Judicial Attitudes and Those of Legislators and Administrators" (Paper presented to the 1962 annual meeting of the American Political Science Association).

[9] McCulloch v. Maryland, 46 Wheaton 316 (1819).

[10] U.S. v. Butler, 297 U.S. 1 (1936).

[11] Adkins v. Childrens Hospital, 261 U.S. 525 (1923).

held that a Louisiana statute placing restrictions on insurance companies was a violation of the "liberty contained in that amendment." [12] The reading of this new liberty into the Fourteenth Amendment had been continued in *Lochner* v. *New York* but had not become a part of litigation involving the Fifth Amendment.[13] Nevertheless, Sutherland, citing the *Allgeyer* case, but ignoring several other cases which might have had a bearing on the subject, declared that "the right to contract about one's affairs is a part of the liberty of the individual protected by this clause is settled by the decisions of this court and is no longer open to question." [14]

This determination to protect the rights of property, or as Sutherland phrased it, "the good of society as a whole," characterized the second period of the Supreme Court's history according to the Miller-Howell scheme, and persisted as late as 1936. During the 1930's, a conservative bloc consisting of Justices McReynolds, Butler, Van Devanter, and Sutherland voted consistently against the New Deal legislation of President Franklin Roosevelt. Generally in support of the President were Justices Stone, Cardozo, and Brandeis. Somewhat in the middle, but with greater identification with the Anti-New Deal Faction, were Justice Roberts and Chief Justice Charles Evans Hughes.[15] It was in this situation that Roosevelt's "Court-packing" plan was proposed. The Hughes Court had invalidated twelve New Deal laws within four years and three Presidential acts within a period of six months. Arguing that "the Court has been acting not as a judicial body, but as a policy-making body," Roosevelt proposed to the Congress that whenever a federal judge who had served ten years or more failed to retire within six months after reaching his seventieth birthday, the President would be allowed to appoint an additional judge to serve on that court.[16] Interests which were disadvantaged by the New Deal and protected by the Court opposed the President's plan, but, before the issue became joined, the business community's plea of "hands off the Supreme Court" was settled by the sudden reversal of the Court's position on several key pieces of New Deal legislation. The change

---

[12] Allgeyer v. Louisiana, 165 U.S. 578 (1897).

[13] Lochner v. New York, 198 U.S. 45 (1905).

[14] Adkins v. Childrens Hospital, at 545.

[15] Schubert, *Constitutional Politics*, p. 161.

[16] Senate Report 711, 75th Cong., 1st sess., 1937 (Washington, D.C.: Government Printing Office, 1937), pp. 41-44.

in the posture of the Court was accomplished by the switching of Hughes and Roberts from the "right" bloc to the "left" bloc and thus creating a majority in support of the New Deal. Robert's concept of mechanical jurisprudence was not borne out in his voting behavior.[17]

Today, as was the case during the Court-packing episode, the Supreme Court is under attack. Those who disagree with the main thrust of the Warren Court's decisions in race relations, federal security programs, conducting congressional investigations, and the prosecution of subversives are proposing limitations upon the jurisdiction of the Court.[18] In language reminiscent of Roosevelt's, the southern legislators who signed the Southern Manifesto of 1956 declared: "We regard the decision of the Supreme Court in the school cases as a clear abuse of judicial power. It climaxes a trend in the federal judiciary undertaking to legislate, in derogation of the authority of Congress, and to encroach upon the reserved rights of the States and the people." [19] Interest groups which defended the Court against Roosevelt began to support various proposals such as those of Representative Howard Smith of Virginia and Senator William Jenner of Indiana to limit the jurisdiction of the Court.[20] The Chamber of Commerce and National Association of Manufacturers have turned upon the Court while the AFL-CIO and NAACP have become its staunchest defenders. Although, like the Roosevelt Court-packing plan, most of this legislation was not adopted, its impact is noticeable. During the 1956 term, when criticism was not yet at its peak, the Court rejected civil liberties claims in 26 per cent of the cases decided by a full opinion but this figure rose to nearly 49 per cent during the 1958 term.[21] Withdrawals were also negotiated in the fields of internal security and race relations. In

[17] For an argument maintaining no relation between Roosevelt's action and the subsequent behavior of Justice Roberts *see* Felix Frankfurter, "Mr. Justice Roberts," *University of Pennsylvania Law Review*, CIV (Dec. 1955), 311-317.

[18] For a categorization of hostile reactions *see* Louis H. Pollak, "The Supreme Court Under Fire," *Journal of Public Law*, VI (Fall, 1957), 428-430 and Walter F. Murphy, *Congress and the Court* (Chicago: University of Chicago Press, 1962). Copyright (1962) by the University of Chicago.

[19] *Congressional Record*, CII (Mar. 1956), 4460.

[20] *See* Murphy, *Congress and the Court* (Chicago: University of Chicago Press, 1962), pp. 127-241, for the particulars of these proposals.

[21] *Ibid.*, p. 246.

Watkins v. *United States*[22] and *Sweezy* v. *New Hampshire*[23] the Court imposed severe limitations upon state and federal investigations of subversive activities but *Barenblatt* v. *United States*[24] and *Uphaus* v. *Wyman*[25] represented clear retreats from these earlier decisions. The Court's upholding of the Alabama pupil placement law and its refusal to sustain a lower court's decision that Virginia's anti-NAACP laws were unconstitutional supply additional evidence of a retreat.

The parallel between the shifting attitudes on the Warren Court and the Hughes Court of 1936 are striking. Glendon Schubert's analysis of voting patterns in the two sets of cases involving investigations of subversive activity, *Watkins, Sweezy, Barenblatt,* and *Uphaus,* reveal that a 6-1 majority in favor of the defendant in the first two cases became a 4-5 minority in the latter two. Schubert notes that there was no change in the position of a majority of the Justices, and changes in the personnel of the Court could not account for the differences between the sets of cases. In order for the Warren bloc (Warren, Black, Douglas, and Brennan) to lose control it was necessary for two justices to switch their votes. Justices Frankfurter and Harlan, having voted for the defendants in the *Watkins* and *Sweezy* decisions of 1957, voted against the defendants' claims in the *Barenblatt* and *Uphaus* decisions of 1959.[26] In 1936, Roberts and Hughes switched, shifting the balance of power in the Court, and in 1959, Frankfurter and Harlan accomplished the same feat. In both situations the Court was under heavy attack from dissatisfied interests (including organized groups), and in both situations the Court reduced the hostility by modifying its policy decisions. Rather than being neutral observers of a political warfare being waged beneath them, courts actually assume the role of partisans in the struggle. This partisanship is not the result of a conscious evaluation of political advantages on the part of judges, but rather is a natural consequence of the position of courts in our political structure.

---

[22] Watkins v. United States, 354 U.S. 178 (1957).

[23] Sweezy v. New Hampshire, 354 U.S. 234 (1957).

[24] Barenblatt v. United States, 360 U.S. 109 (1959).

[25] Uphaus v. Wyman, 360 U.S. 72 (1959).

[26] Judicial behavior during these decisions is discussed in Schubert, *Constitutional Politics,* pp. 633-638.

Selecting Judicial Personnel

Since courts make decisions involving the political well-being of interests, the affected groups may be expected to utilize every resource at their command to insure that these decisions are "satisfactory." The status of the courts and the persistence of community values in defense of judicial isolation from the political process make it impossible for the "normal" group tactics to be employed. Direct and overt solicitation of judges by interest groups would be looked upon as an alarming violation of the rules of the political game, yet more indirect methods can be equally satisfactory. Peltason has categorized these methods under three headings: (1) influencing the selection of judges, (2) influencing the content of decisions, and (3) maximizing or minimizing the effects of decisions as they are implemented.[27] The first method, influencing the selection of judges, is one in which interest group activity is readily discernible. The Constitution provides that federal judges are to be nominated by the President and approved by the Senate. Some of the states have provided for the election of judges by the electorate or the legislature, and some, notably California and Missouri, have sought a compromise between election and appointment. Whatever the method of selection, there has been little success in isolating judges from political influences.[28] The President, in submitting his recommendations to the Senate, will obviously select candidates whose views of the public interest are in harmony with his own, even though Presidential expectations may not be borne out by the behavior of the judge once he has been appointed. In the case of a Supreme Court appointment, the President is less restricted by custom than is true when lesser federal appointments are contemplated. Inferior court appointments are subject to the rule of senatorial courtesy, meaning that the President is placed in a position of approving the decision of the Senator or local party organization in the area in which the proposed judge is to serve. However, even

---

[27] Peltason, *Federal Courts in the Political Process,* p. 29.

[28] *See* Henry J. Abraham, *The Judicial Process* (New York: Oxford University Press, Inc., 1962), pp. 26-88 for a description of the various methods of selecting judges.

without the restrictions of senatorial courtesy, appointments to the Supreme Court have become the center of intense group conflict which is concentrated at the Senate Judiciary Committee. Schmidhauser writes that "a president is . . . subject to pressures which emanate from private groups which, although national in their organization attributes, may be excessively narrow and self-serving in their public policy objectives." [29]

TWO EXAMPLES OF GROUP INFLUENCE

The two most frequently discussed examples of group pressures on the process of Supreme Court appointments are the cases of Louis Brandeis and John J. Parker. Brandeis, who had made a substantial reputation as a lawyer for various progressive causes such as the regulation of utilities and limitation of work hours, was opposed by groups that had been able to resist the tide of regulatory legislation by relying upon a friendly court. Particularly anxious to block the nomination was the American Bar Association which argued that Brandeis did not have "judicial temperament." However, the meaning read into such a nebulous phrase varies with the values of the group using it. Brandeis had a long and active career in the practice of law, but his clients were most often those who were challenging the dominant business ideology of the time. In support of Brandeis were trade associations and other organizations conspicuous in voicing the protest. The intensity of the ideological conflict centering around the nomination of Brandeis is reflected in the absolute partisanship of the vote in the Judiciary Committee and on the Senate floor. President Wilson, who viewed his own chances for re-election as somewhat dependent upon his ability to avoid an open re-election of his leadership by the Senate, worked vigorously in Brandeis' behalf and was rewarded by a straight party vote in the Judiciary (ten Democrats voting for confirmation, eight Republicans opposing) and in the Senate (forty-four Democrats and three Progressives opposed by all twenty-one Republicans and one Democrat).[30] While business-oriented groups were unsuccessful in defeating the nomination of Brandeis in 1916, the NAACP and organized labor were able to prevent the con-

---

[29] Schmidhauser, *The Supreme Court,* 13.

[30] Joseph P. Harris, *The Advice and Consent of the Senate* (Berkeley: University of California Press, 1953), pp. 99-114.

firmation of John J. Parker in 1930. A Republican nominated by
Hoover, Judge Parker was serving on the Fourth Circuit Court
of Appeals. In this capacity he had written an opinion sustaining an
injunction issued by a lower court to enforce a yellow-dog contract.
This decision incurred the animosity of the American Federation of
Labor which did not accept Parker's reasoning that the Supreme
Court decision in *Hitchman Coal and Coke Company* v. *Mitchell*
left him no alternative.[31] Also, as Republican candidate for Governor of North Carolina in 1920, Parker had been charged by the
Democrats with intending to enfranchise Negroes. In response,
Parker stated that "the participation of the Negro in politics is a
source of evil and danger to both races and is not desired by the
wise men in either race or by the Republican Party of North Carolina." The charges that Parker was anti-Negro and anti-labor were
enough to bring about his defeat in the Senate Judiciary Committee, which voted six to ten against confirmation. The unfavorable
recommendation of the Judiciary Committee was supported in the
Senate by a coalition of Progressive Republicans, Republicans from
states with large Negro and labor populations, and northern Democrats. The vote was 39-41 against confirmation with seventeen Republicans voting against the President's nominee.[32]

These examples of group conflict over confirmation are rare
because most Presidents give consideration to the possibilities of
Senate acceptance before nomination. There have been occasions of
withdrawals of nominations in anticipation of rejection, but usually
nominees to the Supreme Court are men whose public life is sufficiently neutral to insure Senate approval. Such approval would
seem to guarantee that Supreme Court Justices will be political
moderates who have not "offended powerful groups." [33] Exactly
who these groups are is not a simple problem of identification since
power is relative to the position of other groups. In the years following the Civil War, during which the influence of large corporations upon governmental policy-making was unchallenged, the influence of railroads in Supreme Court appointments was noticeable.[34] Today, such influence is lacking.

---

[31] Hitchman Coal and Coke Company v. Mitchell, 245 U.S. 229 (1917).
[32] Harris, *op. cit.*, pp. 127-132.
[33] Carl Swisher, *American Constitutional Development* (Boston: Houghton
Mifflin Company, 1943), p. 113.
[34] Schmidhauser, *op. cit.*, p. 13.

THE AMERICAN BAR ASSOCIATION'S COMMITTEE
ON THE FEDERAL JUDICIARY

However, there is one group whose claims to legitimacy in the nomination of federal judges has been firmly established: the American Bar Association. The Association has for years been concerned with judicial appointments because "lawyers are the only group of citizens that are in daily contact with the courts, they are the only group that are really able to judge qualifications necessary for good judicial material." [35] This statement has been accepted by the federal government to a considerable degree. Although the ABA has always sought influence, in 1949 it took a step toward institutionalization of its deliberations. In that year, the Committee on the Federal Judiciary was created to "promote the nomination and confirmation of competent persons for appointments as judges of the courts of the United States and to oppose the nomination and confirmation of persons deemed by it to be not sufficiently qualified." [36]

Prior to 1949 the ABA had constituted a Special Committee on the Federal Judiciary, but this body enjoyed only limited access. There was no way it could present its recommendations until *after* the prospective judge's name had been submitted to the Senate Judiciary Committee. Although the Special Committee had established cordial relations with the Senate Committee, the organized bar sought influence *prior* to submission. The Department of Justice, which assumed the role of handling most lower federal court appointments during the Eisenhower administration, was the agency with which the ABA's Committee on the Federal Judiciary had to establish rapport. Progress in this direction was begun during the last few months of the Truman administration and by 1952 an arrangement had been made whereby all persons being considered seriously for appointments were examined by the Committee on the Federal Judiciary before actual nomination. This procedure did not apply to appointments to the Supreme Court. When

---

[35] Edward J. Fox, Jr., "The Selection of Federal Judges: The Role of the Federal Judiciary Committee," *American Association Journal*, XLIII (Aug. 1957), 685. The above quotation is taken from an introduction to the article by the editor.

[36] *Ibid.*, 685.

a vacancy on the Court was created by the death of Chief Justice
Vinson, the Committee offered its services in screening potential
replacements and was told that "the appointment of a Justice to
the Supreme Court was a personal appointment of the President
and that if the help of the Committee was needed it would be
consulted." [37] This decision was continued with the appointment of
John Marshall Harlan in 1955, but with the appointment of William
J. Brennan in 1956 a new victory for the ABA was achieved:

> Deputy Attorney General Rogers, speaking in Baltimore before
> the regional meeting of the Association in October, 1956, said that
> when Mr. Justice Brennan's name was discussed with the Presi-
> dent, he asked what the American Bar Association thought about
> him. When he was told that the Committee had not been asked
> for its opinion, he directed that the nomination be held up until the
> Committee could report.[38]

Such an ideal situation is recognized by the ABA as not necessarily
permanent. While enjoying semiofficial status, the Committee on
the Federal Judiciary is still subject to the decision of the Attorney
General as to the degree of participation. A case in point is President Kennedy's nomination of Arthur Goldberg to replace Felix
Frankfurter. On the day the nomination was made public, Attorney
General Robert Kennedy called the chairman of the Committee on
the Federal Judiciary who arranged a telephone conference with
the other members of the Committee who approved Goldberg. The
ABA was not consulted until the President had made an initial
choice, but was called upon before the Senate Judiciary Committee
began its deliberations.

On what basis does the Committee on the Federal Judiciary decide whether a proposed judge is "competent"? Judging from ABA
pronouncements, the sole qualifications are totally divorced from
political values. The ABA is opposed to the rule of senatorial
courtesy because "political tags do not belong on judges." [39] Since
the approval of the Senator is obtained prior to submission of a
name to the ABA, it might also be argued that the practice represents a diminution of the influence of the bar. It has urged that
federal nominations be made by an independent commission which,

[37] *Ibid.*, 688.
[38] *Ibid.*, 761.
[39] *Ibid.*, 688.

Schmidhauser maintains, "would in fact insure American Bar Association control of the federal judicial selection process." Similar efforts to remove "politics" from the selection process can be inferred from the ABA's consistent recommendation that judges at the state level be appointed rather than elected. Here, as with the independent commission idea, the influence of the bar would be increased. The ABA, as has been noted previously, is essentially a conservative body whose leaders have traditionally voiced laissez-faire attitudes on economic questions and have defended the ideological position normally associated with defense of the traditional powers of states against federal interference. The defense of states' rights, now a fundamental aspect of ABA official policy, is a relatively recent development. Schmidhauser has described at length the gradual shift in emphasis from federal to state courts which accompanied the Supreme Court's assumption that economic regulation is necessary. Until the Supreme Court's basic shift in policy following the Roosevelt reorganization effort, the ABA "felt that the important economic interests and ideological values were more reliably safeguarded by the federal courts." [40] Here the ABA was throwing its support to defenders of economic conservatism. As state courts began to defend identical doctrines, the ABA became more critical of the Supreme Court and anxious to protect the integrity of the states. In a sense, the state courts have adopted the policies held by the Supreme Court prior to 1937. This idea is supported by the research of Nagel who found that state supreme court justices tend to be "substantially more conservative than both the administrators and the legislators on the economic issues and free speech issues." [41]

Competence, then, is not to be defined entirely in terms of judicial experience and honesty, but also as a reflection of the ideology of the potential appointee. The ABA has been critical of the Warren Court to the extent that Chief Justice Earl Warren decided to resign his membership. On the other hand, the criticism of the Court by the ABA has been more restrained than that of nonlegal groups. The canon of ethics of the ABA declares that "Judges, not being wholly free to defend themselves, are peculiarly entitled to

---

[40] Schmidhauser, *op. cit.*, p. 79.

[41] Nagel, "Judicial Attitudes and Those of Legislators and Administrators," *op. cit.*, p. 6.

the support of the Bar against unjust criticism and clamor." [42]
Thus, although the Association supported a bill to end the doctrine
of pre-emptive federalism, it opposed the Jenner bill, which would
have restricted the appellate jurisdiction of the Supreme Court. The
hostility of the Association toward the content of the decisions of
the Warren Court is tempered by its traditional identification with
defence of the judiciary branch. Such cross-pressures are illustrated
by the debate in the ABA House of Delegates concerning the Jenner
bill in 1958. Walter Murphy described this meeting:

> Meeting in February in Atlanta, the ABA's House of Delegates had
> before it a resolution from its Board of Governors to have the
> association go on record against S.2646. A strange and fascinating
> debate ensued, with the lawyers struggling to avoid the sharp
> horns of an ethical and political dilemma. On the one hand, many
> members felt obliged to rally to the defense of the Court as an
> institution, if for no other reason than to appear consistent with
> their 1937 opposition to FDR and their later support of the con-
> stitutional amendment to freeze the size and jurisdiction of the
> Supreme Court. On the other hand, a great number of lawyers,
> especially those from the South, were totally out of sympathy with
> the Warren Court's jurisprudence and, in fact, could be much
> harsher in their criticism of the High Bench than Jenner had ever
> been. [43]

The final result of this internal conflict was a resolution which,
while disapproving the Jenner bill, did not provide a firm support
of the Court. The main thrust of ABA opinion has thus been critical
of the Court and has thrown the Association into conflict with
groups such as the NAACP, American Civil Liberties Union, Americans for Democratic Action, and AFL-CIO, which have been
pleased with the decisions of the Warren Court and vigorous in its
defence.

Influencing Judicial Decisions

Influencing judicial appointments is not automatically translated
into influencing judicial decisions. As Presidents have frequently

---

[42] Cited in Murphy, *Congress and the Court*, p. 255.
[43] *Ibid.*, p. 164.

discovered, their expectations at the time of appointment have not been fulfilled in the later performance of the justice. If we examine the social background of Supreme Court Justices, there is a degree of homogeneity which is not converted mechanically into decisional consensus. Schmidhauser has provided us with a collective portrait of Supreme Court Justices:

> Throughout American history there has been an overwhelming tendency for presidents to choose nominees for the Supreme Court from among the socially advantaged families. The typical Supreme Court justice has invariably been white, generally Protestant with a penchant for high social status denomination, usually of ethnic stock originating from the British Isles, and born in comfortable circumstances in an urban or small town environment. In the earlier history of the Court, he very likely was born in the aristocratic gentry class, although later he tended to come from the professionalized upper-middle class. Whereas nearly two thirds of his fellows were selected from politically active families, a third of his fellows were chosen from families having a tradition of judicial service. In college and legal education, the average justice was afforded opportunities for training and associations which were most advantageous. It seems reasonable to assume that very few sons of families outside the upper, or upper-middle, social and economic classes have been able to acquire the particular type of education and the subsequent professional, and especially political, associations which appear to be unwritten prerequisites for appointment to the nation's highest tribunal.[44]

While there is no question that the personal biases of judges, as nurtured by their social backgrounds, play a role in the motivational activity surrounding a decision, there is the limiting factor of identification with the Court as an institution. The judicial role is more explicitly formulated than, for example, the legislative role. There is a feeling of obligation to the Court as symbol of impartiality and impersonality which has grown from the common law tradition.[45] This commitment to the abstract ideals of justice, which is presumably developed after service on the Court, can serve to explain the failure of judges, when compared to legislators, to present a high

[44] Schmidhauser, "The Justices of the Supreme Court—A Collective Portrait," *Midwest Journal of Political Science,* III (Feb. 1959), 45.
[45] Peltason, *Federal Courts in the Political Process,* pp. 21-22. *See also* Schmidhauser, "Judicial Behavior and the Sectional Crisis," *Journal of Politics,* XXIII (Nov. 1961).

correlation between personal values and backgrounds and the content of decisions.[46] While such factors are important, they are less satisfactory as predictive devices than is the case in the legislature. Consequently, groups which have been almost powerless at the legislative level of the political struggle are sometimes able to achieve success before the courts. Indeed, Walter Murphy has argued that wealth, status, and potential voting power, which may be decisive during conflicts over legislation, may actually be disadvantages during the judicial process.[47] The ideal of equal justice under law has clearly been a factor in the extraordinary success of the Jehovah's Witnesses, organized into the Watchtower Bible and Tract Society. A religious sect drawing most of its membership from underprivileged classes, the Witnesses have been successful in forty-four of fifty-five cases before the Supreme Court.[48] Expectations attached to the role of judge also help to explain the effective use of the courts by the NAACP. Neither of these groups have enjoyed much good fortune in the legislative process but have found in the federal courts an influential check upon the power of groups who are in a position to achieve better access to the legislature.

OBSTRUCTIONS TO ORGANIZATIONAL ACTIVITY

If institutionalization of the judicial role operates to the advantage of specified types of interest groups, there is still a considerable problem to be faced in the form of technical obstructions. Individuals lack the necessary financial resources required to pursue a federal question through the lengthy process of adjudication. Professor Clement Vose has noted that the average Supreme Court case requires four years, assuming that the path from the lower courts is unobstructed.[49] While some cases are the result of the initiative of individuals, most are supported by organizations which can provide a staff of lawyers able to devote continuing attention to the legal problems involved. However, to acquire "standing to

---

[46] Nagel, "Judicial Attitudes and Those of Legislators and Administrators," *op. cit.,* p. 12.

[47] Murphy, "The South Counterattacks: The Anti-NAACP Laws," *Western Political Quarterly,* XII (June 1959), 372.

[48] Clement E. Vose, "Litigation as a Form of Pressure Group Activity," *Annals of the American Academy of Political and Social Science,* Sept. 1948, p. 22.

[49] *Ibid.*

sue" it is necessary to establish that an individual is personally damaged by a statute or some other form of official decision. Justice Frankfurter explained the position of the Court in *Coleman* v. *Miller:* "we can only adjudicate an issue as to which there is a claimant before us who has a special, individualized stake in it. One who is merely the self-constituted spokesman of a constitutional point of view cannot ask us to pass on it." [50] The immediate problem of the interest group in the judicial process is, then, to recruit a person who both is willing to undergo the strenuous ordeal of extended litigation, and who meets the requirements as stated above. There is also the additional problem of mootness. If an individual plaintiff's standing to sue is dependent upon a particular set of circumstances, a change in these circumstances might result in a loss of standing. For example, if the parents of a Catholic child complain that the teaching of the Church forbids the distribution of the King James version in public schools, but before the trial begins the child withdraws from school, the question is moot.[51] These problems can be overcome by the use of test cases and by reliance upon the Federal Rules of Civil Procedure which provide for "class action." Under rule 23a it is possible to institute action not only for a single individual but for all persons who are "similarly situated":

> If persons constituting a class are so numerous as to make it impractical to bring them all before the court, such of them, one or more, as will fairly insure the adequate representation of all may, on behalf of all, sue or be sued.[52]

TEST CASES

The use of class action—which, while somewhat unclear and subject to dispute in its application, is relied upon to enjoin an official from enforcing a statute—eliminates the problem of mootness since a plaintiff who has lost standing can be replaced by one who has not, without suspension of the original litigation. The

---

[50] Coleman v. Miller, 307 U.S. 433.

[51] This possibility is explored in Will Maslow, "The Legal Defense of Religious Liberty—The Strategy and Tactics of the American Jewish Congress" (Paper presented to the 1961 annual meeting of the American Political Science Association), pp. 12-13.

[52] "Class Actions: A Study of Group-Interest Litigation," *Race Relations Law Reporter,* I (Oct. 1956), 991.

advantage of class action is most noticeable in the case of the NAACP, which has made the test case the foundation of its legal strategy. Rather than operating primarily to provide support for individuals already involved in legislation—a technique used frequently by the American Civil Liberties Union—the NAACP has developed a strategy designed "to secure decisions, rulings and public opinion on the broad principle instead of being devoted to merely miscellaneous cases." [53] The deliberate creation of litigation has advantages over spontaneous action which a well coordinated interest group can maximize. Questions of timing, for example, can be brought more readily to advantage. To illustrate, the American Jewish Congress prefers to begin its objections to Christian celebrations in public schools well in advance of holidays such as Christmas or Easter rather than during the holiday season when an unfavorable climate of opinion might be more expected.[54] Proper timing can also be determined by the group's evaluation of the attitudes of the members of a court at a particular time. Rather than face certain defeat, it might be wiser to avoid litigation and the consequent building of unfavorable precedent, until the personnel or attitudes of the court have changed. Such planning is revealed by the efforts of the NAACP to have the Supreme Court declare restrictive covenants a violation of the Fourteenth Amendment. In seeking a writ of certiorari, which requires the approval of four justices, the NAACP had been denied the writ on numerous occasions. However, in 1945 the NAACP learned that Justices Murphy and Rutledge were willing to grant a writ, and sought to provide the "leverage with which to bring two more justices to their side. . . ." [55] During this time, test cases had been initiated in various cities; and at conferences held by the NAACP, lawyers for the plaintiffs compared notes in order to produce a consistent trial record, since there was no certainty as to which case would be the basis of a writ. Also, attention was given to the details of each case

[53] Herbert Hill and Jack Greenberg, *Citizen's Guide to De-Segregation* (Boston: Beacon Press, 1955), pp. 56-57. Cited in Vose, "Litigation as a Form of Pressure Group Activity," *op. cit.*, p. 23.

[54] Maslow, "The Legal Defense of Religious Liberty—The Strategy of the American Jewish Congress," *op. cit.*, p. 9.

[55] Vose, "The Impact of Pressure Groups on Constitutional Interpretation" (Paper presented to the 1954 annual meeting of the American Political Science Association). Cited in Schubert, *Constitutional Politics*, p. 78.

in order to determine which would have the best chance for a favorable decision once a writ was granted.[56] The ultimate victory of the NAACP in the restrictive covenant cases attests to the effectiveness of organizational preparation of cases.

The use of the test case is the device of a disadvantaged group that is trying to challenge the products of hostile legislatures. Groups whose access to the legislature assures that no such laws will be passed have no need for this technique, yet are placed on the defensive. One solution to this problem is the reduction of the ability of the protesting organization to use its resources to create a constitutional issue. In the South, the attack upon the NAACP illustrates the technique of keeping an issue out of court and hence perpetuating the existing statute. Since the NAACP has demonstrated its access to federal courts, the strategy is to keep the organization from making use of this access. Southern states have attempted this not only by such harassments as legislative investigations to force publication of membership lists and prosecution under corporation and tax laws, but also by the invocation of laws against barratry, champerty, and maintenance.[57] Such laws, which prohibit the participation in litigation of parties with no demonstrable interest and forbid the solicitation or encouragement of unjustified litigation, strike at the heart of the NAACP, which readily concedes that it uses litigation to achieve advantages for Negroes. In defending itself against these charges, the NAACP has avoided the state legislatures in favor of the courts. In preparing its briefs, the NAACP has argued that an interest group has a constitutional right to use the judicial process to achieve its goals and that such a group has standing to sue even though it cannot reveal the names of individual members. In *NAACP v. Alabama*, Justice Harlan, speaking for the Court, declared:

> The association both urges that it is constitutionally entitled to resist official inquiry into its membership lists, and that it may assert, on behalf of its members a right personal to them to be protected from compelled disclosure by the State of their affiliation

---

[56] Vose, *Caucasians Only* (Berkeley: University of California Press, 1959), pp. 156-157.

[57] Murphy, "The South Counterattacks: The Anti-NAACP Laws," *op. cit.*, 373. *See also* Peltason, *58 Lonely Men* (New York: Harcourt, Brace & World, Inc., 1961), pp. 56-78 and American Jewish Congress, *Assault Upon Freedom of Association* (New York: American Jewish Congress, 1957).

with the association as revealed by the membership lists. We think that petitioner argues more appropriately the rights of its members, and that its nexus with them is sufficient to permit that it act as their representative before this Court. In so concluding, we reject respondent's argument that the association lacks standing to assert here constitutional rights pertaining to the members, who are not of course parties to the legislation.[58]

This decision recognized the group basis of litigation, and if the NAACP arguments are introduced with sufficient tenacity the judge-made rule of standing to sue may be modified. In any event, an important part of the judicial process is the maneuverings of litigants to get the right case into the courts at the right time.

PLACING AN ARGUMENT BEFORE THE COURT

Once the case is begun, the attention of groups turns to the best possible way of securing a favorable decision. The rules of the game prohibit, even if written laws do not, the exhibition of overt group pressures. If the Supreme Court were deluged by telegrams during its deliberations it would not take much imagination to estimate their effect. Therefore more indirect methods have been devised. The National Consumers' League, which was active in defense of state labor legislation during the early years of this century, was a valuable ally of state attorneys general when their offices were given the assignment of defending state laws regulating conditions of labor. The League provided legal help (notably Louis Brandeis), assisted in the preparation of briefs, and guided or actually presented oral arguments for the state.[59] Since 1954, the segregationists' groups of the South have developed a similar relationship with attorneys general, who usually begin barratry proceedings.[60] In addition to such assistance, groups seek to achieve as much publicity for their position as possible, in the hopes that the nurturing of a wider public sympathy will enhance the possibility of success. One method of publicity aimed at the judges as a specific audience is the use of law reviews. Newland has shown that

---

[58] NAACP v. Alabama, 357 U.S. 449 (1958).

[59] Vose, "The National Consumers' League and the Brandeis Brief," *Midwest Journal of Political Science*, I (Nov. 1957), 267-290.

[60] Samuel Krislov, "Constituency Versus Constitutionalism: The Segregation Issue and Tensions and Aspirations of Southern Attorneys General," *Midwest Journal of Political Science*, III (Feb. 1959), 75-92.

the citation of legal periodicals by the Supreme Court is on the increase and has been accepted by the justices as a legitimate source of information and opinion.[61] It is indeed natural for judges to consult the writings of legal scholars, published under the auspices of law schools. Consequently, a group might reason that one avenue of access to the Court is through these periodicals. When the precedents in a case are unsettled, or when the precedents run counter to the goals of a group, such sources as will give arguments some form of learned status may be valuable. To construct a body of legal opinion in support of its goal of securing a judgment against restrictive covenants, the NAACP began a campaign to have articles critical of adverse decisions and emphasizing the social and economic inequities of covenants placed in law reviews.[62] Between 1946 and 1948 more than thirty articles urging the Court to reverse the substantial body of precedents which operated to the advantage of whites and their restrictive covenants appeared in law reviews.[63] The strength of the whites lay in the opinions of previous courts; the strategy of the Negroes was thus to provide a contrasting aggregate of legal theory. The same technique was used by interests which favored the state control of offshore oil. After the Supreme Court held in *U.S. v. California* that states did not own the submerged and oil rich land bordering their coasts, critical articles appeared in the law reviews of the affected states, encouraged by the National Association of Attorneys General. However, Newland points out that in most cases the citation of law review articles is a minor part of the written opinion.[64]

THE AMICUS CURIAE BRIEF

By far the most frequently used technique of getting the policy position of a group before the court is the *amicus curiae* brief. Under the rules of the Supreme Court, organizations are permitted to file briefs in support of one of the litigants even though the or-

[61] Chester A. Newland, "Legal Periodicals and the United States Supreme Court," *Midwest Journal of Political Science*, III (Feb. 1959), 58-74.

[62] Vose, *Caucasians Only*, p. 161.

[63] Peltason, *Federal Courts in the Political Process*, p. 52.

[64] Newland, *op. cit.*, 73. However, Newland does believe law review articles can be influential on some occasions, as in *Erie Railroad Co.* v. *Tompkins*, 304 U.S. 64 (1938). In this decision Justice Brandeis relied heavily on legal periodicals in overruling a ninety-six year old precedent.

ganization is not an actual party to the suit. *Amicus curiae* briefs may be filed with consent of both parties or by permission of the Court if consent is denied. In most state courts, consent of the court is required. The trend before the Supreme Court, until 1949, was to pay little attention to the rule of consent; and motions for permission to file were granted as a matter of routine. The latitudinarian construction immersed the Court in a flood of briefs, many of which were of little value in that they merely parroted the position of a litigant or stated preferences without achieving much more than emotionalism. After the "Hollywood Ten" case, involving refusal to testify before the House Un-American Activities Committee, produced forty briefs on behalf of the defendants, the Court adopted a new rule which drew careful attention to the rule of consent.[65] This tightening of the rule reduced the number of *amicus curiae* briefs substantially, especially since the United States government, as a party to about half the cases before the Court, refused consent in nearly every case. However, the strenuous objections of Justices Black and Frankfurter lead to a further modification on the part of the Solicitor General of the United States. Consent is now given when the applicant has a clear interest in the decision and when the brief contains arguments or other material which would not otherwise come to the attention of the Court. This balancing between the two extremes has had an effect upon the number of briefs. In 1949, the last year of the Court's failure to insist upon the rule of consent, ninety-one *amicus curiae* briefs were filed but this number had declined to nineteen by 1952. In the years following the modification of the policy of the Solicitor General in 1952, an average of thirty-six briefs per session has developed.[66]

The *amicus curiae* brief represents group involvement in the judicial process even when the group has not been involved in the institution of a case and has no control over timing and other strategic considerations. According to Vose, the following organizations

---

[65] Fowler v. Harper and Edwin D. Etherington, "Lobbyists Before the Court," *University of Pennsylvania Law Review,* CI (June 1953), 1172.

[66] Peter H. Sonnenfield, *Participation of Amici Curiae by Filing Briefs and Presenting Oral Arguments in Decisions of the Supreme Court, 1949-1957,* Michigan State University Bureau of Social and Political Research, Working Papers in Methodology, no. 2 (East Lansing: Jan. 1957). Cited in Schubert, *Quantitative Analysis of Judicial Behavior,* p. 74.

are most active in the use of *amicus curiae* briefs: the American Civil Liberties Union, American Jewish Congress, AFL-CIO, and the National Lawyers Guild.[67] Each of these organizations is equipped with legal talent capable of developing arguments that may have been overlooked by the parties to the litigation, and, although the specific impact of a particular brief is difficult to ascertain, evidence of the value of a carefully prepared brief is available to the extent that judicial decisions make use of the material presented or judges base a decision upon an argument made in an *amicus curiae* brief. For example, in *Illinois ex rel. McCollum* v. *Board of Education*, in which the Supreme Court ruled that the use of public school facilities for religious instruction violated the establishment of religion clause of the First Amendment, the brief of the American Jewish Congress was relied upon by Justice Frankfurter during the oral arguments and in his concurring opinion.[68] Frankfurter's acceptance of the arguments of the American Jewish Congress may be contrasted with Justice Jackson's reaction to a brief of the American Newspaper Publishers Association in *Craig* v. *Harney:*

> Of course it does not cite a single authority that was not available to counsel for the publisher involved and does not tell us a single new fact except this one: "This membership embraces more than 700 newspaper publishers whose publications represent in excess of eighty percent of the total daily and Sunday circulation of newspapers published in this country. The Association is vitally interested in the issue presented in this case, namely, the right of newspapers to publish news stories and editorials on cases pending in the courts."
>
> This might be a good occasion to demonstrate the fortitude of the judiciary.[69]

A good example of the maneuverings surrounding the submission of *amicus curiae* briefs can be found in Westin's case study

---

[67] Vose, "Litigation as a Form of Pressure Group Activity," *op. cit.*, p. 30. *See also* "Private Attorneys-General: Group Action in the Fight for Civil Liberties," *Yale Law Journal*, LVIII (Mar. 1949), 574-598.

[68] Illinois ex rel. McCollum v. Board of Education, 333 U.S. 203 (1948). *See also* Harper and Etherington, *op. cit.*, p. 1173 and Maslow, "The Legal Defense of Religious Liberty—The Strategy and Tactics of the American Jewish Congress," *op. cit.*, p. 16.

[69] Craig v. Harney, 331 U.S. 367 (1947).

of *Burstyn* v. *Wilson*.[70] A motion picture distributor had challenged
a decision of the New York State Court of Appeals upholding the
state censorship law, under which the Italian film *The Miracle* was
denied the permit which was necessary for public showing. Defending the statute was the New York Catholic Welfare Committee,
which was ready to submit its brief to the Court. However, shortly
after the decision of the New York State Court of Appeals decision
in October, 1951, an opposing Catholic group, the Committee of
Catholics for Cultural Action, was organized with the intention of
filing a brief urging the Supreme Court to reverse the New York
ruling. While the Church was trying to prevent this occurrence, the
attorneys for the motion picture distributor were anxious to have
the Catholic Committee for Cultural Action present its arguments
in the expectation that a display of disagreement among Catholics
would strengthen their case. The situation was complicated by the
refusal of the New York Solicitor General to give consent to the
filing of more than one *amicus curiae* brief for each contestant. The
American Civil Liberties Union, having received such consent, was
prepared to speak against the statute on the basis of its violation of
freedom of expression. However, the attorneys for the appellant
were especially concerned lest the brief of the American Jewish
Congress, which emphasized that film censorship was a use of state
power to enforce religious beliefs in violation of the First Amendment, be kept from the attention of the court. The film, which describes the seduction of a retarded Italian woman by a stranger
whom she believes to be St. Joseph, was denied a permit on the
basis of its sacrilegious nature. To get this argument before the
Court, it was originally suggested that the American Jewish Congress join in the brief of the American Civil Liberties Union, but the
latter organization refused on the grounds that its purely civil liberties position should not be amalgamated with sectarian arguments.

Still having consent only for the ACLU brief, the attorneys for
the plaintiff wrote the State Catholic Welfare Committee of their
refusal to permit presentation of a brief by that organization. Confronted with the loss of its major supporting brief, New York re-

---

[70] Burstyn v. Wilson, 343 U.S. 495 (1952). This account is taken from Alan
Westin, "The Miracle Case: The Supreme Court and the Movies," in Edwin
A. Bock and Alan K. Campbell, eds., *Case Studies in American Government*
(Englewood Cliffs, N.J.: Prentice-Hall, Inc., 1962), pp. 111-115.

lented and offered to allow two briefs: one by the ACLU and another by all remaining organizations. However these groups would not agree to this offer and, since the New York Catholic Welfare Committee had already been refused permission, the New York Solicitor General decided to withdraw consent from all organizations. Upon learning of this decision, the ACLU changed its position and agreed to allow other groups to join its brief. The ACLU was then informed that New York would consent if the anti-censorship interests would agree to the filing by the New York Catholic Welfare Committee. However, consent for this filing could be achieved only if the Catholic Committee for Cultural Action could also file. These conditions were accepted and it appeared as if the matter would be finalized with two briefs (ACLU and its collaborating groups and the Catholic Committee for Cultural Action) attacking the censorship statute and one (New York Catholic Welfare Committee) defending the law. Still further negotiations were to follow. The Archdiocese of New York was able to persuade the Catholic Committee for Cultural Action to withdraw its brief; and the American Book Publishers Council and National Lawyers Guild, which were denied consent by New York, were granted leave to file by the Supreme Court. In May 1952, the Supreme Court, by unanimous decision, reversed the decision of the Court of Appeals. Justice Clark, writing for the Court, distinguished between the claim that the New York statute violated the Fourteenth Amendment as a prior restraint upon freedom of speech and press and the contention that the statute violated the guarantee of separation of church and state with consequent protection of the free exercise of religion. Clark stated: "As we view the case, we need consider only the appellant's contention that the New York statute is an unconstitutional abridgment of free speech and a free press." Clark's opinion would thus seem to have made the arguments of the American Jewish Congress superfluous. However, while building his opinion upon the conclusion that motion pictures are included within the free speech and free press guarantees of the First and Fourteenth Amendments, Clark nevertheless maintained that the banning of a film on the basis of its alleged sacrilegious nature "might raise substantial questions under the First Amendment's guaranty of separate church and state with freedom of worship for all." Justice Clark reasoned that a censor, armed only with authority to prohibit the showing of sacrilegious films, would be "set adrift upon a boundless sea amid a myriad of conflicting currents of religious views, with no charts but those provided by the most vocal and powerful orthodoxies."

The Consequences of Judicial Decisions

A decision by the Supreme Court does not settle a question of public policy finally and for all time. At the most visible level, the Supreme Court itself can change its mind and overturn a previous decision. Some examples of judicial retreats from earlier decisions have been presented earlier in the chapter. However, explicit reversals of precedents have been accomplished on as many as seventy occasions, one of the most noteworthy being the Flag Salute cases. In *Minersville School District* v. *Gobitis* the Court ruled that public school children could be compelled to salute the flag and recite the pledge of allegiance even though the children and their parents believed that this ritual violated their religious beliefs.[71] This case involved the Jehovah's Witnesses, as did the decision three years later, in *West Virginia State Board of Education* v. *Barnette,* which specifically reversed the earlier decision.[72] Usually, the overturning of precedents can be explained by changes in the personnel of the court, as for example in *Brown* v. *Board of Education*[73] which reversed *Plessy* v. *Ferguson.*[74] However in the Flag Salute cases, three justices who had joined in the opinion of the Gobitis case publicly stated their error and practically invited the witnesses to try again.[75]

METHODS OF CIRCUMVENTION

Granted that groups which have been defeated in one court decision can win in another, a more pressing question is the degree

[71] Minersville School District v. Gobitis, 310 U.S. 586 (1940).
[72] West Virginia State Board of Education v. Barnette, 319 U.S. 624 (1943).
[73] Brown v. Board of Education, 347 U.S. 483 (1954).
[74] Plessy v. Ferguson, 163 U.S. 537 (1896).
[75] In *Jones* v. *Opelika,* 316 U.S. 584 (1942), Justices Black, Douglas, and Murphy, in a joint dissenting opinion, declared "since we joined in the opinion of the Gobitis case, we think this is an appropriate occasion to state that we now believe that it also was wrongly decided."

to which a Supreme Court decision, considered as the law of the
land, actually has an impact on policy. On this subject, Peltason has
written:

> A court decision has to be enforced, the judges' opinion requires
> interpretation. What a decision means is determined by group
> conflict after a decision has been announced and the opinion
> read. All this activity—enforcement, postdecisional interpretation,
> possible reversal by some other agency or the judges themselves—
> which follows a judicial decision is part of the story of group con-
> flict, the story of the political process.[76]

What are the methods whereby a Supreme Court decision can be
circumvented? In addition to the obvious technique of amending
the Constitution itself, a long and complex process, interests which
have lost the battle in the Supreme Court can win the war by
modifying the application of the decision. This process can occur
either in the Congress, where interests not satisfied with a decision
can achieve by means of legislation what amounts to a reversal,
or in the lower courts that normally are given the responsibility of
interpretation and application of High Court rulings. For example,
in *Federal Trade Commission* v. *Cement Institute,* the Court ruled
that the basing point system of pricing, maintained under the
auspices of the Cement Institute, was a combination in restraint of
trade. However, the cement and steel industries were able to "rally
fresh groups to their support to revise or overrule the Supreme
Court decision" by legislation protecting the basing point system.[77]
Another illustration of appeals to Congress by groups seeking to
reduce the effects of Supreme Court decisions is the tidelands oil
dispute. State control interests had been told by the Court on
three occasions that the national government had title to the submerged lands. However, when Eisenhower was elected in 1952, the
state control interests were afforded an ally. President Truman
had vetoed legislation establishing state ownership, but Eisenhower
made good a campaign promise and in 1953 signed the Submerged
Land Act, which was declared constitutional by the Supreme Court
in 1954. On this subject, Lucius Barker notes that "by passing the

---

[76] Peltason, *Federal Courts in the Political Process,* p. 55.
[77] Federal Trade Commission v. Cement Institute, 333 U.S. 683 (1948).
Earl Latham, *The Group Basis of Politics* (Ithaca: Cornell University Press,
1952), p. 59.

Submerged Lands Acts in 1953, Congress and the President gave to the state-control interest that which the Court had specifically denied to them, and in effect that which the Court had given to the national-control interest." [78]

Turning to the possibility of avoiding the consequences of Supreme Court decisions through access to lower courts, we must first consider the wide discretion allowed these courts. This discretion provides initially defeated interests with the opportunity to salvage much of what they lost before the Supreme Court. The basic advantage, discretion in application of rulings by lower court judges, is gained from the right of lower court judges to raise new legal questions after the case has been returned. Once new issues are created, the process of litigation can actually be begun again, with a final result that is not necessarily consistent with the original ruling. Of one hundred and seventy-five cases returned to state courts between 1941 and 1951, forty-six involved further litigation, and in slightly less than half of these cases the interests that enjoyed a favorable ruling by the Supreme Court suffered a reversal in the state courts. [79] Even without the raising of new issues, lower court judges have on occasion behaved in a manner that constitutes overt refusal to follow a specific Supreme Court Ruling. After *Minersville School District* v. *Gobitis,* Judge John J. Parker of the Court of Appeals for the Fourth Circuit held the ruling invalid. Parker called attention to the confession of error on the part of three of the justices in the *Gobitis* case and the retirement of two others, leaving only three justices who still supported the decision. Parker therefore reasoned that the Supreme Court would support his ruling on appeal, which it did. [80]

Such examples of resistance are of perhaps less significance than the gradual erosion of Supreme Court decisions by hostile interpretation. The behavior of the United States district judges in the segregation controversy has had precisely this result. Whereas the *Brown* v. *Board of Education* decision represented a clear victory for anti-segregation interests, the directions of the Supreme Court

---

[78] Lucius J. Barker, "The Supreme Court as Policy-Maker: The Tidelands Oil Controversy," *Journal of Politics,* XXIV (May 1962), 363.

[79] "Evasion of Supreme Court Mandates in Cases Remanded to State Courts Since 1941," *Harvard Law Review,* LXVII (May 1954), 1251-1259.

[80] Murphy, "Lower Court Checks on Supreme Court Power," *American Political Science Review,* LIII (Dec. 1959), 1026.

concerning the methods whereby integration of public schools was to be accomplished were a concession to Southern states. After the initial decision, the Court declined to issue a decree covering all school districts and stated that all cases would be returned to district judges for the promulgation of explicit plans for integration. The instructions to the district judges made it clear that primary responsibility for integration was in the hands of the local school authorities, provided a "prompt and reasonable" effort toward compliance was made. Southern district judges, who like most Southerners feel the *Brown* decision was a mistake, are naturally responsive to local segregationist pressures and are not inclined to risk overt violation of local belief systems unless there is no alternative:

> The judge can never forget that any action of his against segregation will threaten his easy and prestigious acceptance by the community. He has become a convenient target for political leaders anxious to impress the electorate with their own soundness on segregation. The judge who delays injunctions and avoids anti-segregation rules is, on the other hand, a local hero; he will hear himself referred to as one of the nation's "great constitutional scholars," a man of courage willing to risk reversal to defend the right.[81]

Although the response to local pressures can be mitigated by a strong perception by the district judge of his role as participant in the legal tradition, the delay in creating situations consistent with the *Brown* decision can be partially attributed to the willingness of many district judges to sanction skillful methods of evasion. Indeed, one writer has concluded that appreciable changes in the educational status of Negro children have occurred in areas which would probably have begun remedial action even without the *Brown* decision.[82]

A final method of circumvention is simply noncompliance. A court decision is similar to any other form of governmental decree in that the extent to which it actually effects a discernible alteration in the distribution of values and forms of behavior within a political community depends upon the conformity of the declaration with the interests of dominant groups within that community.

---

[81] Peltason, 58 *Lonely Men*, p. 9. *See also* "How Southern Judges Look at Segregation," *U.S. News and World Report*, Apr. 27, 1956, pp. 48-52.

[82] Robert J. Steamer, "The Role of the Federal District Courts in the Segregation Controversy," *Journal of Politics*, XXII (Feb. 1960), 419.

Consequently, many decisions mean little since "unconstitutional" forms of behavior are continued as if no official word had been spoken. Although *Illinois ex rel. McCollum* v. *Board of Education* held that the use of public school facilities for religious instruction violated the First Amendment prohibition against the establishment of religion, "no changes were made as a result of the decision in some of the communities which had programs of religious instruction held in school buildings during classroom time." [83] In some states, noncompliance was based upon rulings by attorneys general that no changes were necessary, but in others the decision was quietly forgotten. Where the dominant coalition of interests, institutionalized in state legislatures and other state agencies responsible for the administration of public schools, opposed the decision, compliance was left in the hands of those groups and individuals who had been responsible for creating the religious instruction initially. In rare instances were adherents of the decision successful in imposing enforcement of the *McCollum* decision.

In New York City, children were released from school time to be given religious instruction off the school premises, a distinction which the Supreme Court approved in *Zorach* v. *Clauson*.[84] Having granted the legality of religious instruction off school premises, did the Court thereby reduce noncompliance? It is estimated that about one-third of the religious instruction was being held in school buildings seven years after the decision.[85] Further, the *Zorach* decision has been used to justify injection of religious instruction into school training in a manner which is in no way related to the specifics of the decision. Bible readings and recitations of the Lord's Prayer were justified on the basis of *Zorach* v. *Clauson* even though such actions were undertaken on school property. On the basis of this evidence, Frank J. Sorauf concludes that "especially in religiously homogeneous communities where there are no dissident elements strong enough to protest or begin court action, the *McCollum* and *Zorach* rules are evaded and ignored.[86] In a case originating from New York, the Supreme Court has struck down the required read-

---

[88] Gordon Patric, "The Impact of a Court Decision: Aftermath of the McCollum Case," *Journal of Public Law,* VI (Fall, 1957), 455-464.

[84] Zorach v. Clauson, 343 U.S. 306 (1952).

[85] Frank J. Sorauf, "*Zorach v. Clauson:* The Impact of a Supreme Court Decision," *American Political Science Review,* LIII (Sept. 1959), 785.

[86] *Ibid.,* 791.

ings of prayers in schools, but this decision is merely the most recent round in the struggle, for there is ample evidence that noncompliance will continue to be the rule.[87]

These comments are not intended to suggest that the Supreme Court does not make policy, but rather that the policy which it does make is either a reflection of dominant interests or a fulcrum for values which, though separate from the dominant interests, are not in conflict with them. Although it is untenable to argue for a permanent structure of political power on a national scale, it is as untenable to maintain that all interests are represented in each government agency to the same degree. As the relative position of interests alters, the Supreme Court can both encourage rising groups to continue their efforts and provide such groups with institutional support against the attacks of other interests.[88] The process of policy formation is continuous; ultimate resolutions are rare. Decisions achieve finality to the extent that they reflect dominant community sentiment, a sentiment which, irrespective of the pronouncements of formal law, will be able to maintain a favorable allocation of resources and values.

---

[87] Engel *et al.*, v. Vitale *et al.*, 370 U.S. 421 (1962).

[88] This argument is pursued in Dahl, "Decision-Making in a Democracy: The Supreme Court as National Policy-Maker." *Journal of Public Law,* VI (Fall, 1957), 293 and Peltason, *Federal Courts in the Political Process,* pp. 55-64.

Index